T0313692

Ahmedabad

Ahmedabad

SHOCK CITY OF TWENTIETH-CENTURY INDIA

HOWARD SPODEK

Indiana University Press
Bloomington and Indianapolis

This book is a publication of

Indiana University Press
601 North Morton Street
Bloomington, Indiana 47404-3797 USA

iupress.indiana.edu

Telephone orders   800-842-6796
Fax orders   812-855-7931
Orders by e-mail   iuporder@indiana.edu

Manufactured in the United States of America

Library of Congress Cataloging-in-Publication Data

Spodek, Howard, [date]
Ahmedabad : shock city of twentieth-century India / Howard Spodek.
p.   cm.
Includes bibliographical references and index.
ISBN 978-0-253-35587-4 (cloth : alk. paper)   1. Ahmadabad (India)—History—
20th century. 2. Ahmadabad (India)—Economic conditions—20th century.
3. Ahmadabad (India)—Politics and government—20th century.
4. Ahmadabad (India)—Biography. I. Title.
DS486.A4S76   2011
954'.75—dc22
2010046733

1 2 3 4 5   16 15 14 13 12 11

To my many, many friends in Ahmedabad,
for gifts beyond measure

Afoot and light-hearted I take to the open road . . .

Walt Whitman, "Song of the Open Road"

CONTENTS

ACKNOWLEDGMENTS

Ahmedabad has been my second home for almost half a century. Many of the central actors in this book are friends and colleagues. My sense of gratitude to all of them is overwhelming. I hope they feel that this book repays in small part all that they have contributed over the years to the book and to me personally.

Even before I embarked on my first trip, in 1964, I had been prepared for my studies especially by Profs. Ainslee Embree at Columbia University and Stephen Hay at the University of Chicago. When I returned to Chicago, Profs. Barney Cohn and Brian Berry helped me to process and build on what I had learned. In India, Dr. Olive Reddick, Director of the Fulbright Office, made the fateful decision that Ahmedabad would be my posting. R. P. Sharma came out from Delhi from time to time to check that all was proceeding properly. (On later trips, Pradeep Mehendiratta, Director-General of the American Institute of Indian Studies, was my shepherd through the bureaucracies.) Of the young Fulbrighters in that first voyage, some have remained lifelong colleagues and friends, especially Richard Schiro and Philip Oldenburg (and, later, Phil's wife, Veena).

Similarly, among my colleagues and friends at H.K. Arts College, 1964–66, several remain among my closest friends. From the faculty: Jayant Joshi and, later, his wife, Neela, and their entire family—parents, children, and grand-children; Ilaben Pathak and her family. Bharat Bhatt, a geographer at HK who soon left for study in the States, taught me about the tensions between the two experiences. From among the students: Bension Agarwarkar, and his family, continue as close friends, and Sudhir Khandekar and M. G. Hiragar as memorable from the classroom and continuing as friends.

I became, and, thankfully, remain a part of the extended family of Burhan and Iqbal Siddiqui, in whose home I lived in 1965–66, including parents, children, and grandchildren. In their home I experienced an Islam of love, as they actually lived their faith. Prof. Varis Alavi and his family opened additional windows into more Westernized and academic perspectives on Islam, and on Gujarati literature. Nirubhai Desai and his wife, Nirmalaben—freedom fighters, socialists, political and social activists—welcomed me into their family as well, and their children and grandchildren continue in my circle of friends. Esther David introduced me to two communities in Ahmedabad—artistic and Jewish—and her son Robin and his wife, Raheel, guide me today through the world of Ahmedabad journalism. Dwijendra Tripathi always chuckles as he reminds me that he and I both arrived in Ahmedabad for the first time in 1964—he to become professor and, later, dean at the Indian Institute of Management. His family and circle of friends and colleagues have always welcomed me warmly. Father Joseph Heredero coached me then on the workings of Indian politics, and continues to do so even now. He found for me at St. Xavier's College my first Gujarati teacher, Prof. Chimanbhai Trivedi, and my first Gujarati coach, P. D. Chavda. Later teachers have included Prof. Raymond Parmar, also of St. Xavier's, who has welcomed me to his home and family, and Prof. Arvind Bhandari of Gujarat University, met most recently, in 2009. Father H. and Raymondbhai—through their discussions and their lives—have also offered different and fascinating perspectives on the Christian community of Ahmedabad.

Harinarayan Acharya, General Secretary of the Ahmedabad Millowners Association, opened the doors and the archives of the AMA's headquarters, built by LeCorbusier, and invited me to tea and conversation in his office more often than I can remember. Years later, I introduced him to my children as "my Ahmedabad grandfather." As I studied Ahmedabad's textile industry, Arvind Buch, general secretary of the Textile Labour Association (TLA), gave me personal insights into the workings of Ahmedabad's most important Gandhian institution. S. A. Kher at Calico Mills and Chandraprasad Desai at Arvind Mills guided me on management perspectives. On subsequent trips, B. K. Majmudar, at ATUL products, enhanced that perspective, and unveiled to me his remarkable balancing act between industrial management and socialist politics. Dinkarbhai Trivedi owned and managed Ahmedabad's remarkable New Order Book Store, with its superb collection of older treasures, and kept me alert to the books I needed to read. Two Western academics I met in India on that first trip also became dear friends as well as perceptive guides, John Wood of the University of British Columbia and the late Prof. Leo Jakobson of the University of Wisconsin–Madison. With friends, guides, and colleagues like these, Ahmedabad had already become a new home for me.

Subsequent trips brought new friends, colleagues, and guides. In 1974–75, I first met the leaders of SEWA, the Self Employed Women's Association, still a wing of the TLA, but later to emerge independent and strong. Elaben Bhatt subsequently became one of my closest friends in Ahmedabad. She welcomed me into her family and introduced me to the amazing group of women who were beginning to build SEWA into an organization of worldwide importance. Some I came to know especially well and to cherish as good friends: Renana Jhabvala and her husband, Harish Khare; Mirai Chatterjee, her husband, Binoy Acharya, and later their three daughters; Reema Nanavati, and her husband, Mihir Bhatt (Elaben's son), and their children; and Namrita Bali. SEWA provided a home within a home.

On that same trip, I had the privilege of interviewing Kasturbhai Lalbhai for some fifteen hours over a period of several weeks. I had also begun to meet members of the city's leading industrial and civic families: Shrenikbhai Lalbhai, Mrinalini Sarabhai and her children, Mallika and Kartikeya, and people who worked with them in their various enterprises, including the Nehru Foundation and the Darpana Academy. Padmanabh Joshi was especially helpful with the Vikram Sarabhai archives.

In 1981, under the auspices of the United States Office of Education, I led an academic tour of urban India for several faculty members of Temple University and the University of Pennsylvania: George Claflen, George Deaux, Herb Ershkowitz, Tom Fogarty, Joel Gerstl, Mark Haller, Lane Johnson, Jon Lang, Sarah Jane Moore, Denise O'Brien, Luci Paul, and Loraine Sexton. We spent three weeks in Ahmedabad and I learned much as they shared their insights. We met Pragnesh Parikh, our liaison with the School of Architecture; he subsequently came to study at Temple and has been a lifelong friend. In 1982, with support from the National Endowment for the Humanities, I made a documentary film on Ahmedabad. Prof. Joe Elder, at the University of Wisconsin–Madison, mentored me in the art and craft of arranging filmmaking in India. Norris Brock, the cinematographer, opened for me new visual perspectives on the city.

B. V. Doshi and his colleagues at the School of Architecture (now CEPT University) instructed me in new ways of understanding Ahmedabad's architectural treasures, historic and contemporary. In his Municipal Corporation office, in his home, and in the field, N. R. Desai introduced me to issues of city planning and administration. Prof. Devavrat Pathak of Gujarat University, and later the Gujarat Vidyapith, mentored me in Gujarat politics and civil liberties, joined John Wood and me as senior colleague in translating Indulal Yagnik's six-volume autobiography from Gujarati to English, and welcomed me into his home and family. In Philadelphia, Panna Naik, Gujarati poet, librarian at the University of Pennsylvania, and a good friend for many years, helped me with issues both bibliographic and linguistic.

Academic contacts multiplied, and most of them merged personal friendships with professional relationships, accompanied by many dinners and teas: Usha Thakkar in Mumbai, first at SNDT University, later of the Gandhian center, Manibhavan, and a frequent host in Mumbai; Narayani Gupta, the historian of Delhi and friend and guide to me and many others traveling through Delhi; Jan Breman, social scientist and social critic from the Netherlands, and several of his students and colleagues following him to Ahmedabad; Achyut Yagnik, journalist, commentator, and NGO leader, whose office and library have become a key contact point for so many scholars of Ahmedabad and

Gujarat; Ghanshyam Shah, sociologist, who helped build the Center for Social Studies in Surat into one of the Gujarat's most important academic centers; Makrand and Shirin Mehta, historians at Gujarat University; Prof. Sujata Patel, sociologist, then writing her dissertation from Jawaharlal Nehru University, New Delhi, now Head of the Department of Sociology at the University of Pune; Israeli Ornit Shani, studying for her Ph.D. at Cambridge, now at Tel Aviv University; Riho Isaka, studying for her Ph.D. at the University of Tokyo, now on the faculty there; Rajani Kothari, Ashis Nandy, and D. L. Sheth at the Center for the Study of Developing Societies, New Delhi. The circle of international academics with interests in Ahmedabad and Gujarat was expanding and brought new colleagues and friends, joining with local scholars: Prafulbhai Anubhai, Aparna Basu, Harald Bekkers, Paul Brass, Alice Clark, Marcia Frost, Parvis Ghassem-Fachandi, Abby McGowan, Ami Shah, Kunjalata Shah, Pravin Sheth, Edward Simpson, Nikita Sud, and Arafaat Valliani.

Each visit to Ahmedabad brings new insights inspired by new colleagues, and new friends who have opened their homes and their hearts. In more recent years, these have included Rita Kothari and her husband, Abhijit; Darshini Mahadevia and her husband, P. R. Shukla; Indira Hirway and her husband, Ashoka; Dinesh Awasthi and Amita Shah; Hanif Lakdawala; Debashish Naik; Bijal Bhatt; Rajendra Joshi; Rajesh Shah; Sudarshan Iyengar; Girish Patel; P. U. Asnani; Navdeep Mathur; Dr. Dilip Shah and his family; Sonia deOtto; Pranlal Patel; Prem and Madhu Pangotra and their daughter, who befriended me and my wife, and provided refuge when the floods of 2000 overwhelmed my apartment. Among these newer friends, Bimal Patel, his wife, Ismet Khambatta, and their family, hold a special place. They have hosted me and welcomed me as a member of their family. Bimal, architect and urban planner, has shared with me his unrivalled understanding of change in contemporary Ahmedabad. His office staff have helped with materials and Rajiv Raghavan and Siby Bijoy, especially, have gone out of their way repeatedly to look after me.

In the United States, among my colleagues most helpful in interpreting the evolving history of Ahmedabad have been Carolyn Adams and Sanjoy Chakravorty at Temple University, Michael Adas at Rutgers University, Lynn Lees at the University of Pennsylvania, Owen Lynch at New York University, and Doug Haynes at Dartmouth College. All of them have read parts of this manuscript. Lynn, Owen, and Doug have read earlier drafts of the entire manuscript and made immensely useful suggestions.

My thanks to Indiana University Press, especially to my sponsoring editor, Rebecca Tolen, who accepted this book on their behalf, and guided the early editorial efforts; Miki Bird, managing editor, who supervised final stages; Karen Hellekson, my patient copyeditor and June Silay, project manager.

Over the years I have held many fellowships for study in Ahmedabad, from Fulbright (now the United States–India Educational Foundation), the American Institute of Indian Studies, the National Endowment for the Humanities, the Smithsonian Institution, the United States Office of Education, the American Philosophical Society, the Danforth Foundation, and Temple University. I am grateful to all of them.

Finally, thanks to my family: my wife, Lisa Hixenbaugh, and my children, Susie, Josh, and Sarah. Each has special, personal ties to India and to Ahmedabad. In so many ways, each has helped me to see Ahmedabad afresh. And each has provided inspiration and support to see this book through to completion.

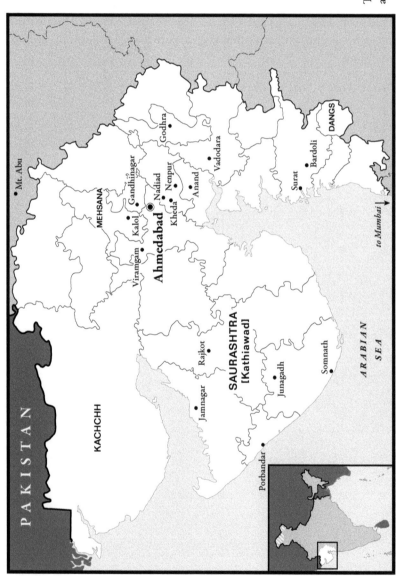

The state of Gujarat and its major cities.

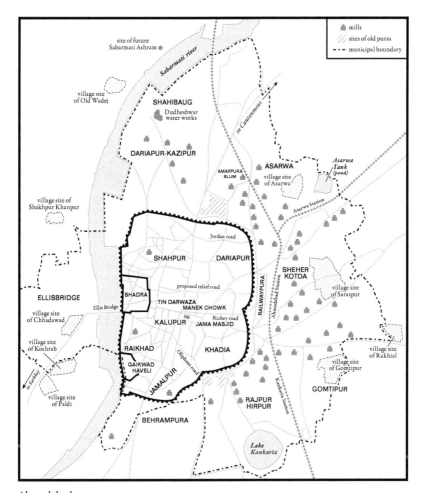

Ahmedabad, ca. 1917.

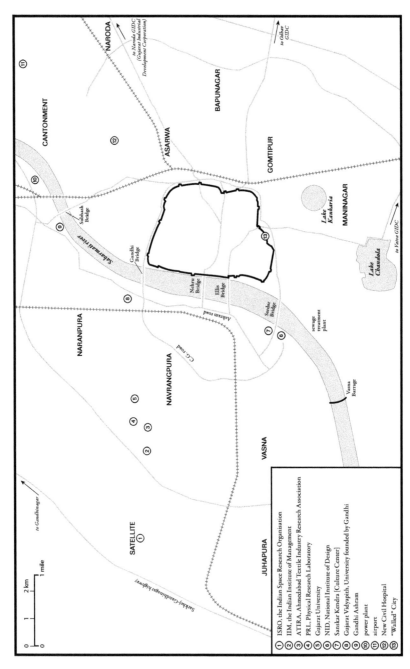

Ahmedabad, ca. 2000.

SATELLITE
①

to Gandhinagar

Sarkhej-Gandhinagar highway

JUHAPURA

VASNA

NARANPURA

NAVRANGPURA
④
③
②
⑤

C.G. road

Sabarmati river

Subhash
Bridge

Gandhi
Bridge

Nehru
Bridge

Ellis
Bridge

Sardar
Bridge

Ashram road

sewage
treatment
plant

Vasna
Barrage

⑧

⑨

⑩

⑬

⑦

⑥

CANTONMENT

⑪

⑫

ASARWA

to Naroda GIDC
(Gujarat Industrial
Development Corporation)

NARODA

to Odhav
GIDC

BAPUNAGAR

GOMTIPUR

MANINAGAR

Lake
Kankaria

Lake
Chandola

to Vatva GIDC

0   1   2 km
0   1 mile

① ISRO, the Indian Space Research Organisation
② IIM, the Indian Institute of Management
③ ATIRA, Ahmedabad Textile Industry Research Association
④ PRL, Physical Research Laboratory
⑤ Gujarat University
⑥ NID, National Institute of Design
⑦ Sanskar Kendra [Culture Center]
⑧ Gujarat Vidyapith, University founded by Gandhi
⑨ Gandhi Ashram
⑩ power plant
⑪ airport
⑫ New Civil Hospital
⑬ "Walled" City

Ahmedabad

Introduction

I arrived in Ahmedabad in 1964 to teach English. As a first-year graduate student at the University of Chicago, specializing in modern Indian history, I had been awarded a Fulbright fellowship to teach and carry on research in India. There were forty people in my group; we were dispatched to ten different centers across north India. Because my interest was industrial history, the Fulbright director, Dr. Olive Reddick, sent me to Ahmedabad, "the Manchester of India," the country's second largest manufacturer of textiles after Bombay. So, in the monsoon season of 1964, along with four other young Fulbrighters, I arrived in Ahmedabad to begin teaching at H. K. Arts College and to research industrial history. I had been briefly coached in the methods of teaching English as a second language. I was twenty-three years old, innocently eager to learn, and highly impressionable.

And there was much by which to be impressed. We were met at the Ahmedabad station after our 500-mile, twenty-four-hour rail journey southwest from New Delhi, then driven from the eastern edge of the old walled city one mile through to the western edge. The heart of old Ahmedabad, the walled city, held almost half a million people in slightly more than two square miles, and all of them seemed to be out in the streets, taking advantage of the late July evening air after a scorching day, visiting friends and shopping, dodging our car and the multitude of autorickshaws, cows, and pedestrians jostling for space on Tilak Road. This main east–west street was more commonly known as Relief Road—for the relief it was to give to traffic. In the process of its construction two decades earlier, however, neighborhood and commercial interests managed to reduce it from a straight-cut thoroughfare to a twisting, crowded street only half its planned width, echoing with the petulant cacophony of horns.

This oldest historic part of Ahmedabad housed the families of professionals, clerical workers, small business owners, and artisans—Hindus and Muslims, too, but often in different neighborhoods. From the main streets, such as Relief Road, lined with pulsating bazaars, we could not see their homes, tucked back in twisting, residential streets, or *pols*. We could not see the gates at the entrances of the *pols,* which could be locked at night to preserve the safety and security of their neighborhoods if violence were to break out.

We arrived at the H. K. Arts College dormitory, newly built, outside the walls, on the east bank of Ahmedabad's Sabarmati River, where we would spend the next few nights until we found an apartment. Our students to be watched our arrival. They were apprehensive, but friendly and eager to meet us. We were the same. They were not much younger than we, but I did not yet realize that many of us would develop warm friendships—some, lifelong friendships. We said our hellos, enjoyed the tea and biscuits graciously provided for us, and went to sleep.

First thing in the morning, after more tea and biscuits, we drove across the Ellis Bridge to the area of the new suburbs, named Ellisbridge. Our hosts pointed out that while we were traveling via the first modern bridge (1870, destroyed by flood and rebuilt in 1892) to cross the Sabarmati, about a half mile up the river stood the Nehru Bridge, which had opened just two years before and was one of the largest concrete bridges in Asia. They were proud of the progress. Yet lining the riverbank were hundreds of shacks, the housing for thousands of squatters.

Our hosts dropped us off at the colleges where we would be teaching: three of us in the historic government-run Gujarat College, which had moved to its new home in Ellisbridge in 1897, when the land was still farmed and jackals could be heard in the distance. One colleague and I were deposited at H. K. Arts College, right along the west bank of the river, established in 1955 by wealthy industrialists responding to the growing demand for college education. As we looked from the college compound across the Sabarmati River, we saw clearly that Ahmedabad had outgrown the confines of the old walled city. Ellisbridge, with its educational institutions, was the city's commitment to its future.

Among those educational institutions were some of India's finest and newest. During the next few days, we met a few faculty members who had come on assignment from Harvard University to help in the creation of the Indian Institute of Management, India's premiere business school, then and now, established in 1961 and still under construction when we arrived. One by one, we discovered the others, several of them nationally and internationally famous institutions still in various stages of construction: the Ahmedabad Textile Industry Research Institute, the Physical Research Laboratory, the Darpana Academy for the Performing Arts, the B. M. Institute of Mental Health, and the National Institute of Design. For a more local population, Gujarat University, founded in 1950, was rapidly constructing new facilities for its expanding student population in its spacious, tree-adorned campus area.

From the days of its founding in 1411 as a new capital for the sultans of Gujarat, Ahmedabad has produced superb architecture. The walled city contained beautiful gems, especially its mosques: the central Jumma Masjid, the delicate Rani Sipri and Rani Rupmati Masjids, and the Sidi Saiyyed Masjid, with its floral window tracery, often reproduced as Ahmedabad's logo. The brooding Bhadra Fort, dominating the western side of the old city, proclaimed the power of Ahmed Shah, the second sultan of Gujarat and founder of Ahmedabad. Opposite the fort, across about 100 meters of busy traffic circles, the ornate sandstone Three Gates, Tran Darwaja (Tin Darwaza in Hindi), marked the main passageway to the city's central mosque and markets. Traffic entering and leaving the central markets of the old city—mostly rickshaws, pushcarts, and donkeys piled high with merchandise, and pedestrians—was still controlled by these gates, half a millennium after they were built.

Outside the city wall, to the southeast, Ahmed Shah II, grandson of the city's founder, built the seventy-two-acre, thirty-four-sided Kankaria Lake as a reservoir and garden for his evening pleasure, especially in the summer, when local temperatures routinely reach 110°F. More than 500 years later, it still served as a choice location for an evening stroll for rich and poor alike. Five miles southwest of the city, at Sarkhej, Sultan Mahmud Begada, in the mid-fifteenth century, built a mausoleum for Ahmed Khattu Ganj Baksh, the Sufi saint who had advised Ahmed Shah, and adjacent to it, another man-made lake. Mahmud Begada constructed his retreat around the lake's perimeter, a tranquil and beautiful complex of palaces along with the saint's mausoleum and an adjoining mosque. Later his own mausoleum was installed here as well. In 1964, the site was far enough from Ahmedabad that it was usually deserted, except for the supplicants who came to pray at the mausoleum of the saint, and a few women from nearby villages who came to beat their laundry, with rhythmic thuds, on the stone steps that led down to the water.

Now, five and a half centuries later, new treasures were being added to Ahmedabad's architectural heritage, most, but not all, in the new suburban area. The American architect Louis Kahn had just designed the Indian Institute of Management campus, with its monumental brick construction. At the request of Ahmedabad's mill owners, French-Swiss LeCorbusier came to the city, from designing the Punjab's new capital of Chandigarh, and introduced modernist design in the Ahmedabad Millowners Association headquarters (now the Ahmedabad Textile Mill Association), the Sanskar Kendra Cultural Center, and a few private homes. Indian architect Charles Correa emphasized attachment to the earth in his elegant, simple, award-winning museum at the Gandhi ashram, where the Mahatma had lived for the better part of fifteen years. Naturally enough, a new school of architecture of Ahmedabad's own, one of the very best in India, had been established in 1962 by Balkrishna Doshi along with Rasubhai Vakil and Bernard Kohn. Most private homes in Ellisbridge were not architect-designed, but they were comfortable and spacious, many with small gardens and carports quietly announcing the success of the professional and business leaders who lived inside.

Their ranks were growing, not only with the expansion of industry, but also with the opening of political opportunity. Independence from British control had arrived in 1947. Then, with considerable local pride, and after four years of struggle, occasionally violent, on May 1, 1960, Gujarat had become a state in its own right. While a new state capital, Gandhinagar, was under construction some twenty-five miles away, temporary offices of the new government were established in Ahmedabad. Virtually all of these new cultural, educational, and governmental institutions, monuments, and campuses were on the west side of the Sabarmati River.

Standing atop the roof of our college, we could see back across the Sabarmati, over the roofs of the walled city—almost no building in the city was more than five stories tall—to the active smokestacks of the textile mills to the east. Clustered around the mills lived most of the mill workers. The city provided less lavishly for these everyday working people, the overwhelming majority of its population. Industrial workers and their families lived in brick-built *chawls,* two-room walk-through, ground-level apartments, sometimes provided with running water and plumbing, usually without, and in slum hutments, of baked mud and scavenged building materials, scattered among the sprawling textile mills and along the railway lines that serviced them. The labor union, the Textile Labour Association, to which almost all the mill workers belonged, took pride in the relatively high pay and job-related benefits the workers received, and workers boasted of their upward mobility. The Congress Party, which had a virtual lock on the politics of the city, took pride in the relatively good, and improving, standard of services—water, sewerage, electricity—that Ahmedabad provided as compared to other cities in India. In addition, the city had also recently constructed new facilities that were in or adjacent to the working-class areas. On land surrounding Lake Kankaria, the municipality had created a zoo, one of the best in India; a children's play garden, the Balvatika; and, on a somewhat different note, a new municipal dairy, funded in part by the United Nations Children's Fund and dedicated to providing milk to Ahmedabad's children.

Challenging the boasts of union and political leaders—often the same people—politicians on the left hammered away at the disparities between the luxury of Ellisbridge and the poverty of the mill areas. They conceded that the union had won benefits for its workers, but they labeled these workers "the aristocracy of labor" and noted that an even greater number of workers in the unorganized sector did not have protected salaries, fixed benefits, and upward mobility. They lacked access to adequate water, sewerage, and toilets. The populist politicians claimed that the prosperity and elegance of a small minority of Ahmedabad's 1.25 million citizens, and the relatively satisfactory conditions of many thousands more in the union, were built on the backs of these laborers.

A Shock City for Twentieth-Century India

I did not realize it immediately, but I had arrived in India's "shock city" of the mid-twentieth century. The term had been coined only the year before by British historian Asa Briggs in his 1963 book, *Victorian Cities*. He applied the phrase in his account of Manchester, England. For Briggs, a shock city

> was a centre of problems, particularly ethnic and social problems, and it provoked sharply differing reactions from visitors. . . . Manchester was the shock city of the 1840s, attracting visitors from all countries, forcing to the surface what seemed to be intractable problems of society and government, and generating as great a variety of opinions as Chicago did later or Los Angeles did in the 1930s and 1940s. Every age has its shock city.[1]

In the heart of England's Midlands, in the 1830s, Manchester stood at the cutting age of the industrial revolution that was transforming England, with its multiplying productivity (which increased disparities in power and wealth), exploited working poor, and ecological disasters. On the other hand, by the mid-1840s, Manchester was among the first to seek, and find, solutions: government action to protect public health, clean up rivers and streams, create a social welfare system, and tame the worst excesses of the capitalist system. Its workers formed unions and social organizations that improved their economic and social conditions.

Ahmedabad had earned its title as the "Manchester of India," and it equally deserved the designation of "shock city." It too was on the front lines of the problems of its nation. Having won its independence in 1947, India was at last free to build its economy in its own way. Prime minister Jawaharlal Nehru, who headed the new government for its first seventeen years, made clear his view that his nation should create urban industry alongside its rural agriculture. Already one of the most industrialized cities in India, Ahmedabad faced two of the biggest problems of industrialization: how to expand industry in new directions, and how to achieve satisfactory relations between labor and capital in an economy of scarcity. Nehru led his old–new nation in Western cultural directions. Himself the product of a British education at the Harrow School, Trinity College Cambridge, and the Inner Temple for legal studies, Nehru advocated science and technology to move India forward.[2] In all these arenas—expansion of industry, mutually acceptable labor relations, Westernization in education and culture—Ahmedabad was on the cutting edge.

In the mid-1960s, Ahmedabad's 133,000 textile workers were 10 percent of the city's total population, about one-third of its total adult male population. About an equal number worked in ancillary industries. No city in India had a more industrialized labor force. (Bombay had a larger textile industry, but a much smaller percentage of its total labor force worked there.) Also, 103,000 of Ahmedabad's textile workers were unionized in the Ahmedabad Textile Labour Association, a unique union created with major input from Mahatma Gandhi that generally eschewed the weapon of the strike in favor of negotiation and arbitration. Critics decried the TLA as a company union; advocates touted the victories it won for its members. As India moved toward independence, the TLA became the model union for one of the national associations of unions, the Indian National Trade Union Congress—the anticommunist association that competed for members and power against the All India Trade Union Congress, its more left-wing rival.

Although Ahmedabad was still a one-industry town, it was beginning to diversify. Here too it was a shock city. As independence had come closer, multinational companies had approached Ahmedabad's leading industrialists with offers of collaboration. Textiles required chemicals, and chemicals were also essential to the manufacture of pharmaceuticals. Ahmedabad's textile magnates began to enter into licensing agreements with companies like Geigy of Switzerland and American Cyanamid. As independent India sought to join the industrialized world, Ahmedabad provided a model. Prime minister Nehru himself came in 1952 to Valsad, south Gujarat, to inaugurate the new ATUL chemical plant, established by the Ahmedabad industrialist Kasturbhai Lalbhai in collaboration with American Cyanamid. ATUL was the first of many private-sector initiatives that Nehru inaugurated across India.

Ahmedabad's civic leaders, most of them drawn from the families of the mill owners, sought to establish the Ahmedabad Municipal Corporation as a model for India in the provision of services to the poor and working classes. They declared themselves successful in this effort, although not everyone went along with their claims. The antagonist who argued most persuasively that they were failing, Indulal Yagnik, was elected to the Lok Sabha, the lower house of India's parliament, four times from 1957 until his death in 1972. Clearly Ahmedabad evoked conflicting opinions about the intractable problems of its economy and society, and the government's role in seeking solutions.

Finally, Ahmedabad's aggressive, and successful, pursuit of prestigious national educational, cultural, and research institutions marked it as a shock city. Ahmedabad was betting that India's future would be Westernized, at least in some form, and it put its chips on the line to secure a prominent place in that future.

The era of the 1960s was actually Ahmedabad's second experience as a shock city in the twentieth century. In 1915, on his return to India from South Africa, Mohandas Karamchand Gandhi, later known as the Mahatma, or Great Soul, established his ashram home in Ahmedabad. This served as his principal residence until 1930. Throughout those years, Gandhi's activities made Ahmedabad a shock city.

The city was much smaller then, with 250,000 to 300,000 people. Two-thirds lived within the walled city. Most of the rest lived to the east, around the mills. The textile industry already employed some 50,000 workers in about sixty mills, about 15 percent of the total population. Across the river, Ellisbridge was home to only about 2,000 people. Formal, official plans for its development were just being drafted. Gujarat College formed one of its principal anchors. Gandhi chose to build his ashram on this side of the river, first slightly downriver at Kochrab. Two years later, he moved about three miles upriver to the west bank location where it still continues today, primarily as a museum and research library. The decision to locate in Ahmedabad seemed a strange choice for someone who had declared himself, in *Hind Swaraj* (1909), thoroughly opposed to the modern industrial–urban world. The choice would have profound effects on the future Mahatma and on his adopted city.

Gandhi made Ahmedabad a shock city for India during his tenure by directly confronting four of the most significant problems of his day. His ashram in Ahmedabad became one of the national headquarters of India's growing Freedom Movement. Gandhi groomed Ahmedabad's leading lawyers, Vallabhbhai Patel and Ganesh Vasudev Mavalankar, into national leaders. He persuaded many of Ahmedabad's industrialists to support the movement with their prestige and their finances. Together, they demonstrated how a city could mobilize effectively for political protest. In 1930, Gandhi brought international attention to the city by launching his Salt March to the sea—the most dramatic single campaign of the entire independence movement—from his Ahmedabad ashram,.

Second, in a city where one in every seven citizens worked in the cloth mills, Gandhi was the indispensable catalyst in creating the Textile Labour Association. In 1918, Gandhi intervened in a strike and lockout in the Ahmedabad mills that threatened labor and management with great losses. He declared his first public "fast unto death" to force both sides to compromise. Two years later, emerging from this agreement, the Textile Labour Association was born. Following Gandhian principles, the union rarely called for strikes, always pushed for negotiation, and supplemented its collective bargaining activities with many social welfare projects for its members, including insurance, a bank, reading rooms, and educational activities. In this city of textile mills, no institution could have

been more important. Over the years, as Bombay racked up a distressing number of strikes and days lost to strikes, Ahmedabad's industry generally proceeded
peacefully. Some denounced the TLA's lack of militancy, but its wage rates and
labor conditions were in line with Bombay's, without the drama and strife.
The TLA's insistence on negotiation and compulsory arbitration became the
standard for the noncommunist labor movement in India.

Third, by the time Gandhi arrived in Ahmedabad, progressive leaders
throughout India had recognized untouchability as a scourge. They had begun
their efforts to undermine this designation of about 10 to 15 percent of India's
population as "untouchables," outside and beneath the caste system of hierarchy, unworthy of any physical contact with caste Hindus, and generally at
the very bottom of the social–economic hierarchy as well. Gandhi entered the
struggle head on by inviting an untouchable family into his ashram, on equal
terms with the other residents, even at the risk of losing the ashram itself.

A few months after Gandhi founded his ashram, he welcomed the family of Dudabhai, a teacher from Bombay, his wife, Danibehn, and their tod-
dler daughter, Lakshmi, to join him. Ahmedabad was a socially conservative
city, especially the mill owners, and this act cost Gandhi the financial support they had pledged. But just as Gandhi began to plan closing his ashram,
one mill owner, the young, successful Ambalal Sarabhai, came to his rescue
and saved the new institution and its mission. Gandhi made sure that the
TLA union also included untouchables. Indeed, most of the spinners were
untouchables, and they remained the most loyal to all of Gandhi's programs.
Later untouchable leaders would claim that Gandhi was patronizing toward
untouchables, but by integrating them into his ashram and into the union, he
again made Ahmedabad a shock city, a place where the condition of untouchables was improving as a result of nongovernmental policies consciously chosen,
defended, and implemented.

Finally, Gandhi transformed Ahmedabad's culture. Gujarati literary critics
define the era before Gandhi's arrival as the Pandit Yug, the age of the educated
elite, the pandits. Gandhi reoriented the concerns of literature and education
much closer to the common man. He began with his *Autobiography*, written
in such a straightforward, simple, elegant style that it opened a new chapter in
Gujarati literature. He founded a new university, the Gujarat Vidyapith, also
located in Ellisbridge, about a half mile from his ashram, to provide an education in Indian culture as an alternative to the government-run Gujarat College.
The faculty, which included the essayist Kishorelal Mashruwalla and the poet
Sundaram, began to craft a new Gujarati literature, one concerned with the
everyday affairs of everyday people, including urban workers. Daily prayers
and spinning were part of the curriculum. Gandhi established his own journals,

Navajivan and *Young India,* and his own printing press, also called Navajivan, "new life."

Gandhi's insistence on spinning, weaving, and wearing khadi (hand spun, hand woven) cloth introduced to the city a new fashion statement. The municipality, controlled by the nationalist political leaders, although under British supervision, dressed its employees in khadi. Even mill owners wore khadi. When Ahmedabad hosted the Indian National Congress' annual meeting in 1921, the main tent in which the representatives from all over India met and the cloth ground cover on which they sat were made of khadi.

In selecting Ahmedabad, Gandhi chose to live in a new urban–industrial age, and for all his concern for village India, he responded by making his adoptive hometown a shock city in culture, social concerns, labor–management relations, and nationalist mobilization.

In many respects, the shock city of 1915–30 had paved the way for the shock city of the 1960s. Although nationalism and reverence for Indian culture were more evident in the earlier period, while capitalist business and Western cultural orientation predominated in the latter, continuities between them were also clear. Businessmen dominated the society in both eras. Indian nationalism and Gujarati regionalism were present in both. Both eras valued local cultural traditions and some openness to the outside world, although the balance between the two shifted. In both eras, a relatively small group of leaders made the key decisions in urban political and economic life. Some of the most important industrialists and civic leaders, especially Kasturbhai Lalbhai and Ambalal Sarabhai, spanned both eras, as did their left-wing antagonist, Indulal Yagnik.

By the 1970s, many of the continuities that had persisted through the age of Gandhi and the age of the industrialists were coming to an end. The national issues were new. As democratic mass politics took root, Indians began the search for a new political center. As global economic forces demanded attention, India was forced to establish a new liberalized economic regime. In confronting these two challenges, political and economic, at the local level, Ahmedabad once again took a leading role.

Through the late 1980s, with Rajiv Gandhi (Nehru's grandson, but no relation to the Mahatma) as prime minister, India began to take small steps to reduce government control over the national economy and to allow more independence to private initiative. The breakthrough occurred, however, in 1991. With dwindling reserves of foreign currency, India was compelled to seek a loan from the International Monetary Fund. IMF loans came with many strings that required borrowers to open their economies to global imports, capital investment, and competition. The national currency had to be made convertible in the international marketplace. Cutbacks were required in government expenditure for providing employment and welfare. As the IMF imposed these rules, India was forced into the international marketplace. Several key local industries—especially chemicals, pharmaceuticals, diamond polishing, and denim production—made the switch effectively. Ahmedabad's financial sector, incuding its stock exchange, also made the transition successfully, supporting Gujarat's industrial entry into the global economy. Ahmedabad did not develop back-office call centers, as Bangalore and other cities did. Some said its educational levels were not adequate. But its international business successes were no less important.

Ahmedabad's leadership in the new economy came late. The Ahmedabad textile industry virtually closed down in the 1980s, a victim not of international competition but of an internal domestic restructuring of the industry from large composite mills to smaller spinning mills and power looms. Indian industrial policy favored the smaller-scale enterprises. Their taxes were lower, and they could employ lower-paid, nonunion labor. Employment in Ahmedabad's textile mills dropped from 155,000 in 1981, to 72,000 in 1987, to 35,000 in 1995. TLA membership dropped proportionately, effectively terminating the power and significance of the union. The once-thriving municipal corporation verged on bankruptcy. The generation of civic leaders attuned to Gandhian values died off. The central pillars of the Gandhian synthesis—the textile industry, the TLA, the municipal government, and the civic leadership—crumbled and passed away. In 1987, the city's civic, academic, and industrial leaders convened a seminar with the title: "Is Ahmedabad Dying?"

As Ahmedabad restructured its economy, however, a new kind of city emerged, one that could and did avail itself of the opportunities of a global market. By the mid-1990s, its economy had shifted to pharmaceuticals, chemicals, diamond polishing, denim, and financial services. The new opportunities did not bring back jobs for the laid-off textile workers, nor were their pay and working conditions usually equivalent to the unionized jobs that had been lost. This downgrading of labor was a by-product of globalization everywhere. Nevertheless, Ahmedabad was once again a leader in India's transformation, returning to its position as a shock city in India's economic restructuring.

In politics, Ahmedabad's role as pioneer was much clearer, although often the direction it led was problematic. Ahmedabad was a political shock city three times over between 1974 and 2002. With independence, India entered the era of democratic electoral mass politics, but under Nehru, the ethos of a closely held polity controlled by a relatively small group of elites continued. By the time of his death, however, that control was breaking down, and the search for a new political regime at the national level began, proceeding in three stages and lasting at least until the early twenty-first century. In the first stage, the stability of India's democracy was at stake as government confronted demands to curb it own corruption. Indira Gandhi, the daughter of Jawaharlal Nehru and prime minister from 1966 to 1977 and again from 1980 to 1984, became so fearful that she would be turned out of office, either on charges of corruption or by rejection at the polls, that she suspended democracy. In 1975, she had the president of India declare an "emergency" under which she ruled the country with dictatorial powers for almost two years. When she called an election in 1977, she was voted out of office, although she was voted back in 1980.

Ahmedabad played a catalytic role in this drama. The Nav Nirman (Reconstruction) movement in Ahmedabad, 1974–75, had evoked Mrs. Gandhi's fears and triggered her response. Nav Nirman began as a movement to enlist Gujarat chief minister Chimanbhai Patel in a popular struggle against high prices. University students and professionals led the movement, abetted by masses of ordinary people, especially housewives, frustrated by the difficulty of balancing family budgets. But Chimanbhai proved to be part of the problem rather than the solution. Further investigation suggested that he was in league with farmers to keep food prices high, that he controlled much of the higher education bureaucracy for his own purposes, and that he bribed, threatened, and cajoled members of the state legislature to support him. Leaders of the Nav Nirman movement now ignited protests against him, which turned violent, especially in Ahmedabad. An official total of 104 people (120 unofficially) were killed. Chimanbhai was forced to resign, and the state government fell. Through the intervention of nationalist leader Jaya Prakash Narayan, the movement spread geographically to attack corruption in the eastern state of Bihar as well. Mrs. Gandhi's fears that the movement would next spread to Delhi pushed her to declaring the emergency—the first, and only, official abridgement of national democratic politics in independent India. The movement that began in Ahmedabad climaxed in Delhi.

A second stage in the search for a new center came with an attempt to build a class-based political movement at the national level. It focused on the struggle over reservations for "other backward classes" or "other backward castes" (OBCs). The Indian constitution reserves a total of approximately 22 percent of places in colleges, government employment, and elected offices for members of "scheduled castes and scheduled tribes"—that is, ex-untouchables, and *adivasis,* or aboriginal people of India, many from remote and mountainous regions. But what about people on the next level up, the OBCs? The government agreed that they should also be awarded reservations, but it put off making the designations and awarding the reservations until a later unspecified date.

The contentious issue rested for twenty-eight years, until 1978, when the Janata government, a non-Congress coalition government, appointed a commission under a former member of parliament, Bindheshwari Prasad Mandal, to determine the composition of the OBC category and to recommend specific reservations for implementation. After Mandal's submission of the report in 1980, the hot-potato issue lay dormant again for almost another decade until 1989. Then prime minister V. P. Singh, of the National Front coalition government, began implementation of the report's recommendations. The action boomeranged. Met by a furious backlash from the upper castes and classes, only part of the report was implemented. Singh's government fell in 1990.

The government of Gujarat state had already addressed the issue of reservations. It blundered into a minefield. As early as 1981, it expanded reservations in its medical schools for scheduled caste and scheduled tribe students, and by 1985 and 1986, it declared its intention to expand them throughout its educational and administrative organizations. More, the state's chief minister from 1980 to 1985, Madhavsinh Solanki of the Congress Party, attempted to build a ruling coalition based on groups considered to be backward. He implemented the KHAM strategy, favoring Kshatriyas (generally low castes), Harijans (scheduled castes, ex-untouchables), Adivasis (scheduled tribes), and Muslims. He gave them the major portfolios in his government, to the almost total exclusion of upper-caste Hindus.

The backlash in 1981 forced Solanki to backtrack on the reservations. The backlash in 1985 forced his resignation from office, but only after 275 people were killed, thousands injured, tens of thousands rendered homeless, property damage reached US$1.75 billion, and Ahmedabad lived in chaos for six months. Most of the rioting and loss of life and property centered on Ahmedabad, the largest city in the state and the cockpit of state politics. Ahmedabad's experience demonstrated why national leaders were so apprehensive about implementing reservations for OBCs and restricting the opportunities of the upper classes and castes. Such policies might win OBC votes, but they evoked the wrath of upper castes and classes. Ahmedabad's experience from 1981 to 1986 presaged the all-India response at the end of the decade. (OBC reservations are still not fully implemented.)

Coalitions built on class and caste interests, usually proposed by the Congress and by parties friendly to it, proved explosive. Others—notably the Bharatiya Janata Party (BJP) and its militantly Hindu allies—attempted to build a coalition on the basis of *Hindutva,* a merger of militant Hinduism and politics. In 1990, BJP Hindutva militants led a procession across north India designed to reach and destroy a 500-year old mosque. They believed that it had been built on exactly the spot where an earlier Hindu temple had marked the birthplace of Lord Rama. They failed to reach their goal because the procession was halted and its leader briefly jailed for endangering the peace of the state. In 1992, however, the militants succeeded. They destroyed the mosque. The procession in 1990 and the destruction in 1992 triggered riots across India in which thousands were killed. On the other hand, they consolidated the power of the BJP. Hindu militancy proved popular at the ballot box. The BJP's electoral seats in parliament rose steadily from 2 in 1984, to 85 in 1989, to 119 in 1991, to 161 in 1996, to 182 in 1998, making it the largest single party in Parliament and enabling it to build a coalition to govern India.

Ahmedabad was a shock city in this ascent of the BJP and Hindu militancy as well. Its experience with Hindutva politics preceded Delhi's. After the rejection of the class-based KHAM strategy in the riots of 1985 and 1986, Ahmedabad rebounded in 1987 by electing to the Ahmedabad Municipal Corporation a BJP majority, which remained in power until 2000. At the Gujarat state level, the BJP entered into a ruling coalition in 1990, and it captured the state legislature on its own in the elections of 1995, winning 122 of a total of 182 seats. The party proclaimed Gujarat its "Hindutva laboratory" for India. In regard to militant Hinduism in politics, Ahmedabad set the pace as a shock city.

The political divisions, coupled with the closure of most of the mills, increased the segregation of Ahmedabad's population on a communal basis. Hindus and Muslims had tended to live in somewhat separate neighborhoods. But the mills had helped to keep the vast number of textile workers living in proximity to one another. They did not live in fully intermixed neighborhoods, for even the union was divided into subsectors according to job specialization, and these often reflected caste and community distinctions. Spinners, for example, tended to be scheduled castes; weavers, Muslims. The closure of the mills left the workers less reason to live near the mills and near one another, and the riots of 1985–86 encouraged them to flee and to segregate for the sake of safety.

In 2002, Ahmedabad, and Gujarat, experienced one of the worst Hindu–Muslim riots in India since the partition riots of 1947. Approximately 2,000 people, overwhelmingly Muslims, were killed, about half in Ahmedabad. Some 140,000 were rendered homeless, about 100,000 of them in Ahmedabad—again, overwhelmingly Muslims. At the outbreak of the violence, the state government did not intervene for several days as the riots built in intensity and as the death toll rose. This decision to allow the riot to become a pogrom represented a calculated wager that the attacks on Muslims would pay off in votes for the BJP in the coming state elections. They did. The BJP won a strong majority in the state assembly. Its greatest victories came in the parts of the state—including the city of Ahmedabad—where the violence was most extreme.

The riots further intensified residential segregation. A huge sector of western Ahmedabad, Juhapura, along the road to Sarkhej, developed as almost exclusively Muslim. Even before, but especially after, the pogrom of 2002, Juhapura expanded as a huge subarea of the city, with about 250,000 people, almost without exception Muslim. Juhapura was so large that it contained a cross section of classes within its all-Muslim population. As the pressures to segregate for safety continued, another area, called Bombay Hotel, was hastily constructed across the Sabarmati from Juhapura, in the southern outskirts of Ahmedabad. By 2003, it already held about 2,500 slum houses, mostly for refugees from the riots, virtually all Muslims. In its communal social and geographical divisions, as in its Hindutva politics, Ahmedabad was a shock city.

To what degree was Ahmedabad at the turn of the twenty-first century living out the legacies of Gandhi and the industrialists? With a population in the urban agglomeration now reaching 4,700,000, it held sixteen times the population of Gandhi's day, more than three times that of the mid-1960s. The urbanized area had grown from the 10 square miles of Gandhi's day to 135 square miles. The walled city now held about 370,000 residents, somewhat more than the 250,000 to 300,000 of Gandhi's day. But then this was two-thirds of the population of the entire city; now it was only about 6 percent. The old walled city no longer served as the nerve center of political, economic, and commercial life. Most of these institutions were now located in the western sector of the city, across the Sabarmati. Indeed, the wall itself was almost entirely gone. As in many old cities around the world that had left their historic core behind in the process of suburbanization, Ahmedabad's old city now drew attention for its history. Historic preservation and sightseeing tours through its winding lanes and precious architectural treasures became part of its daily life.

With the collapse of the textile industry, the industrial labor force declined. The old textile mills themselves were deserted, despite their access to water, sewerage, electricity, and commercial rail transport. A combination of unresolved legal claims of creditors and laid-off workers plus ecological legislation forbidding further industrial development within city limits prevented its recycling. Later, however, industrial employment rebounded as pharmaceuticals, chemicals, soaps and detergents, diamond polishing, and denim manufacture provided new jobs on new land slightly farther east. By 2001, 2.5 million people lived in the eastern industrial part of Ahmedabad, with another 200,000 further out, in the urbanized area beyond the official city limits. As the eastern region sprawled outward, middle management personnel built homes there, rather than commuting to the walled city or the western city. New service sectors also grew up in the east, including one of the first of Ahmedabad's many shopping malls. New Hindu temples were rising. Construction of the first college in the eastern sector was under consideration.

The western part of the city, across the Sabarmati, held 675,000 people within the city limits and another 700,000 in the urbanized area beyond them. The large numbers outside the city limits reflected the inability of city planning and provision of services to keep up with the population growth. Private builders constructed their luxury apartment complexes illegally, providing their own septic tanks and bore wells—often with construction materials that did not meet official code standards—years before the city managed to create its plan for more systematic development. In the early years of the twenty-first century, the construction of malls, cinema complexes, and posh clubs to service the upper end of the upscale population had just begun. A ring road, intended to mark the outer edge of urban development, was soon surpassed. The twenty-five-mile highway connecting the city with the new state capital in Gandhinagar, with its 375,000 residents, was filling in with commercial establishments, educational institutions, and private housing.

In light of the sheer demographics, morphology, economy, and consumption patterns of early twenty-first-century Ahmedabad—not to mention the city's stunning failure in intercommunal, interreligious accommodation—one could argue that the city's historic continuities had been mostly broken. But all these changes also provided continuity—the continuity of dynamic change. Ahmedabad had been throughout the twentieth century a pathbreaking shock city for India, and its vitality and energy continued. In its economic development and in its search for a new political center of gravity—however cynical and violent that search became—it built on its earlier foundations.

This book presents and analyzes almost a century of development in this shock city. It explores the sometimes surprising continuities and discontinuities. It reveals links between Ahmedabad's development and that of India. In light of the importance of leadership in determining the directions of Ahmedabad's development, and to put a human face on them, it employs biography as a central means of conveying its arguments.

Although the arguments of this book examine Ahmedabad's role as a shock city primarily for India, on a broader canvas, Ahmedabad has also been a shock city in world terms. Gandhi's campaigns, not only for national independence, but also for unionization, against caste discrimination, and for local culture, resonated with similar campaigns by others around the globe. The multinational agreements of the industrialists, and their advocacy for Western education and technology in the mid-twentieth century were also symptomatic of globalization everywhere. By the first years of the twenty-first century, creative responses to a globalizing economy, coupled with disastrous failures in intergroup relations, made Ahmedabad once again a shock city to the world. For in this mismatch between economic dynamism and human shortcomings it was surely not alone—as, for example, the Rodney King race riots in Los Angeles in 1992, and the class and ethnic riots in the suburbs of Paris and other French cities in 2005 demonstrated all too clearly. We do not focus primarily on Ahmedabad's place in the world beyond India, but that, too, is surely an important part of the city's contemporary history.

A Note on Method

Readers who are familiar with the literatures in urban history and theory will find tacit allusions to many of the classics in the field: the German School—of Georg Simmel, Max Weber, and others—with its concern for the ethos of urban life[3]; the Chicago School, with its interest in the relationship between central business district and neighborhood, between immigrant and native born, and the significance of the "City as a Way of Life"[4]; the Los Angeles School, with its critique of disparities between the high levels of economic productivity and the degrading quality of life of the (often immigrant) poor[5]; Sam Bass Warner's account of three stages in the life of Philadelphia, 1770–1930, marked by transformations in technology, immigration, and transportation[6]; Floyd Hunter's study of elites[7]; and numerous official and unofficial studies of poverty and squatter settlements, especially in the developing world.[8] Perhaps most comparable will be the studies of leadership regimes, undertaken by scholars such as Clarence Stone[9] and Karen Mossberger and Gerry Stoker.[10] I argue that from the age of Gandhi until the 1970s, Ahmedabad had a small circle of leaders who guided the city's development while for the most part respecting the wishes and needs of the citizens, and that since that time the city has been unable to find leaders who can successfully combine economic progress with social justice and peace, and win at election time. This book lays out the ways in which one city has been a crucible in the development of an entire nation—a shock city—and how its leadership has made it so.

PART I

The Gandhian Era, 1915–1950

The Gandhian Era, 1915–1950

Ahmedabad's historian, Ratnamanirao Bhimrao Jhote, notes that in 1915 both Gandhi and electricity arrived in Ahmedabad. Seen from 1929, when he wrote, this glowing comparison makes sense, but when Gandhi first arrived to found his ashram, the consequences were by no means predictable. His public activities, however, soon distinguished him as a new kind of leader, and the old leadership ceded the field to him.

Gandhi wanted Ahmedabad in the forefront of many of India's agendas, including the struggles for independence; an end to untouchability; harmonious relations between Hindus and Muslims; a clean and safe city; peaceful, cooperative labor relations; an educated citizenry, with an emphasis on moral education and civic awareness; compassion and support for the poorest of the poor; hand spinning and weaving of cotton cloth, providing work for almost anyone who wanted it; and the use of khadi by rich and poor alike. These were the local components of Gandhi's many evolving goals for India.

Gandhi was an institution builder. To achieve his goals in Ahmedabad, he helped to establish the Gujarat Provincial Congress Committee out of the earlier Gujarat Sabha; the Harijan Sewa Trust for the uplift of untouchables; the Majoor Mahajan, or Textile Labour Association (TLA); the Gujarat Vidyapith, his university; and the Navajivan Press and its periodicals, *Navajivan* and *Young India*. He encouraged his allies to gain control of the Ahmedabad Millowners Association and the Ahmedabad municipality, although ultimate control of that government institution was in British hands until independence.

To build these institutions, Gandhi needed allies. He created networks among Ahmedabad leaders and their followers. Through these institutions and networks, Ahmedabad became a Gandhian city, and a shock city for India, especially from 1915 to 1930 when Gandhi lived in the city, and continuing in substantial measure for almost half a century afterward. Gandhi's Ahmedabad networks were a precursor and a microcosm of those he forged at the national level.[1] Chapter 1 portrays the city of Ahmedabad on the eve of Gandhi's arrival, focusing on the relationships he built with its leaders and masses. Chapter 2 traces the main contours of the alliances Gandhi built with five new, rising leaders in Ahmedabad. It sketches a collective picture, for it was by working together that this group created the Gandhian city. Chapter 3 analyzes the contributions of each of the five individually in greater depth.

CHAPTER I

Gandhi Chooses Ahmedabad

I had a predilection for Ahmedabad.

—M. K. GANDHI, Autobiography

Mohandas Karamchand Gandhi's father, and his father before him, served as high-ranking administrative officers in various princely states in Kathiawad, the western peninsula of Gujarat. The British ruled Kathiawad indirectly—that is, they kept the local rulers of its small states in place, but under close supervision. Mohandas's father, in the course of his career, served under several of the rulers in several of the states. Politics was the family business. In his autobiography, Gandhi credits his mother, too, for her political interests (as well as her piety): "My mother had strong common-sense. She was well informed about all matters of State, and ladies of the court thought highly of her intelligence."[1] So two years after his father's death, when a friend of the family urged sending the eighteen-year-old Gandhi to study law in England as a means of maintaining the family's political heritage, the family reluctantly agreed. Mohandas leapt at the opportunity. He had learned his politics in the petty squabbling and intrigues of local principalities, administered under local rulers, subservient to British supervision. Suddenly, wider horizons were opening.

When Mohandas returned in 1891 from his three years of legal studies in London, the family expected that he would excel either in the politics of the princely states or in private practice, but he succeeded in neither—not in Bombay, and not in Kathiawad. Two years later, when a request for his temporary legal services came from a Muslim businessman in South Africa, Gandhi accepted. He had no idea that South Africa would become his adoptive country for twenty-one years, and that he would find his métier not in private legal services, but in leading struggles for civil rights for his fellow Indian immigrants. His personal, direct experience of racial discrimination in South Africa impelled him from the quiet, private life of a commercial lawyer to the national and international spotlight as an innovator in methods of nonviolent mass civil resistance, which he named *satyagraha,* or "firmness in truth."

Near Durban, he established an ashram, traditionally the residential and operative headquarters of a religious sect, but in his case the home and headquarters of a political movement. He founded his own printing press to publicize his movement. Gandhi's efforts in organizing thousands of Indians in South Africa, arguing through legal channels in court, staging public demonstrations and marches, burning identification cards, refusing to pay taxes, and astutely using the media attracted a huge following. The Indians in South Africa came from diverse backgrounds—Punjabis from the north, Tamils from the south, Gujaratis from his home region; Hindus and Muslims; indentured laborers, and prosperous businesspeople. Gandhi got to know them all, and to gain some fluency in their many languages and jargons. By the time he returned to India in the last days of 1914, at the age of forty-five, Gandhi had a national reputation in India. Political leaders there waited eagerly, and often imploringly, to see what role he would choose to play in the ongoing nationalist movement for independence.

First he had to decide where to live—to establish his new home, perhaps an ashram, as in South Africa. In many ways, it is surprising that he chose a city. He began with a sharply critical perspective on the cities of India. He felt strongly that Indian cities, in conjunction with the British government, exploited the rural population. After he had lived in Ahmedabad for a few years, he made these views explicit:

> Little do town dwellers know how the semi-starved masses of India are slowly sinking into lifelessness. Little do they know that their miserable comfort represents the brokerage they get for the work they do for the foreign exploiter, that the profits and the brokerage are sucked from the masses. Little do they realize that the Government established by law in British India is carried on for this exploitation of the masses. No sophistry, no jugglery in figures can explain away the evidence that the skeletons in many villages present to the naked eye. I have no doubt whatsoever that both England and the town dwellers of India will have to answer, if there is a God above, for this crime against humanity, which is perhaps unequalled in history.[2]

Despite this condemnation of Indian cities and their citizens, Gandhi's choice of Ahmedabad as his headquarters made him a suburbanite of a large city struggling with the problems of industrialization and urbanization compounded by colonial rule.

In choosing Ahmedabad, Gandhi weighed several alternatives. His oft-cited explanation, given in his autobiography, reveals an important part of his thinking, although not all of it. In some respects, and for no clear reason, his statement seems misleading:

> When I happened to pass through Ahmedabad [in 1915], many friends pressed me to settle down there, and they volunteered to find the expenses of the Ashram, as well as a house for us to live in . . .

> I had a predilection for Ahmedabad. Being a Gujarati I thought
> I should be able to render the greatest service to the country through
> the Gujarati language. And then, as Ahmedabad was an ancient centre
> of handloom weaving, it was likely to be the most favourable field for
> the revival of the cottage industry of hand-spinning. There was also the
> hope that, the city being the capital of Gujarat, monetary help from
> its wealthy citizens would be more available here than elsewhere.[3]

Several of Gandhi's stated reasons for choosing Ahmedabad seem quite realistic: the attractions of Gujarati language, culture, and wealth, with the latter helping him with expenses for his family, ashram, and movement. In South Africa, Gandhi had lived and worked among Indians from all throughout the subcontinent. (In the first group of twenty-five men and women who came from South Africa to settle in the Satagraha ashram in Ahmedabad, thirteen were Tamilians.[4]) But now he was returning to his home. His home within India was Gujarat, and Ahmedabad was its chief city. In addition, the city's industries were growing rapidly, and its industrialists certainly possessed financial resources that might be tapped.

Early support from the city's businessmen gave him immediate encouragement. For example, despite the reluctance of many of Ahmedabad's financial leaders to receive Gandhi into their homes because of police surveillance surrounding this man who had challenged British power in South Africa, Sheth Mangaldas Girdhardas, Ahmedabad's most prominent senior mill owner of the day, received him warmly as a houseguest.

The third of Gandhi's rationales, reviving hand spinning, however, seems somewhat far-fetched. Ahmedabad was a center of industrialized machine spinning, not hand spinning. In fact, as he reveals later in his autobiography, "Even in 1915, when I returned to India from South Africa, I had not actually seen a spinning wheel."[5] Only after two years, after Gandhi had "poured out my grief about the *charkha* [spinning wheel]" to Gangaben Majmundar at the Broach Educational Conference in late 1917, did "that remarkable woman" search for a spinning wheel and finally discover a few discarded ones in the lofts of some homes in Vijapur, Baroda state.[6] Only then could Gandhi begin his campaign for spinning. So Gandhi's vision of reviving hand spinning seems somewhat quixotic as a reason for choosing Ahmedabad. Perhaps even more surprising was his later success in this mission.

Gandhi does not directly discuss alternatives that he did not choose—the roads not taken—but we may nevertheless consider three of them for a moment. Why not settle in a village? Gandhi's love for village India might have suggested a village home, and in fact, later, after he departed Ahmedabad in 1930, he chose the village of Sevagram, near Wardha, in central India. In 1915, however, Gandhi was intensely aware of the need for communication and publicity. In South Africa, he had founded his own printing press. Now, in Ahmedabad, he started his own publications, *Navajivan* and *Young India,* two years after he established his ashram. By 1930, when he was the world-famous Mahatma, Gandhi could set up in a village and the world would seek him out. But in 1915, he needed the communication facilities of a large city.

The same need for relatively easy communication probably ruled out Kathiawad, where he had been born and raised. As a land of princely states, this peninsula was far more suppressed politically than British India and infested with petty politics that Gandhi could neither tolerate nor master. He had had his fill of Kathiawad in 1892, when he returned from England with his law degree in hand and attempted to establish a private practice in Rajkot, the political capital of the region. He finally gave up because the political "atmosphere appeared to me to be poisonous, and how to remain unscathed was a perpetual problem for me."[7] He left for South Africa. On a brief return from South Africa in 1902, Gandhi once again settled briefly in Rajkot but found it too small for his legal talents and his practice. He was in the process of moving to Bombay when he was recalled to work in Durban and left immediately.

What about Bombay, 300 miles south of Ahmedabad—the commercial capital of India, the political capital of western India under British rule, a major port city on the Arabian Sea? Although not in Gujarat, Bombay was home to many Gujaratis, many of them businessmen, some of them wealthy enough to fund Gandhi's projects. But Bombay was too cosmopolitan, too sophisticated, too professionalized for the ascetic Gandhi. When he had first returned from London in 1891, he had attempted to establish his law practice in Bombay—and failed. His autobiography gives his own account of his first professional appearance in the small causes court in Bombay. The case was simple, but Gandhi lacked the courage to stand up and properly represent his client. He felt disgraced. Believing that he would not be entrusted with any further cases, he applied for a job as an English teacher in "a famous high school," but he was turned down because he was not a college graduate. After these setbacks, he left for Rajkot, where he also failed.[8]

Twenty-four years later, in 1915, on returning from South Africa, Gandhi found that he was much better able to cope with the sophisticated Gujarati society of Bombay. But would it be worth the effort? Could Bombay be home? He describes his experience on arriving in India, at a reception in his honor in Bombay. Everyone was speaking in English:

> The receptions in Bombay gave me an occasion for offering what might be called a little Satyagraha. At the party given in my honour at Mr. Jehangir Petit's place, I did not dare to speak in Gujarati. In those palatial surroundings of dazzling splendour I, who had lived my best life among indentured labourers, felt myself a complete rustic. With

my Kathiawadi cloak, turban and dhoti, I looked somewhat more civilized than I do today, but the pomp and splendour of Mr. Petit's mansion made me feel absolutely out of my element. However, I acquitted myself tolerably well, having taken shelter under Sir Pherozeshah [Mehta]'s protecting wing.

Then there was the Gujarati function. The Gujaratis would not let me go without a reception, which was organized by the late Uttamlal Trivedi. I had acquainted myself with the program beforehand. Mr. Jinnah was present, being a Gujarati, I forget whether as president or as the principal speaker. He made a short and sweet little speech in English. When my turn came, I expressed my thanks in Gujarati explaining my partiality for Gujarati and Hindustani and entering my humble protest against the use of English in a Gujarati gathering. This I did, not without some hesitation, for I was afraid lest it should be considered discourteous for an inexperienced man, returned home after a long exile, to enter his protest against established practices. But no one seemed to misunderstand my insistence on replying in Gujarati. In fact I was glad to note that everyone seemed reconciled to my protest.

The meeting thus emboldened me to think that I should not find it difficult to place my new fangled notions before my countrymen.[9]

In sophisticated Bombay, Gandhi could cope; in Ahmedabad, he could reign.

What, then, was this city of Ahmedabad that Gandhi chose as his home in 1915?[10] Demographically, the city was growing rapidly, by more than a quarter in just ten years, from 217,000 in 1911 to 274,000 in 1921. The textile industry, situated along the railway tracks east of the city walls, accounted for most of the city's economic and demographic growth. The number of mills held steady at about fifty, but they were expanding their internal capacity, and the number of daily workers increased during the decade from 30,013 to 43,515. Ahmedabad was earning its nickname as the Manchester of India. Its industry attracted young, single men in search of work. The ratio of women to men dropped rapidly from 888 per thousand to 796 in a single decade.

The historic city center, dating back to the city's founding in 1411, held two-thirds of the city's population within its walls. The walls still stood. They would not be torn down until the 1930s and 1940s. Afterward, the "walled city" became just a figure of speech designating this oldest part of the city; but when Gandhi first arrived, the walls were real.

Only slightly south of the geographical center of the walled city, in Maneckchowk, the central markets for gold, jewelry, financial stocks (the stock market, or share bazaar), cloth, grain, and vegetables, surrounded the central mosque and the tombs of the founder of the city, Ahmed Shah, and his wives. Khadia, adjoining the southeast edge of these institutions, remained the elite residential neighborhood. The Bhadra area, however, adjacent to the historic fort in the western sector of the walled city, was rapidly rising to prominence as another center of cultural and political life.[11] Wealthier families immigrating to and expanding within the city's walls pushed poorer working-class residents to lower-lying areas, first inside the walls and then to the industrial suburbs outside.

To preserve open space within the crowded city, the municipality introduced some restrictions on land sales within the walled city. In 1899, it designated sixteen acres to be set aside as open-air spaces planted with trees and shrubs. Gardens were planted within the walls in the Karanj, between the Bhadra Fort and Three Gates, and outside at Kankaria. In 1902, the Victoria Memorial Garden was opened adjacent to the city side of the Ellis bridge.

A trickle of upper- and middle-class residential movement to suburban locations outside and to the north of the walls, and even across the river to Ellisbridge, had also begun. The chairman of the Committee of Management of the Municipality commented favorably to the collector of Ahmedabad on this expansion in 1911: "There is a marked tendency among the well-to-do people to build residential bungalows in the open area outside the city walls and the new buildings which have been constructed in the Shahibaug and Dhulia Kot suburbs during the last decade indicate the spirit of urban life is developing."[12] The British took credit for the move outside the walls as a tribute to the law, order, and feeling of safety that their takeover in 1818 brought to the city, and as the maps indicate, the city was steadily acquiring land outside its walls. In 1911, in addition to annexing the industrial area of Gomatipur to the east, it also turned north to annex the Shahibaug area and, for the first time, to the west, across the Sabarmati, to annex the suburban land of Ellisbridge. ("Ellis Bridge" denoted the actual bridge over the Sabarmati to the new development. The new development itself was designated "Ellisbridge.") The buildings of the Gujarat College had been constructed there in 1897, and a railway station on the Ahmedabad–Dholka line had been opened in 1911. But even in 1921, the population of Ellisbridge was only 2,044.[13]

A residential pattern that would hold in general terms almost to the present was taking shape: middle-class business people lived and worked in the old walled city; their four- and five-story townhouses were situated in unbroken rows in *pols* (called *mohallas* in north India), narrow, twisting streets and side streets, that could be closed off with gates in times of trouble in the city. Outside the walls, to the east, industrial laborers worked in the mills and lived in *chawls,* or walk-through row homes of two or three rooms or in makeshift shacks, with only public water and toilet facilities. Wealthier businesspeople and professionals were just beginning their migration to more spacious, often freestanding homes to the west, across the Sabarmati River.

Socially and economically, Ahmedabad was long famous for the wealth and acumen of its businessmen of the Jain religion and of Hindu Vaishnava sects, and the new industry grew within, rather than in defiance of, the city's historic commercial culture and institutions. Family-run firms provided careful supervision of the finance and administration of the mills, just as they had of earlier preindustrial investments. Family honor and managerial integrity were two sides of the same coin. The Indian Tariff Board of 1927 confirmed that in Ahmedabad,

> there are very few agents with more than one or two mills to look after. Their offices are on the mill premises and their constant attendance at the mill enables them to keep that close watch on incomings and outgoings which is essential if costs of production are to be kept down to the lowest possible limit and also to maintain close contact with possible customers and to make arrangements for manufacture to suit their requirements.[14]

Ahmedabad's business life was built on close-knit castes and guilds, especially among the Vania castes.[15] E. W. Hopkins, a scholar of guilds in India, characterized turn-of-the-century Ahmedabad as "the center of guild life."[16] New commercial enterprises organized along guild lines: the Ahmedabad Millowners Association was founded in 1891 when Ahmedabad had nine mills.[17] The Ahmedabad stock exchange opened in 1894. Three cloth-trading guilds were established; one of them, Maskati Cloth Merchants, founded in 1906, still exists.

Ahmedabad historian Ratnamanirao Bhimrao Jhote asserted that even the government could not function without the support of these guilds. He gave the guilds credit for keeping foreign businesses and businessmen out of Ahmedabad's entrepreneurial life. (This was not true of the technical side of mill operation, where many of the supervisory personnel were British. Only in 1910 was the Ranchhodlal Chhotalal Technical Institute established to train local technical personnel.) Ahmedabad's mill owners were acutely aware of their heritage as financiers and businessmen. They knew that financial elites, especially the *nagarsheth,* the city's leading businessman and chief civic representative, had played historic roles in safeguarding the welfare of their city.

Gandhi drew support from the Ahmedabad business community, with its tightly woven organization, its historic traditions, and its Gujarati nationalism. This was a city that already knew how to not cooperate with foreign political rulers when it chose. When properly motivated, it had on some occasions in the past staged effective *hartals,* in which businessmen shut down their enterprises throughout the city to protest against government policies and assert their own political agenda.[18] In the 1870s, businessmen in Ahmedabad formed a *swadeshi mitra mandal,* an association dedicated to promoting indigenous manufactures and discouraging the use of imported goods.[19] In 1905, when Bengalis, especially, launched the *swadeshi* movement, which was similarly dedicated to promoting indigenous products, the Ahmedabad mill owners did their share by building new mills.[20]

When Gandhi chose to settle among them, they noted with approval that he, a Vania, or businessman by caste, like themselves, managed his own organizational establishment with prudence and efficiency, keeping track of his finances to the penny. Gandhi and the financial elites of Ahmedabad appreciated in each other the insistence on personal honor in business and public life.

Ahmedabad's business community believed, correctly, that Gandhi's nationalism and concern for the poor, would ultimately help their businesses and not turn into an anticapitalist movement. Although Gandhi frequently criticized business leaders for improprieties, a tendency to cut financial corners, and a general insensitivity to the needs of poor people, he saw businesspeople as allies rather than antagonists in the struggle for independence. He came to exempt them from the blanket condemnation of Indian businessmen he had leveled in *Hind Swaraj,* in 1909: "Moneyed men support British rule; their interest is bound up with its stability."[21] After his early interactions with Ahmedabadi businessmen, however, he advanced a very different point of view. Compare his praise for them in 1917: "It is my view that until the business community takes charge of all public movements in India, no good can be done to the country. . . . If businessmen elsewhere start taking livelier interest in political agitation, as you in Ahmedabad are doing, India is sure to achieve her aim."[22] In return, Ahmedabad's Vanias felt safe with him, as they did not with several other national leaders.

Ahmedabad was important not only for its business. The city had become also the headquarters of Gujarati culture and regional identity,[23] partly thanks to British intervention. Alexander Kinloch Forbes had established the Gujarat Vernacular Society (later renamed the Gujarat Vidya Sabha) "to lift up the language of the province from its present ignoble condition."[24] By Gandhi's time, Ahmedabad had surpassed Nadiad as the capital of Gujarati culture.[25]

In comparison with other large cities, British rule rested lightly on Ahmedabad. Of the largest cities of India, it was the most Indian, the least influenced by British rule. The three largest cities of the time—Calcutta, Bombay, and Madras—were essentially creations of British rule. Delhi was an ancient Indian city, but New Delhi was designated and planned as the new British capital only after 1911. Hyderabad and Bangalore, though less clearly than Delhi, were also dual cities, with newer British administrative and military headquarters constructed alongside indigenous segments that went back centuries. Ahmedabad, the next largest city after these six and always in the shadow of Bombay, the British capital for western India, played a smaller role in British administration. The presence of British officials was limited mostly to the few administrative buildings near the Bhadra Fort, the military cantonment to the north of the city, and the *sadar* bazaar, or civilian area attached to it. These British areas were suburbs of Ahmedabad, not dual cities, and their British populations numbered in the scores, not the hundreds or even thousands of these larger cities.

The shift in the relationship between British rule and local politics at the time of Gandhi's arrival becomes evident in the careers of three of Ahmedabad's leading public figures and their families. Two were industrialists; one was an intellectual and administrator. All participated actively in politics. All began working along with Gandhi in the public life of city politics, administration, and business. But as Gandhi, and Ahmedabad, began to move in new directions, they were left behind in a sweeping generational shift. In one case, a family failed to keep up its position among the leading circles of the city. In the other two, the leaders continued to be prominent, but they found Gandhi and the institutions he was building too revolutionary for them.

Chinubhai Madhavlal presided over Ahmedabad's first public reception in Gandhi's honor on February 2, 1915.[26] Born in 1864, five years before Gandhi, Chinubhai was knighted in 1910 and was the first Hindu to be awarded the title of baronet, in 1913. Chinubhai's grandfather, Ranchhodlal Chhotalal (1823–98), had pioneered Ahmedabad's first textile mill in 1861—an unusual business activity for a person of the Nagar Brahmin caste, who would most typically be involved in administration and the professions rather than business—and was the first president of the Ahmedabad Millowners Association, which formed in 1891. Ranchhodlal also gained a heroic reputation for his contribution to civic affairs.

Following the new policies on local self-government introduced by the viceroy, Lord Ripon, Ahmedabad was given the right to elect half the members of its municipal commission. The first election under the new policy was held in 1883. The elected commission then elected Ranchhodlal Chhotalal as chair of the managing committee, and the government confirmed this election. When the government sought to introduce piped water and an underground sewage system to the city, Ranchhodlal supported these improvements, and they were generally implemented, despite the opposition of the elected commissioners and the scorn and public abuse of the citizens. A historian of Ahmedabad covering this period, Kenneth Gillion, points out Ranchhodlal's heroic efforts for the health and progress of the city, but concludes that "Ripon's local self-government scheme was ultimately a failure in Ahmedabad. Without government support, Ranchhodlal would not have been able to succeed."[27]

The dependency was mutual. After Ranchhodlal's death in 1898, the municipality functioned poorly. In 1909, the commissioner of the northern division accused the municipality of an "almost criminal lack of business method" and called for it to be superseded—that is, dismissed and its functions taken over by the government.[28] This was done in 1910.

In 1915, coincidentally the year of Gandhi's arrival, the right of election of the municipality was restored, with an appointive municipal commissioner presiding. Of the twenty-seven municipal councilors, thirteen were nominated by the government, twenty-two were elected in wardwide elections, four were elected by a special constituency of the educated classes, and one was appointed by the Millowners Association. In 1920, after the Montague–Chelmsford reforms, the municipality selected its own municipal commissioner, but from 1922 to 1924, the government once again superseded the municipality in reaction against the nationalist noncooperation movement. The Congress was doing its best to shut down the public school system and replace it with their own schools. The supercession of 1910 had been blamed on the lassitude and inaction of the elected municipality, the supercession of 1922 resulted from its commitment and action—in opposition to British policies.

Ranchhodlal's son, Madhavlal, died only three years after his father, so he had little time to make his mark, but Chinubhai, born in 1864, carried on the traditions of his grandfather in both industry and public works. Chinubhai died in 1916, however, just one year after Gandhi's arrival. His widow, and subsequently their children, did not match the accomplishments of their forebears, and this family lost its leadership role in Ahmedabad. They faded from importance just as a new era of confrontation between the British and the Indian National Congress was opening in Ahmedabad.

As that confrontation sharpened, Ramanbhai Nilkanth found that he could not continue with the Congress. His loyalty to the British and to constitutional process weighed more heavily in his consideration. Ramanbhai, like Chinubhai, was a Nagar by caste, a president of the Ahmedabad municipality, and a member of the Indian National Congress. Born to the educational and social reformer Mahipatram and his wife, Parvati, in 1868, just a year before Gandhi's birth, Ramanbhai took a government job as clerk of courts and then became a local administrator, a *sherastadar*. A successful lawyer and civic activist, Ramanbhai earned his greatest distinction as a literary scholar. He was considered the most eminent Gujarati man of letters of his generation, the center of the cultural life of Ahmedabad.

Ramanbhai published twenty-four humorous essays and novels, most notably *Bhadhrambhadhra,* a bitterly satirical attack on the conservative religious pandits of his time. The book is still widely read today. With the publication in

1904 of *Sahitya ane Kavita* [Literature and Poetry], a 700-page anthology of his critical essays, Ramanbhai earned his reputation as the leading literary critic in Gujarat. He wrote poetry and plays as well, most notably 1914's *Raeeno Parvat,* a drama that reinterprets a nineteenth-century folk legend to emphasize the importance of individual conscience and to espouse both love marriage and widow remarriage—important components of the upper-caste feminist agenda of his day. In 1903, Ramanbhai founded the Gujarat Sahitya Sabha, the Gujarat Literary Society, and in 1905, he chaired the reception committee at the first meeting of the Gujarati Sahitya Parishad, the Gujarati Literary Conference. He edited several literary journals.

Ramanbhai served in public life as well. He was elected to the municipality in 1897–98 for the first time, and he often served as member or advisor to the municipality's law, schools, sanitary, and managing committees. When the government dismissed the elected municipal committee in 1910, it appointed Chinubhai Baronet as president of the managing committee and Ramanbhai as its vice president. In 1911, the British government awarded him the title of Rao Bahadur for his services. When the municipality was reconstituted as a popular body in 1915, Ramanbhai was elected to it, and he served as president from 1916 to 1922.

From 1922 to 1924, the government again dismissed the municipality because of its complicity in the nationalist (Gandhian) Congress noncooperation movement to oppose government schools and replace them with nationalist ones. By this time, however, Ramanbhai had broken with the Gandhians. He accepted the government appointment as chair of the Committee of Management.

In Gandhi's first few years in Ahmedabad, he and Ramanbhai developed deep personal respect for one another. Both were lawyers, knowledgeable of British law in India, and believers in the British commitment ultimately to leave India. Both were deeply involved in public life. Both took strong public stands against untouchability. In 1912 Ramanbhai had participated in a celebrated dinner in Bombay hosted by the Aryan Brotherhood, in which two untouchables also participated. Under threat of outcasteing, most of the upper-caste participants later denied their participation; claimed not to have eaten; argued that they had eaten in a different room, away from the untouchables; or undertook the prescribed ritual penance. Ramanbhai proudly proclaimed his participation and was outcasted.

Until 1918, Ramanbhai and Gandhi seemed to share a common political perspective. In that year, when Gandhi launched the Kheda satyagraha, urging farmers to break the law by not paying taxes in protest against British policies, Ramanbhai resigned his presidency of the Gujarat Sabha; Gandhi then assumed that position. Following World War I, the British passed a series of laws, the

Rowlatt Acts, also known as the Black Acts, which curtailed freedoms of the press and assembly and inflamed political opinion in India. Ramanbhai chaired the first anti–Rowlatt Act meeting in Ahmedabad. Later in the year, however, after a British army commander massacred hundreds of Indians gathering peacefully in Jallianwala Bagh, in Amritsar, Punjab, a thoroughly disillusioned Gandhi led the Congress into declarations of noncooperation with the government and direct civil disobedience. Ramanbhai did not go along. Civil disobedience transgressed his limits. He especially opposed the Gandhians' noncooperation with the municipal school system. He saw those schools as a key to India's future. Their paths split irrevocably. While Gandhi took the path of satyagraha—nonviolent civil disobedience—Ramanbhai remained a moderate, still committed to the methods of formal petition and constitutional change. With other Ahmedabad conservatives, he founded the League for Peace and Progress. In the emerging political environment, however, Ramanbhai was left behind. [29]

Gandhi displaced Ramanbhai in literature as well as politics, as he introduced an entirely new style and content into Ahmedabadi and Gujarati culture. The history of Gujarati literature is conventionally divided into a series of ages. Ramanbhai is one of the markers ending the Pandit Yug, or age of the pandits, the highly educated scholars who sought to synthesize the best of traditional Sanskritic culture with the best of the new Western learning they were encountering in the new British colleges and universities in India and England. Beginning with Govardhanram Madhavram Tripathi (1855–1907) and his classic four-volume novel, *Saraswati Chandra,* and ending with Ramanbhai, these pandits tried to find in their literature, as in their private lives, paths between the indigenous Hindu cultural traditions and the new teachings coming from the West. Their concerns and their audiences were drawn from the highest, most educated classes and castes of Gujarat. Their language was often philosophical and bookish. Ramanbhai often mocked that culture as excessively conservative, yet he was a part of it.

Gandhi, by contrast, simply left it behind. He wrote essays addressing the concerns of common people in lucid, elegant, but simple Gujarati, which became a new model for the development of the language. His *Autobiography: My Experiments with Truth* holds a unique place in world literature and had a pervasive influence on Gujaratis as a new way of understanding life as an honest, open, truthful engagement with problems, from the ills of child marriage, to the search for solutions to mass poverty, to personally evaluating the essential teachings of religion and culture, and to combating discrimination, whether based on caste or colonial arrogance. Gandhi also introduced into literature a new focus on ordinary people. Gandhi did not produce fiction or belles lettres, but many who followed him did. Sundaram (1908–91) wrote several of his most beloved short stories about impoverished, low-caste, and untouchable communities and individuals struggling for their existence in the streets of Ahmedabad. Umashankar Joshi (1911–88), who asked in 1930 "Am I a man or a slave?" and wrote a few of his early poems in sympathetic observation of simple people—a beggar, an oil presser, a blacksmith, a cobbler in Ahmedabad's Victoria Garden. Both Sundaram and Umashankar studied with Kaka Kalelkar (1885–1981), a professor of literature in the Gujarat Vidyapith, the nationalist university founded by Gandhi in Ahmedabad. Gandhi conquered Ahmedabad not only politically but also culturally. In literature, as in public life, the new era beginning about 1915 is named for him: the Gandhi Yug, or "the age of Gandhi."

Nevertheless, Gandhi continued to pay respect to Ramanbhai. As Ramanbhai approached the end of his life, he was knighted in 1927. By that time, the Congress had condemned the acceptance of such honors from the British, but in the case of Ramanbhai, even Vallabhbhai Patel, Gandhi's staunchest supporter, sent his congratulations. Gandhi himself continued to visit Ramanbhai at his home through his final illnesses and composed a touching eulogy at his death in 1928. Gandhi imposed a style in Ahmedabad politics that was civil, tolerant of differences of opinion based on individual conscience, and respectful of honest opponents. In Ramanbhai, he had found a kindred spirit.

The public activities of Ramanbhai's wife also contributed to the graciousness of interactions among the leaders. Vidyagauri served as a bridge among them. She worked actively for the welfare of untouchables through the Gandhian Harijan Sevak Sangh and for women's education through the Gujarat Kelavani Mandal, and in 1932 she served as president of the All India Women's Conference, closely associated with the Indian National Congress.

The third of Ahmedabad's leaders who would be displaced by Gandhi was Mangaldas Girdhardas, the most prominent mill owner of the day and Gandhi's host in his first few days in the city. Born in 1862, Mangaldas was the leading representative of the traditional Vania caste members who had entered into industrial life. He encouraged and supported others of his caste who wished to enter industry, recognizing that their social and economic progress would go hand in hand. A gregarious and friendly man, Mangaldas enjoyed his postion at the social and economic center of his circle of friends and colleagues.

Mangaldas apparently participated actively in the club life that was taking root in Ahmedabad. Ahmedabad housed three important clubs for its professional and business elites, one at Bhadra, one at Khadia, and one in the new northern suburb of Shahibaug. (Ahmedabad's first cinema hall, the Alexandra, opened in 1912, and by 1921 the city housed six movie theaters. They screened English-language films with a running narration in Gujarati.[30])

Mangaldas completed his high school education, and with the help of his father, who ran a business in the cloth trade, he found a managerial job as a keeper of the stores in one of Ranchhodlal's mills. In the late 1800s, Ahmedabad's expanding mill industry offered the potential of upward mobility. As he learned the business, Mangaldas envisioned owning his own mill. He formed a partnership with another young man of his own caste, also a high school graduate and also working for Ranchhodlal, as a salesman. Together, they enlisted the support, and the capital, of Ranchhodlal and of a Jain Vania financier, and in 1892, they floated the Aryodaya Spinning Mill. Later, the two young entrepreneurs separated their business holdings, but Mangaldas created more mills of his own and encouraged other Vanias to invest in mills of their own as well. From the outset, Mangaldas reserved first choice of the jobs in his mills for men of his own caste. At one point, he served on the boards of nineteen mills. After the death of Chinubhai Baronet, Mangaldas was the most important single mill owner in Ahmedabad. He served as president of the Ahmedabad Millowners Association from 1920 to 1924. His brother, Chamanlal, succeeded him from 1924 to 1934.

As president of the Millowners Association, it fell to Mangaldas to negotiate union contracts on several occasions. Often this meant negotiating with Gandhi, who represented the workers. As a man to whom caste identity was important, Mangaldas noted, "Gandhi is a Vania; I am a Vania; we will be able to work this out."[31] In fact, however, they were not always able to negotiate agreements without outside adjudication, and on at least one occasion, in 1920, agreement could be reached only after a brief strike.

Until his death in 1930, Mangaldas remained a key participant in Ahmedabad's public life, but as time went on, it became clear that he too represented an older generation that was beginning to lose its dominance in politics, social life, and business. Politically, Mangaldas had taken interest in emerging nationalist concerns and had chaired the reception committee of the Bombay provincial Congress meeting in Ahmedabad in 1916. But he was not an activist. In 1921, when the Indian National Congress was to have its nationwide annual session in Ahmedabad, Mangaldas suggested himself once again as chairman of the reception committee. This request put the organizer, G. V. Mavalankar, in a quandry. A few days later, however, Mavalankar reported with relief, Mangaldas withdrew his request, remarking that he was not the proper person for the job and acknowledging that it should go to Vallabhbhai Patel. Mangaldas realized that a new political era had opened between 1916 and 1921, and he was not an active participant in it.

In social life, the treatment of untouchables was also emerging as a central issue, and Mangaldas was not reconciled to recognizing the full human rights of untouchables, as Gandhi demanded. Mangaldas had promised financial support to Gandhi's ashram but then withdrew it when Gandhi welcomed an untouchable family. At least in his early years, after visiting his mill sheds and the untouchables who worked the spinning departments, he would take a ritual bath to purify himself before eating lunch. In the early 1920s, as the Gandhians began to establish their own school system, he was reluctant to allow space within his property in the industrial areas of Ahmedabad for their use lest untouchable children enter the premises. Mangaldas relented only after assurances from Mavalankar and Vallabhbhai Patel that the school would be moved if untouchable children came to attend.[32]

On the other hand, Mangaldas wanted to treat his workers with decency. Shankarlal Banker, an early supporter and spokesman for the Textile Labour Association, commented repeatedly and warmly on Mangaldas's responsiveness to workers' needs for adequate food, facilities such as drinking water and toilets, and some time off from work for celebrating religious and cultural festivals. When people he respected, such as Anasuyaben Sarabhai and Gandhi, called his attention to workers' hardships, Mangaldas responded compassionately and directly, and he urged his fellow mill owners to do likewise. Within the paternalistic system, which was being challenged, Banker saw Mangaldas as a caring, if old-fashioned, employer.[33]

Mangaldas did not believe in the usefulness of collective bargaining, and he led the forces against it within the Millowners Association. He was willing to make an exception in negotiating contracts with Gandhi, presumably because both were Vanias, but otherwise he was opposed. He lost his fight against unionization to two younger, more progressive mill owners, Ambalal Sarabhai and Kasturbhai Lalbhai, but only after bruising battles.

These biographical and institutional sketches afford some insights into the Ahmedabad that awaited Gandhi in 1915. The city was increasing in population and expanding in area as the textile industry opened new opportunities for employment and entrepreneurship. Its business leaders were serious about their industry, and they tended it carefully. Its prosperity, and the willingness of some of the entrepreneurs to encourage newcomers, offered upward mobility, especially to young men of the Vania castes. Cultural opportunities expanded within the clubs of the elites and the movie theaters of the masses.

In many ways, however, many of the older elites looked comfortably backward, or at least were unwilling to accept the more edgy challenges of the future. Many of them, such as Chinubhai and Ramanbhai, would continue to pay devoted allegiance to the British. They might challenge specific policies, on imports for example, but not the entire premise of colonial rule. Like Ramanbhai, cultural and literary leaders would continue to produce a literature critical of the upper castes, yet addressed to those castes and written from within their perspectives. Mill owners, such as Mangaldas, would continue to treat both colleagues and employees paternalistically and according to conventional caste rules. They were most comfortable when the people around them knew their place and accepted it.

Many mill owners promised financial help to Gandhi as he established his ashram, but this support dried up when Gandhi first took in untouchables, a move that shocked the sensibilities of Ahmedabad's financial elites. Mangaldas, for example, withdrew his support. Gandhi wrote in his autobiography that he was on the verge of closing his ashram and moving to one of the untouchables' neighborhoods in Ahmedabad.

But a real change was coming. One of the youngest and most progressive of the mill owners, Ambalal Sarabhai, came to Gandhi's rescue with a completely unexpected donation of Rs. 13,000. With this contribution, the ashram had enough resources to subsist for another year, and soon financial support from the more conservative businessmen resumed. Gandhi saw this renewed support as a great victory: "The fact that it is mostly the real orthodox Hindus who have met the daily growing expenses of the ashram is perhaps a clear indication that untouchability is shaken to its foundation."[34] Ahmedabad's public life was in flux. A new generation, led by a middle-aged mahatma, as Erik Erikson referred to Gandhi,[35] was beginning to assert its leadership.

CHAPTER 2

Gandhi Assembles New Leadership

*I was strengthened by the impartiality and
breadth of Gandhi's point of view, and by his
trust in his co-workers. Because of these special
qualities Gandhi was able to bring together
people of many different natures, attitudes,
and thoughts.*

—G. V. MAVALANKAR, Sansmarano

Gandhi's arrival in Ahmedabad in 1915 precipitated a remarkable generational shift in the city's leadership. The three dominant leaders at the
time—Mangaldas Girdhardas, Ramanbhai Nilkanth, and Chinubhai
Madhavlal—had all been born between 1862 and 1864, only a few years before
Gandhi, in 1869. But by 1930, all three had died, while Gandhi lived on until
1948.

The new leadership cadre that gathered around Gandhi were younger than
Gandhi—some almost a full generation younger. They began to work together
in their formative years of public activity, and their influence on the city continued well into the 1970s. They were not always in agreement with one another,
but they had a strong sense of common purpose and a general faith in Gandhi's
ability to resolve their differences fairly and effectively for the benefit of the
whole. We introduce them in the chronological order in which they began their
working interaction with Gandhi and trace their subsequent relationships with
Gandhi, with each other, and with the city of Ahmedabad.[1]

Ambalal Sarabhai

Ambalal Sarabhai, one of the younger members of the new order, was a
wealthy benefactor who saved Gandhi's ashram after Gandhi welcomed in an
untouchable family. Ambalal was already becoming the voice of progressive
culture and politics, and he was Ahmedabad's wealthiest industrialist. His family would earn the informal title of the Medici of Ahmedabad.

Ambalal was the great-grandson of Maganbhai Karamchand (1823–64),
one of Ahmedabad's wealthiest Jain financiers. Maganbhai had made his

AHMEDABAD LEADERS

DATE OF BIRTH	NAME	DATE OF DEATH
	The Old Guard	
1862	Mangaldas Girdhardas	1930
1862	Ramanbhai Nilkanth	1928
1864	Chinubhai Madhavlal, Baronet	1916
	The New Order	
1869	Mohandas Karamchand Gandhi	1948
1875	Vallabhbhai Patel	1950
1885	Anasuyaben Sarabhai	1972
1890	Ambalal Sarabhai	1967
1892	Indulal Yagnik	1972
1894	Kasturbhai Lalbhai	1980

fortune in long-distance trading across India and, in part, from profits in the early nineteenth-century India–China trade in opium. He had invested in Ahmedabad's very first textile mills with Ranchhodlal. A social reformer, Maganbhai financed Gujarat's first school for girls and contributed to Gujarat College. He was awarded the title of Rao Bahadur by the British government. He founded a Jain religious school and supported Jain temples. Maganbhai combined two sets of concerns that were usually separate: the business and religious interests typical of the Jain financier, and contact with the British and their social reforming concerns, more frequently associated with the Nagar Brahmins.

Both of Ambalal's parents died when he was only five years old, and he and his two sisters, Anasuya and Kanta,[2] were raised by their uncle, Chimanbhai, until he also died, when Ambalal was eighteen. Ambalal left his studies in

Gujarat College and went to work managing the family's mills, especially the Calico Mill, which his great-grandfather had purchased in 1880.

Two portraits, one a painting and the other a verbal description, give some insight into the young man's early character and rarefied heritage. Ravi Varma, one of India's outstanding artists, painted an oil portrait of Ambalal at age twelve with delicate features and soft, expressive eyes, standing beside a world globe. He is dressed in velvet trousers, full-length coat, tie, and a gold embroidered velvet cap studded with jewelry and topped with an ostrich plume; he wears a heavy gold chain around his neck.

Indulal Yagnik, a fellow student, describes Ambalal about five years later, in 1907, as he entered Gujarat College:

> In the hostel there were, of course, caste differences, but the differences based on class were not felt. But one day a young student of about sixteen or seventeen came to the hostel. He was handsome and well built and so fair that he appeared somewhat different—like an Englishman with pants, coat, collar, and hat. Even more strange, he had brought along with him his beautiful bed, several trunks, camping bags, and his own servant. For his convenience two rooms at the end of the hostel were made available to him.
>
> In his appearance and belongings he was very much like a white gentleman. He remained aloof from other students and lived, ate, and moved alone. The most surprising thing about him, we heard, was that he had been admitted to the college as an exception since he had failed in the matriculation examination. After staying in this royal style for a few weeks, one day he left. In conversation I found out that he was Sheth Ambalal Sarabhai and that he had ended his studies just as he was starting because of the sudden death of his uncle.[3]

At the age of twenty-one, in 1910, Ambalal was appointed by the government to the Ahmedabad municipality. In the same year, he married Sarladevi, the daughter of a well-educated advocate practicing in Rajkot. In 1912, Ambalal sailed to England for a ten-month trip, partly to explore English culture and partly to learn about the textile industry. Ambalal was preparing to expand his family's Ahmedabad Manufacturing and Calico Printing Company Limited into the largest and most modern textile mill in the city. Accompanying him on the trip were his wife, their newborn daughter, Mridula, and several relatives and friends. Ambalal's older sister, Anasuyaben, was already there. She had arrived the year before for premedical studies. Ambalal and his family lived the life of upper-class English aristocrats with an English butler, chauffeur, valet, and maid in a rented house in Richmond. Photographs show that Ambalal and Sarladevi also dressed the part. Their second daughter, Bharati, was born in London. On their return to Ahmedabad in 1913, Ambalal shifted the family residence from their house in Mirzapur, within the city walls, to the "Retreat," a huge bungalow that Chimanbhai had built in 1904 in the northern suburb of Shahibaug, well outside the city walls, halfway to the British cantonment.

By 1915, at the age of twenty-five, when he met Gandhi and saved his ashram, Ambalal was already among the leaders of Ahmedabad in industry, civic and cultural life, and social reform. His leadership took many forms, including support for both feminism and unionization; he respected his sister Anasuyaben's decision to guide mill workers in a strike against management generally, and his own mills in particular. He also financially supported her decision to establish schools for children of untouchable mill workers.

Although not a disciple of Gandhi, Ambalal treasured forever the memory of their earliest encounters. Even as he explained in a letter to the Mahatma in 1926 why he could not support the noncooperation movement directed against British rule, Ambalal credited Gandhi's inspiration in his own life and work. He reminisced emotionally:

> It is something to be alive at a time when it is possible to come in contact with you, to study from close quarters activities which you consider beneficent, to watch their effects on man-kind. I attribute my good fortune in this respect to some good deeds in past lives. Ever since I had the privilege of meeting you for the first time on the platform at the Railway Station at Ahmedabad, your sacrifice, great [words not clear], burning desire for service of all lives, your simplicity, with great force drew me to you. It made me anxious to come in close contact with you, with the object of benefiting by it.[4]

Ambalal's leadership of Ahmedabad's mill owners combined commercial and nationalist goals. In 1922, Ambalal installed in the Calico Mills a complete fine-count spinning, weaving, and processing mill. Economically, this strengthened the company's position. It moved Ahmedabad into the upscale market and demonstrated that the highest profits were to be made by supplying rich consumers. It led to the introduction of quality-control procedures, which were later adopted in some of Ahmedabad's other mills as well. Whether by intention or not, it also meant that Ambalal and those who emulated him would not be competing with the producers of hand-spun, handwoven khadi cloth, which was usually of low quality. Politically and psychologically, Ambalal's innovations demonstrated that Indians could produce goods of quality equal to those of technologically advanced foreign countries. Beginning in the late 1920s, Ambalal began to professionalize Calico Mills' management, bringing in college-trained personnel on a permanent basis for almost the first time in India.[5]

Indulal Yagnik

Indulal Yagnik (1892–1972) founded no deep and lasting institutions, yet his unruly voice for individual dignity for even the lowly and poor brought him into a love–hate relationship with Gandhi, and won him his place as one of Ahmedabad's most beloved orators, writers, and, paradoxically, organizers.[6] Indulal's six-volume autobiography lays out the details of his multivariegated life with a depth of emotional reflection and revelation, often quite painful, which gives it a special place in Gujarati literature.

Indulal was born in 1892 in Nadiad, about twenty miles south of Ahmedabad, at that time the center of Gujarati literary culture. He was the first child of his parents, born when his father was nineteen years old and his mother fifteen. His Nagar caste was ritually the highest and educationally the most advanced in Gujarat, but its cultural traditions were conservative at the time. It provided many administrators to the princely states of Kathiwad, Gandhi's homeland, the politically conservative western peninsula of Gujarat.

Indulal's father went off to Bombay to study medicine and died there in a plague when Indulal was only twelve years old. Indulal was left in Nadiad, raised more by his mother's father's sister than by his mother, who plays only a shadowy role in his autobiography. He compensated for "an overwhelming feeling of loneliness" through constant explorations of the Nadiad bazaars and by-lanes and, later, through the company of books. A brilliant student, Indulal passed his college matriculation examination at age fourteen, winning a scholarship as well. At Gujarat College, in Ahmedabad, he stood first in his class and won additional scholarships. In order to study science, he transferred to St. Xavier's College, Bombay, in 1909. He later wrote, "I could see before me in Bombay the tremendous physical progress based upon rationality and science and I began to recognize its value" (1:154–55). Indulal recognized clearly the intellectual and cultural contrast between the more traditional Ahmedabad and the more dynamic Bombay.

Indulal continued with his studies, earning his B.A. first class and receiving a Dakshina Fellowship to continue on for an M.A. in chemistry. Separately, he also began to study for a law degree. But then he decided to study philosophy, so he gave up his fellowship, switched courses, and, to support himself, took on assignments as a translator and reporter for the *Mumbai Samachar,* a Gujarati daily newspaper in Bombay. In 1913, he received his law degree and began practice, but he did not enjoy the profession. Indulal could find neither a job nor a home that suited him.

In 1915, Shankarlal Banker, a wealthy young businessman who provided funding, and Kanaiyalal Munshi, a creative young writer who provided inspiration, joined Indulal in launching *Navajivan* [New Life], a journal of culture and politics, affirming Indulal's early, and lifelong, concern with journalism and print communication. The pages of *Navajivan* carried new writers who were beginning to tire of the Pandit Yug style of elitist literature and to address issues of Indian and Gujarati nationalism, cultural rebirth, and institutions of education and governance. Indulal also helped inspire, and contributed to, a new English-language weekly called *Young India,* sponsored by Annie Besant, an Englishwoman who had come to India, founded the Home Rule League, and become a hero to India's nationalists. Both new publications were based in Bombay.

In the same year, Indulal joined B. K. Gokhale's Servants of India Society, headquartered in Poona, taking a vow of service to the nation. One of Indulal's incentives was that Gandhi was joining at the same time. He wrote later, "From the day in 1915 when I took the vow of national service and joined the Servants of India Society, the walls and roof of my personal life, as of my own private house, blew away. Gujarat became my home and I took refuge under the sky in my own faith in myself" (1:12).

The prospect of Gandhi's contributions to Indian public life excited Indulal from the moment he heard of his work in South Africa. When Gandhi arrived in India at the very end of 1914, Indulal wrote an article welcoming him and hoping that he would use his "new weapon" of satyagraha for furthering the fight for freedom in India. At the end of 1915, Indulal helped to arrange a lecture by Gandhi in Bombay, "to introduce him to the city" (1:12). Gandhi spoke on the condition of Indians in South Africa. This session provided Indulal with his first opportunity personally to size up Gandhi. He came away deeply impressed:

> His insistence on the strict observance of his principles, his clear understanding of the ebb and tide of popularity, and his readiness to suffer all by himself—I was greatly moved when I recognized these qualities in him. (vol. 1, chap. 12)

In 1916, Indulal began to visit Gujarat intensively, meeting a number of leaders, especially the advocates of educational and social reform. By now confirmed as a member of the Servants of India Society, he dedicated himself to "the uplift of village life in Gujarat" (vol. 1, chap. 13), and he chose as his first project the planning of a Gujarat education conference. It would directly follow the Bombay Provincial Political Conference's annual meeting, to be held in Ahmedabad. Indulal went to Ahmedabad in the monsoon season of 1916 to begin the preparations. Not only did he meet the local educational and cultural leaders, especially Dr. Sumant Mehta and his wife, Sharadaben, but he also engaged the wealthier financiers who provided funds.[7]

Indulal's education conference criticized government for not carrying out its educational promises and called for education for girls and women at all levels; it also called for education for villagers, laborers, farmers, and untouchables. Its agenda included physical education. Gandhi's keynote address demanded education in Gujarati, a theme repeated throughout the conference. At its close, the conference resolved to establish a permanent Gujarat Education Society with a large standing committee to implement the resolutions of the conference.

As soon as the education conference ended, a social reform conference began, and here Indulal met Anasuyaben Sarabhai. She gave a paper on the condition of the textile workers and their children, with whom she was working in Ahmedabad. Indulal published her paper in *Navajivan.* A few days later came the annual meeting of the Gujarat Sabha, forerunner of the Gujarat Pradesh Congress Committee, and here "my young friend and sincere worker, the pleader Ganesh Vasudev Mavalankar, was elected Secretary of its Political Conference" (vol. 1, chap. 14). (Mavalankar's career would ultimately make him speaker of the Lok Sabha, the lower house of India's parliament.)

In the course of just a few months, Indulal had met most of the leaders of Gujarat's most important social, educational, cultural, and social service institutions. He had begun to make his own contributions in journalism and in organizing. He was earning recognition as a rising young leader in his own right.

In 1916 and 1917, Indulal had his introduction to national and international politics. At the 1916 annual session of the Congress, he was shocked to see the opulence of many of the leading delegates, and he published in *Navajivan* Gandhi's criticisms of their elite lifestyle: "Can such a Congress ever solve the country's problems? Could we ever attain freedom by wearing such foreign clothes, speaking the English language, and living in their affluent style? All these styles and ways of life will have to be changed" (vol. 1, chap. 15).

In 1917, the government decided to send a delegation of Indian journalists to Iraq to report on the conditions of Indian soldiers there and, they hoped, to dispel negative accounts of their treatment. Indulal was accepted as a member of the delegation. Although he fell sick during most of the visit to Iraq, Indulal did get a firsthand view of another part of the world and for the first time became aware that other colonized regions also wanted an end to colonialism. He began to recognize the Indian freedom movement as part of a more global awakening.

When Indulal returned to Gujarat, he found the local political situation transformed and vibrant. The imprisonment of Mrs. Annie Besant, the English head of the Home Rule League, had enraged Gujaratis. Thousands turned out to protest at public meetings throughout the region, including 10,000 who thronged a huge public demonstration in the central vegetable market of Ahmedabad in August 1917. Indulal writes, "I was considerably encouraged when I heard from the mouth of Gandhiji his first political speech and when I saw the first really huge meeting of people in the capital city" (vol. 2, chap. 10). Indulal's evaluation of the rising tide of national feeling, however, attributed more to Besant and to those who denounced the government for its oppressions than to Gandhi, who had not yet abandoned his faith in Britain's fundamental dedication to justice and its openness to constitutional petition.

Within Ahmedabad, Indulal enjoyed many friendships. The closest seem to have been with Dr. Sumant Mehta, his wife, Sharadaben, and Shankarlal Banker. Most of his time, however, was spent trekking through villages, raising public awareness about national politics and the need for social regeneration.

Indulal was the principal organizer of the second Gujarat Education Conference held in Bharuch, October 20–21, 1917, and he conferred at length concerning arrangements with Gandhi, who was the president. In his keynote address, Gandhi spoke of the importance of Hindi as the national language; of Gujarati as the mother tongue of the region and the language in which education should be transmitted; of history as a means of teaching patriotism; and of local games like hockey, *moidandio, kho kho, hu tu tu tu, kharopat, navnagalio, and saat tali.* He lost his fight against cricket (which he himself had played in England). He encouraged women's education and declared at the end of the conference, "In education lies the key to swaraj." To carry out its work on a permanent basis, the conference created the Gujarat Kelavani Mandal (Education Society). Gandhi was its president and Indulal one of its secretaries.

A few days later, the Gujarat Political Conference opened its annual meeting in Godhra. From Ahmedabad came Mangaldas Girdhardas, Ramanbhai Nilkanth, Vallabhbhai Patel, Ganesh Vasudev Mavalankar, and Ambalal Sarabhai. At the end of this conference, a standing committee was established to implement its resolutions. Its president was Gandhi. Indulal was one of its secretaries, along with Vallabhbhai Patel and Haribhai Amin. The conference passed no special resolutions regarding untouchables, but at its conclusion, "an historic meeting was held in the Bhangivas [an untouchables' neighborhood] of Godhra on the night of the last day thanks to the efforts of Mama Phadke [an untouchable leader from Maharashtra] and Thakkar Bapa [a Gandhian leader of untouchables in Gujarat]. . . . This was the first time in Gujarat that sheths, lawyers, traders, and other gentlemen mingled with the untouchables and Bhangis" (vol. 2, chap. 2). A proposal was accepted to begin a school in Godhra for Bhangis, parallel to the municipal school. Ambalal Sarabhai pledged Rs. 500 to the effort.

For raising funds, Indulal had numerous encounters with the *shethias* of Ahmedabad. He found them more accessible and more generous than those of Bombay, but apparently more timid in the face of government power. Indulal and Dr. Sumant Mehta approached Ambalal Sarabhai for Rs. 5,000 for spreading

physical education and creating gymnasiums in Gujarat, and they were immediately promised the money. Then they approached Mangaldas Girdhardas for
Rs. 5,000 to fund village libraries; again, they were immediately pledged the
money. Indulal described the men and the occasion:

> Thus in one day, within half an hour, we obtained Rs 5,000 each
> from two outstanding rich people of Ahmedabad for the service of
> the people. The nature and the life styles of both of them were dif-
> ferent. Mangaldas was an outstanding senior representative of the old
> generation of millowners; Ambalal was a bright son of the new genera-
> tion. Mangaldas was a religious gentleman of old orthodoxy; Ambalal
> was an independent minded young man. Mangaldas wearing a clean
> dhoti and loose shirt used to sit on his *gaddi* [padded mat and cushion
> placed on the ground] among friends and traders in his drawing room.
> Ambalal used to wear pants, collar, tie, and hat and would meet people
> individually by appointment in his bungalow at Shahibag furnished
> in Western style. Fortunately, in the heart of both of them there was a
> deep regard for the welfare of the people. (vol. 2, chap. 3)

Indulal seemed pleasantly surprised by the courtesy and hospitality of the
two leading *sheths*. They invited him to their homes, sometimes to dine, sometimes giving him a place of honor among other visitors: "From the moment I
arrived in Ahmedabad, these two gentlemen of old and new generations helped
me a great deal for work in the villages" (vol. 2, chap. 3). Of Ambalal in particular, Indulal writes:

> As our personal contact grew, he invited me to dine at his house in
> Shahibag and I met often with his wife Sarladevi and other family
> members. After free discussions with me in his huge drawing room he
> would drop me at my place in his motorcar. At that time he was the
> richest man, with crores of rupees, while I was a servant of society with
> absolutely no means. Yet he treated me as a friend of equal status and
> helped me in the best possible manner. (vol. 2, chap. 3)

He compared the Ahmedabadis with the *shethias* of Bombay and found them
more accessible and more generous, but more frightened of the government:
"I had the first experience of the strange combination among the rich in
Ahmedabad of economic prosperity, fear of government and pride in their
superior position" (vol. 2, chap. 6). Personally he found them helpful, welcoming, and tolerant, if not accepting, of his independent ideas:

> I had no heart to see any rich persons in Bombay and there was no
> occasion for it. But in Ahmedabad at that time, very wealthy millown-
> ers used to stay mostly in the city and kept good relations with the

middle class. Thus we could easily reach the two rich businessmen and they also had welcomed us in an appropriate fashion. While pursuing public activities in Ahmedabad my contact with industrialists and traders increased. But on account of my independent nature I refused to come under their influence. I used to meet them and conduct discussions with them with full freedom and complete equality. At times I used to quarrel with them but mostly I succeeded in my work of service with their cooperation. (vol. 1, chap. 5)

At the end of 1917, Indulal decided to move his home and headquarters to Ahmedabad: the rich *sheths* were there, this would be the center for his travels and works among the villages of Ahmedabad, and the *Navajivan* monthly was also now being transferred there. Gandhi, Indulal, and the two main financiers of *Navajivan*, Shankarlal Banker and Umar Sobani, all decided that *Navajivan* could serve as the principal Gujarati periodical to carry Gandhi's thought and message. They shifted it to Ahmedabad, increased its frequency to weekly, made Gandhi its official editor, and retained Indulal as its managing editor. At about the same time, they also shifted *Young India* to Ahmedabad to serve as the principal English-language periodical; Indulal was a frequent contributor. They bought a press in Ahmedabad from which both journals could be published.

In January 1918, Indulal made the move to Ahmedabad. He stayed until 1924. Years later, in his *Autobiography*, he reflected on the changes that he experienced in his personality and in his life as a result of the transfer. In Ahmedabad, he became less intellectual, less edgy, warmer, more loving, more obedient, and simpler:

At first I enjoyed the comparatively orthodox society and contacts in Ahmedabad because I enjoyed the novelty of it. My habit of study and gaining new knowledge decreased. Although I stayed in the city, I traveled daily in villages and . . . while my heart got larger with my love for the village, my intelligence and imagination got more constricted. I was like a lover of an illiterate but beautiful woman. . . . my old scientific flights of intelligence became less frequent. . . . My heart and my nature became warmer. . . . And now my devotion to my political guru Gandhiji was very intense. He worked 24 hours and asked the same from others. My love and daily contact with the brothers and sisters of Gujarat roused my heart a great deal. In the new circumstances as my old thoughtful intelligence cooled, my warm love for men inspired my capacity for work, my nature, the tempo of my daily activities, and my power of performance. (vol. 2, chap. 5)

If a man with such independent mind and warm heart had to stay in the simple atmosphere of Ahmedabad and work with colleagues of varied natures he should cultivate a very conciliatory attitude. In my own way I began to compromise in several matters. But on important principles I remained completely unyielding. Some close friends appreciated this, while others regarded it as unconsidered. (vol. 2, chap. 5)

Vallabhbhai Patel

Vallabhbhai Jhaverbhai Patel[8] became Gandhi's principal lieutenant in Ahmedabad and in Gujarat, where he ran the Congress Party, excellent preparation for his career as party boss of the national Congress. He was one of the most powerful men in the politics of India's freedom movement and after independence as well. Like Indulal, Patel was also an immigrant to Ahmedabad, but the two men differed greatly in background, philosophy, and temperament—and, ultimately, in political affiliation. Indulal's *Autobiography* captures their first meeting in 1917, just before Patel joined Gandhi's circle. Both were traveling to Borsad to spread propaganda for their organizations, Indulal for the more radical Home Rule League, Patel for the more constitutionally oriented Gujarat Sabha. Their train pulled into the Nadiad station:

> At somebody's suggestion I entered Vallabhbhai's second class compartment. Seeing him in perfectly foreign dress, I was surprised. In his well-ironed silk pants, half coat, collar, tie, and hat he appeared very formal. His shirt collar touched the top of his neck and a foreign cap covering his forehead set off his fighting eyes. Because of this he appeared a high ranking sahib. Looking at my indifferent dress, I immediately became somewhat embarrassed. Taking a look at my wheat-colored dhoti, a rumpled, black-buttoned, khaki half-coat from Iraq, and a Kashmiri cap of dust color, he welcomed me with an ironical smile.
>
> Recognizing me from the description of mutual friends, Vallabhbai raised his eyes and asked me, "Are you Indulal?" Feeling somewhat one-upped by this question, I asked him with a slight smile, "Are you Vallabhbhai?" After this verbal duel we started talking. . . . Later on, with smiles, we began to understand each other's point of view. I found him a redoubtable, witty, and clever diplomat. He recognized me as an impatient, over-enthusiastic young man. After a three- or four-hour journey we adjusted to each other. I stayed at a big house along with him at Borsad. (vol. 2, chap. 1)

Vallabhbhai had arrived in Ahmedabad in 1913 to practice law. By the time he shifted his headquarters to Bombay in the 1930s, he had served as president of the Ahmedabad municipality from 1924 to 1928, and as president of the

Gujarat congress from the time of its formation in 1920 until his imprisonment during the Quit India movement in 1942.

Born in Karamsad, in the rich, well-watered Charotar region of the Kheda district, some forty miles south of Ahmedabad, Vallabhbhai was a member of one of the most vigorous, and most highly politicized, caste communities of his time. The Patidars of Charotar had reached a comparatively comfortable standard of living by the late nineteenth century, and they meant to preserve it. They were farmers of some substance, holding tenure over private plots of land large enough to allow them to taste comfort but not to enjoy luxury. Frequently, in addition to farming their individual plots under individual tenure, they also acted as headmen for villages or groups within villages, gaining familiarity with the power and the administration of local government. They were usually described as extremely hardworking and blunt. By the late 1800s, as increasing population pressure threatened their modest economic gains, they began to emigrate in large numbers to East and South Africa, where they sought prosperity and adventure.

The Kheda district was also known for violence. Vallabhbhai launched one of his first major political campaigns, the Borsad Satyagraha of 1923–24, to persuade the government to remove a special punitive police tax on areas of the district where violence was so endemic that extra police were assigned.

Vallabhbhai's background was thus quite different from that of most of the lawyers, professionals, and intellectuals who dominated nationalist politics at the time of his maturing—and different, too, from the cautious, urban Vania-caste business people who controlled the major financial institutions of Gujarat. His rural, agricultural, Patidar caste styles and values would influence Patel throughout his life. They were also representative of the Patidar community generally—a community that was beginning to assert its importance not only in agriculture, but also in the urban life of Gujarat, especially in Ahmedabad, sometimes in the face of upper-caste scorn and resistance.

Patel chose law as his profession, mastered it, and found a niche for himself among the leading criminal lawyers of Gujarat. He explained that reading law provided the quickest, cheapest path to a lucrative career, perfect for a man of his wit, quick judgment, and forceful personality. He spent ten years, from 1900 to 1910, successfully practicing in the various courts of central Gujarat. His district pleader's certificate, however, did not allow him to practice in higher courts. He therefore decided to pursue further training in London's Middle Temple.

Vallabhbhai set sail for London in 1910. On board the ship, he wore Western clothes and used a knife and fork for the first time. Patel channeled all his energies into his work; he donned blinders so as to not be distracted. He completed his courses in just under two years instead of the usual three and finished with first class honors in his examinations, winning a prize of £50. During the six-month compulsory reading period that followed, he traveled in England. The day after he completed his academic requirements, in February 1913, he embarked for India.

When Patel returned from England in 1913, at the age of thirty-eight, he chose not to follow his older brother, Vithalbhai, to Bombay. He set up his practice, quite successfully, in Ahmedabad, the nearest large city to his home in the Kheda district. Patel had gained considerable experience in the towns and villages of central Gujarat. He had matriculated from Nadiad and practiced law in Godhra in the Panch Mahals district, and Borsad and Anand in Kheda. His contacts in all these places would now be of immense help in his legal and political work. Patel took a lawyerly interest in the constitutional and parliamentary politics of the day. In 1916, he attended both the Gujarat Sabha, the local nationalist association, and the annual session of the Indian National Congress, which met that year in Lucknow. He was also a member, and sometimes the joint secretary, of the Gujarat Club, a social center for professional and business elites of the city.

Within the Ahmedabad municipality, civically conscious people were chafing at the cavalier disregard of the city's interests exhibited by the British municipal commissioner, J. A. Shillidy. In 1914, the government of Bombay had required municipalities of larger cities to employ a municipal commissioner of the highest rank, the Indian civil service (ICS). As chief executive of the municipality, the municipal commissioner could overrule the general body of municipal councilors. In 1916, the Bombay Presidency Political Conference, which met in Ahmedabad, opposed this requirement as too costly for small municipalities. They also feared that an ICS officer would control and intimidate the municipal councilors. Shillidy confirmed their fears. His salary was high and his bureaucratic rank intimidating. Shillidy granted to a friend rights to use a pond owned by the Ahmedabad municipality for private industrial purposes at no charge. Shillidy's chosen subordinate staff was not very competent. He made special provisions for supplying water to the British cantonment even though the walled city itself—the only area for which he was legally responsible—suffered from scarcity.

When a seat in Ahmedabad's Dariapur ward was vacated through the death of the incumbent, Vallabhbhai ran for the office.[9] After a first election was invalidated, Vallabhbhai ran unopposed in the second and was elected a municipal councilor in 1917. He took his responsibilities seriously. While he was still running for office, he intervened in the choice of a supervisor of a Muslim school to ensure that the appointee had the proper formal qualifications even though

Shillidy, and even some of the councilors, were willing to turn over the post to an unqualified candidate.[10] Chosen to chair the municipal sanitary committee, he spent three to four hours every day walking the streets of the city, examining their condition and soliciting comments from citizens. When plague broke out later in 1917, Patel impressed Ahmedabadis by staying in the city, sticking to his job, walking his rounds, and remaining faithful to his trust despite the danger to his own health.

From his base as city councilor, Vallabhbhai also conducted a campaign against Shillidy. The opposition to Shillidy within the municipal council became so great, on the part of both the government-nominated and the elected councilors, that the government finally transferred him out of Ahmedabad and subsequently acquiesced to the request of the municipality, canceling the entire office of municipal commissioner (ICS) in favor of a lower-salaried Indian municipal chief officer. Patel emerged as the organizer of the nationalist members of the municipality. At the time, he only wanted to have Shillidy dismissed, not radically change the colonial system that had brought him. Patel played the role of the British-trained lawyer pursuing limited constitutional goals.

For Patel, as for so many other nationalist leaders, Gandhi showed the way toward a broader conception of the rights of Indians and methods to attain them. But not right away. In 1915 and 1916, Gandhi had occasionally visited the Gujarat Club to meet with some of Ahmedabad's professional leaders. Vallabhbhai, who frequented the club regularly, paid him little attention and less deference, speculating (negatively) mostly on Gandhi's potential at playing cards. On one of these occasions, Mavalankar got up to listen to Gandhi speak, but Vallabhbhai made fun of Gandhi: "What are you going to learn from him? He doesn't even understand the Third Law of Nature. [This sarcasm was directed at Gandhi's vow of *brahmacharya,* sexual abstinence.] If he sits with us and learns to play bridge he will come to know a little more about the ways of the world."[11]

Events in the Champaran district marked the turning point in Patel's perspective. In early 1917, the workers in the indigo fields of Champaran, Bihar, in eastern India, contacted Gandhi, informing him of their exploitation at the hands of European plantation owners and asking him to provide leadership for their protest. Gandhi accepted the challenge. First he went to the scene, visiting village after village, and prepared a report on the situation. He identified with the plantation workers, dressed as they did, and enabled them to feel at one with him. He had a carefully chosen, limited objective. He paid close attention to his subordinates and the local people while he rubbed raw the local grievances. He risked threats on his life and courted possible arrest as he carried out his survey. Finally, he presented his findings to the government, invoking their sense of honesty and fair play. He succeeded in having the conditions of labor in Champaran revised. Gandhi's successful shift of emphasis from urban elite issues to those of the rural masses gave birth to a new era in Indian nationalism. When news of Gandhi's success in Champaran reached the Gujarat Club, the members all agreed that he should be invited to serve as the president of the Gujarat Sabha, the forerunner of the Gujarat Congress. When Gandhi returned to Ahmedabad from Champaran, they made the offer, and he accepted. Patel could now see that urban and rural protests could reinforce one another, and he had the experience to lead both.

In late 1917, when Gandhi launched a satyagraha campaign in Kheda, Vallabhbhai's home district, Vallabhbhai joined him immediately. Gandhi had again chosen a rural issue, this time the need for tax relief for the peasants and landowners during the famine year of 1917. Again Gandhi identified with the peasantry, dressed like them, walked among them, organized them, and carried out detailed survey work. Vallabhbhai accompanied him as chief lieutenant. Like Gandhi, Patel began once again to wear village clothes, dhoti and kurta (shirt). Reorienting toward his rural roots, Vallabhbhai found it easy to talk the language of the peasants and establish a rapport with the landowners—a rappport that lasted throughout his life. At times when Gandhi had to leave Kheda to return to Champaran, Vallabhbhai assumed day-to-day leadership of the local movement. In addition to his work in the municipality, he earned his credentials as a new kind of rural leader. Vallabhbhai combined leadership in the municipality with leadership among the peasantry.[12]

Although Gandhi usually left issues in the administration of the municipality to Patel, sometimes he did intervene to support his lieutenant. On January 1, 1918, he chaired an Ahmedabad civic meeting on water supply at which he not only called for improvements in urban sanitation, he also held the British government to account for inadequacies in the water supply. He reinforced the position Vallabhbhai Patel had staked out that the municipal government— even if in British hands—should be responsive to the citizens. Gandhi also ended on a note sure to endear himself to Ahmedabad's businessmen:

> We meet here today on a matter which is important because it is but an aspect of swaraj. In saying this, we are guilty of no exaggeration. Swaraj means rule over oneself. A meeting which asks whether the Ahmedabad Municipality is able to manage its affairs well is surely a meeting in the cause of swaraj. The subject to be discussed at this meeting has a bearing on public health. Doctors say that bad air is more harmful than bad water. Inhalation of bad air is harmful by itself and this is the reason we (sometimes) need change of air. Next comes water. We are generally very careless about it. If we were to be sufficiently careful about air, water and food, the plague would never make its appearance among us. Some parts of Ahmedabad

have been experiencing difficulties about water during the last eight years. For these three months, the whole city has been in difficulty and we have assembled here to protest against this to the Collector of Ahmedabad, the Commissioner of the Northern Division and the Municipal Commissioner. From now on we must take up the effort to secure water. Councillors are servants of the people and we have a right to question them and, if they fail to discharge their responsibilities properly, even to ask them to resign. Under one of the sections of the (Municipal) Act, the Municipal Commissioner is appointed by the Government. We are also entitled to call the Municipal Commissioner and the Municipal Engineer to account; we have assembled here to take even further steps, if necessary. The larger the attendance at a meeting like this, discussing an issue of public importance, the weightier will be its protest. I should like to request you all not to rest till you have succeeded in this effort. If we approach every problem as seriously as we would a task of the highest importance, we are bound to succeed. We have the right to demand our money back.[13]

For several years to come, the task of making the municipality into an instrument of the nationalist struggle rested with Vallabhbhai, as Gandhi's principal lieutenant in Gujarat.

Anasuyaben Sarabhai

Daughter of Ahmedabad's richest family, Anasuyaben Sarabhai devoted her life to the needs of the poor, especially the working poor in Ahmedabad's mills.[14] Ultimately, with Gandhi's blessings and the assistance of her brother, Ambalal, she helped to found one of Ahmedabad's most important institutions, the Textile Labour Association, with its unique Gandhian perspective on the desirability of labor–management harmony.

Born in 1885, Anasuyaben was orphaned in 1895. Like her brother, Ambalal, who was five years younger, she was then raised by her uncle, Chimanlal. Anasuyaben's parents had been devoted to her education as a wealthy, cultured young woman. They had arranged her engagement while she was still a child, and when she reached puberty, her uncle carried through with the marriage. It proved disastrous. Her husband's family was beneath her own in class, and apparently she found the transition difficult. In addition, she wanted to enjoy the pleasures of a sheltered childhood before embarking on the life of a housewife. Finally, her husband was failing in his studies, and so she was not permitted to continue with her own. She looked forward to each visit with her brother at their original home, and during those visits, she sat in on his tutorials. At the end of each visit, she resisted returning to her husband. Finally Ambalal brought her back to their own family home permanently, although there never was a formal divorce.

Anasuyaben remained deeply religious and philosophical throughout her life, with a special appreciation for the teachings of Ramakrishna Paramahansa and and Swami Vivekananda, both of whom combined a love of the spiritual with a concern for the lives of the poor and downtrodden. For a time she considered becoming a Jain *sadhvi,* or nun. Then, in 1911, partly to satisfy Anasuyaben's desire for further study and partly to ensure that her husband did not pursue her or her inheritance, Ambalal agreed to send her to London to study medicine.

In London, she stayed in a hostel for vegetarian students run by the Theosophical Society. Seven of the residents were from India, three from Gujarat. One day, as she was walking in London, she saw a calf's head hanging in a butcher shop and decided that medicine was not for her. She transferred to studying social work at the London School of Economics. She stayed for about a year and a half. Then, just short of completing her exams, she returned to India in 1913 at the death of her younger sister, Kanta.

Anasuyaben and Ambalal talked about common interests. She wanted to work for the benefit of the mill workers, and he owned a *chawl,* a worker's neighborhood, outside Delhi Gate, adjacent to the Jubilee Mill, which he also owned. Sanitation was minimal, education for the children nonexistent. Ambalal would supply space in the *chawl,* watchmen from the mill for protection, and necessary financing. Anasuyaben would do the work of education and hygiene among the children. She accepted the challenge and was joined by Jashodaben, a childhood friend and a child widow. On March 14, 1914, they opened a school for the children of the Amarpura *chawl.* Decades later, reminiscing about the experience, Anasuyaben recalled, "Working among you I began to understand your dreadful condition. The picture of men and women making their way home after working for 24 to 36 hours in the mill is still vivid before my eyes. Even small children were compelled to work for 12 hours then!" On another occasion, she recalled, "We noticed before us emaciated and despondent children, their bodies naked and covered with dirt and unkempt hair. We commenced our work in right earnest. We would bathe them and comb their hair after applying oil when innumerable lice would come out."[15]

As the new school became accepted in the community, it added a head teacher and two assistant teachers. Later it added adult education courses; an ayurvedic *vaidya,* or doctor practicing traditional Indian medicine; and a cooperative credit society. The workers themselves began to organize *bhajan mandalis,* or neighborhood associations for singing religious hymns in the evening. In 1916, Anasuyaben, her friend and colleague Shankarlal Banker, and some other upper- and middle-class reformers established the Majoor Mitra Mandal

(Friends of Labour Society) to encourage further social work.[16] The workers accepted Anasuyaben as a friend. In 1917, they asked her to provide leadership for a strike.

By this time, mill workers and their families formed more than half the population of this most industrialized city. The census of 1921 enumerated 87,965 people connected to the cotton textile industry—47,618 workers and 40,347 dependents. A total of 1,469 worked in their homes; all the rest were mill workers. Another 52,925 workers and dependents relied on additional industrial jobs, bringing the entire industrial population in Ahmedabad to 51 percent of the city total. Men made up 72 percent of the mill labor force, women 15 percent, and children 13 percent. Accommodating the working classes peacefully and politically was perhaps the most important issue confronting Ahmedabad's leaders.[17]

As early as the last years of the nineteenth century, Ahmedabad's industrial workers were beginning to demonstrate greater commitment to their urban homes and jobs than could be found anywhere else in India. Ahmedabad's mill workers had already attenuated their ties to their villages and land. The 1892 Bombay *Provincial Report on the Working of the Indian Factories Act* noted that "Ahmedabad appears to be the only great center of the cotton industry that possesses what may be called a separate mill population." The 1929 Royal Commission on Labour reported that Ahmedabad's mill workers showed lower rates of absenteeism than Bombay's and suggested that the reason was their greater independence from village ties. By 1929, 20 percent of the workers had been born in Ahmedabad city itself; 25 percent in other parts of Ahmedabad district; and 35 percent in other parts of today's Gujarat state. These 80 percent were classified as permanent laborers. Of the remainder, 10 percent came from Marwar, in today's Rajasthan; 5 percent from the Deccan and Konkan; and 5 percent from other parts of India.[18]

Jobs in the mills were allocated largely by caste. Some of the workers were of higher castes—Brahmans, Vanias, and Kunbis—but most were Kolis, Marathas, Pardesis, Bavchas (printers), Vaghris, Marwadis, and Muslims—generally a poor working-class community in Ahmedabad, subdivided into its own castes. Some untouchable castes were recruited into the industry for their skills, especially Dheds, who were weavers of coarse cloth displaced from hand-loom weaving into the mills, and Vankars, also traditional hand-loom weavers who now moved off the land to take industrial jobs in Ahmedabad. In the 1920s, Muslim weavers and Dhed spinners represented almost 20 percent of the labor force in the mills. The 1929 Royal Commission reported that the Vankar untouchables were employed in the spinning sections of the mills, separate from workers of higher castes. It also noted that most of the weavers were Muslims, along with Koli Patels and some higher castes. Generally the weavers were better paid than the spinners.[19]

Much of the recruitment and work discipline was left in the hands of *mukkadams*, or jobbers. These men usually hired workers who shared their own caste and village backgrounds. They also looked after the welfare of newer, younger recruits—at a price. They expected kickbacks. Independently, and under orders from higher-level management, they often beat the workers like animals. One manager argued, "When we beat the workers, the mills work better."[20] The jobbers had a reputation for sexually exploiting the women working under their control, sometimes breaking up the families of the women in the process. Shankarlal Banker cites this exploitation as one of the reasons that Gandhi urged women not to work in the mills, but to stay home and nurture their families if this was financially feasible.[21]

So long as the mill owners did not wish to invest in employing middle-level supervisory and management personnel, these jobbers—"uneducated, corrupt, and tyrannical," as Ambalal Sarabhai characterized them—had a powerful place in the mills. They were also the best paid. Kacharabhai Bhagat, an early union organizer, reported weekly pay rates in 1912 as follows: doffers, Rs. 2–8–0; warpers, Rs. 5; wefters, Rs. 5–8–0; *mukkadams*, Rs. 7; oilers, Rs. 6; and jobbers, Rs. 30–35.[22]

Working conditions in the mills and living conditions in the neighborhoods surrounding them were abysmal. Mortality in Ahmedabad was 50 per thousand in 1921; infant mortality was 360 per thousand. Rates in the mill areas were higher. The Royal Commission on Labour heard testimony that the mills sometimes released wastewater into the areas of workers' housing and slums. Workers' housing invariably lacked adequate sanitation, water supply, and toilet facilities. Work in the mills went on dawn to dusk. When electricity was introduced into the mills in 1905, ten years before a public electricity supply was installed in the city, some mills began to open as early as 5 AM, and some closed as late as 9 PM. A single shift might run fifteen hours.[23]

Government legislation in 1881 and 1891 limited women's and children's hours. Children below the age of nine were not permitted to work in the mills, but sometimes their parents brought them along to add to the family income. Children between nine and twelve were permitted to work a half day in each of two mills. The younger children wandered around during the day, after hunting in garbage heaps or begging from wealthier people for scraps of leftover food.[24] Men's hours were reduced to twelve per day only by the Indian Factories Act of 1911. In Ahmedabad's dry climate, humidification was necessary in the mills. Some introduced steam humidification. In the hot summer months of May and June, when temperatures routinely reach 110°F, the mill atmosphere was intolerable. One mill worker told the Indian Factory Labor Commission of 1908, "We have to work in that great heat and are exhausted so much so that at times men faint in that hot weather and have to be taken home in carts."[25]

In about 1917, Shankarlal Banker assessed the expenditures and income of a typical mill worker. He studied a two-loom weaver, a Muslim with a wife and two young children. The children might have been of school age, but so few workers sent their children to school that Banker did not include any estimates for educational expenditures.[26] The expenses were basic, yet they exceeded the worker's income. The total monthly expenditure for this family of four, Rs. 24-12-0, did not include expenditures for childbirth, illness, accidents, marriage, betrothal, death, almsgiving, dinners on festive occasions, gifts, insurance, education, or recreation. In addition, most families had more than two children. Bottom line: the workers could not make ends meet. They were deeply in debt to moneylenders. As Banker explained,

> A worker's earnings have been calculated at Rs. 22 per month but the worker cannot always earn that amount. He cannot work all the twelve months of the year as the work is hard. Further, incapacity, illness, and unemployment intervene, so that on an average he works only for eleven months in a year. His income should therefore be really calculated at Rs. 20 per month. Most of the workers are deep in debt. They have to pay heavy interest. The amount of this interest is not included in the above estimate. It is not possible to give a full idea of the pathetic plight to which a needy worker is reduced when he is in the claw of *savkar* or Pathan [moneylenders].[27]

Thousands of workers' families lived near the mills in *chawls,* walk-through lines of tenement housing, usually allowing one room per family. In 1881, there were about 1,300 households residing in thirty-seven *chawls,* constituting about 4 percent of the total number of households in the city. By 1911, the number of households residing in *chawls* had risen to about 20,000 and constituted about 38 percent of the total number of households. By 1941, almost 48,000 households constituting 44 percent of the total were residing in 880 *chawls.*[28]

As president of the Ahmedabad municipality in the 1930s, G. V. Mavalankar visited and described the horror of these *chawls:*

> I saw a chawl built by a wealthy gentleman. It was built without a finished plinth foundation, and the floor of the room was about one and a half feet lower than the surrounding ground level, allowing water and other materials to drain into it. The structure was built not of baked bricks, but of strips of iron. The strips were not fastened with metal nails, but were stood up and held in place by wooden rafters. There was not enough space in this room for a five and one-half foot man to stand erect, nor could he stretch out full length to sleep. The rent (at that time) was Rs. 3/month. The chawl had no special facility for water. There were so few toilets, and the ones that existed were so dirty,

EXPENSES

MONTHLY EXPENSES

Rice (1 maund)	2-12-0
Pulses (½ maund)	1-3-0
Wheat (2 maunds)	4-8-0
Mutton (4 lbs.)	0-8-0
Fuel (4 maunds)	1-4-0
Vegetables (1 anna/day)	1-14-0
Oil, condiments	1-0-0
Ghee, gur, sugar	1-0-0
Tea and milk	2-0-0
Hair oil	0-3-0
Soap	0-4-0
Shaving	0-6-0
Bidis, betel	1-8-0
Rent	1-8-0
Kerosene	0-6-0
Monthly expenditure	20-4-0

ANNUAL EXPENSES

Pants 4	4-0-0
Coats 3	3-12-0
Shirts 4	3-4-0
Shirts (special variety) 2	1-14-0
Turban 1	1-5-0
Boots 4 pairs	12-0-0
Umbrella 1	2-2-0
Cap 1	2-6-0
Trousers 4	2-0-0
Shirts 4	3-0-0
Coats 4	2-4-0
Short saris	2-4-0
Peshwaj 1	4-8-0
Women's trousers	3-0-0
Women's shirts 4	3-0-0
Chappals (sandals)	0-8-0
Bangles	2-0-0
Girls' saris	1-14-0
Annual expenditure	54-1-0
Annual expenditure on a monthly basis	4-8-0
Total monthly expenditure	24-12-0

Expenses are expressed in rupees, annas, and pies; 1 rupee
= 16 annas; 1 anna = 12 pies.

that if you wanted to give a description of hell you need go no further. I was so overwhelmed with disgust that the words blurted out of my mouth, "Oh, God, how can it be that the wealthy man who profits by keeping poor people in this hell is not punished for this sin?" There is justice from God in this world. The next year the wealthy owner of the chawl went bankrupt and lived in poverty for the rest of his life.[29]

Banker reports a shockingly similar visit to the industrial areas by pandit Madan Mohan Malaviya, vice chancelor of Banaras Hindu University, who came to Ahmedabad in 1930 to learn firsthand about labor issues:

> Malaviya was told about the difficulties of the workers in regard to housing, water, and toilets. When he told a meeting of workers that they ought to bathe every day, he was met by laughter. He asked, "Why are you laughing?" They said, "We don't have enough water for drinking. How can we arrange for baths?!" The next day Malaviya went into the workers' chawls to see for himself. He saw a line of women carrying pots to fill with water from a single tap.

Malaviya later addressed a meeting of the Millowners Association:

> I have returned to Ahmedabad not to make speeches but to see the condition of the workers. I have seen the workers' chawls. How can the Ahmedabad Municipality allow such chawls in the twentieth century? There ought to be an arrangement for housing the workers. If they have no facility for drinking water, where will they get water for bathing?! Without bathing they cannot do good work. The lack of toilets is also painful. Form a plan for housing the workers.[30]

Literacy was very low among the workers. The collector of Ahmedabad district, W. T. Doderet, testified before the Factory Commission in 1907 that the class from which the mill workers came did not usually receive formal education. Doderet did not regard this as a problem because they were likely to spend their entire lives working in the mills. As late as 1930, a TLA survey among 3,926 families of mill workers found a literacy rate of 20.9 percent. The first school that would accept Harijan children was the Jamalpur (Christian) Mission School. When the municipality later opened a school for Harijan children at Ghee Kanta and three more schools at Khasipur and Lal Darwaja with funds from the Lalshankar Umayashankar Trust, only Christians and Muslims came as teachers. "Other teachers did not come."[31]

Despite the wretched living conditions, laborers committed to a lifetime of work in the mills, suggesting that alternative employment opportunities were limited and worse. Strikes broke out periodically. In 1892–93, the mill owners of Ahmedabad introduced wage cuts, and all the mills were shut down by strikes. Because Ranchhodlal Chhotalal was the principal mill owner, the workers unleashed their anger on him. They damaged machinery in his mills and gathered in protest outside his home, but he was not there. The strike was unsuccessful. In 1895, the Millowners Association decided to pay weavers every two weeks instead of weekly. A massive strike resulted, but it also failed. The inspector of factories wrote,

> I must report on one of the largest strikes of mill operatives ever known in the Presidency which occurred in Ahmedabad in the first week of February. All the weavers in the mills struck work without notice, and other mill workmen joined them . . . There must have been at least 8,000 men on strike at the time. The strike lasted ten days and for days afterwards the weavers were slow and dissatisfied at their work. It was fully a month before everything was again working smoothly.[32]

Localized strikes in individual mills over wages, hours, and conditions were frequent, but they were not viewed as industry-wide threats. Sometimes, however, violent demonstrations threatened the peace of the industry and of the city. In one instance, the army was brought in to keep the peace. A violent demonstration in the Raipur mill in 1914 went on for eight days and was successful. The doffers received a pay increase of 266 percent, while the warpers and the weft piecers got 100 percent raises. The raises could be so large because the wage bill was a relatively small proportion of the total cost of production.

Labor unrest was not limited to the mills. On September 14, 1911, the sanitation workers of Ahmedabad went on strike. These men and women of the Bhangi, or lowest untouchable, sweeper caste, had not received their pay for two months. The toilets, drains, and roads of Ahmedabad remained uncleaned for several days. Three of the strike leaders—Kashiya Deva, Mafatiya Mana, and Dhana Baluni—were arrested and sentenced to one month's rigorous imprisonment. To recruit alternative labor, the municipality dispatched telegrams to Nadiad, Kheda, Bharuch, and even as far away as Pune. As strikebreakers began to arrive, the Ahmedabad workers returned to their jobs, and the municipality found funds to pay them their back salary.[33]

The workers in this industrializing city were making themselves heard, but the powerful elites were not prepared to listen. How could the poorly fed, poorly clothed, exhausted, illiterate, low-caste, untouchable, and Muslim manual laborers make their demands stick? Anasuyaben Sarabhai provided an answer to this question. She could represent them, and she had the ear of the exclusive group of Ahmedabad leaders. Indeed, her brother was becoming the biggest mill owner of them all, and a respected member of the city's leadership regime.

In 1917, a group of mill workers asked Anasuyaben to provide leadership for a strike. A plague was sweeping through the filthy lanes of Ahmedabad.

Workers began to flee the city, and the mills were threatened with closure. To keep the workers on the job, the mill owners offered a plague bonus of 75 percent of salary, but their offer did not include the workers who were already city dwellers and had nowhere to flee: the Muslims, Vanias, Brahmans, and the warpers. The warpers decided to ask for an increase of 25 percent. They asked Anasuyaben to attend their meeting and offer guidance. She suggested that the warpers submit a written demand—which she also signed—and give the owners forty-eight hours to reply. Not only did the mill owners refuse the demand, but they began to recruit strikebreaking workers from Bombay. Some violence ensued between the strikers and the strikebreakers. Anasuyben offered financial help from her personal funds to the strikers. After two months, the owners offered 24 percent, and the strike ended. From that time on, the mill workers of Ahmedabad have celebrated December 4, the first day of the strike, as Majoor Din, Laborer's Day.

In February 1918, however, as the plague ended, the mill owners sought to terminate the plague bonus, and a new strike broke out. This was the famous "Righteous Struggle" described by Mahadevbhai Desai,[34] the strike that provoked Gandhi's first political fast in India and fifty years later provided the setting for Erik Erikson's psychobiographical account, *Gandhi's Truth*.[35] The negotiations pitted Ambalal Sarabhai as the representative of the owners against his sister, Anasuyaben, as the representative of the workers.

All three interested parties—government, mill owners, and workers—asked Gandhi to intervene. The Ahmedabad district collector, G. E. Chatfield, representing the government, asked him to advise the mill owners and keep the peace: "I am informed that the millowners will, if at all, only heed your advice; you are sympathetic to them and you are the only person who can explain their case to me."[36] Ambalal, speaking for the mill owners, asked Gandhi to restrain the workers and keep the peace. Anasuyaben asked him to lead the workers and keep the peace. Here was the Ahmedabad leadership regime in action. All groups sought the peaceful resolution of a dispute. All saw the need to maintain a flourishing economy based on the textile industry. By this time, even Gandhi agreed on this. All saw the need for comprehensive negotiations. All looked to Gandhi to provide a workable, peaceful solution. Because the dynamics of the strike have so well described elsewhere, the account here will be brief.

As rumors of the termination of the plague bonus spread throughout Ahmedabad, an agreement was reached to establish an arbitration board. Ambalal was one of the three negotiators for the owners. (Mangaldas Girdhardas, who was the president of the Ahmedabad Millowners Association at the time, had removed himself from the negotiations by accepting the workers' salary demands within his own mills.) Gandhi, Vallabhbhai, and Shankarlal Banker represented the workers. Although the workers had turned to Anasuyaben for leadership, she had asked Gandhi to intervene, and she herself was not part of the negotiating committee.

Even as the negotiations were in progress, some workers went on a wildcat strike. The mill owners responded by declaring a lockout of all workers who would not accept a reduction in the plague bonus to 20 percent of salary. This was their negotiating position. Gandhi met with Anasuyaben, Banker, and the workers. He gathered data on the cost of living as well as the financial position of the mills. He concluded that a 35 percent salary increase was justified. A meeting of 100 workers' representatives wanted to push for 50 percent, but they were willing to accept Gandhi's judgment that 35 percent was a reasonable midpoint.

Gandhi was presenting himself as both workers' representative and mediator. Most of the workers accepted this conflicted position, but the mill owners did not. They rejected Gandhi's offer. The strike began on February 22. In response, the owners declared a lockout. The warpers' strike in 1917 had involved about 500 men, mostly untouchables. The 1918 strike began with 15,000 weavers, mostly Muslims and Patels. The lockout affected 40,000 workers. Anasuyaben, Banker, and Chhaganlal Gandhi visited the workers daily in the *chawls*. Mohandas Gandhi addressed them daily in public meetings at the Sabarmati riverbed. As many as 10,000 workers attended these meetings. A new style of consultation and accommodation was evolving between the workers of Ahmedabad and the people who would lead and represent them.

On March 12, the owners lifted the lockout and took back all workers who accepted a 20 percent pay increase. By March 15, the strike seemed headed toward failure. Workers directed their frustrations at Gandhi and Anasuyaben: "They come and go in their car. They eat elegant food while we suffer death agonies. To attend meetings does not keep us from starvation."[37] Stung by the workers' bitter criticism, Gandhi responded by undertaking to fast until the workers' demand for a 35 percent increase was met, or until he died. He claimed that he was fasting to rouse the flagging spirits of the workers, but the owners understood Gandhi's fast as coercive. On March 18, the third day of the fast and the twenty-second day of the strike, a compromise was reached by which the workers would receive a 35 percent increase on the first day back at work, a 20 percent increase on the second, and after that an amount to be determined by an arbitrator.

Gandhi clearly recognized the coercive element in his fast, and therefore the very peculiar nature of this experiment in labor–management relations. He spoke at his ashram a few hours before the compromise was announced: "Deny it emphatically as I may, the people cannot but feel that the millowners have acted under pressure of my fast and the world at large will not believe what I say. My weak condition left the millowners no freedom."[38] Despite the coercive element, Gandhi appears to have emerged from the strike and the fast with the same reputation for fairness as he had enjoyed at the outset. At a public meeting marking the end of the strike, Ambalal said, "If the workers revere Gandhi Sahib, the millowners do no less. On the contrary, they revere him even more. I hope that mutual good will among us will remain for all time."[39] Government, too, found nobility in Gandhi's leadership of the workers. The Commissioner of the Northern Division said, somewhat patronizingly,

> It pleases me very much that there is a settlement between you. I am thoroughly convinced that as long as you follow Gandhi Sahib's advice and do what he tells you, you will fare well and secure justice. You have to remember that Gandhi Sahib and his associates—both men and women—have suffered much, taken a great deal of trouble, and shown love and compassion for you. You should remember that always.[40]

The strike inspired the formal establishment of several unions of different groups of workers by specialization: weavers; folders; throstle workers; sizers; winders; card room, blow room, and frame department workers; oilmen and firemen; and mill jobbers and *mukkadams.* Of the labor force of 43,500, some 17,500 joined the union. To consolidate all the unions, the TLA was established in February 1920 with Anasuyaben as president, a position she held for life. Gandhi, who always chose his symbolism and rhetoric with great care, named the union in Gujarati "Majoor Mahajan," the workers' *mahajan.* If the business organizations of the wealthy Vanias were called *mahajans,* often translated as "guilds," then the workers should appropriate the same terminology: "We already have mahajans of Banias and Brahmans. Kshatriyas, too, have theirs. The time has now come to form a mahajan in which weavers, blacksmiths, workers in the throstle department and others can join."[41]

Despite the opposition of more conservative colleagues, the more progressive mill owners, like Ambalal, welcomed the creation of a union, especially one favoring arbitration over strikes and nonviolence over violence. They had before them the example of strike-ridden Bombay, and they sought to avoid it. In addition, Ambalal feared that the violence and chaos of the Russian revolution might spread to India; he embraced Gandhi's and Anasuyaben's policies of discipline, peace, and moderation.

The potential for violence among the workers, and the general population as well, emerged full blown in 1919. The issues were more political than economic. In large part, they reflected popular affection and respect for Gandhi and Anasuyaben. At the end of World War I, India had expected that the British government would fulfill its promise to move the colony toward increasing self-government. Instead, the government issued the Rowlatt Acts, which restricted freedom of expression and the press. In addition, although not related, prices of basic commodities continued to rise sharply despite the end of the war, and adding to the pressures, a lethal influenza pandemic spread with special severity throughout India, ultimately killing approximately 12 million people (and another 8 million in the rest of the world). Protests against the Rowlatt Acts and against the lack of government action to curb rising prices and to control disease were organized throughout the country. In Ahmedabad, the moderate Ramanbhai Nilkanth presided over the first opposition meeting.

In this atmosphere of national distress and feelings of betrayal, the British banned meetings of public political protest. At Jallianwala Bagh, a public park in Amritsar, Punjab, however, Indians gathered to protest British policies. Brigadier General Reginald Dyer brought in the army and gunned down approximately 379 peaceful, unarmed protesters and wounded another 1,200. Although he was censured by the British government, Dyer received a hero's welcome on his return to England. Jallianwala Bagh marked a turning point in Indian nationalism. From this point on, few Indian continued to trust in British good faith and goodwill. They began to think that constitutional protest would never bring them home rule. Gandhi declared his first national satyagraha campaign. In Ahmedabad, on April 6, 1919, between 50,000 and 100,000 people gathered for a procession and a public meeting of protest. All classes were represented, and the shopkeepers shut down their businesses in a general strike. Gandhi set out by train to Delhi and the Punjab, where conditions were tense, to investigate for himself. On April 8, Gandhi was removed from the train and detained by the British. When the news reached Ahmedabad on the April 10, inflamed mobs of people went wild in the streets.[42] Ahmedabad's mills stopped work and shops closed. In the general rioting, an Indian policeman was killed.

At the time, Anasuyaben was in Bombay, and false rumors reached Ahmedabad that she too had been arrested. The next day, crowds of up to a thousand people gathered in various parts of the city. Most were mill workers, and they came with kerosene. They burned down the collector's office, the government record office, the main telegraph and post office, additional government buildings, and many police posts. A European sergeant of police was killed and the houses of two Indian officials were wrecked. The police and the military opened fire. Official accounts list 28 people killed and 123 injured. Vallabhbhai and Indulal observed, met, and discussed, but they could not control the mobs. Only the presence of Gandhi and Anasuyaben could help, but he had been arrested and she was in Bombay. Indeed, Gandhi's arrest and the (unfounded) rumor of Anasuyaben's arrest had been the triggers of the mob fury.

On April 13, disturbances spread to Viramgam, approximately 60 kilometers (forty miles) away, while in several places in the Kheda district, telegraph wires were cut, and a troop train was derailed en route to Ahmedabad. The next day the disturbances ended abruptly as Gandhi was returned to Ahmedabad and the population saw that he was safe and unharmed, but the raw power of the mob, and especially of the mill workers, had been demonstrated.

However, the city leaders were not yet prepared to admit the workers as equal participants in their contract negotiations, nor were the workers prepared to represent themselves. They regarded Gandhi and Anasuyaben as their representatives. In May 1920, workers in the throstle sections threatened to strike for shorter hours and higher wages. They came to Anasuyaben and she agreed to lead them. Ambalal and his allies within the Millowners Association immediately agreed to send the issue to arbitration and to keep their twelve mills running pending a settlement. Mangaldas, who was at the time the president of the Millowners Association, refused arbitration. He wanted direct negotiations with Gandhi. (At this, Ambalal temporarily quit the Millowners Association.) But Gandhi and Mangaldas could not reach a compromise or agree on an arbitrator. A ten-day strike of the throstle workers resulted, and in the end, arbitration brought a reduction in hours and a raise in pay. Gandhi thought that the result demonstrated the wisdom of arbitration, which could prevent such strikes: "One good principle has emerged as a result of this strike, namely, arbitration. The workers will not, I hope, go on strike hereafter, but, whenever there are any differences between them and the employees, the two will always resolve their differences through arbitration."[43]

Gandhi spoke too soon. He was too optimistic too early about the acceptance of both the union and of arbitration. But for the moment, he was riding a crest. In the long run, the strike had convinced the owners that they would do better to accept arbitration from the beginning, and they agreed to do so. Gandhi believed that the principle of peaceful deliberation and negotiation would accommodate both labor and management, the two largest organizational forces in Ahmedabad.

Critics of the TLA policy of negotiation and compromise note that the workers were more militant than their leaders. They point to a wildcat strike of 9,000 spinners in twenty-nine mills in 1922 that was not endorsed by Anasuyaben. Indeed, she closed the throstle workers' union and resigned as its president. After the strike failed, the workers who wished to recreate the union had to pay a fine, apologize, and submit to TLA discipline. But the TLA did not give up the strike as a weapon of last resort. In 1923, the TLA called an industry-wide strike over a proposed wage cut and the failure to pay a bonus that had been agreed upon. A total of 43,000 workers struck in fifty-six mills for sixty-four days. The strike failed and cost the TLA severely. Most of its members quit. It took years of organizational efforts among the workers, especially in the "constructive work" of providing education and social services, to make up the losses in membership. Later, however, the TLA found new ways to secure its position as the powerful and representative union of Ahmedabad's textile workers. In the process, it transformed the legal structure of labor relations throughout India.

Kasturbhai Lalbhai

Kasturbhai Lalbhai, the youngest of the new generation, proved the most enduring, and the most secure link, among all the leaders. Along with Ambalal, he became one of the two most important industrialists in Ahmedabad, with vital concerns for the city's business climate and industrial relations.

Kasturbhai was a descendent of one of India's richest and most illustrious Jain merchant families. He traced his lineage directly back to Shantidas Jhaveri, born around 1590, one of the greatest merchant princes of Gujarat, with powerful business and political ties to the Mughal imperial government. Shantidas's grandson, Khushalchand, in Ahmedabad, earned the newly created title of *nagarsheth*—that is, the *sheth,* or leading businessman, of the *nagar,* "city." From this time onward, the informal title stayed with his family. Kasturbhai belonged to one branch of that family.

Kasturbhai's grandfather made his fortune in cotton speculation in the late 1860s, just after the American Civil War, which had introduced great instability into world cotton supplies and prices. His father invested the family wealth in the new textile industry, which began to grow by the end of the century. Kasturbhai was intensely proud of his family legacy, both in business and in the leadership of the Jain religious community. When Kasturbhai succeeded to leadership of his family, the family was prosperous but not without financial problems. Kasturbhai raised its economic level virtually to that of Ambalal's.

When his father died in 1912, Kasturbhai was seventeen. His mother asked him to leave his studies at Gujarat College and work in the management of the mills. She did not trust that her brother-in-law, Kasturbhai's father's brother, would treat her and her children fairly. Kasturbhai regretfully left his studies to help administer the Raipur Mill, although he had virtually no experience in the mills. After six months, he took over as cotton purchaser, one of the key jobs in the mills because the quality of cotton is the chief determinant of the quality of the final cloth product. Kasturbhai personally toured the cotton fields to learn the touch of evaluating cotton quality. In 1916, he was made a member of the board of directors of the Raipur Mill. During the war years, the mills of Ahmedabad, including the Raipur Mill, earned unprecedented profits, and the young Kasturbhai came to the notice of many leaders, especially Ambalal Sarabhai, who was only four years his senior. They became close friends as well as neighbors, and Ambalal's son, Suhrud, married Kasturbhai's niece, Manorama. Especially after the death of Mangaldas in 1930, these two men were recognized as the leading businessmen of Ahmedabad.

In Gandhi's Ahmedabad, public political affairs were everyone's concern. Indulal noted Kasturbhai's presence at the mass public protests against the arrest of Mrs. Besant in 1916. During the 1918 strike, meetings of the mill owners were frequently held at his city residence at Pankor Naka. He accompanied Ambalal to Anasuyaben's house, where Gandhi was staying during his fast, to tell him that "we had won the fight and he was coercing us into an agreement by fasting."[44] Impressed by Kasturbhai's role during the strike, Ambalal invited him to join the managing committee of the Ahmedabad Millowners Association. The young businessman later referred to this invitation as the beginning of his public career. That career expanded later in the year when he was named one of the secretaries of the Famine Relief Committee appointed by the Gujarat Sabha in the wake of both famine and influenza. The other secretaries were Vallabhbhai, Indulal, Ganesh Vasudev Mavalankar, and Krishnalal Dalal. Kasturbhai went out each day to collect donations from other mill owners and the rich *mahajans* of the city, and then to arrange for the purchase and delivery of supplies. He was as careful in the management of relief operations as in his mill operations.

Participation in the famine relief operations generally unified the dominant elites, but some disagreements over policy also emerged. Indulal prepared a report highly critical of government policies and administration, and he proposed to publish it. Kasturbhai objected and successfully prevented its going to the local newspapers, although Indulal later published it in *Navajivan*. On the other hand, Kasturbhai's relationships with Vallabhbhai were smooth and mutually supportive. The constitutional reforms of 1919 had authorized the Ahmedabad Millowners Association to elect one member to the Central Legislative Council. In 1923, Vallabhbhai urged Kasturbhai to enter the contest and supported his candidacy. Kasturbhai won the election among the mill owners.

In Delhi, Kasturbhai met and mingled with some of the leading nationalists from all over the country. He represented the interests of his constituents and learned the workings of parliamentary bodies. Most notably, he successfully led the fight to remove the countervailing excise duties that had been imposed on Indian textile exports in 1892. In this struggle, he needed the support of the Congress Swaraj Party representatives in the council. In March 1924, Kasturbhai and Ambalal Sarabhai met with Motilal Nehru, the Swaraj Party leader (and father of Jawaharlal), and several leading Bombay mill owners. Motilal agreed to back Kasturbhai's proposal if the industrialists could supply his party with Rs. 5 lakhs: Rs. 3.5 lakhs from Bombay, and Rs. 1.5 lakhs from Ahmedabad. At first Kasturbhai hesitated, but Ambalal persuaded him to undertake the responsibility. The Ahmedabad mill owners supported him, and with the backing of the

Swaraj Party, the export duties were suspended in 1925 and abolished in 1926. As a further result of his service on the national scene, Kasturbhai became one of the pillars of "a major, if intangible and informal nationalist lobby" that included G. D. Birla in Calcutta, Sir Purshottamdas Thakordas in Bombay, and Lala Shri Ram in Delhi.[45]

By providing such mutual support for one another, the Ahmedabad leaders ultimately reaped benefits for themselves individually and collectively, as well as for their city. Kasturbhai, the youngest of the leadership group, was perhaps the most responsive to changing conditions and challenges. He was certainly the most long lived, and he continued to play the role of city father, informal *nagarsheth,* almost until his death in 1980. Thus the effects of his early involvement in Ahmedabad's leadership circles and his interactions with Gandhi, Patel, Anasuyaben, Ambalal, and Indulal shaped his life and the life of his city for sixty-five years.

The Ahmedabad leadership circle was, of course, not a formal association, but simply a group of men and a woman backed by the tens of thousands of constituents they represented. By 1922, they had transformed the institutional structure of the city. They created the TLA and had begun to transform the Ahmedabad Millowners Association into a counterpart organization for establishing viable, peaceful labor–management relations. On the foundations of the earlier Gujarat Sabha they created the Gujarat Pradesh Congress Committee as a nationalist organization committed to satyagraha—militant, nonviolent, civil disobedience—and also to the Gandhian agenda of promoting *swadeshi,* economic self-reliance, primarily through the production and consumption of khadi cloth; ending untouchability; instituting prohibition; expanding the use of Gujarati as the medium of instruction in the schools and as the language of cultural and political expression; and fostering Hindu–Muslim unity. They captured the municipality and turned it into a platform for launching nationalist programs and challenging British authority. They shaped major policies of the city into the 1970s.

Others participated in the leadership group as well, perhaps most notably Ganesh Vasudev Mavalankar (1888–1956), who served formally and informally as friend, advisor, and lawyer to Mangaldas, Patel, and Kasturbhai. He was trusted by all sides. Even the leader of Ahmedabad's Communist Party, Dinkar Mehta, reflected in the 1940s on Mavalankar's honesty in describing political events.[46] Mavalankar served as president of the Ahmedabad municipality, 1930–33, vice president, 1934–35, and again as president, 1935–36. After independence, he was elected to parliament and served as first speaker of the Lok Sabha. Mavalankar's activities in Ahmedabad, however, were mostly in support of the activities of the leaders discussed here. The sisters, Sharadaben Mehta and Vidyagauri Nilkanth, played important roles in women's education; Muldas Vaishya in Dalit activities;

Khandubhai Desai and Gulzarilal Nanda as leaders of the TLA; and Balvantrai Thakore in education. But the small group of people discussed in this chapter, meeting collectively, in pairs, and in small groups, evolved the major policies that expressed their individual and collective vision for the city. Concomitantly, this mutual participation shaped their lives.

Each of the major leaders had his or her own vision of what the city ought to become. They learned to talk among themselves, to express their agendas, and to negotiate. They also provided encouragement and assistance to one another. Ambalal and Kasturbhai financed Vallabhbhai and Indulal; Vallabhbhai encouraged Kasturbhai to enter the national political scene; Kasturbhai and Ambalal prevailed upon their mill owner colleagues to negotiate with Anasuyaben's TLA, and they supported her social welfare projects in the *chawls* and slums. Anasuyaben encouraged workers to be more conservative, deliberate, and effective in their demands and methods. All of these accommodations seemed possible because of the charisma of Gandhi, who was respected, even beloved, by all these leaders, and who often acted as both convener and mediator of the proceedings.

Gandhi, too, was transformed by his Ahmedabad experience. His view of businessmen, at least of Ahmedabadi businessmen, began to mellow. In 1909, in *Hind Swaraj,* Gandhi had written, "Moneyed men support British rule; their interest is bound up with its stability."[47] After his interactions with Ahmedabadi businessmen, however, he advanced a very different point of view. Compare this evaluation from 1917: "It is my view that until the business community takes charge of all public movements in India, no good can be done to the country. . . . If businessmen elsewhere start taking livelier interest in political agitation, as you in Ahmedabad are doing, India is sure to achieve her aim."[48]

His views on industry also changed. Backing away from his earlier blanket condemnation of industrialization, Gandhi began to accept coexistence between the power machinery of the mills and the spinning wheels of the masses. The two forms of production could complement one another. This was especially true in Ahmedabad, where the most successful mills produced high-quality textiles, which did not compete with the rough khadi cloth that Gandhi advocated. Ahmedabad drew Gandhi into one of the key issues of the industrial age: labor–management relationships. He became both a principal leader of the mill workers and an advocate of harmonious relationships between them and the mill owners. In Ahmedabad, Gandhi would pioneer new methods of labor organization, negotiation, and arbitration.

Through his experiences with the citizens of Ahmedabad, a new vision evolved that was more favorable and less condemnatory of cities and their potential. In 1935, at the centennial celebration of Ahmedabad's earliest taste of self-government, Gandhi dispatched this hopeful message:

> The latrines of the city will be as clean as a library; its pols [neighborhood streets] will be a model of cleanliness; all of its children will be going to school; its contagious diseases will be minimized; there will not be divisions between labor and owners, between high and low; the president of the Municipality should be able to sleep in the houses of the workers—someday the Municipality will be like this. And I will get to see it. It is in the power of the citizens to achieve it.[49]

Gandhi achieved much of his new urban agenda, but to this day, this 1935 projection has remained a utopian vision.

Another of Gandhi's goals—Hindu–Muslim cooperation—was achieved only intermittently. Unfortunately, the Ahmedabad elite leadership group included no Muslim leaders. Very little has been written of the public life of the 10 percent of Ahmedabad's population that was Muslim. Siddharth Raychaudhuri's dissertation is one of the few exceptions.[50] Raychaudhuri points out that at least until the 1930s, Ahmedabad's twentieth-century Muslim community was not internally cohesive as a community. Most Muslims were a part of the industrial working classes, and as workers, they were represented by the TLA. The union, however, was composed of subgroups, and sometimes the Muslims, who were clustered most strongly in the weaving department, followed different agendas from the Harijans, who were predominantly in the spinning sections. In the 1920s and 1930s, the Harijan spinners were the TLA's most loyal members while Muslim weavers were somewhat more attracted to the Lal Vavta (Red Flag) communist union, as we shall see in the next chapter.

The small middle class of Muslim businessmen and professionals—Vohras, Memons, Khojas, Syeds, and Shaikhs—was not well integrated with the working-class Muslim community, and in the early years of the century, they did not attempt to organize or represent a unified Muslim community. There were no Muslim mill owners and hardly any Muslim industrialists. Lacking internal cohesion and points of commercial contact with the mill owners of Ahmedabad, Muslims were not represented in the city's leadership regime.[51] When nationalism began to sweep through Muslim India after the 1920s, the political and cultural fissures that opened between Hindu and Muslim in Ahmedabad could not be fully contained. After independence, those fissures could be, and were, cynically exploited by politicians for electoral gains. Gandhi had created around himself an outstanding cadre of interactive leaders, but despite his best efforts, he had not succeeded in reaching everyone.

CHAPTER 3

Vallabhbhai Patel Builds
the Congress Political Machine

*But with the work of the Congress, power
politics was introduced into our circles.*

—INDULAL YAGNIK, Autobiography

*The Gujarat Congress was completely Sardar
Patel's Congress, not Gandhi's.*

—DINKAR MEHTA, Parivartan

When Vallabhbhai Patel was elected councilor from the Dariapur ward in 1917, he began his new political career with two goals in mind. As a resident of the city, he wanted Ahmedabad to be healthy and clean, with adequate facilities for water, drainage, sewerage, lighting, and roads. As a nationalist, he wanted to limit, and ultimately to terminate, British domination of the municipality. After he joined with Gandhi in the rural Kheda satyagraha for the suspension of taxes, also in 1917, Vallabhbhai was well on his way to making politics his full-time career. By yoking together young, assertive leaders of both rural and urban interest groups, he crafted a political style of great power, ultimately creating for himself the informal position of political boss of the Indian National Congress during the freedom struggle.[1] After independence, he served as home minister and deputy prime minister, the second most powerful politician in India.

Managing the Muncipality

In 1920, as chairman of the sanitary committee of the municipality, Vallabhbhai drew up plans for extending proper drainage and water facilities throughout the walled city. As president of the board of the municipality during 1924–28, he implemented them. The government plans implemented when Ranchhodlal Chhotalal was president of the municipality, a generation earlier, had mistakenly provided water before drainage (a situation repeated in the industrial areas of the city in the 1950s and with variations in the western suburban areas in the 1970s and 1980s). Only one-third of the walled city had proper drainage, often resulting in waterlogging and flooding. Vallabhbhai extended drainage to the entire walled city: "The pumping station and the sewage farm which went with the drainage, were greatly expanded, re-equipped and modernized."[2] Then he diverted water from the Sabarmati to proper wells and purification facilities to augment the water supply throughout the walled city. The plans received government sanction and assistance in the form of a loan of Rs. 45½ lakhs. The sanitary engineer of the Bombay government monitored the progress. To ensure the continued backing of the board, Vallabhbhai invited all of the members to meet with the sanitary engineer on his visits. Vallabhbhai was praised for his early accomplishments in these areas by the local weekly newspaper, *Praja Bandhu* (albeit a publication closely linked to the Congress):

> The services which Vallabhbhai Patel is rendering to our city as President of the Municipality are unforgettable. The expedition with which he is carrying out the schemes of underground drainage and water supply has received the admiration of friend and foe alike. But for him, these schemes would have taken years, if not decades, to be carried out and Ahmedabad would have continued to be a hell on earth. Now with the completion of these schemes, Ahmedabad will be a place fit for human habitation.[3]

A staunch Gandhian, Vallabhbhai also called for self-reliance. He not only demanded that government implement programs for urban sanitation, but he also called on the citizens individually and collectively to modify their behavior. In words very similar to those of Gandhi (cited in chapter 2), he addressed these issues as president of a conference on local self-government, convened in Surat in 1927. He spoke from experience:

> Our cities are neither cities nor villages. Though living in cities, many of our people behave as they would amidst rural conditions. Half the buildings have no latrines, and there is no place even to throw the garbage from the houses. Although they live in houses in narrow streets and in thickly populated areas, they do not hesitate to keep cattle. Large numbers of apparently unowned cattle are left to wander about in the streets. Ordinarily, people are very lax in observing even the most ordinary rules of health and cleanliness, and indeed in such matters they neither appreciate what their duty is to themselves nor their duty to their neighbours. They do not consider it wrong to throw the rubbish from their own houses in front of the doorsteps of their neighbours. They do not hesitate to throw from the windows of upper storeys of their houses dirt and other rubbish or dirty water. A foreigner on studying our Local Self-Government institutions or when entering our cities would discover no evidence of real self-government. People spit

where they like, they ease themselves where they feel like, and generally consider themselves free to cause nuisance, irrespective of time or place. Conditions in the villages are no better than in the cities. . . . In such circumstances, I regard it as a great sin not to do anything ourselves but merely wait for the Government to mend matters.[4]

In 1929, Ahmedabad's historian, Ratnamanirao Bhimrao Jhote, confirmed Vallabhbhai's jaundiced view: "In Gujarat's capital, a city of three lakhs population, considered in the first rank of India's leading cities, there is no good garden, no good place for a playground, nor an open parade ground, no museum, no art collection, and no central library. This is sad!"[5]

The expansion of the city brought some welcome changes, but these were mostly across the Sabarmati River. The Maneklal Jethabhai (M.J.) Library opened in 1938, ten years after Vallabhbhai left the administration. It was funded with an initial donation from M.J.'s son to house Gandhi's library lest it be seized by the government along with the rest of the ashram. In 1939, the Mangaldas Girdhardas town hall opened next door to the library. Both buildings were in the newly developing area of Ellisbridge, on the west bank of the Sabarmati River, just at the foot of the Ellis Bridge. Two additonal bridges were constructed: the Sardar Patel Bridge, opened in 1939, and the Gandhi Bridge, opened the next year. A small but growing proportion of the city's population could enjoy the spaciousness of semi-suburbia, although their new homes in Ellisbridge separated them geographically, economically, and culturally from the majority of citizens who lacked the resources, and perhaps the desire, to make such a move.

As to the walled city and the industrial areas, despite all of Sardar's contributions, in 1941, the municipal engineer of Ahmedabad remarked to Narhari Parikh, Sardar's biographer, "We are trying to build roads and houses to provide other amenities in Ahmedabad on the most modern lines, but the mental outlook and the habits of the greater part of the citizens greatly add to our difficulties." Parikh continued, "The position has not materially altered even today [1953]."[6] We have already seen through the eyes of Ganesh Vasudev Mavalankar and Madan Mohan Malaviya the horrific conditions of the residential areas surrounding the mills, where most of the industrial workers lived. As Gandhi recognized, Vallabhbhai's personal and political concerns were more for the professional, business, and artisan classes of the walled city and Ellisbridge than for the working classes of the mill areas.

Politicizing the Muncipality

In 1919, Vallabhbhai helped to organize local demonstrations against the Rowlatt Acts, which restricted political freedoms in India after World War I, at the very time Indians had expected greater liberalization. Then, after the massacre of unarmed peaceful protesters at Jallianwala Bagh, in the Punjab, the municipality publicly expressed its censure and anger. Under Vallabhbhai's leadership, the municipality canceled its scheduled celebration of the British victory in World War I, for which it had sanctioned Rs. 6,000.[7]

For the next decade and longer, the municipality regularly demonstrated its increasing antagonism towards the British government. The municipality voted to keep its principal records and its correspondence in Gujarati, with an English translation provided on request.[8] It named the main section of the municipal headquarters building Gandhi Hall. It resolved to purchase and use *swadeshi* goods and machinery whenever possible, and to require khadi for its uniforms.[9] The municipality had the national flag printed on its official stationery and painted it on official vehicles and public property throughout the city.[10] It sent letters of support for the Bardoli satyagraha, a no-tax campaign in 1928 in a district of southern Gujarat, officially recognized Vallabhbhai's victory there—for he coordinated that rural protest movement, and earned, from Gandhi, the informal title of *sardar,* military commander, for his efforts—and offered formal congratulations to him in a ceremony at municipal headquarters.

On February 28, 1929, Gandhi raised the national flag over the municipal headquarters building and also unveiled there a statue of the nationalist hero, Bal Gangadhar Tilak. On August 15, 1930, students at several government schools, especially at the government girls' school, raised national flags—illegally—over their school buildings.[11] The municipality voted not to observe the emperor's birthday in 1930. In 1931, as part of the Salt March agitation, the Ahmedabad municipality voted to boycott India's decennial census operation. The boycott was so effective that the government itself stated in its official census report that the statistical data from Ahmedabad city were invalid. It conducted a recount in 1932.[12] These actions were largely symbolic, and the British officials with ultimate supervisory power over the municipality did not intervene. In some cases, as with noncooperation with the census, they could not intervene.

Vallabhbhai combined service to the municipality with service to the Indian National Congress. He chaired the reception committee for the 36th annual Indian National Congress session, which met in Ahmedabad in 1921, infusing the proceedings with the city's Gandhian style. The Ahmedabad session used only khadi furnishings: the tent, the ground cover, and even the small bags that members had to purchase to carry their shoes into the tent—since, for the first time, the delegates sat on mats on the ground rather than on chairs. The use of khadi made an important statement about the values of the Congress and saved tens of thousands of rupees in expenses. "When the accounts of this session were closed, there was sufficient money left to enable the local Congress organization to build present Congress House in the City."[13] In light of the city's need for a new hospital, Vallabhbhai had the V. S. Hospital and C. C. Nursing Home built on the site of the Congress meeting and had the municipality take over their administration. Several women of locally prominent families served as volunteers at the Ahmedabad Congress session, marking a general trend of greater female participation in nationalist politics.[14]

As the Indian National Congress accepted Gandhi's leadership in new noncooperation campaigns, Vallabhbhai raised over Rs. 1,000,000 (including Rs. 350,000 from Ahmedabad's mill owners and Rs. 45,000 from its workers) in 1920, and recruited 300,000 new members of Congress as his contribution to the Tilak Swaraj fund for supporting Congress programs. He called for the creation of the Gujarat Vidyapith, a private Gandhian university, which opened in Ahmedabad in 1920, and he collected Rs. 1,000,000 for it in a campaign that took him as far as Rangoon in 1922. The meeting to draft the constitution that transformed the Gujarat Sabha into the Gujarat Provincial Congress Committee was held in Vallabhbhai's home,[15] and he served as committee president from 1920 to 1942. In 1921, during the first noncooperation movement, he presided over two celebrations of burning foreign cloth, the first on September 18 and the second on Gandhi's birthday, October 2. Both took place on the banks of the Sabarmati, outside Khanpur Gate, following processions through the city. The second *holi,* or cloth burning, according to the *Praja Bandhu* newspaper, brought some 50,000 to 60,000 Ahmedabadis to watch and participate.[16]

The government did not intervene in these expressions of nationalist sympathy. The dispute over control of Ahmedabad's public schools evoked a harsher response. Under Vallabhbhai's leadership, the municipality contested control of the public school system. On February 3, 1921, the Ahmedabad municipal board refused to accept the annual government grant for funding the public schools. The board argued that financial self-reliance would bring control over the schools' budget, curriculum, and administration. The board claimed the right to refuse government inspection of the schools. (Nadiad had preceded Ahmedabad in this action on October 20, 1920. Surat followed on July 4, 1921.) In actuality, the schools continued to run more or less as before. Sometimes inspectors were allowed to administer examinations, sometimes not. Government retaliated by withholding funds from some projects that the municipality wished to undertake. The government demonstrated that it too could "noncooperate."

Ambalal Sarabhai, who did not approve of the strategy of noncooperation, attempted to mediate the struggle. In late November, he hosted a tea between Dr. Raghunath Paranjpe, minister in charge of education in the Bombay government, and Vallabhbhai Patel, who attended along with Mavalankar and Balvantrai Thakore. However no agreements were reached.

In mid-December 1921, the municipality closed the schools for a month. On the next day, December 17, the government took possession of the schools and ordered the teachers to teach and the students to study. About 200 teachers reported for work; about 175 did not. These included about eighty Hindu men, thirty Hindu women, and sixty-five Muslim men and women. This was the time of maximum Hindu–Muslim cooperation, the period of Gandhi's *khilafat* agitation in support of continuing the religious office of the Muslim caliph in Istanbul even after the British had defeated the Ottoman empire in World War I and proposed to abolish it.

The government responded on February 6, 1922, by suspending the municipality for two years. (It suspended the Surat municipality for three.) For two years, two parallel school systems ran in Ahmedabad, that of the government and that of the Prajakiya Kelavani Mandal, the People's Primary Education Association. They traded claims about which was larger and the degree to which they commanded the allegiance, or the fear, of the teachers and students.

At the end of two years, when the municipality returned to an elected board, Vallabhbhai was elected president. A new understanding, more deferential to the municipality, was reached concerning the terms for government inspection and examination of the schools. The director of education, northern division, wrote:

> When the inspectors deal with the Municipal schools, they should scrupulously maintain the honour and dignity of the Municipal Board. Municipalities have been empowered to run their own schools. Ordinarily, the Education Department's attitude toward the authorities of the Municipal schools should be one of offering suggestions and opportunities for joint deliberation. And interference in the administration of the Municipal schools is to be strongly deprecated. The inspectors, therefore, should avoid coming into collision with the Municipality and should exercise every care not to do so.[17]

The schools episode had tested the commitment and will of some 350 to 400 teachers and some 10,000 students and their families. It had forced the literate, educated classes to take sides, at least temporarily.

In preparing to contest the 1924 elections to the restored municipality, the selection committee of the Ahmedabad city Congress committee fielded a slate of its candidates under the title Rashtriya Paksh (Nationalist Party). Each candidate had to subscribe to a fourteen-point pledge that included freeing education from control of the government; favoring Gujarati in the municipal administration; propagating khadi and *swadeshi;* reducing tax burdens; providing local amenities such as education, water, latrines, and lighting for the working class; and promising party loyalty and discipline, expressed in an oath: "If, after accepting the Committee's resolution in regard to the choice of candidates, I fail to be selected as a candidate, I shall not stand for election from any seat."[18] The municipality had sixty seats in total. Twelve were reserved for government appointees. Ten were reserved for Muslim candidates to be elected only by Muslim voters. The Khilafat Samiti, allied with the Congress, won six of these. Of the thirty-eight remaining seats contested by the general electorate, Congress won thirty-three. The newly elected board met on February 9, 1924, and elected Vallabhbhai president. He was reelected each year through 1928.

During these four years, the municipality had to respond to new town planning schemes proposed by A. E. Mirams, the consulting surveyor to the government of Bombay, in accord with the Bombay Town Planning Act of 1915. Vallabhbhai Patel showed that he could cooperate with the British government when he thought the plans would benefit the city, and he could object vigorously, and obstruct, when he thought they did not. The town planning schemes for bringing electricity and increased water supply and sewage lines in Jamalpur and Kankaria incurred no strong opposition and were implemented easily. The plan for the Ellisbridge area, on the west bank of the Sabaramati River, met opposition both from farmers who would be displaced and from residents of the area who believed that they were not receiving adequate compensation for lands that were taken, and that they would be charged excessively for the proposed new municipal services.

Expansion west of the river was, however, important to Vallabhbhai.[19] It would reduce congestion in the city—always a priority—and would benefit mostly upper-income people who would build new homes there. Therefore, in addition to his position as president of the Ahmedabad municipality, Vallabhbhai took on the position of chairman of the joint town planning board of the Ahmedabad municipality and the Ellisbridge Notified Area committee. He got the scheme approved. The Ellisbridge expansion opened up the development of new suburban neighborhoods built to new, higher standards of spaciousness; physical, social, and cultural amenities; and cleanliness. By 1927, the first cooperative housing society, the Brahmakshatriya Society, named for and based on that specific caste group, was in place. About ten others had been registered, and like the Brahmakshatriya Society, most were organized by and for people of high castes.

On two other planning schemes, Vallabhbhai was much less eager to cooperate, and they were not implemented during his administration. Pulling down the city wall had been suggested by government officials at least as early as 1875, and repeated by the collector in 1888, the sanitary commissioner in 1894, the police in 1911 (who wanted the walls replaced by police lines in some places), and by a government committee in 1915. The committee's city wall improvement scheme, however, was controversial on three different grounds. As first proposed by the government, it included not only provisions for pulling down the wall and constructing a ring road—procedures that ultimately were implemented in the 1930s and 1940s—but also for planting gardens and installing an electric tram along at least part of the road's length. These latter plans were considered too expensive, and they were never implemented. Pulling down the wall also offended the sensibilities of Ahmedabadis who did not want this tie with history destroyed. Some Muslim Ahmedabadis, especially, saw the wall as a link to the days of the sultanate and Mughal administration. Also they feared that Muslim cemeteries alongside the wall might be uprooted. Finally, the plan to pull down the wall also included provisions for pulling down some adjacent housing, and the owners protested. In the face of this opposition, Vallabhbhai was not prepared to make this project a priority, and it languished for more than a decade.

The plan for building a relief road from the Kalupur railway station in the east to the riverbank in the west was even more controversial. To relieve the traffic congestion on Richey Road, the city's only east–west through street, the plan proposed a second relief road to be built parallel to the first through the Kalupur section of the city. This road would cut through numerous north–south *pols*, destroying their geographic, social, and cultural cohesion. Many residents were bitterly opposed. The city Congress committee, under Vallabhbhai's direction, chose to harness this opposition to the plan to its own efforts at political mobilization. The Congress included as one of the fourteen pledges required of each Congress candidate to the municipal election of 1924: "I shall strive to cancel the Kalupur Relief Road Scheme."[20]

Vallabhbhai's opposition was not to the idea of the road, but to the British insistence on pushing it forward without adequate public discussion. At a political rally on October 7, 1923, he declared,

> Let me make it clear that our opposition does not mean that the scheme should be scrapped or that it should be dropped. Our clear demand is to postpone it till the people's representatives are returned to the Municipality and they explain the scheme to the people after examining it in terms of the risks and expenses involved.[21]

Mavalankar and Kasturbhai Lalbhai spoke in support of Vallabhbhai's position. After the 1924 election, Vallabhbhai did return to supporting the relief road plan, but the opposition persisted, and construction could not actually begin until 1933. By that time, Vallabhbhai was gone from the municipality and the width of the road was scaled back from eighty feet to sixty feet, and individual residential considerations transformed it from the straight line of the planning map into the crooked, twisting road that now exists. Ahmedabad's leaders could succeed only when their followers were willing to accept their leadership. Even Vallabhbhai, the strongest political leader, learned that lesson.

In some fields, Vallabhbhai found noncooperation inappropriate. He worked with the British government in supplying drinking water and in working on health, hygiene, street cleaning, and sanitation. In 1927, as president of the Gujarat Congress, he directed flood relief operations throughout the region—as he had directed famine relief in 1917—and won support and praise from Gujaratis and from the British government. Kasturbhai and Mangaldas each gave Rs. 11,000 as an outright contribution, and each also contributed Rs. 40,000 to an interest-free revolving loan fund. They both also worked actively, along with Mavalankar, in organizing the flood relief efforts.

The flood relief projects extended to the rural areas of Gujarat. Vallabhbhai and the Congress worked with the British here as well. The British relied on the Congress's network of rural contacts to deliver supplies in regions where the government had little representation. Ultimately Vallabhbhai was in charge of delivering Rs. 1 crore of relief supplies throughout Gujarat, earning the thanks of the viceroy.[22] Vallabhbhai had demonstrated that the Congress was more closely connected with the people, and more able and efficient than the government in delivering services.[23]

Crafting a Political Style

Beginning with the Kheda Satyagraha, Vallabhbhai became Gandhi's chief lieutenant in Gujarat, but his political style differed sharply from the Mahatma's. They shared, of course, the desire for independence from the British and a pride in their own heritages. In confronting imperial policies, they were equally courageous. But in forging the Congress into a mass movement. Gandhi attempted to welcome everyone, at least to the extent he was able. Vallabhbhai's task, personality, and methods were different. His responsibility was to discipline and mold the Congress into an organization capable of successfully confronting and defeating a powerful colonial government and then, after independence, to restructure it into a political party prepared to fight elections and to govern. Gandhi understood and approved of Vallabhbhai's mission and often autocratic methods, believing them to be compatible with his own. Gandhi wrote:

> Let us understand the functions of the Congress. For internal growth and administration it is as good a democratic organisation as any to be found in the world. But this democratic organisation has been brought into being to fight the greatest imperialist power living. For this external work, therefore, it has to be likened to an army. As such it ceases to be democratic. The central authority possesses plenary powers enabling it to impose and enforce discipline of the various units working under it. Provincial organisations and provincial parliamentary boards are subject to central authority.[24]

As independence drew closer, Gandhi seemed to change his mind on the importance of contesting elections and governing. He advised the Congress not to take government positions, but to continue to act as a gadfly, as an extragovernmental movement dedicated to struggle and development, just as it had been under the British. Vallabhbhai did not share this belief; nor did any of the major national leaders of the Congress. Vallabhbhai admired power and authority, and he saw Congress as the means to attain them. He adopted methods that forced people to take sides, either with or against him and the Congress, as he did in the 1921–22 confrontation with the British over the educational establishment in Ahmedabad.

He adopted similar strategies in rural satyagrahas against government taxation policies in Kheda, Borsad, and Bardoli, where he countered the British threats of confiscation of land and property with his own threats of outcasteing. In Ahmedabad, during Gandhian picketing campaigns against liquor shops, the police often came through the bazaars in the morning and forcibly opened shops that had closed; in the afternoon, Congress members would come through and shut them down again. Vallabhbhai played hardball.

In evaluating his opportunities to implement the British town planning schemes, he backed those he knew would pass—Jamalpur, Kankaria, and Ellisbridge—and soft-pedaled those that confronted opposition not worth antagonizing—the relief road and town wall schemes. Sometimes, however, Vallabhbhai underestimated his opponents, or he fought for principle without regard for the results. As president of the municipality after 1924, he began aggressively to collect overdue taxes. He published the names of the nonpayers and the amounts they owed. This helped in the collections, but it lost him the support of several of the councilors in the municipality.[25] On the other hand, it gained him the support and respect of many others, who had grown resentful of the delinquents.

Although Vallabhbhai could be a devoted and caring friend, even his relationships with the other members of Gandhi's Ahmedabad leadership circle were based in large part on considerations of financial and organizational power. His methods brought some of the close, personal relationships to an end and introduced in their place a hard-driving political machine. Where Gandhi often succeeded in establishing warm personal relationships even with political enemies, Vallabhbhai sometimes created enemies even out of political friends.

Consider Vallabhbhai's relationships with Indulal Yagnik. We noted in chapter 2 the first meeting and early friendship between the experienced, composed, senior Vallabhbhai, and the impetuous, effervescent, junior Indulal. During the period of famine relief operations, 1918–1919, and during the 1919 satyagraha against the Rowlatt Bills, Indulal was periodically Vallabhbhai's houseguest. In this early relationship, Vallabhbhai protected and defended his younger colleague. During the relief operations of the 1918 famine, Indulal reported that he had the responsibility for purchasing food grains to be sent to the famine-stricken regions. He and the *shethias,* who had to pay for the purchases, usually reached agreements, balancing Indulal's firsthand knowledge of rural conditions and the shethias appreciation of budget and market realities.[26]

But sometimes Indulal and the *shethias* quarreled. Vallabhbhai, impressed with Indulal's boldness and bravado, came to his defense. When Indulal found an especially favorable offer of 1,000 tons of wheat and another 1,000 tons of millet to be delivered over several months, he made arrangements for their purchase, with the bill to go to the Ahmedabad committee for famine relief. This committee used to meet at Vallabhbhai's home. When the Ahmedabad committee learned of the purchase, Ambalal in particular responded with astonishment and some irritation: the order was too large, and if a single bill arrived, it could be for Rs. 5 lakhs—perhaps beyond the financial capacity of the committee to pay. Indulal described the confrontation:

> Ambalal, Kasturbhai and other members collectively presented this matter in the committee, proposed a resolution that no Secretary should enter into a deal for purchasing any foodgrain without the resolution of the committee. The language of the resolution was gentle, but its sharp point was aimed at me. A blow struck my heart when this resolution was passed. For some time, there was absolutely no communication between my critics and myself. When Ambalal asked Vallabhbhai about it, he frankly told him. "What! Do you think Indulal is your salaried servant? What he did was quite proper and if he asked for a little more foodgrains, should you overreact this way?"[27]

In fact, as Indulal had supposed, the shipments of the supply arrived in installments, and so did the bills. The finances worked out without a problem.

Vallabhbhai came to Indulal's defense once again during the same famine relief campaign when Indulal wrote a rather blunt letter to the Ahmedabad collector. Once again, the big *sheths* objected. They

> asked Vallabhbhai not to send such a rude letter to the Collector. But what did Vallabhbhai care? While both of them went on talking Vallabhbhai said, "Everything is all right," quietly put his signature on the letter, and sent it. Within a few days when an understanding Collector sent a full formal answer, Vallabhbhai told me, "Let them read it so that they will understand."[28]

When Indulal posed a direct challenge to Vallabhbhai's authority, however, Vallabhbhai quickly and directly cut him down to size so brutally that Indulal resigned his positions as secretary of the Provincial Congress Committee, secretary of the District Congress Committee, and secretary of the reception committee for the upcoming 1921 national Congress session in Ahmedabad.[29] Finally he quit the Congress altogether.

Beginning in 1917, Indulal had visited and worked among the impoverished Bhil *adivasis* (tribals) in the Panch Mahals district, about 100 miles east of Ahmedabad. He founded a Bhil ashram and school at Mirakhedi in 1920, and he also took interest in other schools and ashrams for Bhils and for untouchables in Dahod, Nadiad, and elsewhere. He sent a bill for their annual operation to Vallabhbhai at the Congress's untouchable office. Despite Indulal's impassioned arguments for the education and empowerment of the Bhils and the untouchables, in accordance with Gandhi's proposed programs, Vallabhbhai rejected Indulal's budget, but he advised him to take it to the Vidyapith, where he might find a warmer reception. (Meanwhile, Indulal secured a loan of Rs. 5,000 from Anasuyaben Sarabhai to continue day-to-day operations.)

By the time he reached the Vidyapith, Indulal had pared his budget to Rs. 22,000, but only a fraction of this sum was granted. Vallabhbhai arranged a meeting at which the faculty of the Vidyapith and members of the ashram explained their decision. Unconvinced and isolated, Indulal resigned his three positions with the Congress.

Indulal describes the public meeting in Ahmedabad at which his resignation as secretary of the provincial Congress was considered. Gandhi summarized the issue. In the conflict between Vallabhbhai and Indulal, Indulal would have to go:

> There is no doubt that there is no other person as industrious as Bhai Indulal. There is also no doubt that one would not easily come across a sincere person like him. Gujarat cannot afford to lose him. But on account of their different natures he and Vallabhbhai cannot work together. Therefore, it is my suggestion to accept Bhai Indulal's resignation with great regret.[30]

Indulal later reflected more deeply on the power politics that now infused Ahmedabad:

> I started looking at Vallabhbhai as the symbol of the politics of Ahmedabad city. The separation from Vallabhbhai marked the difference of nature, of opinion, and of outlook from my colleagues in the city. As long as I worked with them for the Political Conference and the Association, Kheda Satyagraha and famine relief—in other words the work pertaining to the village and the peasant—till then our regard for each other had gone on increasing. But with the work of the Congress, power politics was introduced in our circles, while my heart continued to move in the old direction.[31]

Decisions about money—raising it and allocating it—divided the two men. Indulal argued that as Vallabhbhai controlled ever more funds, he and the Gujarat Congress were isolating themselves from the common people:

> Money then naturally began to pour into our office from all sides from the beginning of April 1921. . . . A veritable downpour began by the end of April and the beginning of May. . . . I saw Mr. Vallabhbhai Patel, our President, for the first time attending our office punctually at noon every day from the middle of April, ready to collect the money as it poured in from all sides . . . Evidently a new barrier had been raised between us. Collecting money raining on the Congress table—thanks to Mr. Gandhi and his propaganda in his great political movement—and influenced by the conservative and petty-minded counsels of his new-found allies, sitting at the headquarters, stationery and immobile like a great god, he increasingly tended to develop into a bureaucratic and centripetal force, charged with the onerous responsibility of guarding the people's treasure in the name of the great Mahatma. While, though I had made Ahmedabad the headquarters of all my public and political activities, I instinctively represented the centrifugal tendency and could not help identifying myself with the needs, the views, and the feelings of the mass of the workers and people in the districts and villages.[32]

Indulal stayed on in remote areas of Gujarat for another three years, supported by some Congress contributions and by special donations, but generally isolated from the mainstream of nationalist activity.

Indulal had revolted not only against Sardar's tightly held politics, but also against the narrow culture in which they flourished. For Indulal, the requirement that each member spend time every day spinning and weaving, imposed in 1923–24 during a lull in active political campaigning, symbolized the rejection of free thought in favor of mindless discipline:

> During 1916–17, when I used to meet lawyers and traders, educated, cultured women and men in Ahmedabad and other cities, with what great curiosity they all presented all kinds of plans for the overall progress of society! At the same time, with what rising interest they used to discuss all kinds of ideas current in and outside the country! . . . By and large, the rosy air of intellectual life and free discussion of 1916 was replaced by the superficial *charkhaism* [Gandhi's emphasis on the *charkha*, or spinning wheel, as the major expression of Indian nationalism] and badly-tuned frivolousness.[33]

In 1924 Indulal gave up his work in Ahmedabad and Gujarat. For the next six years, he would work in Bombay. He contrasted the two cities:

Here, nobody was subjected to anyone's pressure or influence on any subject. Nobody could rule single-handedly. Free discussion about principles and policy went on. Here different kinds of lively thoughts flowed, sometimes together, sometimes in different directions. Compared to Ahmedabad, life flowed here, constantly assuming new forms, with lively and impartial vigor, providing knowledge and inspiration to all students. . . . when I returned to Ahmedabad I felt as if I had come down into the darkness of a small oil lamp from the light of electricity. Here, when I met some friends they appeared to be extremely busy only in religion and philosophy, ancient literature and studies, having left all the desires of this world. . . . If you talked with them about the progress of Europe they would treat it merely as violent and would praise our non-violent civilization. . . . Their intellect and knowledge appeared to be stagnant. As I remembered all the kinds of books that I had read in Bombay, and its thoughtful scholars, these people appeared like frogs in a well.[34]

Vallabhbhai Patel's confrontations with Indulal spanned a spectrum of issues: personality clashes, disputes over the proper collection and disbursement of funds, choice of appropriate target populations for assistance, the spinning and weaving requirements, openness to the outside world, philosophical and cultural orientation. Similar confrontations repeated consistently, over many years, although perhaps less emotionally, with other left-wing members of the Congress in Ahmedabad and nationally. When a socialist faction emerged within the Congress in the mid-1930s, Vallabhbhai did his best to squelch it. Vallabhbhai claimed that his Congress organization was nonideological. He claimed it was centrist and Gandhian, attempting to include everyone in the nationalist struggle for independence. His critics on the left argued that in fact he included only groups that already controlled resources of wealth, or numbers, or political awareness. The Congress, they countered, might represent the political center of those with available resources, and this group might be much larger by the 1920s and 1930s than ever before, but it remained, relative to the total population, a small, elite group.

In 1935, the newly formed Gujarat Congress Socialist Party, in an attack on Vallabhbhai's philosophy and methods, asserted that India's peasants could not be won over to the Congress through a policy of patronage from benevolent landlords. Vallabhbhai retorted with scorn for their "remote idealism," "vain academic discussion," "claptrap and catchwords." Vallabhbhai regarded the socialists as inexperienced in the realities of political power and explained to his own loyal followers, "You who have tasted the sweet experience of a life of silent service for a period of fifteen years can have no attraction for mere learned talk."[35]

In his autobiography, *Parivartan,* Dinkar Mehta, a staunch Gandhian who later become a Marxist, and still later would become the first and only communist mayor of Ahmedabad (1965), paints a stark picture of Vallabhbhai's suppression of the socialists in the Gujarat Congress:

> Sardar Patel was released from jail [1941] at a time when they, [several younger leaders of the Congress] were undecided about their political ideology. Patel received a detailed report on the formation and the activities of the Socialist Party in Gujarat and at the very next meeting of the Provincial Committee he issued a harsh attack on us, on the Socialist Party. "In the land of Marx [the USSR], Marxists are being shot," he said while waving his hand and shooting an imaginary pistol. "And here these people are talking of Marxism! They are spreading Marxist ideology! They want to incite workers to class war against owners! I am warning them, I will never allow any of this!"
>
> This was the first shot. Those, like Nandaji [Gulzarilal Nanda] and Morarji [Desai] who had been wavering, now immediately turned back and withdrew. They stopped even taking the name of socialism and began to work against socialist activities as zealously obedient servants of Sardar. I had understood even before how difficult it was to work for socialism in Gujarat. Now I began to get concrete experience. . . . The Congress of Gujarat was completely the Congress of Sardar Patel, not of Gandhi.[36]

Vallabhbhai's (and Gandhi's) Congress was, however, the party of the freedom struggle, and it commanded respect, if not support. Even Indulal came to recognize this. In 1957, after he was elected to parliament from Ahmedabad representing the Maha Gujarat Janata Parishad, a party opposed to the Congress, he urged prime minister Jawaharlal Nehru and parliamentary officials to install an oil painting of Vallabhbhai in the central hall of parliament—a mission finally accomplished only in 1998.

Although the scholar-journalist Indulal lacked the resources to confront Vallabhbhai effectively, the wealthy mill owner Ambalal Sarabhai did not. Although they often worked cooperatively on issues of civic and national welfare, temperamentally, these two powerful, strong-willed men sometimes clashed. Each was accustomed to being the boss, but of different kinds of organizations, with different styles. One headed an industry, the other a political party. Ambalal later wrote of Vallabhbhai, "With all his good qualities he is very jealous of power, intolerant of differing views and prefers that both quality and quantity of the Congress work suffer with 'yes' men to improving the quality of work and getting capable men who will not on all occasions say 'yes.'"[37]

The stage for a confrontation was set on December 27, 1927, as Mavalankar and Chandulal Bhagubhai Dalal tell the story, when Ambalal, a member of the municipality appointed by the government, created the Swatantra (Independence) Party to compete with Vallabhbhai's embryonic Rashtriya Paksh (Nationalist Party). Ambalal was president, Kasturbhai was vice president, Pestonji Vakil was the whip, and Gulzarilal Nanda was secretary. Fourteen members of the municipal board joined. The new party claimed no ideological differences with Vallabhbhai. It sought only to make the municipality more efficient and democratic by limiting terms of office, by disciplining its own members, and by setting an example to others of proper attendance at meetings and of expeditious dispatch of municipal business.

In fact, the board was not working well at the time, as even Vallabhbhai lamented. He had himself resigned as president in September 1926 because of the "indiscipline and irresponsibility" of the board.[38] He withdrew the resignation only after councilors belonging to different factions agreed to cooperate with him. In late 1927, he was elected to a fourth one-year term as president, following his nomination by Kasturbhai.

Skirmishing began over the election of officials to the board and climaxed with the voting for a new municipal chief officer in April 1928. Vallabhbhai wanted Harikrishna Divan for the post, but he indicated that he would also be satisfied with Morarjibhai Desai as a compromise candidate. He threatened to resign his presidency, however, if the third candidate, Ishwarlal Ranchhodlal Bhagat, a political enemy, was elected. Ambalal, who had originally favored Bhagat, agreed to back Morarjibhai, nominated him, and voted for him. But both parties fragmented, and in the end, Bhagat was elected, with thirty-two votes against twenty-one for Morarjibhai. Mavalankar and Dalal saw in this vote a clear slap at Vallabhbhai. So did he. He resigned immediately and left Ahmedabad the same night to continue his leadership of the noncooperation movement in the Bardoli satyagraha in south Gujarat.

Ambalal, Kasturbhai, and others, imagining that Vallabhbhai's threat had been only a bargaining ploy, quickly asked Vallabhbhai to return, but this time he remained firm in his decision. He never returned to his post as mayor. Kasturbhai resigned from the Swatantra Party by the end of the year. The administration of the municipality decayed further. Vallabhbhai resigned from the municipality completely in 1929, and Ambalal followed the next year. (Ambalal, as a government appointee, resigned on May 5, 1930, in protest at the arrest of Gandhi the previous day.) Also in 1930, after Vallabhbhai was jailed for civil disobedience, Ambalal sent him some books and a chair.[39] The Bhagat episode demonstrates how difficult it was to construct and hold together a political party and to run the Ahmedabad municipal administration effectively, even for the most powerful of India's political bosses. Individual leaders felt free to go their own separate ways, and second-tier political representatives felt free to choose among them, or even to oppose them all.

When Vallabhbhai resigned as president of the municipality in 1928, and from the municipality altogether in 1929, he left behind a local political organization in shambles. It could be resuscitated, however, especially when nationalist programs were revived, as in the period 1930–34. So, for example, city elections throughout the early 1930s brought two of Vallabhbhai's client supporters as presidents of the municipality: G. V. Mavalankar, 1930–33 and 1935–36, and Balvantrai Thakore, 1933–35. When the national movement cooled, however, the Congress did less well. Much depended on the Congress's phases of campaigning. When it actually led militant confrontations against the British, for example in the noncooperation campaigns of 1920–22 and the Salt March and subsequent campaigns of 1930–34, it could count on wide political backing. When it pulled back from direct confrontation and concentrated instead on "constructive work," various programs of social and economic uplift within Indian socieity, its attraction dimmed.

In 1935, a new constitution for India called for new elections and powers at every level in the colonial administration. The Ahmedabad municipal Congress established in 1936 a parliamentary board to choose candidates for election. They would stand together as a party, not just as individuals. Vallabhbhai spelled out his intentions:

> We want to send our representatives in the Municipality because it is impossible to carry out any programme of work without the agreement of a majority. There are 60 members. If they are of diverse opinion, they cannot do work. The result would be that the City would suffer. It has already suffered enough in the past. No improvement was made for a number of years till the Swarajya Party under my presidentship took up into its hands the work of constructing gutters and many other works of public good. But that Swarajya Party did not consist of members pledged to a vow nor were there any rules and regulations of their programme of work. A great difficulty was therefore experienced many a time when the questions affecting persons of influence came for consideration. A party is therefore required to work on the basis of common principles for the speedy betterment of the city.[40]

The candidates again had to proclaim their allegiance to the party and its principles. The Congress apportioned its workers throughout the city ward by ward and even street by street, but it did not do as well as it had expected, winning only twenty-one of the thirty-five seats it contested. Within the municipality, however, the Congress forged working agreements with the Muslim councilors, and several members of the opposition Swatantra Party quit their party and joined the Congress. In the 1941 Ahmedabad municipal elections, the party did much better, winning fifty-one of the fifty-two seats it contested.[41]

During the Quit India movement of 1942, the municipality was once again suspended by the British. The suspension, which lasted until 1944, gave Congress the opportunity to demonstrate the power of its organization over the city. As the municipality was superseded and many city leaders were jailed, Jayanti Thakor was informally designated by the Congress as "city *suba*" or "chief officer of Free Ahmedabad." He had a chain of command of nineteen ward leaders in fourteen wards. Thakore asked for donations to a war fund. A total of Rs. 21,000 was collected. The center of political activity shifted to the Khadia neighborhood, with its highly educated, high-caste activists. Women participated actively. In nine of the wards, they volunteered for committees to look after the needs of families whose members were in jails or hospitals during the movement. Seventy-six women were detained, and nine of them were imprisoned. A total of 80,000 students boycotted school for 250 days. In a student demonstration at Gujarat College, Vinod Kinariwala was shot dead by police, achieving martyr status, as he tried to raise the Indian national flag. Leaders of the Textile Labour Association (TLA) and the Ahmedabad Millowners Association agreed on a strike and shutdown of the mills, and their valuable wartime production, which lasted for 105 days.

Congress lost control over the Quit India movement. Violence broke out throughout the city. Ahmedabad witnessed a total of sixty-six bomb explosions, including three set up by women. Police stations and telephone and telegraph offices and wires were sabotaged. During the movement, 1,057 people were arrested; 397 were sentenced under the Defence of India Act and 430 on other charges. Several underground newspapers were cyclostyled and published. Despite Gandhi's preference for direct civil disobedience and courting arrest, several political leaders chose to go underground.[42]

The municipality was briefly returned to Indian control in the new elections in 1944. The Congress won all fifty-two non-Muslim seats it contested, but all the Muslim reserved seats went to the Muslim League. Even when Gandhi had lived in the city, the Ahmedabad leadership had failed to include Muslim representatives. Two decades later, Hindus and Muslims were still not working together effectively. After little more than a month, the government again dismissed the municipality and ruled through a committee of management.

Vallabhbhai, the Congress, the Municipality, and the Muslims of Ahmedabad

How did Vallabhbhai, and the Congress, relate to the Muslims of Ahmedabad? Pathak and Sheth, in their survey of Vallabhbhai's leadership within Ahmedabad, claim that he treated them just as he did everyone else.

Pathak and Sheth note that many Muslims thought him biased against their community, but they argue that "Vallabhbhai's seeming insensitivity to minority feelings was informed by larger perspectives embracing the whole city."[43] They note that he "used to personally supervise the digging of the [Muslim] graves that had been irregularly and arbitrarily razed when they came in the way of construction of roads in the city."[44] And he posed no objection to taking down the city walls even though Muslims expressed much emotional attachment to their historic significance. But Pathak and Sheth argue in his defense that Vallabhbhai was equally unsentimental with all groups. He did not seem to exhibit favoritism toward his own caste in appointing municipal officials. He ordered rats killed during the plague even though some Jains objected. He pushed for having a Harijan mill worker as a counselor in the municipal government, despite the early opposition of high-caste congressmen. Pathak and Sheth view him as even-handed toward all, regardless of caste, religious, or communal feelings. Other observers might say that in a country as diverse as India, such administrative even-handedness was, in fact, a mark of insensitivity. Many Muslims in the city saw it that way.

As independence appeared on the horizon, national politics impacted Ahmedabad ever more strongly. Tensions escalated between Hindus and Muslims, and especially between the politics of Vallabhbhai's Congress and the Muslim League of Mohammed Ali Jinnah. For example, when the British government officially took India into World War II in 1939, the Congress protested by resigning all its offices in provincial governments throughout India, but the Muslim League declared a day of national delivery.

The Congress and the Muslim League arranged mass assemblies and neighborhood meetings in Ahmedabad to attract members to themselves and away from one another. In 1937, Jawaharlal Nehru, then president of the national Congress, came to address a meeting arranged by Muslims who opposed the Muslim League. Fifteen thousand Muslims and five thousand Hindus were reported to be in attendance. In 1938, the Bombay provincial Muslim League conference met in Ahmedabad, with 10,000 members attending. On November 27, 1938, the political leader Shaukat Ali died suddenly. The Muslim League asked the Millowners Association to close the mills for one day as a mark of respect. The association refused. But when the TLA and Congress made the same request, the owners closed the mills the next day.

Mavalankar and Dalal, recounting the history of the Ahmedabad municipality at that time, note that by the period 1939–40, communal feelings among Muslims had grown strong. When a new bridge to open in 1939 in Ahmedabad was named Sardar Patel Bridge, the majority of the Muslim members of the municipality proposed instead that it be called Jamalpur Bridge. The bridge that was to be opened in 1940 and named Gandhi Bridge should be named instead

Sir Chinubhai Madhavlal Bridge. Neither name change was accepted. Muslim councilors argued that because Muslim employment in municipal government was below the Muslim proportion in the city's population, hiring should be 50 percent Muslim until the proper proportion was reached. This proposal was rejected. They proposed that the municipal president be elected each year on a rotating basis by community. Again, rejected. Each year, the municipal schools held a parade on Gandhi's birthday. Muslim members asked, unsuccessfully, to have the parade moved to a different day. Siddharth Raychaudhuri, basing his account on records of the government of Bombay and the pro-Congress *Bombay Chronicle* newspaper, adds another issue.[45] Some Muslim political leaders who were also newspaper owners protested that the municipal board, controlled by Congress, was not placing enough advertising in Muslim newspapers. Mavalankar and Dalal, staunch Congressites frustrated by Muslim sensitivities, concluded that "the Muslim members of the municipality demonstrated the attitude that their only purpose was to oppose and not to assist in whatever the nationalist party might do."[46]

The competition for Muslim support intensified and grew violent. On January 27, 1940, 35,000 people attended a meeting in Ahmedabad addressed by Mohammed Ali Jinnah, leader of the movement for a separate Muslim homeland, and the next day he addressed 4,000 students in the town hall. In the January 1941 elections to the municipality, Congress captured all fifty-two unreserved seats. The Muslim League captured all twelve reserved seats. Three months later, a riot broke out lasting six days, April 18 to 24, and resumed again briefly in the middle of May. Sixty-five people were reported killed and 300 injured. Officially, all seventy-three of the city mills were open, but the *Bombay Chronicle* reported that only three were actually functioning. Hindus could not enter Muslim majority areas such as Kalupur and Jamalpur; Muslims could not enter Hindu majority areas such as Khadia and Raipur.[47] Fifty thousand people fled the city.[48]

On April 21, an Ahmedabad citizens' peace committee formed, convened at the home of and chaired by Chamanlal Girdhardas, brother of the late Mangaldas Girdhardas. Among those attending were Manilal Chaturbhai Shah, the mayor; Sir Mehbub Kadri and Faiz Mohammad Khan, both members of the Muslim League and the latter also a member of the Bombay legislature; and Kasturbhai Lalbhai, who soon emerged as the leader of the group. Later this group would expand. Among the additional members was Mridula Sarabhai, Ambalal's eldest child. They set up committees to tour each ward of the city and an overall coordinating committee for the whole city. Some went by foot, others in cars lent by the mill owners. Four representatives went in each car: one Hindu, one Muslim, one civic guard, and one member of the Ahmedabad Rotary Club. They circulated during the riots, dispelling rumors and encouraging peace. On

May 27, representatives of sixty-seven *mahajans* met in Manek Chowk, Ahmedabad's most central business district, under the presidency of Kasturbhai. They called for an impartial tribunal to inquire into the origins and responsibilities of the riots. They decided that they would reopen businesses by the end of the month, an act they were not willing to risk individually but that they did undertake collectively. In June, the annual Rath Yatra, a Hindu procession through the streets of the walled city, was conducted peacefully, thanks to intense coordination among various city and neighborhood leaders. By the end of June, Ahmedabad was peaceful.[49]

In a long letter to Gandhi, Mridula Sarabhai, who had been elected in 1936 as a member of the All India Congress Committee from Gujarat and who served for a time as one of the secretaries of the city Congress committee, referred to the Gujarat Congress as a party divided between the more conservative wing under Vallabhbhai and a newly growing socialist wing. The party organization collapsed during the riots. Mridula criticized the Congress for a Hindu bias. She had nevertheless found some Congress leaders who were noncommunal and constructive, especially the leaders of the TLA, such as Khandubhai Desai. Other commentators praised the actions of nonpolitical Gandhian social workers such as Ravishankar Maharaj, Mahadev Desai, Narhari Parikh, and two women, Indumati Chimanlal and Pushpaben Mehta, all of whom moved directly among the rioters, calling for peace.

Mridula apportioned blame widely for the outbreak and continuation of the riots: on the British, who, she claimed, had ordered Muslim Pathan police officers to instigate violence in Ahmedabad in order to punish its citizens for not contributing adequately to the war fund; on Muslim *goondas* (hoodlums), who had set fires and looted in the Khadia, Manek Chowk, Gandhi Road, and Pancha Kuva areas of the city; on the Muslim League, whose local president and secretary witnessed systematic attacks on cars passing through the Astodia neighborhood and did nothing to stop them; on Muslim police, who did not take action to halt the violence; and on Hindus, who had retaliated with violence equal to that of the Muslims.[50]

Gandhi, who cited the Ahmedabad violence as part of a larger national breakdown, shared Mridula's dismay and disgust. He wrote in the *Congress Bulletin*:

> Individual cases apart, the Congress produced little or no influence over either the Muslims or the Hindus in the affected areas. From the accounts received it seems that Muslim fanatics in Dacca [Bengal] and Ahmedabad did their worst in inflicting damage on Hindu property by looting and burning with a deliberation that showed premeditation. Hindus, instead of boldly standing up and facing the mischief makers, fled in their thousands from the damage zone. And where

they did not, they were as barbarous as their assailants. These were all untouched by the Congress non-violence. And yet these are the men who form the bulk of the Congress meetings.[51]

Evidence of the communal divide continued. When the municipality voted to support the 1942 Quit India movement, thirty-nine voted in favor, thirteen abstained, and all twelve Muslim councilors voted against the resolution. In the 1944 municipal elections, Congress again captured all fifty-two non-Muslim seats; the Muslim League won all twelve Muslim reserved seats. The municipality, however, was dismissed within two weeks, after only two meetings. (It was restored on February 8, 1946.)

On July 1, 1946, riots broke out again, this time in the path of the annual Rath Yatra Hindu religious procession through the city. Scuffles began as members of Hindu and Muslim *akhadas,* gymnasium societies, taunted one another. In the heated political atmosphere of the time, antagonisms flared into repeated assaults, looting, and stabbings along the route of the procession, and spilled over into other parts of the city.[52] Over the next few days, at least thirty-two people died, including two young peace workers, Vasantrao Hegishte and Rajab Ali, one a Hindu and one a Muslim, who were killed together in the rioting and became martyrs for communal harmony. (Ahmedabad's Vasant-Rajab High School and Vasant-Rajab Chowk commemorate their memory even today.) Vallabhbhai and his political successors were even less successful in bringing the Muslim community into their political machine than Gandhi had been at bringing them into the Ahmedabad leadership group.

Vallabhbhai and the Business Classes

With the business classes, on the other hand, Vallabhbhai had probably his greatest success, although it was not total. As noted above, during the famine relief programs of 1918 and 1927, Vallabhbhai chaired committees that included the richest *shethias* of Ahmedabad. They gave their time, money, and expertise. They believed so much in the importance and value of the projects that they came to Vallabhbhai to volunteer; he did not have to go to them to recruit. They trusted his honesty and his efficiency. Vallabhbhai Patel benefitted from Gandhi's legacy, and he earned his own excellent reputation as well. When Vallabhbhai's fund-raising turned to national causes, such as the Tilak Swaraj Fund and the Vidyapith, wealthy people opened their purses to him. Vallabhbhai's crackdown on tax delinquents in Ahmedabad, although it alienated the particular men whom he exposed, increased his reputation for honesty and efficiency, and in the long run it benefited him and his political machine.

Of all the Ahmedabad *shethias,* Kasturbhai had the closest relationship to Vallabhbhai. As a young man of twenty-four, in 1918, Kasturbhai played a key role in organizing famine relief and raising funds under Vallabhbhai's direction. In 1923, Vallabhbhai urged Kasturbhai to contest for the Ahmedabad mill owners' seat to the central legislature and lobbied for him among the mill owners, dramatically advancing Kasturbhai's entrance into India's political and economic life. As a nominated member of the Ahmedabad municipality, in 1927, Kasturbhai returned the compliment by nominating Vallabhbhai to a second term as president. In a more risky role, Kasturbhai agreed to serve as treasurer for at least some of Congress's funds in 1930–31, when the organization was outlawed. Kasturbhai's general manager, Chandraprasad Desai, told me in an interview in 1975 that during that period, Kasturbhai's office at Pankor Naka, in the walled city, was raided by government officials searching for Congress funds. Kasturbhai had received a phone call from Lala Shri Ram, the Delhi industrialist, warning him of the impending search and of possible imprisonment. When the government inspectors arrived, they found nothing, and Kasturbhai remained a free man.

The friendship between the political organizer and the *sheth* remained lifelong, and during Vallabhbhai's last visit to Ahmedabad, two months before his death in 1950, he was Kasturbhai's houseguest.

In the period 1915–47, Ahmedabad was Gandhi's city—the preeminent Congress city in India, and India's political shock city. Tens of thousands of people dressed in white khadi. The Indian national flag flew, and it was posted around the city, legally or illegally. The municipality bought *swadeshi* goods, dressed its employees in khadi uniforms, fought for control of its school system, and resisted British government demands it found inappropriate. The mill owners supported the Congress financially and guarded its treasury when necessary; many of them wore khadi even while their mills were producing more cotton fabric than any other city in India except Bombay. The major labor union, one of the most powerful in India, was thoroughly allied with the Gandhian Congress.

Vallabhbhai's machine politics consolidated power and wealth for the Congress in the struggle for independence, yet they also created deep rifts among the politically active population. Indulal, Mridula, and the entire left-wing Congress Socialist Party were pushed out, while fence-sitters such as Morarjibhai and Gulzarilal Nanda were coerced into breaking with some of their leftist friends and rejoining the mainstream. Cultural life narrowed. Muslims deserted the Congress for the Muslim League, mirroring a national phenomenon. *Adivasis* (tribals) were largely left out. Most Harijans, organized as mill workers in Ahmedabad's TLA, were in. Vallabhbhai had great respect for people who controlled wealth, power, and organization and much less regard for those without. With Vallabhbhai's Congress, power politics came to dominate the public life of Ahmedabad and Gujarat.

Vallabhbhai's experiences in Ahmedabad proved formative as his organizational responsibilities expanded far beyond the municipality. As president of the Gujarat Provincial Congress Committee, he was in charge of the whole Gujarati-speaking region of British India, and as principal member of the Congress National Parliamentary Board, he had the central responsibility of converting the Congress from a protest and welfare organization into a political party capable of fighting and winning elections—and ultimately of governing India. As home minister of India, he faced and mastered the challenge of integrating India's princely states into the new federal republic. In Gujarat, he earned the popular title of *sardar,* military officer; in India he earned the nickname Iron Man of India. Vallabhbhai's experiences in Ahmedabad established the framework for his later political achievements—and shortcomings.

CHAPTER 4

Anasuyaben Sarabhai Engages Ahmedabad's Working Classes

Sometimes there are those we regard as opponents. Sometimes they may turn out to be friends.

—GANDHI to ANASUYABEN

At the time of Gandhi's arrival, half of Ahmedabad's population were of the industrial working classes. Anasuyaben Sarabhai saw their poverty, oppression, and need for help. Her vision began with compassion and manifested itself in social work. Her dedication attracted Gandhi and engaged his own orientation toward the poor and the underdog. Together, the efforts of Anasuyaben and Gandhi inspired the establishment of the Ahmedabad Textile Labour Association (TLA), and reassured employers and the Ahmedabad Millowners Association (AMA) that they could trust the new union. As it grew, the TLA attracted members not only through its ability to win higher wages, shorter hours, and better working conditions, but also through its schools; child care facilities; housing programs; cooperative societies; anti-untouchability campaigns; lobbying in the municipality for basic facilities of light, water, toilets, sewerage, and streets in the workers' neighborhoods; and participation in the nationalist organization for independence.[1]

In the 1918 strike, the presence of Anasuyaben at the head of the workers and of her brother, Ambalal Sarabhai, at the head of the owners seemed to incarnate Anasuyaben's and Gandhi's vision of a family relationship between labor and ownership. But the relationship between sister and brother is not what either actually had in mind. Gandhi spoke, rather, of the paternal relationship between father and child. Even following a long, bitter, unrewarding strike in 1923, Gandhi addressed this advice to the workers: "Owners and workers ought to be in a relationship of father to son. We ought to understand that to the extent that we have not reached that stage, several kinds of difficulties will come directly or indirectly. Despite the difficulties we should not become bitter. We have been wise, courteous, tested, and loyal. If you remain loyal and firm, the employers will not desert you."[2]

Anasuyaben's social work activities stemmed from a similar point of view. The leaders of the AMA also accepted that view sometimes, but often they seemed to envision instead a patron–client relationship, the relationship between the head of household and the family servants. Gandhi, too, suggested that even this relationship might be appropriate if it were accepted by both sides:

> There was a time in India when servants used to serve in the same household from father to son for generations. They were respected and treated as members of the family where they served. They shared the misery of the employer and the employer was with them in their joy and sorrow. When this was the state of affairs the social order in India was simple, and it lasted for thousands of years on that basis. . . . Servants did not ask for higher wages when there was a dearth of servants, and masters did not reduce wages when supply was plentiful. This was mainly due to mutual regard, discipline, courtesy and affection.[3]

These parent–child, patron–client views of management–labor relations ultimately determined the strategies of the TLA. On the one hand, the union challenged owners to manage their businesses with a sense of responsibility, of "trusteeship," and to regard their employees with respect as "copartners": "What I expect of you, therefore, is that you should hold all your riches as a trust to be used solely in the interests of those who sweat for you, and to whose industry and labour you owe all your positions and prosperity. I want you to make your labourers co-partners of your wealth."[4] On the other, it produced a union that was described by the Royal Commission on Indian Labour in 1931 as "managed more for the workers than by the workers."[5]

Anasuyaben and Gandhi's vision of labor–management relationships did not go unchallenged, even in Ahmedabad, Gandhi's stronghold. The communist leader Dinkar Mehta expressed a counter viewpoint and tried to build an alternative union. In Mehta's Lal Vavta (Red Flag) Union, "we had become not the uplifter of the workers, but their companions, friends, and comrades."[6] These alternative visions of labor–management relations competed with one another during the thirty years covered in this chapter, 1918–48, with the TLA's philosophy consistently dominant. In 1938, its vision was incorporated into law in the form of the Bombay Industrial Relations Act, which encouraged arbitration rather than strikes in resolving industrial disputes.

The core around which the future TLA first organized was Anasuyaben Sarabhai and the schools and day-care centers that she organized, first in the Amarpura slums and then more widely in various Ahmedabad mill neighborhoods. The fact that a daughter of one of Ahmedabad's richest families came to work personally among them and for them touched the workers deeply. The fact that she was the sister of one of the city's largest employers and had access to his ear also weighed in her favor. The spontaneous rioting of 1919 in response to the news of Gandhi's detention in the Punjab and the false rumors of Anasuyaben's arrest in Bombay attested to the workers' zealous devotion to both of them.

Through the years, Anasuyaben's most active interventions in union development were on the side of social welfare structures within the union: the creation of youth organizations for child laborers in 1927; of unions of the untouchable Bhangi sweepers, also in 1927; of special literary centers for women, called Mahila Mandirs, in 1939; and of a special union for women working in winding and spinning in the mills, also in 1939. Anasuyaben integrated a dual vision of struggle and development, with more emphasis on development, which in many ways was closely related to social work.

Gandhi understood Anasuyaben's humanitarian interest in the labor movement, and in 1920, in speaking to the mill workers, he characterized it as follows:

> Anasuyaben has not dedicated her life to you merely for the purpose of securing for you better wages. Her object in doing so is that you may get enough to make you happy, to make you truly religious, that you may observe the eternal laws of ethics, that you may give up bad habits such as drinking, gambling, etc., that you may make good use of your earnings, that you may keep your houses clean and that you may educate your children.[7]

Anasuyaben's crackdown on a "lightning" (wildcat) strike among the spinners in 1922 demonstrated that she did not always back workers' economic demands and actions. While the TLA and the AMA were in negotiations over wages, 9,000 workers in twenty-nine mills struck work. Their job action violated existing arbitration agreements, and Anasuyaben reacted sharply, with Gandhi's support, resigning from and closing the throstle workers' union. Without the backing of Anasuyaben and the union, the workers lost their strike. Only after they agreed to apologize, accept TLA discipline, and pay a fine of 4 annas each did Anasuyaben agree to reconstitute the union and resume service as its president.[8]

The TLA consistently opposed lightning strikes. In 1925, the newspaper *Majoor Sandesh* criticized workers for participating in them: "Lightning strikes, often called out on petty issues, involve mills as well as labour in a big loss. They also create an ill-will between them. Since the betterment of workers is dependent upon the prosperity of mills, workers should not impulsively take steps that entail losses to the industry. We therefore cannot support a strike called out without prior consent."[9]

Anasuyaben envisioned the TLA as a powerful vehicle for the conventional union demands for higher wages, shorter hours, better working conditions; as a social service agency; and as a lobby within government. By skill and temperament, her own leadership role was largely in social service provision. Others could supply the other components. One of the others, Shankarlal Banker, the young, wealthy Bombay businessman who had become a Gandhian, became Anasuyaben's leading representative in union affairs, especially in negotiations. In addition, almost from their first meeting in 1917—they were introduced by Gandhi—Shankarlal lived in her house when he was in Ahmedabad; later in their lives, that became his permanent address.

In the early days of the founding of the union, from the strikes of 1917 and 1918 to 1920, when the union was formally founded, the personal relationships among union, management, and government were indispensable to success: Gandhi, Ambalal, Anasuyaben, the workers, and Commissioner G. E. Chatfield. Even Mangaldas, who had strong reservations about the role of a union in Ahmedabad, had warm relationships with Gandhi and Anasuyaben, and was won over by the TLA's humanitarian activities. At several points in his account of the development of the TLA, Banker notes his own appreciation for the support offered by Mangaldas Girdhardas, Ahmedabad's senior *shethia* of the time. Gandhi usually kept all these relationships on an even keel.

Gandhi supplied a new rhetoric to give voice to the new relationships. By giving the new organization the Gujarati name of Majoor Mahajan, the *mahajan* (guild) of the workers, he was implicitly arguing that the status of the workers should be on par with that of the owners. This was a new concept for both. In contrast to Gandhi's otherwise paternalistic rhetoric, the very name of Majoor Mahajan suggested a relationship of some equality.

Gandhi also worked to ensure that the nationalist movement, the TLA, and the AMA all supported one another. He wanted workers and owners to see their mutual benefit politically from the freedom movement, economically from the limits on textile imports imposed by continuous *swadeshi* campaigns, and psychologically and spiritually from the emphasis on freedom from subservience and fear. To the extent that both the TLA and the AMA could unite in their nationalism, they could more easily reach agreements on labor–management relations.

The AMA, however, was split in a battle between Ambalal and Mangaldas over the legitimacy of union organization and the establishment of formal procedures for collective bargaining.[10] In 1918 and again in 1919, Ambalal defeated Mangaldas for the presidency of the AMA. Progressive in his outlook on labor–management relations, Ambalal believed that an organized, reasonably paid, educated, and healthy workforce would be good for the industry. In March 1920, in response to a strike, Ambalal and the owners of ten other mills signed an arbitration contract with Gandhi. Mangaldas, accustomed to patron–client relationships, led the rest of the mill owners in refusing to sign such a contract. They wanted to negotiate with the workers directly in small groups, rather than collectively through Gandhi's representation.

Gandhi called an industry-wide strike that lasted for two days until Mangaldas agreed to the establishment of a permanent arbitration board, with Mangaldas and Gandhi as the representatives of owners and workers, respectively. Even then, Mangaldas dragged his feet in negotiations, and some mill owners still did not sign any agreement. In light of this breach of their understanding, Ambalal resigned his presidency of the AMA and soon took his mills out of the association; they remained out until 1939. Gandhi called a second strike of the throstle workers on May 9. Ten days later, Mangaldas agreed to establish a permanent arbitration board that would hear all workers' demands. The workers seemed victorious as wages for spinners were increased from 25 percent to 40 percent, a ten-hour day was accepted, and some water, eating, and toilet facilities were to be provided. But it soon appeared that Mangaldas and his allies had accepted the arbitration board not as a principle but out of necessity. For the moment, however, Gandhi's position was unassailable as he led both the workers' economic struggle and the nationalist freedom struggle at the very height of the 1920–22 noncooperation movement.

The years 1922 to 1924 were a turning point for the TLA, as it was for all four of the institutions we have been emphasizing: TLA, AMA, Congress, and municipality. In the wake of violence in Chauri Chaura, Bihar, Gandhi called off the noncooperation campaign just as it seemed to be mobilizing the nation successfully. He was soon jailed for six years for sedition. The sentence was lifted after two years as a result of his need for surgery to treat appendicitis, but with the understanding that he would not initiate further nationalist campaigns during the remaining four years of his sentence. The excitement of civil disobedience came to a halt as one wing of Congress moved toward contesting elections, while the other concentrated on constructive social work. In Ahmedabad, the elected municipality had been dismissed from 1922 to 1924, and when it resumed, it no longer adopted confrontation against the British as a principal agenda. Meanwhile, the extraordinary war profits in the mills came to an end, and management found itself squeezed by Japanese competition. Ahmedabad, which sold mostly to the domestic market, felt the pressure less than Bombay; profits continued, but only at a small fraction of their wartime highs. The early and mid-1920s called for reorganization in all four institutions.

The TLA grew in size and moved toward professionalization. In 1922, it hired two young men who would be influential in its development for the next quarter century. Gulzarilal Nanda completed his M.A. in economics from Allahabad University and came to Ahmedabad to pursue further studies on union activities. Anasuyaben suggested that he interview Shankarlal Banker in Bombay, and Banker suggested that the young scholar become an activist and join the TLA as a union organizer. Gulzarilal agreed. He became a secretary of the TLA in 1922 and remained until 1946. He went on to serve as minister of labor in the Bombay government, 1947–60, and minister of home affairs for the government of India, 1963–66.[11]

Khandubhai Desai left his B.A. studies in Wilson College, Bombay, to join the noncooperation movement in 1920. He became a professor in a national college in Bombay, but he was dissatisfied with the department chairman and left. Banker met him and suggested that he too should join the TLA, which he did, also in 1922, as assistant secretary. Khandubhai was also elected, 1937–39, to the Bombay provincial legislative assembly, and he became the first general secretary of the Indian National Trade Union Congress, 1947–50, and then its president in 1951. He served as minister of labor in the central government, 1954–57.

Shortly after World War I, India's economy was readjusting downward to postwar conditions. Profits in the Ahmedabad industry had dropped from 50 percent per year on the capital value of the mills during and immediately after the war to 6 percent in 1923. Ahmedabad failed to keep up with the postwar competition of Japanese cloth, and the AMA emphasized the need to cut production costs. Its president, Mangaldas, called for a wage cut of 20 percent. With Gandhi in jail, the economy in stress, and two new young men brought in as organizers, the union responded with a general strike. Unfortunately, the strike resulted in the greatest loss in the history of the TLA.

The TLA, and even the AMA itself, were not prepared. Gandhi and Shankarlal Banker were in jail. Ambalal had resigned from the AMA. The leaders on both sides who had made possible the success of the negotiations in 1918 were absent. Within the AMA, Kasturbhai Lalbhai, a voice for moderation, called for a wage cut of only 10 percent, but he was not yet able to carry the day against Mangaldas. Within the TLA, it fell to Anasuyaben, in consultation with Gulzarilal and Khandubhai, to provide leadership to the restive workers.[12]

The TLA had no strike fund, no alternative employment possibilities, and no leader with Gandhi's charisma and connections. During the sixty-five days of the strike, some 20,000 of the 45,000 workers left the city. A total of 2,370,933 man-days of labor were lost.[13] In the end, the workers had to accept a wage cut of 15 percent, and in the immediate aftermath of this defeat, membership in the TLA dropped from 25,000 to 6,220 in January 1924, dipping briefly to only 1,500, although it rose again to 12,030 by the end of that year and to 17,075 in 1928.

The membership losses also revealed the social, caste, and religious discontinuities that prevailed within the union. Of the 4,000 members of the weavers' union—mostly Muslims and higher-caste Patels—only 778 remained. On the other hand, 4,500 of the 5,000 spinners—mostly untouchable Harijans—remained staunch supporters of the union.[14] Gandhi's union, like Gandhi's efforts generally, was far more successful with Harijans than with Muslims. It took years of organizational efforts among the workers, especially in the constructive work of providing education and social services, to make up the losses in membership. The divisions by caste, religion, and occupational strata within the union were never entirely resolved.

The constructive work of the post-1923 strike echoed Anasuyaben's earliest activities. In 1926, the TLA ran fifteen night schools, eleven day schools, one kindergarten conducted on Montessori principles, and one reading room; published *Majoor Sandesh,* a weekly newsletter on TLA events that distributed 5,000 copies each week; administered cheap grain shops and tea stalls; campaigned against liquor and for prohibition; and, from 1925, began to open savings banks for workers and to make loans available at 6¼ percent interest. In 1927, at Anasuyaben's initiative, the union organized *majoor kumar mandals,* youth organizations for child laborers older than twelve. The TLA also introduced centers for child care and for education for girls and women, but these were limited in the number of workers they could serve. The TLA introduced complaint books throughout the mills and followed up on workers' grievances in negotiations with management. In 1926, a total of 958 grievances were recorded, of which 651 were handled satisfactorily.[15]

The TLA appeared chastened by its 1923 experience, and even the AMA seemed to rethink its position. After Gandhi was released from jail in 1924, the AMA gave him its assurance that there would be no further wage cuts.[16]

The most important new initiative for the TLA in the mid-1920s was its entry into municipal politics, merging the forces of the union with those of the Congress. In 1924, Vallabhbhai Patel saw enthusiasm for the Congress ebbing as the excitement of the noncooperation movement gave way to more sedate and mundane constructive work. He saw the entry of the TLA into politics on the side of the Congress as a means of widening and strengthening his party. He suggested that a union member run for a seat in one of the workers' wards in the 1924 election to the restored municipality. Union leaders, wishing to have workers' interests represented in the city government, had already made such a suggestion earlier, and although Vallabhbhai had been receptive, other Congress members had not. Now they agreed. Their candidate was Kacharabhai

Bhagat, a piecer in the throstle department of the Laxmi Cotton Mills, by caste a Harijan, untouchable. Nominated by a Brahman mill worker and seconded by a Patel, Kacharabhai stood in the Saraspur ward along with two other Congress candidates. All three were elected without opposition. In Kacharabhai, the Ahmedabad municipality had its first labor representative and its first untouchable representative.

TLA members began to take interest in the working of the municipality. During the election campaign, worker voter associations were formed, enrolling 4,000 members, to work the neighborhoods and the streets of the labor localities. These associations became a permanent part of the political landscape, responsible to both Congress and the TLA.[17]

> With Kacharabhai in the Municipality it became easier to call the attention of both the Congress party and the municipal officers to the needs of the workers' neighborhoods for roads, lights, water, toilets, and other facilities. . . . The working classes had been unaware of the responsibilities, and the activities, of the Municipality, on their behalf, and they had suffered from feelings of inferiority. At first when the TLA came to the workers to talk to them about their lack of sensitivity to their own basic necessities, the workers had said, "Yes, it may be like that, but we have no complaints." A welcome change began to occur in that attitude.[18]

In the 1927 municipal elections, the Congress and the TLA again worked together. The TLA, the Congress, and the workers themselves began to realize the value of labor votes. Kacharabhai ran again in Saraspur and won, and he also campaigned there for Gulzarilal Nanda, the TLA secretary, who also won. In this election there was opposition, and the competition for their votes made the workers more aware of their own importance. In subsequent elections, TLA representation in the municipality continued to increase. In 1936, five representatives were elected, two of them from the staff, Khandubhai Desai and S. R. Vasavada, and three from the mill workers, Keshavji Vaghela, Dudhabhai Trikamji, and Naranbhai Ranchhodbhai.[19] In the late 1940s, seventeen TLA members were elected to the municipality.[20]

However, the TLA and its membership did not become a passive "vote bank" for Vallabhbhai's Congress. From the beginning. relations between them were testy. In 1927, Vallabhbhai asked Anasuyaben to run for election as city councilor. She declined. She did not think she would be happy or successful in politics. She distinguished between her own *seva,* or quiet, behind-the-scenes social service for its own sake on behalf of the workers, and *sardari,* or leadership offered for the sake of political power. Her language alluded to some friction between the two. Gandhi supported her in this decision. When Vallabhbhai pushed the issue, Anasuyaben replied that others could represent the mill workers equally well.[21]

In the 1927 division in the municipality between the Rashtriya Paksh (Nationalist Party) of Sardar and the Swatantra (Independence) Party of Ambalal and Kasturbhai, Gulzarilal joined the mill owners. That split was based on personality clashes and methods of work more than on policy differences. Nevertheless, the divisions indicated that the leaders of the TLA and the Congress did not always stand together.

Some conflicts emerged from issues of class and power. Sardar Patel built the Gujarat Congress, and the Ahmedabad Congress, on constituent groups that controlled money and people. The weak and the powerless, and the poor and the unorganized were of little interest to him. We have already seen Vallabhbhai's misgivings concerning Indulal's work among the impoverished tribals, calling it a digression from the central battle against British imperialism and forcing Indulal out of the Congress leadership. Anasuyaben's explanation for declining a nomination for election in the municipality also suggested that Vallabhbhai was more concerned with issues of political power than she was. A lengthy undated letter from Gandhi to Anasuyaben offers Gandhi's perspective and his offer to help in reconciling these two friends and colleagues:

> As regards the workers' matter, you may feel that Vallabhbhai is at fault. Let it be so. But it cannot be said that Gaikwadi [struggle for power] is going on in Gujarat. I can understand your wrath arising out of misery. But from wherever I receive news, I hear praise of Vallabhbhai. Sitting here I am watching all this. Man is full of frailties. Vallabhbhai may be committing errors. If we understand this, it is our duty to draw his attention to them so that he can correct them. Even if he does not, let us be patient. This much as regards your general comments.
>
> Have you and Shankarlal met Vallabhbhai personally? Have you told him what was in your mind? You should not hesitate a bit to do so. You need not entertain any fear of being insulted. In matter of justice you should take up cudgels and settle the matter with Vallabhbhai. Therein lies friendship and moulding of public life. In certain public institutions, sometimes there are those whom we regard as opponents. Sometimes they may turn out to be friends. Regarding both equally, we may demand justice from them. . . .
>
> You are still hesitant to ask of Vallabhbhai what you ought to get through him. Hence let me know so that I can write to him. So far I have not written to him. If you sort out the matter there will be no need for me to write. So think over these two alternatives and inform me. Thereafter I will do what is proper.[22]

Gandhi closed by commending to Anasuyaben several *slokas* of the Bhagavad Gita on nonattachment.

Nevertheless, Gandhi, too, took issue with some of Vallabhbhai's attitudes toward the industrial workers of Ahmedabad. In the same year that Anasuyaben turned down Vallabhbhai's offer and Gulzarilal chose Ambalal's party over Vallabhbhai's, Gandhi confronted Vallabhbhai over the allocation of flood relief supplies in Ahmedabad. Floods devastated Gujarat in 1927, and Vallabhbhai earned almost universal praise from both the British and the Gujaratis for his organization of flood relief throughout the region. But the working-class areas of Ahmedabad were neglected. Banker considered their treatment unjust. Was it a lack of sensitivity to the suffering of the working people? Did the relief committee just not know the situation? Ahmedabad newspapers did not cover the story, so the editors of the *Bombay Chronicle* and *Janmabhoomi* were alerted to the problem. (Banker does not reveal who alerted them, but the implication is that he himself blew the whistle.) Investigative reporters came to Ahmedabad, and the Bombay newspapers told the story. The news reached Gandhi, and he began his own inquiry. Vallabhbhai told Gandhi his side of the story:

> The relief committee knows that the workers have suffered much, but it seems to them that the millowners ought to make independent arrangements for helping the workers.
>
> Gandhi heard this but he did not understand. He was upset. it seemed to him that the relief funds were for all the people, and it was a duty to make them available to everyone who needed help. He said immediately that a conceptual error had been made. If the millowners made their own arrangements, so much the better, but whether they did or did not, it was the duty of the relief committee to supply help and to make the arrangements for delivering it.[23]

In response to Gandhi's views, the relief committee immediately turned its attention to the workers' areas, doing surveys and helping as best they could. This new attitude, Banker concludes, helped to some degree to allay the workers' earlier dissatisfaction. Banker's account strongly suggests that Vallabhbhai believed that the workers had no right to relief assistance from city officials. Municipal agencies had no responsibilities toward them. The workers had to rely only on the goodwill of the mill owners; they had no recourse to the public facilities available to everyone else. No wonder municipal facilities were lacking in the mill areas!

Banker records a further gap in understanding between Gandhi and Patel regarding the obligations owed by public officials toward poorer citizens— issues that were now being raised in union cases. Municipal sweepers, Bhangis by caste, were considered the lowest social and economic stratum even among the outcastes. As Bhangis began to see some of the benefits of unionization for the members of the TLA, they approached Anasuyaben and TLA officials, asking them to help establish their own *mahajan*. As a result, in 1927, the Bhangi Mahajan was founded. Gandhi helped the Bhangi Mahajan establish social improvement services including schools, because they were not given admission to municipal schools. At one meeting with the Bhangis, Gandhi addressed Vallabhbhai directly: "Make a survey of the conditions of the Bhangis. Just as you think about the higher level workers, so you should think about the Bhangis."[24] Presumably Gandhi felt that Vallabhbhai needed this reminder.

By the late 1920s, relationships between the TLA and the AMA had become warmer, and by the early 1930s, relationships with the Congress also improved, in large part thanks to the increasing power of Kasturbhai within the AMA. He was elected vice president, 1923–28 and again 1930–34, and president, 1935–39. From 1925 onward, he seems to have made many of the major decisions. Like Ambalal, Kasturbhai was progressive in his thinking, valuing a strong union and well-paid, well-treated, healthy workers for a stable industry. He also favored collective bargaining and arbitration. Kasturbhai was considered about on par with Ambalal as one of the two most successful and enterprising mill owners, but unlike Ambalal, who resigned from organizations that did not accept his leadership, Kasturbhai saw his role as providing persuasive leadership from within.[25]

In 1928, the TLA won an arbitrated settlement accepting the principle that mill management would deduct union dues directly from workers' pay. The Gujarat Ginning Mill rejected this settlement for six months. Banker recalled the strike that resulted at the mill: "Owners are not willing to implement agreed upon programs. The workers came to realize that the owners and managers thought of them as nothing more than beasts and animals and, were there no union, would certainly oppress them as much as they wanted. They recognized also that to make the union work under such circumstances, they, the workers, would have to suffer."[26]

Ultimately, the AMA executive committee, including Kasturbhai, persuaded the recalcitrant mill to accept the agreement. Encouraged by this support for the validity of the union and for the arbitration procedure, the TLA asked for a wage increase in 1929, the first since the wage cut of 1923. The union argued its case on the principle of a "living wage," adequate to support a family with only one breadwinner, while the AMA argued against the increase on the basis of the health of the industry. The umpire, Justice D. B. Krishnalal Jhaveri, granted an increase of 8 percent to spinners and 5 percent to weavers and accepted in principle the concept of a living wage, but he also took into consideration the statistics presented by the AMA in arguing that the health of the industry should not be harmed. The award was generally considered a victory for labor. The agreement to use the arbitration machinery was considered a victory for both sides.

One of the consequences of receiving a living wage was a reduction in female labor in the mills. The Gandhian ideal for the industrial family had always been that men would work in the factories and women would stay at home. This would create happier families, and it would also keep the women safe from the sexual exploitation of jobbers and *mukkadams*. As wages went up, employment of women went down, although it is not clear whether this represented a change in policies of the employers on hiring, or of the employees on seeking work. Dinkar Mehta heaped scorn on the entire agreement:

> As a result of this agreement the workers did double work and received an increase in pay of 45%. Thus the owners saved 55% per worker. Thousands of workers were left unemployed as a result of this agreement and the owners' profits increased by lakhs of rupees. A second "benefit," that is really a loss, in this agreement was that the women who had been working in the spinning/throstle departments were sent home. In explaining this, the TLA said that with the women staying home the family life of the workers would become happy. The women would be able to look after their children and run the house in a good way for their husbands. When the worker would come home, she would keep hot water ready for his bath! Gandhi himself gave this explanation of the agreement.[27]

From 1928 to 1933, yearly net profits of the Ahmedabad mills on block account varied between 4 percent and 7 percent; from 1934 to 1938, they dropped to between 0.5 percent and 2.41 percent. In this later five-year period of industrial depression, the number of spindles went down slightly from 2 million to 1.9 million; looms went down from 50,000 to slightly below 47,000; the number of daily workers also came down slightly from 78,593 to 77,859.[28] Under this profit squeeze, the mill owners again wanted to reduce wages. In several mills, they did so unilaterally, often triggering wildcat strikes.

The TLA executive feared that the system of arbitration was on the verge of breaking down. The owners were acting arbitrarily and the workers were responding without organized planning. Gulzarilal wrote to Banker in 1933:

> The difficulty is not the particular complaints which are immediately responsible for the strike. It is a more fundamental one. It is the mental reservations on the side of the employer in accepting . . . the procedure of negotiations and arbitration. As long as it is the question of only tolerating the organization [the TLA] as a necessary nuisance when it is too strong for them and of constantly trying to undermine its

strength and influence [when it is weak]. . . . the conditions for successful co-operation do not exist. The best way to settle this is a good, hard strike.[29]

Within the AMA, leadership was divided. A minority accepted Kasturbhai's viewpoint that a strong union and a functioning system of collective bargaining and arbitration served the interests of both labor and management, and that unilateral actions by the owners was short-sighted. Chamanlal Parekh, president of the AMA at the time (and brother of Mangaldas, who had died in 1930), carried the majority in arguing for the owners' rights to independent action, especially in times of economic depression.

Despite Chamanlal's resistance, the collective bargaining and arbitration mechanisms held firm. Backed again by Gandhi's personal intervention and by the willingness of both sides to endure negotiations that dragged on for sixteen months, the so-called Delhi agreement was signed in India's capital, in the presence of Gandhi, on January 17, 1935. The agreement responded to the owners' desire to reduce and standardize wages, and to rationalize production procedures. The TLA accepted an across-the-board wage reduction of 6¼ percent, which effectively wiped out the salary increase of 1929, but the agreement also tacitly responded to the government's decision in December 1934 to cut weekly hours of work from sixty to fifty-four. It guaranteed that weavers' wages would not fall below Rs. 41-4-0 for a twenty-six-day month of ten-hour days, thus taking into a account the principle of a living wage (but based on a sixty-hour week). Both sides were to continue discussions on rationalization. Gandhi endorsed the agreement, which had been reached through hard, difficult bargaining.

As the economic position of the Ahmedabad industry continued to deteriorate, however, both lockouts and strikes occurred, threatening the adjudication procedures. In early 1936, the AMA demanded a wage cut of 20 percent across the board. The TLA resolved to call a general strike if such a cut were introduced. The issue was brought to the permanent arbitration board. A second question was also introduced. The New Manek Chowk Mill resigned from the AMA to circumvent the 1935 Delhi agreement and cut wages. Did the mill have the right to take such a course of action? In the negotiations, Gandhi represented the TLA; Kasturbhai represented the AMA. Kasturbhai, more favorably disposed toward the TLA than were his AMA colleagues, reduced the proposed wage cut to 10 percent. Even so, the two sides could not reach agreement. The issue went to Sir Govindrao Madgaonkar, ex-judge of the Bombay high court, as umpire. Sir Govindrao mostly agreed with the union position on both issues:

> The Mill Owners Association have not proved that a general wage-cut is necessary and advisable for the mill industry taken as a whole, a

conclusion which agrees with Mahatma Gandhi's and not with Sheth Kasturbhai's.[30]

> I hold that the New Manekchowk mills should withdraw the notice of a cut and the lockout of the weavers. This species of conduct shows the somewhat easy character of the membership of the M.O.A. and the consequent weakness of the Association and of the industry.[31]

Many other issues were not addressed, including Gandhi's radical suggestion that "it is vital to the wellbeing of the industry that workmen should be regarded as equals with the shareholders, and that they have, therefore, every right to possess an accurate knowledge of the transactions of the mills." The mill owners refused to give up such information, one of their most cherished prerogatives and signs of their independence. Even investors who lent money to the mills in the form of unsecured fixed deposits were not entitled "to possess an accurate knowledge of the transactions of the mills."[32]

The resumption of civil disobedience against the common enemy of British imperialism revitalized and consolidated the enthusiasm of the TLA, the AMA, and the Congress in the early 1930s. As the mass civil disobedience movement gave way to individual civil disobedience, that enthusiasm and sense of common purpose waned. But a new challenge arose to bring the three groups together again. Left-wing, more radical organizations challenged the philosophy of Anasuyaben and Gandhi that harmony was more important than conflict.

In 1928 and again in 1931, B. R. Ambedkar, himself an untouchable and leader of an important movement of India's untouchables, and after independence the key architect of India's constitution, came to Ahmedabad to address untouchables, many of whom were members of the union of the throstle workers, the largest and most loyal union in the TLA. Anasuyaben's earliest work had been with untouchables, and they supported her devotedly. The throstle workers, composed mostly of Harijans, had always been the key union in the TLA from the time of its founding through all of its vicissitudes, with the largest and most loyal membership. In addition, in 1925, Gandhi had founded the Mahagujarat Harijan Samaj to work for Harijan welfare by changing the behavior of both Harijans and of the larger society. It was headed by an untouchable, Muldas Vaishya.

Ambedkar's policies were much more militant than Gandhi's, calling for untouchables to organize themselves in confronting many different authorities —in government, in Hindu temples, and in workplaces. Ambedkar's base was in his home territory of Maharashtra, immediately south of Gujarat, but some Gujaratis carried his message back to Ahmedabad. Most prominent among them were Nathuram Sharma, Tulsidas Acharya—from their names, presumably Brahmans—and a publicist, Ratanji Vahalji, who went under the name Sevak Savanandji. In the Dariapur area of Ahmedabad, they started an untouchable welfare organization in 1928. Many workers in Ahmedabad hoped to reconcile the philosophies of the two leaders, but mostly they were perceived as rivals. In 1931, Ambedkar returned to Ahmedabad for discussions concerning a "depressed classes" hostel, which Tulsidas Acharya wished to establish in the Khanpur neighborhood. Although Ahmedabad remained firmly Gandhian territory, the visit indicates that not everyone had been persuaded.

Ambedkar was met at the train station on June 28, 1931, by scuffles between supporters who had come to receive him and by some young men waving black flags with signs saying, "Dr. Ambedkar go back!" He proceeded, however, to a warm welcome at the hostel and at a program arranged by the youth committee. Ambedkar's address to his followers blasted Gandhi:

> Even the British government has bowed before Gandhi, and all of you are believers in Gandhi's politics. So I ask you, "What has he done for your benefit? . . . What has he done in providing wells for your drinking water?" You say that we ought to work for the country. But I ask you, "Is this country yours?" You are not considered humans. You are jealous for land and you do not have passable roads. How can such people say that this is our land? Yes, Brahmins, Vanias, and Patidars can say it, but those of whom even the shadow cannot be tolerated, on what grounds can they say that this is my country?[33]

Ambedkar proceeded in the evening to Premabhai Hall, the central meeting hall in the city, at Bhadra, to address a meeting organized by Ahmedabad's untouchables. The proceedings took a different turn. As Ambedkar entered the hall, he was met with calls of "Victory to Mahatmaji and Sardar Vallabhbhai." The chair of the meeting was Muldas Vaishya, one of the leading opponents of Ambedkar's thought. Vaishya addressed him: "Dr. Ambedkar has returned from England and America and has done much work for our peace and welfare. But I want to say that for the most part the Harijans of Ahmedabad believe in Mahatmaji and the Congress. We have no form of attachment at all to the thought of Dr. Ambedkar."[34] (The Dalit leader Rameshchandra Parmar suggests greater complexity. He argues that Ambedkar's 1928 and 1931 meetings with the Dalits were arranged specifically by the *mukkadams* in the throstle departments. The TLA was reining in their power on the shop floor, and they saw themselves losing out to other spinners who were consolidating their own power in the mills, in the TLA executive, and in the Congress.[35])

Ambedkar's movement did not become a force in Ahmedabad. Gandhi's activities on behalf of the union and for Harijan welfare did not leave him much scope. The Gandhians also had many means at their disposal with which to respond to challenges. For example, in 1931, they formed the Organization for Abolishing Untouchability, and they arranged a large public meal at which city leaders ate together with untouchables—quite a different experience from the days of Ramanbhai.[36] In 1932, they established the Harijan Sevak Sangh for Harijan welfare. Gandhi was a local Gujarati, whereas Ambedkar was a Maharashtrian and thus was perceived by most people as something of an outsider. His visit nevertheless indicates a challenge to Gandhi's power and the power of the TLA—a challenge to which they had to respond.

The larger and more serious challenge came from the Communist and Socialist parties, which believed in class conflict rather than class harmony. They threatened to split the union not only along ideological lines, but also along caste and religious lines. The Harijan spinners in general rejected their appeal, just as they rejected Ambedkar's, while the Muslim weavers, already disaffected from Gandhi and the TLA, became the core of the membership of the left-wing unions. Both the AMA and the TLA regarded the communists and socialists as a common enemy, and the challenge encouraged labor and management to work together in Ahmedabad. Not all the challenges were from advocates of change. Conservatives also organized. In 1932, the Sanatan Varnashram Sanrakshan Sabha (Organization for the Defense of the Eternal Caste System) was established in Ahmedabad with the support of some of the mill owners.

In 1928, a general strike in the Bombay mills had taken 200,000 workers out for six months and twelve days. This was precisely the kind of labor conflict the TLA and AMA wanted to avoid. The government of Bombay shared their fears. In November 1934, it declared illegal the communist union, the Mill Mazdoor Mandal, which had organized a few workers in a few mills in Ahmedabad, and arrested several of its officers. The Lal Vavta (Red Flag) Union continued some of its activities underground, and in January 1935, it precipitated a brief strike of several thousand spinners.[37] In the same month, weavers struck at fifty mills, supported by both the Communists and the Congress socialists. Gandhi condemned the strike, but the TLA had little influence over these workers. Of the 40,000 weavers in Ahmedabad mills in 1932, only 3,069 were TLA members.[38] Most of the weavers were Muslims disaffected from Gandhi, the TLA, and the Congress. Many were not Gujaratis but immigrant workers, both Muslim and Hindu, from the Upper Provinces (U.P.) in northern India. Government bans on worker meetings and police violence against the workers brought the strike to an end in only four days. However, the strike revealed caste, religious, and regional fault lines in the mills and labor organizations of Ahmedabad.

In 1934, the Congress Socialist Party (CSP) established its Gujarat branch. Nirubhai Desai, a journalist, was secretary of the Ahmedabad chapter. Dinkar Mehta, who preferred the Communist Party but found it ineffectual in Gujarat, was also a member. So was Kacharabhai Bhagat, the former TLA representative in the Ahmedabad municipality, now no longer a member of the TLA (although he rejoined later).[39] Vallabhbhai, who was president of the entire Gujarat Congress, of which the CSP was a part, resented the CSP and told its members sarcastically, "You would like it if the local millowners were evil minded, but they are of good mind. Here there is love between the owners and the workers, good feeling, cleanliness, a feeling of family for one another. If it breaks, the atmosphere will be poisoned, demonic."[40] But he could not make them accept this viewpoint. In 1935, the CSP revived the banned Mill Mazdoor Mandal and built it into the Mill Kamdar Union.

In 1937, when mill owners declared another reduction in weavers' pay, a twenty-one-day strike ensued. The TLA did not want this strike. It was organized by the banned Communist Lal Vavta Union and the Mill Kamdar Union. While the owners called for wage cuts of 25 percent, these unions demanded a 12½ percent increase for day workers, 25 percent for night workers. At least forty-seven mills were struck by up to 50,000 workers. The core group of the strikers were the Muslim weavers, but ultimately, virtually the whole industry was shut down. By the time the strike ended on November 29, an elected Congress government was ruling in Bombay under the newly promulgated national constitution of 1935. It imposed the law banning meetings of more than five people when public safety was endangered—its first use of repressive measures in Ahmedabad city. It urged the workers to bring the TLA into the negotiations. In addition, the strikers had acted spontaneously. They had made few preparations for a lengthy strike and no arrangements for alternative employment or strike allowances.

The TLA had initially opposed this strike, but now the AMA refused to negotiate with the Mill Kamdar Union and insisted on arbitration only with the TLA.[41] In the negotiations, the TLA persuaded the AMA to restore the 6¼ percent cut of 1935 and to increase wages by 9 percent, in accordance with the recommendations of the Textile Labour Enquiry Committee, established by the Bombay government in 1937 to determine the amount of a minimum living wage and a mechanism for guaranteeing it.[42] With this settlement, the AMA, frightened by unions more demanding and more militant than the TLA, chose to strengthen the TLA and the arbitration machinery.

The TLA, the AMA, and the Congress all shared the wish to marginalize socialist and communist unions, lest they build on their accomplishments in this strike.[43] With the passage of the 1938 Bombay Industrial Disputes and Relations Act, they found the mechanism to achieve their goals. The act grew out of earlier legislation of the Bombay government. When the Congress took control of that government, after the constitutional reforms of 1935 and the elections of 1937, they reexamined that legislation. Each registered trade union was allotted two seats in the Bombay legislative assembly. The TLA sent Gulzarilal Nanda and Khandubhai Desai. Gulzarilal, the TLA secretary, was appointed

the parliamentary secretary for labor in the new government and was charged
with reviewing and revising the legislation already under consideration. As part
of their deliberations, the legislators compared the frequency and intensity of
strikes in Bombay and in Ahmedabad:

> During the eight years from 1926 to 1934 there had been 471 strikes in
> Bombay Province which affected only the textile industry involving
> 735,758 workers with a time loss of 34,849,000 working days. Of that
> time loss, Bombay city alone was responsible for the enormous figure
> of 32 million working days lost whereas the loss in Ahmedabad was
> for only 138 days! Textile operatives in Bombay city suffered a loss of
> about Rs. 427 lakhs while operatives in Ahmedabad suffered less than
> Rs. 2 lakhs.[44]

In light of this track record, they wanted to limit Bombay's militancy and
encourage the Ahmedabad pattern of arbitration. Gulzarilal's revised bill kept
most of the provisions already drafted: only a representative union—that is,
one with a membership of at least 25 percent of the workers—could negotiate
on their behalf; a union could be recognized only if it accepted the principle of
arbitration in any dispute regarding hours, wages, or working conditions; and
strikes and lockouts were banned once arbitration began. Gulzarilal added one
major change, making arbitration compulsory in industries where both parties
accepted it. The bill passed in November 1938 despite strong labor opposition
in Bombay. The revised act represented the TLA–Ahmedabad model of labor
negotiations rather than the Bombay model of strikes.

The TLA was content, but the AMA now was divided. A majority of its
members refused to accept the bill, but instead proposed a unilateral wage cut.
At this, Kasturbhai resigned from the AMA. The general board of the AMA
immediately reconsidered its actions, withdrew the wage cut, and unanimously
accepted the Industrial Disputes and Relations Act. The mediation methods of
the *mahajan* of the Mahatma and of Anasuyaben had been rescued and firmly
institutionalized by the actions of one of the charter members of Gandhi's civic
leadership regime.

The TLA was always associated with a policy of negotiation. It thought
that even the most bitter strike ultimately had to reach a negotiated conclusion,
so why not negotiate in good faith from the beginning to eliminate the need to
strike? But the TLA understood the importance of relative strength in negotiations. It was not so naive as to foreswear confrontation, nor so innocent as to
give up the strike as a weapon of last resort. Although the TLA called no general, industry-wide strike after 1923, Gulzarilal threatened such a strike in 1933,
until TLA demands found acceptable responses from the AMA. The Industrial
Disputes and Relations Act did not rule out strikes, but it mandated negotiation

first. In 1940, in a dispute over increasing the dearness (cost of living) allowance in light of rising wartime prices, the TLA was not satisfied by the AMA's offer, nor with the recommendations of a special conciliator. The AMA refused to go to binding arbitration. Gulzarilal as secretary of the TLA wanted to call a strike. He consulted Gandhi, and the Mahatma agreed, even giving instructions for strike preparations:

> Fellow worker brothers and sisters:
>
> Bhai Gulzarilal has explained the whole situation to me. I feel that your demand is just. If we do not get justice through arbitration or any other method, we have only the remedy of a strike. This weapon is to be used with thought and discrimination. If we are not strong enough, there is no shame in sitting quiet. But once we take this weapon in hand, we must not rest until we secure justice. I have pointed out a solution since years for it.
>
> All of you should learn another trade or occupation whereby you can tide over the period of unemployment. . . .
>
> Moreover, all those who are better placed should help their weaker brethren.[45]

The decision to strike was approved by membership vote, and 65,000 members of the TLA assembled on February 25, 1940, the day before the strike was to begin. Banker made a brief speech, and Anasuyaben herself gave her blessings to the strikers, urging them to act with "discipline and restraint."[46] Faced with this resolve of the workers, the AMA agreed to further negotiations and to final adjudication by the industrial court. The strike was averted at the last moment.

A very different kind of strike took place in 1942, when the TLA, with the agreement and collaboration of Kasturbhai, declared a strike in support of the nationalist Quit India movement. On August 8, 1942, the Congress session in Bombay declared its goal of immediate nationwide resistance to British rule until independence would be achieved. Gandhi was arrested the next day. Also on August 9, the workers in Ahmedabad went on strike, apparently spontaneously. Meanwhile, on the night of August 8–9, Khandubhai Desai and Kasturbhai Lalbhai found themselves on the same train returning from Bombay to Ahmedabad. They decided that a long strike would be a proper contribution to the struggle. Khandubhai agreed that the TLA would issue the strike call and encourage the workers to leave the city so that they could not easily be forced back to work. Kasturbhai agreed that the mills would not reopen even though some workers would doubtless show up. The nationalist effort to close the mills was aided by an untraceable rumor that Ahmedabad might be bombed by the Japanese. About 100,000 workers streamed out of the city. The strike continued for 105 days, until November 22. By then Khandubhai, who was in jail, and Kasturbhai thought no further purpose would be served by prolonging it. The strike is referred to with pride in Ahmedabad accounts, although the communist leader Dinkar Mehta reports that workers came to him protesting against this strike, seeing it as a scheme hatched by the TLA and AMA against the workers' best economic interests.[47]

The 1942 Quit India movement was widely supported in Ahmedabad. Eighty thousand students stayed out of school for 250 days. In a student demonstration at Gujarat College, Vinod Kinariwala was shot by police and martyred as he tried to raise the Indian national flag. As the municipality was superseded and many city leaders were jailed, Jayanti Thakor was informally designated by the Congress as "city *suba*" or "chief officer of Free Ahmedabad." He had a chain of command of nineteen ward leaders in fourteen wards. He issued calls for observing Gandhi's birthday by closing shops and offices, and he issued calls for donations to a "war fund." A total of Rs. 21,000 was collected. The center of political activity shifted to the Khadia neighborhood, with its highly educated, high-caste activists. Women participated actively in the movement. Nine ward committees were appointed in which women volunteered to look after the needs of families whose members were in jails or hospitals during the movement. Seventy-six women were detained, and of them, nine were imprisoned. Three of these women were involved in planting bombs. Ahmedabad witnessed a total of sixty-six bomb explosions. Police stations and telephone and telegraph offices and wires were sabotaged. During the movement, 1,057 people were arrested; 397 were sentenced under the Defence of India Act and 430 on other charges. Several underground newspapers were cyclostyled and distributed. And despite Gandhi's opposition to the practice, several political leaders went underground.[48] In Ahmedabad, support of the Quit India movement united all four of the institutions we have been discussing: the municipality, the Congress, the TLA, and the AMA.

By the time of independence, Anasuyaben's vision of providing education, health care, child care, and compassion to poor mill workers and their children had found considerable fulfillment in the Majoor Mahajan, the occupational association of the workers, the TLA. Her social work ideals had served as a rallying point for workers who pushed her to create a union that enabled them to confront their bosses, including her own brother, in obtaining the benefits of higher pay, shorter hours, and better working conditions. As these issues were beyond her central interests, she involved Gandhi, Shankarlal Banker, and later professional economists and organizers such as Gulzarilal Nanda and Khandubhai Desai. In order for the union to grow, especially in the Gandhian mode of preferring negotiations to strikes wherever possible, the union had to be met by owners and managers who also accepted this model. Fortunately, the

AMA chose leaders such as Mangaldas, who did not wish the TLA to fail, and Kasturbhai, who wished it to succeed. Together, the AMA and TLA brought wage levels in the textile industry in Ahmedabad from 20 percent below those in Bombay in the 1920s to 10 percent higher than in any other textile center in India by the time of independence.[49]

As the TLA increased in power and size, it also warily entered into electoral agreements with Vallabhbhai and the Congress, first in the municipality and later in the Bombay government. As TLA representatives of the Harijan weavers took their seats in the Ahmedabad municipality, they gained increased self-awareness and pride, and they called to the attention of the municipality the needs of the working-class areas for water, sewerage, toilets, roads, and lights. They did not fully succeed in these municipal agendas, but they brought them visibility, legitimacy, and attention. The TLA's web of relationships with the AMA, the Congress, and the municipality—and with Gandhi, Vallabhbhai, Ambalal, and Kasturbhai—enabled it to fend off challenges from other unions. Like Gandhi and the Congress, the TLA drew especially strong support from the Harijan spinners, but it had difficulty holding the allegiance of Muslim weavers. This had not been the initial situation. The industry-wide strike of 1918 that had inspired the foundation of the TLA was a strike of the weavers. The later aloofness of the Muslims may have resulted from a general cooling between Muslims and the Congress after the end of the Khilafat movement, which had brought them together.

Because the TLA never again called a general strike after 1923, it has often been viewed as collaborating with the AMA. The leadership of the two groups did attempt to find negotiated solutions to the inevitable confrontations between labor and management, but the TLA remained vigilant. It called numerous localized strikes, and on at least two occasions issued a strike call that was rescinded only because of last-minute compromise. Also, management frequently disagreed with the decisions of negotiators, suggesting that negotiation did not mean sellout. This was nevertheless far from Bombay's pattern of militant mobilization; nor was it the combative pattern that socialist and communist union organizers preferred. They believed that Gandhi's methods papered over class conflict, just as the Gandhians believed that the leftists failed to take into account the underlying need for accommodation, even harmony, between labor and management. The Ahmedabad TLA became the model and anchor institution of the Indian National Trade Union Congress, founded a few months before independence in 1947 as a Gandhian, anticommunist alternative to the All India Trade Union Congress. Once again, an Ahmedabadi solution served as a model for a national policy.

Shahpur Gate, one of twelve gates in the wall surrounding Ahmedabad, ca. 1935. The walls were dismantled in the 1930s and 1940s. *Photograph by Pranlal Patel. Used by permission.*

Ambalal Sarabhai expanded on the business traditions of his family to become the richest and most innovative of Ahmedabad's textile magnates. *Provided by the Sarabhai Foundation. Used by permission.*

Anasuya Sarabhai, daughter of one of Ahmedabad's
most prominent businessmen, returned from
her studies of medicine and social work in London
to work in the slums of Ahmedabad and helped
found the Textile Labour Association. *Provided by
the Sarabhai Foundation. Used by permission.*

View of a *pol,* from Raipur Chakla, ca. 1935. These narrow, twisting streets, lined by four- and five-story houses, provided the basic residential units for the middle-class, middle- and upper-caste residents of the walled city. *Photograph by Pranlal Patel. Used by permission.*

Gandhi and
Vallabhbhai Patel
(with moustache)
at the annual meet-
ing of the Indian
National Congress
in Ahmedabad, 1921.
*From the author's
collection.*

Kasturbhai Lalbhai, Vikram Sarabhai, and Amritlal Hargovandas, leaders of the business community of the business-oriented city of Ahmedabad and prominent figures
in the religious, educational, cultural, and scientific life of the city, in the 1950s. *From
the author's collection.*

Mass meeting organized by the Maha Gujarat movement, 1956. *Photograph by Shukdev Bhachech. Used by permission.*

From Gandhi's time onward, women participated actively in the public political life of Ahmedabad, as in this procession organized by the Maha Gujarat movement, ca. 1957. *Photograph by Shukdev Bhachech. Used by permission.*

Students hijacked public buses during the Nav Nirman movement protest, 1974. *Photograph by Shukdev Bhachech. Used by permission.*

A still from the documentary film *Ahmedabad*. The film was produced in 1982, but the equipment provides a good idea of what weaving sheds in the mills might have looked like even in the 1940s and 1950s. *Filmed by Norris Brock, copyright Howard Spodek. Used with permission.*

Elaben Bhatt (center), cofounder of the Self-Employed Women's Association (SEWA), which has earned international recognition for its union organization, cooperative bank, microcredit programs, and policy advocacy in local, national, and international arenas, ca. 1972. *Photograph provided by SEWA. Used with permission.*

In 2004 water from the Narmada River was diverted to the monsoon-driven Sabarmati and controlled by dams. Ahmedabad now had a full riverbed year-round. This 2005 aerial photo by Vivek Desai illustrates the results.

PART 2

The Westernizing City, 1950–1980

PART 2

The Westernizing City, 1950–1980

The year 1947 ended the era of colonialism and confronted India with the new challenges of independence. In addressing two of these challenges—building a more productive, more equitable economy and encouraging indigenous culture —Ahmedabad stood out as a shock city.

As one of the most industrialized cities in India, led by one of the most venerable communities of businessmen and industrialists, Ahmedabad took its place as a beacon in the theory and practice of economic development not only in the private sector, but also in creating public–private ventures. Ahmedabad demonstrated that a city could assert itself as a center for new Western forms of professional, commercial, and technical organization and education while retaining traditional cultures.

The city's concern for advancing both business and tradition carried into the political demand for a new state of Gujarat. Ahmedabadis campaigned militantly for a separate, single-language state of Gujarat. They sought to bifurcate the existing Bombay state, to separate the Gujarati-speaking regions of the north from the Marathi-speaking areas of the south. The new state would give them greater control over both their own culture and their own business development.

Both movements—for economic and political/cultural development—had roots in the late colonial era. As independence drew near, the Indian National Congress established a national planning committee under the chairmanship of Jawaharlal Nehru. The committee drew a lesson from Russian planning. Countries that wanted to overcome technological backwardness needed a strong state with control over the commanding heights of the economy: infrastructure, heavy industry, and finance. This emphasis on centralized planning signaled a fundamental break from Gandhi's emphasis on the decentralized, local village economy.

Many of India's leading businessmen concurred that the state would have to play a major role in the economy. At the same time, they affirmed an important role for private business. In 1944, a group of seven of India's leading industrialists —including Ahmedabad's Kasturbhai Lalbhai—drew up the Bombay Plan, which recommended a mixed economy, with the state in charge of the commanding heights of large-scale industry, transport and communication, and finance, leaving private capitalists free to develop lighter and smaller-scale industry and commerce. Many of their recommendations strongly influenced government policies after independence.

In the 1940s and 1950s, as the Congress and private businesspeople were planning for economic growth, Ahmedabad's industry flourished, giving birth to a city quite different from Gandhi's. Three events marked the gestation. First was the fabulous industrial profits of World War II. Ahmedabad's mills ran overtime, and the mill owners reaped profits beyond their dreams, giving them the means to move the postwar, postindependence city in new directions, cultural as well as economic. The new wealth trickled down to the mill workers, represented by the Textile Labour Association, who gained unprecedented new benefits of higher salaries, fewer hours, better working conditions, and the opportunity for at least some of their children to advance into new, white-collar careers. The industrial profits also enriched the tax base of the municipality, facilitating the expansion of city services to new semisuburban developments on the west bank of the Sabarmati River and improvements in some of the services in the mill areas to the east. As the finances of the city improved, and as its population increased by almost 50 percent in one decade (from 595,000 in 1941 to 877,000 in 1951), the government of Bombay raised the status of the Ahmedabad municipality to make it a municipal corporation in 1950, with correspondingly greater control over its self-government and revenues.

Independence in 1947 opened the door to increased foreign economic investment in Ahmedabad and Gujarat. New investments and new investors expanded the horizons of Ahmedabad businessmen, increased their sophistication and worldliness, and encouraged them to develop new kinds of enterprises within and outside of Ahmedabad.

Educationally, the businessmen had been constructing colleges through the Ahmedabad Education Society for more than a decade. These institutions now provided the basis for establishing Gujarat University, conceived in 1946 and founded in 1949. In 1948, the mill owners added the practically oriented Ahmedabad Textile Industry Research Association, and in the 1950s and 1960s, they captured for their hometown such premier national institutions as the first Indian Institute of Management, the National Institute of Design, and the Physical Research Laboratory.

A younger generation of Gandhi's allies was assuming the mantle of leadership in Ahmedabad, perpetuating important values of the Gandhian heritage, but also moving in new directions to meet the new issues of a new age. Ambalal Sarabhai and Kasturbhai Lalbhai, along with younger members of their families, especially Vikram Sarabhai, gave new direction to the city's business community and its civic institutions, while Indulal Yagnik returned to Ahmedabad to lead the fight for a separate Gujarat state and, later, for better conditions in the working-class neighborhoods of the city. Anasuyaben Sarabhai lived until 1972, an icon in the union. Her active influence on Textile Labour Association affairs passed to a more professionalized and politicized leadership cadre. The next two chapters tell the story of Ahmedabad's economic, civic, and cultural transformation through the prism of the new leadership.

As a result of these changes, a newcomer to the city in the 1950s, and even more so in the 1960s, would encounter a city with a strong Gandhian heritage in its politics and organizational life, but also with startling new developments in industry and culture, significant also to India's national development. Ahmedabad had once again revealed itself as a shock city—of a new kind.

Ambalal Sarabhai and Kasturbhai Lalbhai Build an Industrialized, Westernized, Prosperous, Cultured, World-Class Company Town

From the moment of his arrival in Ahmedabad, the *shethias*—the wealthy businessmen—had welcomed Gandhi.[1] Mangaldas Girdhardas hosted him. When Mangaldas withdrew his support because Gandhi brought untouchables into his ashram, Ambalal Sarabhai stepped in. Kasturbhai Lalbhai acted as sometime treasurer for the Congress and as Gandhi's counterpart in negotiations between the Textile Labour Association (TLA) and the Ahmedabad Millowners Association (AMA). The *shethias,* and particularly Ambalal and Kasturbhai, who were the richest and most powerful among them, wanted the independence for India that Gandhi promised, shared the pride in Indian culture that he radiated, aspired to the labor peace that he negotiated, and accepted the social reforms that he advocated. Gandhi had ushered in a new age that they valued for themselves, for their city, for their nation—and for their businesses.

They were not always willing to accept the responsibilities of trusteeship for their workers and their society that Gandhi demanded of them, and Gandhi frequently criticized them for their civic shortcomings. They valued much of Gandhi's agenda, but they were businessmen first. They created in Ahmedabad a new shock city: profit oriented, technologically sophisticated, culturally experimental and progressive, and engaged with world affairs, often from a Gandhian perspective. In this, too, Ambalal and Kasturbhai were leaders. Most of them cherished strong roots in the Hindu and Jain religions. Ambalal, a Jain, was an exception, remaining aloof from religious identification. None of the frontline businessmen in Ahmedabad was Muslim. Gandhi's influence remained strong in the emerging Ahmedabad of Westernizing business, but this was no longer Gandhi's city as it had been when he had lived here.

The *sheths* had prospered even before Gandhi arrived, and they continued to prosper through the years he lived in Ahmedabad. They survived the depression of the 1930s comfortably, in part because of the labor peace that Gandhi encouraged through the TLA, and in part because of the boycotts of foreign goods that he proclaimed.

Gandhi's *swadeshi* campaigns reduced imports, opening uncontested markets for Ahmedabad's products.[2] World War I had cut imports in half, from

3,130 million yards in 1913–14 to 1,470 million yards in 1917–18. In the first year after the war, Gandhi launched his *swadeshi* and noncooperation campaigns, and imports fell by another third, to 990 million yards in 1919–20. As Europe recovered from the war and as Japan increased its competition, imports rose again, but for the next decade, they did not rise above 2,000 million yards per year. Competition in overseas markets was harsh, but Ahmedabad produced mostly for domestic consumption. The city's industry increased from fifty-one mills and 43,500 workers in 1920 to seventy-six mills and 74,000 workers in 1940. Profit margins were narrow, but moderate dividends continued.[3] Even in 1936, several mills ran night shifts employing 11,613 workers.

Several innovations kept Ahmedabad's mills competitive, and the leader in this innovation was Ambalal Sarabhai. In 1922, Ambalal's Calico Mill began fine-count spinning, weaving, and processing. Many Ahmedabad mills followed suit. The innovation had many motives and repercussions. It increased Calico's profits. Ambalal demonstrated that the highest profits were not to be found in supplying the mass of poorer consumers, but rather in the markets of the upper and middle classes. He demonstrated that Indians could produce goods of quality equal to those of European countries and Japan. His move also pleased Gandhians because it led Ahmedabad's mills away from competition for the khadi cloth market.

Second, Ambalal insisted on quality control. Ahmedabad's contemporary historian, Ratnamanirao Bhimrao Jhote, recorded the numerous abuses by other mill agents, selling low-quality, irregular, wrongly packaged, and substandard goods. Writing in 1929 of the shabby tactics of Ahmedabad wholesalers, he lamented, "After taking the goods of Ahmedabad, a merchant cannot sleep peacefully. . . . For the most part the cloth of the mills of Ahmedabad supplies the lowest of the low, the poorest of the poor, and the most ignorant of the ignorant among the population of India."[4] Ambalal's Calico Mills, however, established a different standard:

> This mill years ago moved away from the defects listed above. It competes with foreign or any similarly good cloth with complete confidence. There is no irregularity in the quality of its goods. Standardized goods are put in each parcel; therefore everyone accepts them. It is not often necessary [for the merchant] to show samples. Novel varieties are often introduced in style and some kinds look exactly like foreign types. I have heard from some upcountry consumers that THE mill in Ahmedabad is Calico.[5]

Ambalal employed college graduates in managerial positions at Calico, a third important contribution to the Ahmedabad industry. Until the early 1920s, graduates did not usually consider careers in business, nor did businessmen expect to hire college graduates. Ambalal instituted a new pattern. With a desire to economize, to utilize the highest managerial skills, and to demonstrate the practical possibilities of nationalism, he began to replace foreign technicians with Indians. He established in-house recruitment and training programs to prepare college graduates for careers in industrial management. Then he put them in charge.

For example, when S. A. Kher, a Pune-born Brahman, returned from studying mathematics at Cambridge University in 1928, Ambalal offered him a position as assistant manager in the Calico Mills. Kher accepted this very unusual change of career and ultimately rose to be general manager of Calico.[6] At first, Ahmedabad mocked Ambalal for running a training school instead of an industry, but later, they began to follow his lead. Ambalal's methods paid off. In 1938, he held assets of Rs. 3 crore—heavily concentrated in the single huge Calico Mill.

Kasturbhai Lalbhai, Ambalal's next-door neighbor, a fellow Jain, his close friend, and his junior by four years, began his career in mill management, as Ambalal had, somewhat prematurely and under adverse circumstances.[7] Kasturbhai's father died of a heart attack in 1912. While still in his first year in college, Kasturbhai left his studies and began working in his family's Raipur mill. The family enterprises were not doing well at the time, and the family itself was divided by serious internal conflicts. For two or three years, Kasturbhai left management to others as he set out to learn the ropes. Unlike his office-bound, mill-owning colleagues, Kasturbhai went to the cotton fields to learn to recognize the qualities of the basic raw material of his enterprise. Then he took control of Raipur's management and turned its fortunes around, making the mill one of the most profitable in India.

From the beginning, Kasturbhai took seriously his heritage as a descendent of the family of Ahmedabad's *nagarsheth,* the chief *sheth* of the city (*nagar*). Historically, the *nagarsheth* and his family stood at the center of the economic, political, religious, and social life of his city. We have seen that Kasturbhai was inducted into the leadership of the AMA by Ambalal after the 1918 strike and into national affairs by Vallabhbhai Patel as representative of the AMA in the central legislative assembly in 1923. Kasturbhai also began to take over his father's role as head of the Anandji Kalyanji trust, which funded a number of important Jain temples throughout India. He saw the need to broaden his horizons through foreign travel, and in 1920, he and his brother, Narottam, embarked on an eight-month tour of Europe.

At the very center of Kasturbhai's concern was the unity and welfare of his family—perhaps because the division of the family in the last year of his father's life had been so painful. He wished to establish an industrial empire providing security for the families of his two sons and his three sisters. He built or acquired a mill for each of them. Kasturbhai's seven mills were the largest concentration in Ahmedabad. In 1938, on the eve of World War II, they held 235,060 spindles (13 percent of Ahmedabad's total) and 11,425 looms (25 percent of Ahmedabad's total), and employed 8,619 workers (12 percent of Ahmedabad's textile mill labor force.

In financing most of his mills, Kasturbhai followed a pattern common in Ahmedabad. He raised about a third of the capital from share equity, another 25 percent from his own firm, and about 40 percent from public deposits. These deposits were unsecured, usually issued for one year, at an interest rate anywhere from 4½ percent to 6 percent. This deposit system of finance allowed Ahmedabad mills to be radically undercapitalized. It allowed the managing agents to promote new mills with a minimum investment of their own capital. It relied on great trust by the public: the deposits were unsecured, and the interest rates were comparatively low. The respect of the family, its high public profile, and its record of philanthropy encouraged investors to feel secure.

By 1923, as Kasturbhai's mills and production were increasing, the Ahmedabad market proved inadequate, and Kasturbhai searched farther afield. He added guarantee brokers to his mills. They distributed his cloth to and collected payment from out-of-city agents. Agents in the outlying areas had exclusive contracts with Kasturbhai's mills; they accepted samples of new product lines and designs and reported back on their marketability. Kasturbhai's group was soon selling 50 percent of its production to national markets outside the Ahmedabad region.

In the early 1930s, Kasturbhai, like Ambalal, sought to hire professional managers to run his mills. B. K. Majumdar, who became manager of Arvind Mills and, informally, of all seven mills of the Kasturbhai group, was the first and leading manager. He had trained at the London School of Economics and had returned to join the economics faculty of the Benaras Hindu University. Kasturbhai offered him a job in management, and Majumdar moved to Ahmedabad to accept the new challenge. Chandraprasad Desai joined Arvind Mills in 1933 and rose to second in command to Majumdar. When Majumdar moved to head Kasturbhai's chemical and pharmaceutical enterprises in the 1950s, Chandraprasad took over as principal manager of textiles.

By 1934, Kasturbhai was elected president of the AMA as well as president of the Federation of Indian Chambers of Commerce and Industry, which had begun to emerge as India's main national business organization. He presented evidence before the tariff commissions of 1927 and 1935 on the condition of the textile industry, especially in Ahmedabad. In 1929 and 1934, Kasturbhai served as

India's employers' delegate to the International Labor Organization in Geneva. In 1944, Kasturbhai was among seven of India's most successful business leaders who issued the influential *Brief Memorandum Outlining a Plan of Economic Development for India*. Looking forward to independence, this "Bombay Plan" outlined their recommendations for industrial development under the new government, presenting an enlightened plan calling for rapid industrialization and considerable government direction for the economy.

Kasturbhai relished public life, whereas Ambalal, who was more patrician in his demeanor, did not. After his clash with Vallabhbhai in the municipality in 1928, Ambalal left municipal politics and never returned. Kasturbhai exited briefly, but he continued his close relationship with Vallabhbhai. When Vallabhbhai suggested that he assign someone in his family to serve in city government, Kasturbhai selected his nephew, Chinubhai Chimanbhai.[8] In 1942, Chinubhai was elected to the municipality on the Congress ticket. In 1950, he became the first mayor of the newly chartered Ahmedabad Municipal Corporation, a role he held until 1961.

We have already discussed Kasturbhai's decisive influence in the mill owners' decision to accept and constructively negotiate with the TLA and his contributions to the independence movement in guarding the Congress treasury and in arranging, with the TLA leadership, the long "strike" in the mills during the 1942 Quit India movement. In all of the key institutions we have been considering —municipal government, Congress Party, AMA, and TLA—Kasturbhai or a closely related family representative took a leading and critical role.

Guided by the advice of his lawyer and confidant, G. V. Mavalankar, Kasturbhai also took the lead in constructing a comprehensive new establishment for higher education in Ahmedabad. Kasturbhai, Mavalankar, and the respected businessman Amrutlal Hargovandas sought a nationalistic middle way between the British-oriented, government-run Gujarat College and the Gandhian village- and khadi-oriented Gujarat Vidyapith. They looked forward to a time when the Gujarat region would get its own university, separate from the University of Bombay, and they wanted to establish the foundation on which it might be built in Ahmedabad. In 1935, they established the Ahmedabad Education Society (AES), with 300 life members. Kasturbhai contributed funding and large tracts of land in Navrangpura, the northwest quadrant of the Ellisbridge area, and became chairman of the governing body. In 1936, the AES chartered its first college, the H. L. Commerce College, and in 1937 the L. D. Arts College. World War II and the Quit India campaign for immediate independence, in 1942, postponed expansion, but several additional colleges were added after 1946 with funding from industrial families. The new Gujarat University was accepted in principle in 1946 and officially established in 1949.

Kasturbhai's courageous response to the communal riots that flared in Ahmedabad in 1941 and again in 1946 further consolidated his preeminent leadership position. Relationships between Hindus and Muslims in Ahmedabad were sometimes attenuated by their different class positions within the city, with Muslims overrepresented in the poorer and working classes, underrepresented in the urban elites, and not present at all in the dominant leadership circle. As independence drew closer, the demand for an Islamic homeland, autonomous from India, drove sharp wedges between the two communities.

During the 1941 riots, 65 people were killed, 300 were injured, and an estimated 50,000 workers left the city, leaving only a handful of mills in operation. In response, several groups in the city organized to contain the violence and work for peace. The most important was the Ahmedabad Citizens' Peace Committee, formed on April 21, 1941, at the bungalow of *sheth* Chamanlal Girdhardas. Among those attending were mill owners Manilal Chaturbhai and Nandas Haridas, and Muslim League activists Sir Mehbub Kadri and Faiz Mohommad Khan. Kasturbhai was chosen to head the committee. The committee organized groups of Hindu and Muslim leaders to go round the city, circulating in each ward at least twice each day, investigating rumors and complaints. The coordination committee supervised their activities, secured finances, acted as liaison with government, and issued publicity notices. Kasturbhai himself led a procession through the city urging an end to the rioting and a reopening of business. When riots, which had quieted at the end of April, broke out again in mid-May, the peace committee was prepared to contain them more quickly.[9]

To get the city's business back in motion, representatives of sixty-seven *mahajans* assembled in Manek Chowk to set a date for collectively reopening the closed shops and to call for an impartial tribunal into the riots. Kasturbhai presided. When the rioting ended, the peace committee did not immediately disband. During the monsoon season of 1941, when the city was beset by floods, the committee raised relief funds and urged the government to suppress profiteering and to limit speculation in goods and rents. Kasturbhai acted as the recognized spokesman not only for the city's industry, but also for the peace and welfare of the city. He had informally earned the title *nagarsheth* that had honored his family in earlier generations.

Wartime Profits and New Enterprises

The power and prestige of Kasturbhai, Ambalal, and the Ahmedabad *sheths* as a group increased as the war years brought unprecedented profits to their industry. In 1943, profits reached 125 percent of the capital value of the Ahmedabad mills. In that year, the total value of the mills was Rs. 1,952 lakhs, while profits were Rs. 2,410 lakhs. Such colossal profits were not sustainable, but they remained high throughout the war and continued afterward. The year

1948 was another good year. The value of the mills had increased to Rs 2,322 lakhs, while profits were Rs. 1,608 lakhs.[10]

Kasturbhai and Ambalal now led the way to diversification through multinational ventures. Their first new endeavor was chemicals to be located in central and south Gujarat and Bombay. The new industries required facilities of water and space that Ahmedabad could not provide.

On the other side of the globe, American companies had also profited enormously during the war. They sought to increase their international investments, and India, on the verge of independence, looked attractive. American Cyanamid came to visit India in 1945 seeking to invest in dye manufacture. Later that year, in New York City, Kasturbhai finalized an agreement with them to create ATUL Products.

Kasturbhai chose to site ATUL Products near Valsad railway station, 200 miles (300 kilometers) south of Ahmedabad in a rural but fallow area. The government provided Kasturbhai with 900 acres at an attractive price, and subsequently he purchased 250 more. He created on this spot "a residential colony with all modern amenities,"[11] an attractive, progressive company town. This was "the beginning of the full-fledged dyestuff industry in the country"[12] and a breakthrough for Gujarat. In 1965, the Indian Monopolies Inquiry Committee estimated Kasturbhai's combined industrial holdings as the twenty-first largest group in the country.[13]

Ambalal Sarabhai ranked sixteenth. Ambalal's family extended its international collaborations in chemicals and pharmaceuticals even more boldly. In 1931, Ambalal had opened the Swastik Oil Mills in Bombay. By 1961, this company had collaborated with Mssrs. Tensia (Société Anonyme des Produits Tensio Actifs et Derives) of Belgium, and by 1964 Swastik had assets of Rs. 2.5 crores. In 1943, he opened Sarabhai Chemicals, then a small undertaking in Baroda. New chemical plants were designed and built in Bombay between 1953 and 1961. Agreements for collaboration were signed with several multinational corporations. Ambalal built several of his newer enterprises in Baroda, about 60 miles (100 kilometers) south of Ahmedabad: Sarabhai Chemicals in 1950; Suhrid Geigy in 1955; Sarabhai Merck in 1958; and Synbiotics Limited, the Sarabhai Engineering Group, and Sarabhai Glass all in 1961. Ambalal also took over the management of Standard Pharmaceuticals in Calcutta in 1960. By 1965, the annual sales turnover from Ambalal's pharmaceutical and chemical concerns reached Rs. 25 crores, almost double the Rs. 13.67 crores turnover in textiles.

Finding a common bond in their uncommon wealth, the mill owners intertwined their families in marriage. They also married into elite families outside of Ahmedabad, and sometimes even outside of the business community. The trend had begun long before. For example, Mangaldas's son married Ambalal's daughter. Mangaldas's grandson married Kasturbhai's niece. Across religions,

Jainism and Hinduism, and across the generations, the Mangaldas family and the branches of the other major families of industrial Ahmedabad were linked.

Ambalal Sarabhai had eight children. His oldest son married Kasturbhai's niece. His second son married into the Bombay industrialist family of Khatau. His third son, Vikram, married Mrinalini Swaminathan, the daughter of a South Indian family distinguished in the arts and just beginning her own career as dancer, teacher, and patron of the arts. Two of the daughters did not marry, while one married into the Mangaldas family, one married a British author, and one married into a north Indian industrial family.

Kasturbhai's older son Siddhartha married Vimla Bhogilal, a trained surgeon in her own right and a member of the family that owned Shri Ram Mills in Bombay. A niece married Somendranath Tagore, a nephew of the Nobel Prize–winning poet Rabindranath Tagore. A nephew married Krishna Nehru, the sister of Jawaharlal Nehru, the first prime minister of independent India.

Foreign travel and foreign education became increasingly common among Ahmedabad mill owners. Kasturbhai's older son, Siddhartha, for example, completed a master's degree in chemical engineering from the Brooklyn Polytechnic Institution, while Shrenik completed his master of business administration degree from Harvard. Both sons returned to the family businesses.[14]

The Sarabhai family charted extraordinary paths . Ambalal provided private home schooling up to the college level for each of his children. At his eleven-acre home, he established a complete private school for them. At one time, there was a staff of thirteen, three of whom held Ph.D.s, and three were graduates, all from different European universities. Madame Maria Montessori, the world-famous educator, visited to share her views with the Sarabhai family. The school began in 1921, when the oldest of Ambalal's eight children turned ten, and continued until 1946, when the youngest was twenty-three. The school was maintained only for the Sarabhai children, and therefore there was never more than one child in a class.[15] All three Sarabhai brothers went on to attend Cambridge University.

The children made important contributions to Ahmedabad and to India's national life. Mridula, the oldest, began as a Gandhian and founded Jyoti Sangh in Ahmedabad in 1934, an organization for the betterment of downtrodden and abused women. Jyoti Sangh, provided vocational training, legal and social assistance, and individual and family counseling in dealing with abuse. With Pushpaben Mehta, Mridula founded Vikas Griha in 1937 as a shelter for abused and abandoned women and children. Both organizations continue active in Ahmedabad today. On the national scene, Mridula served on the All India Congress Committee, working to achieve a position of equality for women within the organization.

Bharati married an Englishman and moved to England, where she became a noted writer. Leena, who married into the Mangaldas family, founded and directed the private Shreyas School, noted for its emphasis on individual creativity and artistry. Founded in 1947, it attracted students from some of Ahmedabad's most culturally sophisticated families. Gita helped administer the Bakubhai Mansukhbhai Institute of Psychology, devoted to research and clinical work in psychology. The institute also administered two primary schools: an experimental school structured on Montessori principles, and a school for children with learning disabilities.

Gira, the youngest of the children, helped to create the Calico Museum in Ahmedabad, one of the world's finest museums of textiles. She also helped to bring to Ahmedabad the National Institute of Design, an all-India study center for arts, crafts, and design. Established in 1961, with the assistance of the Ford Foundation of the United States and with the advice of an international team of advisors, especially Charles and Ray Eames, the institute is India's preeminent center for education, research, service, and training in industrial, product, graphic, and communication design.

With a Ph.D. in cosmic ray physics from Cambridge, Ambalal Sarabhai's youngest son, Vikram, became the most wide-ranging of the institution builders. He guided the creation of some of Ahmedabad's most prestigious and important new institutions of science, technology, education, research, and culture. Several of these institutions were sponsored by the central government, and it was in large part thanks to Vikram's efforts that the decisions were made to locate them in Ahmedabad. In virtually all of these undertakings, Vikram had the full support of Kasturbhai, often acting through the Ahmedabad Education Society.

Their first collaboration was in the Ahmedabad Textile Industry Research Association (ATIRA), established in 1947 and opened in 1949 through the cooperation of the government of India and the AMA. The AMA first suggested the idea in 1944 and contributed Rs. 52 lakhs toward its founding, on the condition that it be located in Ahmedabad. The government contributed Rs. 33 lakhs toward capital expenses in two installments, in 1946 and 1957. Annual operating expenses were shared by government and the mill owners. The practical benefits were immediate:

> At the time ATIRA was established, in the majority of the mills there were no Quality Control techniques, few laboratories for testing and control of yarn and chemicals, and no training programmes. The technical departments were staffed by "technicians" who had either a certificate or a diploma in textiles, very few indeed had a graduate degree. The managerial positions were held generally by members of the

entrepreneur family. The introduction of the scientific method in the Ahmedabad textile industry meant bridging the communication gap between scientists and practitioners, between the different generations of managing agents, and between the physical and social scientists.[16]

Sardar Vallabhbhai Patel laid the foundation stone for the ATIRA complex on November 1, 1950, just two weeks before he died. Achyut Kanvinde, one of India's leading architects, designed it. Prime minister Jawaharlal Nehru inaugurated it on completion on April 10, 1954.

Perhaps closer to Vikram's heart was the Physical Research Laboratory (PRL), devoted to pure research in the space sciences and theoretical physics, which he founded in 1948. Vikram specialized in research on cosmic rays; his colleague, K. R. Ramnathan, studied the upper atmosphere. Assistance from the Atomic Energy Commission of India enabled the PRL to add departments of theoretical physics and electronics. The Ahmedabad Education Society provided the land as well as some financial support. Other assistance came from the government of Gujarat (after 1960) and Gujarat University. After 1963, 99 percent of its funds came from the government of India's department of space. In 1966, Vikram was appointed chairman of the Atomic Energy Commission of India, and in that capacity he was influential in bringing to Ahmedabad a branch of the Indian Space Research Organization. The entire section of the western part of the city where ISRO's huge campus is situated became known as "Satellite." In the same year, Vikram founded the Community Science Center to promote scientific education among students, teachers, and the general public.

Vikram also brought to Ahmedabad India's premier school of business, the first of the Indian Institutes of Management. IIM-Ahmedabad was founded in 1961 through the collaboration of the government of India, the government of Gujarat, the Ford Foundation, Harvard University's School of Business Administration, and private industry. The institute was to be located in Bombay, but Vikram persuaded the sponsors to settle in Ahmedabad instead.[17]

Vikram's wife, Mrinalini, a young Bharata Natyam dancer from a Tamil family noted in the arts, established, with Vikram's help, the Darpana Academy for the Performing Arts in 1949. Darpana became a center for training generations of young dancers, performers, and researchers in drama, music, and puppetry. It won national and international acclaim for its success in reviving and revising traditional arts. It helped put Ahmedabad on the international map of the performing arts.

Some Businessmen Depart the City

The most successful Ahmedabad-born industrialist of the first half of the twentieth century, however, was neither Kasturbhai Lalbhai nor Ambalal Sarabhai, but Mafatlal Gagalbhai. The Monopolies Inquiry Committee of 1965, which ranked Kasturbhai's holdings twenty-first largest in India and Ambalal's sixteenth, listed Mafatlal's as fifteenth.[18] An examination of Mafatlal's reasons for leaving Ahmedabad reveals important qualities of the city.

Mafatlal's business ventures outgrew the geographical limits of the city, and socially, he was not among the Vania financial elite. Born in Ahmedabad in 1873 in the Kadva Patel caste community, Mafatlal began working with his father in marketing textiles until, at the age of fourteen, he joined one of Ahmedabad's mills as a clerk. In 1905, he joined with Collinson Shorrock, an Englishman, and with Chandulal Achratlal, a Vania, to finance and staff the Shorrock Spinning and Manufacturing Company in Ahmedabad. In 1912, he purchased a mill in Nadiad, approximately twenty miles south of Ahmedabad, and named it New Shorrock.

Mafatlal continued to move further afield. In 1916, he bought an old mill in Surat and remodeled it. In 1921, he took control of the China Mill in Bombay, and in 1927, he added the Standard Mill, also in Bombay. In 1929, he promoted the Gagalbhai Jute Mills of Calcutta, and in 1930 he established the Mafatlal Fine Spinning and Manufacturing Company in Navsari, in the princely state of Baroda. In 1933, he took over management of Indian Bleaching and Dying and Printing Works Ltd. of Bombay. As Mafatlal's empire expanded, its center was no longer in Ahmedabad. His family moved out of the city in the 1930s, although they retained some degree of influence as they took an interest in one new Ahmedabad mill, became partners in another, and supported some Ahmedabad educational charities. For the most part, however, Mafatlal's enterprise had outgrown the city.

Regional capitals such as Ahmedabad tread a thin line. They must be homey and sociable enough to provide a comfortable style of life, yet open and challenging enough to provide room for creativity and growth. Regional capitals must be attractive to creative and enterprising people in all walks of life without overwhelming them, as a larger, more metropolitan city might, and without stifling them, as a smaller city might. In general, Ahmedabad seems to have succeeded in achieving this balance—but not for everyone.

Quality of Life in the City of Mill Owners and Mill Workers

While Vikram and Kasturbhai were bringing to Ahmedabad elite institutions of a world-class center of education, science, and technology, others confronted the more down-to-earth challenges of governing a city overwhelmingly composed of mill workers. The firm alliance that had been negotiated among the Congress, the mill owners, and the TLA continued to control city government until 1965. Chinubhai Chimanbhai, the nephew whom Kasturbhai chose in answer to Vallabhbhai Patel's call for a civic leader from within his family, was elected to the municipality in 1942 on the Congress ticket. In 1944, he became chair of the standing committee, and in 1949 president of the municipality. In 1950, the Bombay government sanctioned the transformation of Ahmedabad's legal status from muncipality to municipal corporation, a more powerful legal entity with greater administrative powers. As president of the municipality, Chinubhai automatically became the mayor of the new corporation. He held the position until 1961, when another mill owner, Jaykrishna Harivallabhdas, succeeded him and served until 1965.

Through this period, Ahmedabad's population doubled, from 877,000 in 1951 to 1,760,000 in 1971. The increased wealth of the mills, the increased value of land and property, and the increased taxation power of the corporation more than kept pace. In the 1950s, the corporation's income grew, even surpassing expenditures until a reversal in 1973–74.

With new wealth and increased zeal, the corporation transformed large areas of Ahmedabad, both above and below ground. New annexations doubled the area of the city between 1931 and 1941, from twenty-five square kilometers to fifty-two square kilometers. Most of the annexed land was on the eastern side of the city. Those borders held steady for a decade, then increased by another 80 percent to ninety-three square kilometers by 1961, this time mostly on the west side of the river. The 282 kilometers of roads in 1951 were extended to 820 by 1971–72 and the 164 kilometers of drains to 716. The water supply was dramatically increased between 1950 and 1954 at the cost of Rs. 90 lakhs. The twenty million gallons of water per day in 1950 was almost doubled to thirty-eight million gallons per day in 1960–61 and increased by half again, to fifty-nine million gallons in 1965–66. Supply per capita rose from twenty-three gallons per day in 1950 to forty in 1960–61 to forty-six in 1965–66.

Public education received renewed attention. The number of municipal primary schools increased from 195, with 1,608 teachers and 62,813 students in 1950–51, to 364 schools, 3,500 teachers, and 147,000 students in 1965–66. Expenditure rose from Rs. 58 lakhs in 1960–61 to Rs. 121.5 in 1965–66, with the per-capita expenditure per child rising from Rs. 52 to Rs. 83 in those five years.

The municipal corporation built amenities as well as necessities. To create a new municipal cultural center in which the city could take pride, Mayor Chinubhai Chimanbhai invited the world-famous Swiss-French architect Le Corbusier to design the Sanskar Kendra (culture center). Corbu had come to India at the invitation of prime minister Nehru to design Chandigarh, a new capital for the state of Punjab. Sensing that the architect might be enticed to build in Ahmedabad at the same time, Mayor Chinubhai pursued the possibility actively and successfully. While Corbu was in Ahmedabad, the AMA hired him to design a new building for its headquarters, and two mill owners' families engaged him to design their private homes as well. Even before Corbu arrived, architect Achyut Kanvinde had designed the new ATIRA headquarters in 1950. About 1960, Charles Correa designed the new Gandhi Memorial Museum at Gandhi's Sabarmati ashram. In the early 1960s, Louis Kahn designed the campus and buildings of the Indian Institute of Management. In 1962, along with Bernard Kohn and Rasubhai Vakil, Balkrishna Doshi, who had worked extensively with both Corbu and Kahn in Europe, the United States, and India, established Ahmedabad's School of Architecture, which later expanded into the Centre for Environmental Planning and Technology (CEPT), and still later into the CEPT University. Ahmedabad earned a place on the world map of modern architecture, to complement its historic reputation for outstanding fifteenth- and sixteenth-century Islamic architecture.[19]

Beginning in 1951, the Ahmedabad Municipal Corporation constructed a zoo and a children's park, the Bal Vatika, surrounding Lake Kankaria. The zoo, and its director, Reuben David, won national recognition for excellence. The Bal Vatika included pony- and goat-cart rides, a children's zoo, and a fun house of mirrors. Its site at Lake Kankaria, on the eastern side of town, was easily accessible to both working-class families in the mill areas and the more middle-class population of Maninagar. The corporation reconstructed the steps surrounding the man-made lake to make the 500-year-old structure still more attractive. In 1956, the city opened the first of its six municipal swimming pools.

Each of these municipal achievements, however, also had a downside. For example, the increased supply of water overtaxed the drainage and sewerage capacities of the city. The rebuilding of the wastewater collection system did not keep pace. Ahmedabad's first underground sewer line had been laid in the Astodia–Raipur–Khadia area in 1890, and the entire walled city area was completely serviced with sewage lines by 1930. Facilities were extended to the eastern areas outside the wall by 1939, and drainage connections on the Ellisbridge side were completed in 1955. By the end of 1958, the Ahmedabad Municipal Corporation had extended underground sewerage facilities to almost the entire area within its limits. The corporation's assistant engineer, P. R. Shah, asserted proudly, "The AMC was the first Municipal Corporation in India which has completed installing gutter lines in the whole city."[20] But their capacity was inadequate. In many localities, the new sewer lines were simply connected to the existing lines:

> Due to such arrangements the old drainage lines, which were hardly sufficient to take their own discharge, were further loaded with the increased discharge of the extended areas. This resulted in frequent breakdowns due to choking and backing.[21]

> Such a disregard for the basic principle of sanitation had its toll in the form of polluting the river water. There were frequent incidences

of break-downs of old mains due to heavy back pressure; over-flowing of sewers during peak hours occurred at increasing rate; silting of sewer-sections due to stagnancy became common. This over-flown sewage met the river through the nearby separately laid down storm water drains and started polluting the river flow giving rise to a lot of other problems of public health and general sanitation.[22]

Industrial waste pollution added to the problem. The industrial wastes in the sewer lines were "also damaging drainage lines and they get rusted, affecting the drainage system. Even the machinery used for cleaning drainage lines is also affected by these sulphur gases and they therefore become unserviceable in the course of time."[23] The government report alluded to perhaps the most shocking aspect of all: the method of cleaning the drains. Then, as now, Bhangis, sweepers, were lowered by rope, almost naked, into the gutters to clean them by hand, a filthy and extremely hazardous occupation: "The work of drainage line maintenance is also extremely difficult because on account of industrial waste sulphur dioxide or hydrogen sulfide is produced which is fatal to human life."[24]

Inequities in Ahmedabad

The problems of overloaded sewer lines backing up was, however, minimal in Ellisbridge. The sewerage system there was completed only in 1955 and was built to accommodate its needs fully. Expansion to the west, based on new institutions and white-collar populations, proceeded with considerable concern for residential comfort and cultural and commercial development. The elite educational, research, and cultural institutions all concentrated here. Two new bridges facilitated access between them and the older city, the Sardar Patel Bridge, opened in 1939, and the Gandhi Bridge, opened in 1940. On its completion in 1961, the Nehru Bridge became the largest and most central of them all. After the construction of the bridges, the activities of the central business district inside the old walled city began to spill across the Sabarmati onto Ashram Road, the main north–south artery of the west bank. It paralleled the Sabarmati and was zoned for commercial uses. The mostly middle-class residential population of Ellisbridge increased from 110,825 in 1961 to 223,954 in 1971. Many of their new homes were single-family bungalows built of reinforced concrete, with small lawns and carports, enclosed by fences or low walls.

Cooperative housing ventures provided an important legal mechanism to facilitate this middle-class residential expansion. The first cooperative housing society, the Brahma Kshatriya Society, was founded in 1924 in the Pritamnagar neighborhood of Ellisbridge. In 1950–51, there were 110 cooperative housing societies; in 1960–61, 679; in 1965–66, 1,022; and in 1969–70, 1,419, with 45,562 members. Government regulations making land purchase, materials purchase, construction costs, and taxes less expensive for cooperative societies fostered this extraordinary growth. The greatest number of them were located in three wards on the western side of the city, Naranpura, Usmanpura, and Ellisbridge; in one middle-class ward in Maninagar, in the east; and in Rakhial, a working-class area situated among the mills. A survey of cooperative housing society members who had joined between 1941 and 1965 showed about 75 percent of them to be Patels, Brahmans, and Vanias—upper and rising middle castes—in about equal proportions. In terms of their occupations, well over half were white-collar, salaried employees, while about 25 percent were in private business. It was an open secret that the advantages extended to the cooperative societies encouraged builders to create paper cooperatives, which actually masked private housing programs. The government subsidies for cooperatives thus benefited private businesspeople, but on the other hand, new, much-needed housing was built through this deception.[25]

Expansion in the mill areas to the east arose quite differently, marked by the continuing growth of industry and of workers' residences, especially new *chawls* constructed by private builders, the municipality, and the TLA. By 1951, Ahmedabad had almost 1,500 *chawls*. Almost half had no sewage and toilet facilities, and the corporation was not effective in seeking out and forcing improvements. Attempts to force owners to provide these facilities under the Bombay Provincial Municipal Corporations Act usually became mired in litigation.

Owners generally evaded any responsibilities of maintenance and repair of drains, water closets, urinals, baths, and washing places. If the owner failed to heed a directive concerning maintenance issued by the collector, the fine was only Rs. 100, and other penalties were equally nominal. In addition, finding space for installing toilet facilities in the *chawls* was difficult: "All the open spaces around the original *chawl* are taken up by irregular hutments and very little open space is available for providing additional water closet facilities in such *chawls*. . . . Further, the inhabitants of the area often resent the setting up of public latrines near their houses and are able to obtain stay orders from the courts."[26]

Repeatedly frustrated in attempts to force owner compliance, in 1971, the corporation decided to provide sewerage at its own expense, and in five years, it provided sewer facilities and toilets to some 600 *chawls*. (The decision was reminiscent of the arguments from the 1920s between Gandhi and Patel over the locus of responsibility for the cleanliness of the slums.) By that time, the city had an estimated 80,000 huts classified as *kuchha*—that is, built of impermanent materials, usually baked mud. Under a central government–sponsored program for slum clearance and redevelopment, the corporation pledged to build approximately 10,000 tenements for slum families, but this was to be spread over many years. In no single year did the number exceed 800—hardly enough to dent the slum problem of the city.[27]

The inequality of services between east and west drew constant criticism. In 1974, for example, by which time the citywide per-capita supply of water had declined to 38.5 gallons a day, the central zone, including the walled city and the Shahibaug area, received 46 gallons per day per capita; the western zone, including Ellisbridge, 40 gallons; the eastern industrial zone, 31. Although the Kankaria Lake area, with its zoo and the Bal Vatika children's park, stood out as a special gem, elsewhere Ahmedabad's system of recreational spaces was severely overburdened. Prabhakar Bhagwat, a landscape architect and regional planner with the National Institute of Design in Ahmedabad, noted that although the "generally accepted standard for landscape and recreational spaces varies from 4 acres to as high as 6–7 acres per 1000 population, [in Ahmedabad] we have 0.6 acres per 1000 population."[28] In addition, the provision of open spaces was skewed by region of the city. The wide, tree-lined streets of the west bank and the green spaciousness of the huge campuses of the National Institute of Design, Gujarat College, C. N. Vidyalaya (an educational institution devoted mostly to the arts), Gujarat Vidyapith, Gujarat University, the Indian Institute of Management, and the Space Application Center were unmatched in the old walled city, where densities exceeded 300,000 per square mile, or in the crowded, underserviced *chawl* and hutment areas surrounding the eastern mill areas.

The corporation in the 1950s and early 1960s introduced some spectacular projects that brought it international attention, initiated some fine programs of middle- and upper-class expansion west of the river, and was coping, with somewhat less enthusiasm, in the old walled city and the eastern industrial regions. Deputy municipal commissioner N. H. Thacker and town development officer N. R. Desai assessed the situation:

> Compared to other cities, of course, the performance of the Ahmedabad Town Development and Town Planning Committee is better and can legitimately be proud of its performance in spite of various shortcomings and limitations. . . . [But] to be quite candid, the set up of Municipal Corporations is hardly conducive to integrated development. If we speak of Ahmedabad Municipal Corporation, policy decisions are taken by the Town Planning Committee, composed of twelve Corporators. . . . For any planning that this department does, a scheme has to pass through eight stages which, if circumstances are favorable, takes three years. The revision of any part of the scheme has to pass through the same stages. . . .
>
> This calls for a new organisation; a Metropolitan Development Authority, which will be free from organizational weaknesses. Such

authority should be a statutory, permanent, autonomous body armed with adequate powers, financed and equipped with expertise and representing a cross section of population, local authorities surrounding the areas concerned, Corporation, State and the Central Government and the financial agencies like the Life Insurance Corporation, and the Reserve Bank of India.[29]

A metropolitan development authority with the kind of powers that Thacker and Desai were recommending was not created even in the 1960s, a time when the city government was powerful and commanded the strong support of the city's leadership and general population, and a time when the state government was new and brimming with enthusiasm and money. It still does not exist today.

The Electorate Speaks

The 1961 municipal election provides a rich perspective on Ahmedabad at the time of *shethia* dominance—a time when the Gandhian ethics of trusteeship were considered seriously. The election results indicated the degree to which the institutional relationships established by Gandhi, Patel, and Anasuyaben continued to hold—although within a vastly changed economic, political, and ethical framework.[30]

With the growth of the city, the corporation had expanded to seventy corporators. Only the Congress ran candidates for all seventy seats. It won fifty. The Praja Socialist Party ran thirty-eight candidates; eight won. The Janata Samiti, a collection of mostly liberal and leftist groups, ran forty candidates; nine won. Independent candidates won the three remaining positions. None of the other parties—the conservative Jana Sangh, the ex-untouchable Republicans, the Muslim League, the Revolutionary Communists, and the Socialists (Lohia)—won even a single seat.

The Congress won its huge majority through the backing of the TLA. Beginning in 1924, as we have seen, the leadership of the TLA selected candidates for the municipal government and submitted them for approval for the Congress ticket. This electoral agreement began with one candidate in 1924 and two in 1927. In 1961, thirty-one candidates from the TLA were given tickets by the Congress; twenty-nine of them won. Twenty-seven of these working-class representatives were elected from mill areas east of the river, outside the city walls. The party won its other twenty-one seats from twenty-nine other constituencies. Working-class votes were the basis of the Congress' power in Ahmedabad. TLA leaders called for workers to vote Congress, and they did.

On March 27, two weeks before the election, S. R. Vasavada, secretary of the TLA, issued a statement to the membership explaining the decision of the union's executive committee to stand with the Congress. He emphasized the same importance of tight organization in municipal affairs as in union affairs:

> You have built an organization to find solutions to industrial questions. The TLA looks after these questions on a daily basis. But just solving questions of pay, inflation, bonus, and working conditions alone does not bring satisfaction to the workers. The workers' neighborhoods must be clean; when the workers return home at night from the mills, there must be proper roads, and the roads must have street lights; there must be clean water to drink and adequate water for cleaning and bathing; there must be drainage for waste water; there must be arrangements for the children's education. There must be adequate health education and also arrangements for nursing for people who fall sick. Only if such basic facilities are maintained can the workers' world be happy. The Municipality is responsible for carrying out all these tasks and therefore it is of the utmost importance that the members we have chosen participate in the administration of the Municipality.[31]

The Praja Socialist Party (PSP) disputed the TLA–Congress commitment to delivering on these promises. The PSP manifesto condemned the building of new world-class institutions while the majority of the citizenry lacked basic necessities. It called on voters to throw out the Congress:

> THE PSP DOES NOT BELIEVE IN THE KIND OF PLANNING THAT KEEPS THE HUNGRY PERSON HUNGRY WHILE FUNDS ARE USED TO CLOTHE HIM IN SILK.
>
> See how it is! In the name of the workers and the poor the TLA gets thirty seats from the Congress, but the chawls, the hutments, and the other settlements remain as they are.
>
> OH, YES! AT THE TIME OF ELECTIONS, THE POTENTATES OF THE TLA REMEMBER THE SERVICE OF THE POOREST OF THE POOR, WATER TAPS FOR THE CHAWLS AND NEIGHBORHOODS, BATHING FACILITIES, AND OTHER THINGS.
>
> But . . . what have the very representatives of the workers themselves actually done?[32]

The PSP carried eight seats. Seven were in Khadia-1, Khadia-2, and Kalupur-1—among the best-educated and wealthiest wards in the city. One was in Maninagar, a mixed ward. None was in a working-class area. The Janata Samiti, a loose coalition of mostly leftist groups, won nine seats, all within the old, formerly walled city. In the working-class wards, the Gandhian institutions and party continued to hold firm. In 1962, the newly elected corporators, led by their Congress–TLA majority, elected as mayor of Ahmedabad Jaykrishna

Harivallabhdas, a highly successful young industrialist, past member of the Bombay state legislature, and future president of the AMA.

Almost fifty years after Gandhi's leadership circle had mobilized and woven them together, these four institutions—Congress, the TLA, the AMA, and the Ahmedabad Municipal Corporation—continued to hold sway in Ahmedabad. Their cooperation created a new form of shock city: a scientific and artistic center of international renown on one bank of the Sabarmati River and an industrially productive, unequally served company town on the other. The four major institutions had greatly evolved from their early Gandhian days. Then, they had struggled for their existence. Now, they had become the establishment.

CHAPTER 6

Indulal Yagnik Challenges the Gandhian Consensus

*From 1963 till the end of 1966 Indubhai
became the heartbeat of the common people of
Gujarat and especially of the agitation of the
revolutionary workers of Ahmedabad.*

—DHANVANT OZA, introduction to
Indulal Yagnik's Autobiography

Even during Gandhi's time, Indulal Yagnik had fought against establishments. He lost these early battles. Despite Indulal's objections, Gandhi continued to call for daily quotas of spinning on the *charkha* (spinning wheel), and Vallabhbhai Patel continued to set the direction of the Congress.[1] In 1924, at the age of thirty-two, Indulal left Ahmedabad for Bombay feeling "as if my past was obliterated, my political prestige lost, my social service wiped out" (3:266).[2]

Indulal's friend, Bhogilal Gandhi, later remarked to him that "every five or seven years you have changed your entire ideology" (1:2), and Indulal's transformations in Bombay illustrate the point. He quickly found a job as a journalist with the *Bombay Chronicle* and later with the Gujarati daily, *Hindustan*. He gave up khadi and dressed in European-style clothing. He began to read seriously the literature of communism and socialism and became increasingly disillusioned with nationalist politics altogether.

He began making films. He entered the world of cinema by translating titles of a film on the life of the Buddha, then prepared a script for a film on the fortress and temples at Pavagadh in eastern Gujarat. He bought a film studio and a motorcar, but a partnership venture with a German filmmaker lost so much money that Indulal had to declare bankruptcy. Once again, he had to search for new worlds.

In 1930, Gandhi launched the Salt March and was arrested. After receiving the news in Bombay, Indulal broke down in tears. He realized that "whatever rebellion my intelligence had proclaimed against Gandhiji in the intervening period of six years, my heart was perfectly united with him" (5:4). He joined old friends in Congress House, Bombay, and they suggested that he travel in Europe to publicize the Congress goals and programs. Vallabhbhai wished him well in the venture, and in the fall of 1930, Indulal sailed for London and Berlin.

In March 1931, however, Gandhi signed a pact with the viceroy, Lord Irwin, suspending civil disobedience in exchange for the release of political prisoners and promises of constitutional reform. Indulal felt betrayed: "Gandhi had compromised with the Viceroy" (5:4). He resumed his criticism of the Mahatma. He wrote *Gandhi as I Know Him,* one of the most bitter of the early socialist critiques of Gandhi.

In Europe Indulal grew more radical. During a half-year visit in Ireland in 1932, he met leaders of the Irish independence movement and started an Indian-Irish Independence League: "I became a true advocate of a socialist republican state" (5:5). He returned to London in 1933, continued his radical and revolutionary reading, and in 1934–35, he wrote a biography in English of the militant, violent Indian revolutionary Shyamaji Krishnavarma, which remains a standard work.[3] In 1935, he returned to India and to the struggles at ground level.

Indulal went directly to organizing peasants to protest their triple oppression by the British, the landlords, and the moneylenders. Responding sharply, the government externed Indulal from the five districts of British Gujarat in February 1936. He shifted his headquarters to Bombay and continued to organize peasants in the fields of western India. Together with Swami Sahajanand Saraswati of Bihar and Professor N. G. Ranga of Andhra, in 1936 he founded and led the All India Kisan Sabha (Peasant Association) (AIKS). Under India's new constitution of 1935, elections were held in 1937, and a Congress government took office in the Bombay presidency. The new home minister lifted the externment order on Indulal, and he returned to Gujarat. But he did not return to the Congress. Indulal wrote, "In the new age the Congress started running after power and wealth while we of the Kisan Sabha started formulating a program to obtain as much relief as possible by giving the new ministers [in the Congress government of Bombay] an idea of the new power of the kisan" (5:96).

Indulal, however, recognized the power of the Congress and of Vallabhbhai, who had by now won his designation as Sardar (commander). Indulal reflected on the Sardar's power to control the press, an area Indulal knew well: the *Gujarat Samachar,* an important daily newspaper in Ahmedabad, supported a mill worker strike in the city 1937 led by the Mill Mazdoor Union, until "Sardar Vallabhbhai came to Ahmedabad. At his directive, the tone of the paper was changed" (5:113).

Indulal traveled the rural areas, especially in Gujarat, agitating, organizing, and articulating the problems of poor peasants. He campaigned for lower land revenue assessments from the government, lower rents from the landlords, lower interest rates from the moneylenders, and for land redistribution. The fifth volume of his autobiography tells the story of these rural efforts from 1935 to the early 1950s. Class struggle—though not communism—was Indulal's guiding philosophy. His own rejection of possessions and property—apparently as much an aesthetic as a political decision—kept him above reproach. His lack of a permanent home and his frequent dependence on others for his meals left a legend and a legacy in Gujarat of friends who were pleased to host him at one time or another.

Indulal, however, could not build lasting organizations. He won occasional successes, but romantic agitation was usually no match against the power of vested interests and Congress organization. A colleague later wrote of him, "It is true that there was some ideological clarity, but rigid discipline and regulation did not suit him. Because of this, in his long career in public life, Indulal started many institutions—and left them."[4]

The All India Kisan Sabha itself slowly came under the control of the Communist Party. Unable to tolerate the party's dogmatic rigidity, Indulal left the organization to found and work with regional peasant movements. He founded four ashrams in Gujarat, including one at Nenpur, approximately twenty miles from Ahmedabad, where he established his own principal residence. He published a small monthly, *Gram Vikas* (Village Development). Politically, as physically, he was in the wilderness, and he remained there for almost two decades. In 1954, at Nenpur, he began to write his autobiography.

Then came the Mahagujarat struggle—the struggle to create a Gujarati-speaking state of Gujarat, carved out of the huge bilingual state of Bombay. Indulal opens the last volume of his autobiography citing the exact moment of this turning point in his life: "On August 8, 1956, in the afternoon, a procession of hundreds of students in Ahmedabad reached the Congress House [to advocate for the creation of a separate Gujarat state] and at about 1:30 PM bullets were fired at them" (vol. 6, chap. 1). Thus began Indulal's greatest opportunity to work on behalf of his beloved Gujarat—and against his nemesis, the Congress. The sixth and final volume of Indulal's autobiography emphasizes Indulal's role as inspiration, driving force, and chief public spokesperson of the movement. It is an emotional tale full of passion and fury.

Two other authors present alternative perspectives. *Le Ke Rahenge Mahagujarat* [We Shall Not Rest until We Have Mahagujarat], by Brahmakumar Bhatt, tells the story from the point of view of a leader of the Praja Socialist Party (PSP) of that time. Bhatt had been a student leader during the 1942 Quit India movement, and in 1956, the new student generation looked to him for guidance. Bhatt stresses the organizational skills of the student socialists in making a success of the Maha Gujarat Janata Parishad (MGJP), the leading organization of the movement. Indulal was indispensable to the students as the face and the voice of the movement, but, Bhatt suggests, the PSP students were its brains and its nervous system. The second volume of Dinkar Mehta's autobiography, *Krantini Khojmaan* [In Search of Revolution], tells the MGJP story through the eyes of Ahmedabad's leading communist organizer.

All three authors stress the mutual suspicions of the three main factions of the MGJP: ex-Congressites, PSP members, and communists. All three factions had their reservations about Indulal, but they recognized his passion for Mahagujarat, his simplicity and sincerity, his fire as a speaker, and his command over the masses. For all the factions, Indulal was indispensable.

The issue of linguistic states dated back to 1921 when the Congress, at Gandhi's urging, established its regional structures on the basis of local languages as the most effective way of reaching people and as a tool for cultural revival. So, for example, while the British established the Bombay presidency as its regional administrative subdivision, the Congress organized two separate provincial organizations, one in Maharashtra and one in Gujarat. In 1928, the "[Motilal] Nehru Report," produced within and for the Congress, further recommended a federal structure based on linguistic states. Immediately after independence, on November 27, 1947, the constitutional committee agreed to the principle of linguistic states as the prime minister, Jawaharlal Nehru, had also recommended.

In 1952, Bhailalbhai (Bhaikaka) Patel, a respected political and economic leader in central Gujarat, convened a meeting to form a Mahagujarat conference to press for a separate Gujarat state. An Ahmedabad lawyer, Himmatlal Shukla, was named president. Indulal was named vice president. All three men were known for their anti-Congress sentiments, so the movement was perceived from the outset as both for Mahagujarat and against the Congress. In the same year, riots broke out in Bombay City, organized by the Samyukta Maharashtra movement demanding a separate Maharashtra state, with Bombay City included within it. Meanwhile, in other parts of India, linguistic states were being carved out of old British administrative units, often in response to popular agitations.

The key issue in Bombay was the fate of Bombay City. Geographically, it fell in Maharashtra and the mother tongue of most of its citizens was Marathi, but Gujarati speakers dominated much of the economy, and Bombay was the commercial capital of India. The Gujaratis did not want "their" city and its commercial enterprises to go to Maharashtra. Their preferred solution was to create three states: Maharashtra, Gujarat, and Bombay City. The Maharashtrians would have nothing to do with the proposal.

Anticipating the creation of a new state of Gujarat as part of a three-state package—Gujarat, Maharashtra, and Bombay City—the Gujarat Sima Samiti (Border Committee) was established in 1952 to determine the proper borders of Gujarat according to linguistic usages. The areas of greatest controversies with neighboring states were Mount Abu in the north, contested by Rajasthan, and the tribal area of Dangs, in the south, contested by Maharashtra. Kasturbhai Lalbhai chaired the committee.

Kasturbhai was a supporter of the Congress, and he took comfort in Morarjibhai Desai's apparent advocacy, at the end of 1953, for the three-state formula. But on certain other critical issues, he already differed greatly from Morarjibhai. As home minister of the state of Bombay, Morarjibhai had declared that the Dangs was a Marathi-speaking area, contrary to the beliefs and the linguistic research of most informed Gujaratis. Subsequently, as chief minister, Morarjibhai imposed a heavy sales tax that evoked public street processions of protest. Kasturbhai joined in these demonstrations in Ahmedabad. Dinkar Mehta notes that this was the last time that *sheths* joined in such public marches.[5]

Mehta also noted that the Communist Party was quite unconcerned with the demands of the Gujarati capitalists for control of Bombay City. The party identified with the working people, mostly the Marathi speakers of Maharashtra. It therefore joined with the Samyukta Maharashtra committee in advocating two states: Maharashtra, including Bombay City, and Gujarat. Because the two-state formula was ultimately accepted in 1960, Mehta was also arguing, in hindsight, that much bloodshed, destruction, and waste of human energy could have been avoided if this concession had been accepted as the basis for negotiation from the beginning. The entire Mahagujarat movement would have been unnecessary.

A crisis did, however, emerge from the confrontation of different interest groups. It began moving toward explosion on January 17, 1956, as prime minister Nehru announced on All India Radio that the three-state formula had been accepted: Maharasthra state, Gujarat state, and a separate Bombay City state. In Ahmedabad there was rejoicing, but riots broke out in Bombay. In four days, 37 people were killed and 500 wounded. Gujaratis in Bombay feared for their lives and property, and thousands fled the city. Congress ministers from Marathi-speaking areas, indignant over the loss of Bombay City, resigned from the Bombay government.

In the face of this violent reaction, Nehru reversed his position, taking Morarjibhai with him. On August 7, newspapers throughout Gujarat carried the astonishing news on the front page: the bilingual state of Bombay was created by act of parliament, by a vote of 241–40, and the major Congress politicians of Gujarat, led by Morarjibhai, had agreed to it. Indulal wrote, "A sudden shock fell on the dreams of Maha Gujarat which had been entertained by the Gujarati people and supported by Gandhiji and Sardar. The plans for

Mahagujarat were shattered at the final moment. The golden aspirations of the entire people of Gujarat were turned to ashes" (6:20).

Later that day, student leaders came to protest outside Congress House, the party headquarters in Ahmedabad. The next day, August 8, they came again. Some went across the street to the Textile Labour Association (TLA), where one of the officials, Shyamprasad Vasawada, declared disingenuously that the TLA was only a union of workers and was not involved in politics. Some student protesters entered Congress House while others milled about outside. Some of the students threw stones. Without warning, without any prior use of *lathis* (police batons) or tear gas, the police opened fire, killing four people on the spot. Two more died later.[6] About fifty people were wounded. Muslims as well as Hindus were among the casualties, and as a result, Brahmakumar Bhatt explains, the MGJP movement saw both communities participating together from beginning to end.

As the news of the shooting spread, so did the horror. Some of the students placed the skull of the first man killed, Poonamchand, on a plate and carried it across the street to the Gujarat Club. The lawyerly crowd gathered there was shocked and came out to observe, interrogate, and protest. Some came to the Congress House and asked who was responsible for the shooting. No one took responsibility. (The Kotval Commission, appointed to investigate the violence, also did not fix responsibility.) No one from Congress House issued an apology. No one came out to speak with the students and to console them. Later, one of the Congress leaders, Thakorebhai Desai, further inflamed the situation by declaring, "Bullets do not have names written on them."

Student messengers carried the news, and stone throwing against the police began in Raipur and Khadia. It continued in other parts of the city as well, with stone throwing against police posts and municipal bus stands, and gate meetings at several mills. The bazaars and even some mills closed. A curfew from 9 PM to 7 AM was declared, but it could not be enforced. Crowds gathered and threw stones and burned property. Later, Indulal summed up the situation: "A political revolution took place. In one night Ahmedabad, regarded as the fortress of Congress on account of the impact of Gandhiji and Sardar, turned into a bitter opponent of Congress. Within one night the white cap that used to be placed on the head disappeared. If somebody wore it he would be beaten" (6:42). Elaben Bhatt, then working in the TLA office across the street, related in a personal interview that she saw protesters seize people with Gandhi caps on their heads, pour kerosene on the caps, and set them on fire.

Student leaders Harihar Khambholja, Prabodh Raval, Hariprasad Vyas, and others, in consultation with Brahmakumar Bhatt, went around the city urging peaceful protest. On August 9, the bazaars were closed. Private cars were stopped on the streets of the city. A khadi shop was attacked and burned.

There was shooting on Relief Road. Another eight people were killed and forty wounded.

Indulal, reading the news in Nenpur, took the train to Ahmedabad. Eluding the curfew police, he reached the office of the *Jansatta* newspaper to assess the latest developments and then proceeded to Gujarat College for a program arranged by the student committee to pay tribute to Vinod Kinariwala, martyred in the 1942 Quit India movement. Indulal became the principal speaker and "got ready to launch myself into the new struggle. . . . When I went to bed on the 9th night, the direction of my life underwent a change" (6:30, 35).

On August 10, five more people were killed and forty-five wounded. Almost all the mills were closed as the more militant, non-TLA unions called for closure. The military was called out and patrolled the Raipur–Khadia area in police jeeps, armed with Sten guns. Indulal, Mehta, and Bhatt all characterized the events as guerrilla warfare. Indulal reminisced of 1919 and reveled in "The Wonder of the Masses." The people were rising again:

> In 1919 when Gandhiji had been arrested and the first trouble was started in Ahmedabad, people feeling afraid on account of the firing by the army had hidden themselves in their houses. But now, 37 years later, a new history was created. As the firing continued and the tear-gas shells were fired, people continued breaking telegraph poles, milk kiosks, roofs of the buses, and putting them as obstacles on the road. They stopped police vans by throwing brickbats and stones at them. People continued to wage guerrilla war. (6:42)

Many leaders of Congress, including the mayor and deputy mayor of Ahmedabad, submitted resignations both from the party and from office. The Gujarat Chamber of Commerce declared its opposition to the bilingual state. Some of Ahmedabad's most prominent businessmen—including Chinubhai Chimanbhai (the mayor) and Amritlal Hargovandas—published a statement of support for Mahagujarat and condemned the Congress for so completely misunderstanding the temper of the people and so completely mismanaging the situation. A women-only meeting was convened on the grounds of the law college; the speakers, including Sharadaben Mehta and Vinodini Nilkanth, represented some of Ahmedabad's most venerable families.

Women played significant public roles in the Mahagujarat movement. Nalini Mehta was not only Dinkar Mehta's wife, but was also an important organizer in her own right, a speaker, and a candidate of the MGJP and the Communist Party. Ranjanben Dalal, wife of MGJP leader Jayanti Dalal, spoke of her organizational work in neighborhoods of Ahmedabad and across Gujarat, and of the responsiveness of women in those neighborhoods. The women were themselves strong, and many of the male leaders of the MGJP, notably Mehta, Jayantibhai, and Indulal, were strongly feminist in their attitudes and behavior (6:289).

The president and the secretary of the Mahagujarat Student Committee passed resolutions "to spread the struggle of Mahagujarat all over Gujarat, to continue the strike until the objective was attained, and to observe 13th August as Martyr's Day" (6:44). Again, women played important roles. Among the many commemorations of August 13, a group of

> some 500 women of Raipur, incited by police excesses, marched toward the police chowky of Raipur. When they started shouting against the thoughtless oppressions of the police, teargas shells were released on them. Some women brought with them boxes of water and soaked napkins so that they could protect themselves. When the agitation by the women continued, the police resorted to teargas 6 or 7 times and the women, feeling frightened, dispersed. On account of the poison-ous gas even some police fell down. (6:50)

On August 19, Morarjibhai scheduled a mass meeting and public speech in Ahmedabad to present his case. Much of the blame for the loss of the antici-pated Gujarat state had been placed on Morarjibhai—for permitting the loss, for agreeing to it, and for an almost complete lack of communication with Gujarati Congress leadership concerning the proceedings. Indulal and the stu-dents led the growing opposition to Congress in general and to Morarjibhai in particular.

They declared a "Janata curfew," a people's curfew, on the day Morarjibhai was to give his speech. The curfew was to be a complete boycott not only of Morarjibhai's meeting, but of all public activity. Everyone was to stay home. The streets of the city were to remain empty. Indulal wrote, "To make a success of the program, workers of the students committee canvassed throughout the city. Thousands of volunteers were registered in every ward, locality, pol, and lane to make a success of the people's curfew" (6:56). On August 19, the city of Ahmedabad was effectively shut down. Astonished by the discipline and peace of the protest, European and American newspapers published photographs of the deserted city.

So few people showed up for his meeting that Morarjibhai canceled his appearance. He declared that he was beginning a fast to atone for and protest the coercion that he claimed had been used in enforcing the Janata curfew. Although the movement included people from across the political spectrum, including many Congressites who had quit the party over the Mahagujarat issue, he condemned the movement and the curfew as a communist plot to destabilize the government, Morarjibhai broke his fast on August 26 at a public meeting in Ahmedabad at which about sixty public leaders promised a peaceful city—even as students were throwing stones. Mehta reports that listeners to the radio broadcast of Morarjibhai's speech that day heard mostly the sounds of stones hitting the broadcasting equipment.

Now discussions began in Ahmedabad among ex-Congressites, PSP members, communists, and student organizers to institutionalize the movement and give it a political structure. On 9 September, at a public meeting of 1,000 delegates of various political parties and persuasions, and 500 guests, the Maha Gujarat Janata Parishad (MGJP) was created. An office was established on Relief Road. People belonging to many different parties joined, but PSP members were the primary organizers, and they monitored access to the meeting. Mehta reports that some tried to keep communists out of the organization, but because the communists had supported the linguistic state movement from the beginning, they could not now be excluded. Two weeks later, in a speech at Congress House, Thakorebhai Desai, reflecting on the diverse composition of his opposition, asserted that the goal of the MGJP leaders was not the creation of Mahagujarat but the destruction of the Congress. Some MGJP leaders must have harbored both goals.

Who would be the MGJP president? Bhatt noted that the need was not for the long-term organization of a political party, but "for giving an agenda for battle. The time had come to fill the jails. In that situation, everyone felt that the right man for the presidency was Indulal Yagnik."[7] The vote, however, was not entirely lopsided. Many communists on the left and recently resigned Congressites on the right saw Indulal as a captive of the PSP socialists. Others saw him as allied with the communists. Mehsana district to the north voted for its own candidate, Purushottamdas Patel. Ahmedabad, however, was the heart of the MGJP movement, and the Ahmedabad vote carried Indulal to office. The final vote was 389–265 for Indulal.

On October 2, the anniversary of Gandhi's birth, prime minister Nehru was coming to Ahmedabad for a major address at Lal Darwaja. Indulal proposed a parallel meeting that would demonstrate powerfully the popular anger with the central Congress government and solidarity on behalf of Mahagujarat. Everyone would see who would draw the larger crowd—the Congress with Nehru, or the MGJP with Indulal. Frantic preparations ensued, including the mounting of a huge map of Gujarat, its borders lit by electric lights; twenty-five lamps burning with ghee, one for each of the Mahagujarat martyrs; and massive organization to bring out the crowds. Final estimates were that Nehru drew 50,000 to 100,000; the MGJP, 300,000 to 400,000. The MGJP meeting sang new anthems of their new movement, including the richly symbolic "Din Koon Ke Hamare" [The Days of Our Bloodshed], led for the occasion by Nalini Mehta[8]:

The days of our bloodshed, friends, do not let them be forgotten.
In your rejoicing, shed tears for us.
Gunned down by bullets, we sleep in Jallianwalla Bagh.
Light a lamp on our neglected tombs.

The hunter sighted our flowers, and plucked them.
But go on planting flowers in this desolate garden.
Hindus and Muslims, both are burned in the Holi fire today.
Let your clothes be stained in their flowing blood.

Approximately 3,000 Congress students attended Nehru's meeting. Most accounts, however, indicate confrontation, anger, and indignation rising on both sides.

The MGJP used the media effectively. The *Jansatta* newspaper was especially friendly to the new party. In addition, the MGJP reached the masses and the neighborhoods through innovative rituals. During the Navratri festival later in October, new *garbas,* folk songs and dances, were composed praising Mahagujarat, and they were sung and danced throughout the city.

Despite the demonstrations, the publicity, and the mobilization of the population in Ahmedabad and other parts of Gujarat—and in Maharashtra as well—on November 1, 1956, the bilingual state of Bombay officially came into existence. Processions, strikes, and demonstrations took place on the previous day throughout Gujarat. By this time, twenty-four people had been killed in Gujarat, and the demand for a judicial inquiry increased. The MGJP kept the tensions raw through continuing demonstrations, monthly martyrs' day commemorations, and parallel meetings. On December 15, Sardar Patel's death anniversary, the Ahmedabad Congress met in the Manek Chowk bazaar, in the heart of the old walled city, while the MGJP convened a parallel meeting in the adjacent Sankdi Sheri. Pushing, shoving, and stone throwing resulted.

Political attention began to focus on upcoming elections in the first week in March for the state government and parliament, and on April 14 for the Ahmedabad Municipal Corporation. At all levels, but especially at the state level, the selection of party candidates threatened to pull the disparate, improvised MGJP coalition apart. Indulal, always known as a brilliant, charismatic speaker, now exhibited yet another political skill. Bhatt wrote of Indulal's ability to manipulate his audience in a crucial public meeting: "In these circumstances

Indulal broke down in tears. He saw the Janata Parishad collapsing. He may have felt that his tears would have some influence."⁹ Finally, agreements were reached and slates drawn up, although some disappointed contestants later ran as independents.

The manifesto of the MGJP acknowledged its motley membership: "The MGJP does not belong to any party or group but it accommodates within itself all parties and groups which believe in Maha Gujarat." The manifesto demanded a judicial inquiry into the police firing at Congress House. It said nothing about the ultimate disposition of Bombay City, a tacit recognition of agreement with S. M. Joshi of the Samyukta Maharashtra movement, assigning the metropolis to Maharashtra.

On January 3 and the following few days, the police arrested approximately twenty-two non-Congress political leaders, most of them socialists and several of them candidates in the forthcoming election, and sent them to the Yeravada jail, near Pune. Divisional commissioner Sathe announced to the press that the detainees would be released after two months, but for the present, they were a threat to security, law, and order. Large public meetings and many shutdowns and strikes were held in Ahmedabad in protest against what appeared to be a direct intervention in the political election process. On February 5, three of the prisoners—Brahmakumar Bhatt, Jayanti Dalal, and Harihar Khambholja—were freed, to much public celebration. The others remained in jail until after the elections.

Indulal describes the zest of electioneering in Ahmedabad:

> On 6th March, the last Sunday before the elections, the Parishad took out a procession in Ahmedabad city. Thousands of citizens from all the wards joined it and it extended to about 1½ miles. There were 10 camels and 20 horses carrying large election symbols of the cock and lion adorned with live cocks. Besides, there were drums and cymbals and band music playing everywhere. Around 9 o'clock at night, having arrived via different roads, the procession turned into a huge meeting at Manek Chowk. (6:147)

The elections put the MGJP and its relationship with the Congress into perspective. Of 133 seats at the state level, Congress won 101, MGJP 29, and the PSP 3; of the 22 seats for the Lok Sabha from the Gujarat region, Congress captured 17 and MGJP 5. Some of the MGJP victories were quite remarkable. For the Lok Sabha seat from Ahmedabad, Indulal defeated the Congress candidate, Khandubhai Desai, the veteran TLA leader and labor minister in the central government.

The election results revealed the degree to which the MGJP was centered in Ahmedabad and the neighboring Mehsana and Kheda districts. Of the total twenty-nine assembly seats captured by the MGJP, eleven were from Mehsana, nine from Ahmedabad, and five from Kheda; two came from Panchmahals, and one each was from Bharuch and Sabarkantha. Of the five Lok Sabha seats, two came from Ahmedabad, two from Mehsana, and one from Kheda. The MGJP won no seats at all in Saurashtra, Kutch, or Surat.

The political geography of the election was understandable. From the time of independence, both Saurashtra and Kutch had been fashioned into separate political constituencies, reflecting their history as states of princely India rather than of British India. They are Gujarati speaking, but their cultural and historic developmental patterns, like their geography, were separate from the mainland. In addition, their patterns of migration were strongly linked with Bombay. Many Saurashtrians and Kutchis had direct, comfortable relations with Bombay—more so than with Ahmedabad. They did not see a new state, with a new state capital at Ahmedabad, as any more of an advantage than a bilingual state with its capital in Bombay.[10]

Surat district in the south is equidistant between Ahmedabad and Bombay, with many years of experience of looking toward Bombay as its political center. Here, too, the concept of Mahagujarat ignited little political enthusiasm. In addition, Surat was the political base of Morarjibhai. Mahagujarat, with a capital in Ahmedabad or adjacent to it in Gandhinagar, was of maximum interest to the people of Ahmedabad and its contiguous districts of Mehsana and Kheda. Indulal and the MGJP promoted their demand for a new state and a new capital by mobilizing them.

In the 1957 Ahmedabad municipal elections, no candidate was willing to stand on the Congress ticket.[11] Candidates who had resigned from the Congress, candidates from the PSP, and candidates from the Communist Party agreed to abandon party identification for this election. They agreed to contest as individuals on a combined slate called the Nagrik Paksh (Citizens Party), which had as part of its platform the creation of a Mahagujarat state. The head of this slate was Chinubhai Chimanbhai, the popular mayor, who had resigned from his position and from the Congress over the Mahagujarat issue.

Indulal agreed that Chinubhai would choose the remainder of the slate with appropriate representation for all constituent groups, and the MGJP would support it. Any other candidates would have to run as independents. In the end, some of these independents were actually MGJP supporters who thought that Chinubhai's allocation of seats was unfair and therefore broke the agreement. Mehta notes that the only Communist Party member who was given a ticket was his wife, Nalini, who lost. He suggests that the Nagrik Paksh did not give her full support. The Nagrik Paksh carried forty-eight seats, independents eighteen. Seven seats were reserved for candidates of scheduled castes and scheduled tribes.[12]

A clash came somewhat later when Chinubhai, reelected as mayor, declared for the three-state formula. By this time, the MGJP–Samyukta Maharashtra alliance was built on the tacit agreement of the Gujaratis to give up their claims on Bombay City. Indeed, at an election victory celebration on March 19, 1957, Indulal, Bhatt, and Harihar Khambholja stated clearly, "Bombay City is a part of Maharashtra. This is just. The MGJP and SMS [Samyukta Maharashtra Samiti] must shake hands on this so that they can divide up the bilingual state."[13] Chinubhai's statement violated that agreement.[14]

Meanwhile, in other elections of 1957, Bombay City elected a communist mayor, defeating Congress. It was becoming obvious to almost everyone by this point that Bombay City should go to Maharashtra in a unilingual state, while Gujarat should become its own state with its own capital, either Ahmedabad or a new city to be specially built, Gandhinagar. Indulal agreed with this.[15]

The MGJP was ecstatic with its electoral gains—and with the showing of its ally, the SMS. Indulal wrote,

> By adding in the Vidhan Sabha [Bombay state legislative assembly] 130 members of the Samiti with 30 of the Parishad, in all 160 members, we prepared to give a call with one voice for single language states. If that Government would not heed our joint power then we prepared with the chosen brave people of Gujarat and Maharashtra to launch a great non-violent struggle. (6:163)

In his maiden speech in parliament, immediately after the president's address, Indulal discussed the history of the struggle for a Gujarat state and the demand for a judicial inquiry into the shootings. Then he, too, waffled in public on the issue of Bombay City—a surprising lapse from his previous agreements:

> Since there is no demand to include Bombay City in a Gujarat State, these issues are not related to one another. On the other hand, we do take interest in the lakhs of Gujarati people staying in Bombay. Therefore we do not agree to the demand made by Dange—[president of the SMS]—of merging Bombay with Maharashtra. To solve the question of the entire bilingual state I supported the motion to appoint a committee with representation of all the groups. (6:174)

On August 8, 1957, the MGJP arranged a citywide commemoration of Martyr's Day, including the construction of local shrines, a large silent procession ending in a meeting at Martyrs' Garden—today's Sardar Bagh—and the shutting down of traffic and commerce in the city. Mayor Chinubhai was reluctant to grant the use of Sardar Bagh, but ultimately a compromise agreement was reached on the use of part of the space. A meeting of managers of the schools of Ahmedabad, with Kasturbhai Lalbhai presiding, cautioned against shutting down the city and its traffic. The MGJP, however, continued with its more militant program:

> We had requested the municipality not to run its buses, but the Nagarik Paksh insisted on running them. This caused friction with our volunteers who then let out the air from the tires of the buses. As a result, a large number of buses stood still at several places. On the other hand, schools and colleges, all bazaars, firms and offices remained completely closed in the city and there was no friction. (6:192)

The MGJP also urged sisters to tie *rakhi* string bracelets on their brothers' wrists commemorating the struggle, just as they did to claim the protection of the brothers each year on the holiday of Raksha Bandhan, taking place at about the same time of year. Indulal wove together traditional celebrations with his new political goal.

In September–November 1957, in discussions with S. M. Joshi of the SMS mediated by Bhaikaka Patel, Indulal and the MGJP publicly agreed not to push for separate statehood for Bombay City but to allow it to be included peacefully in Maharashtra state (6:207–10). The major stumbling block to the creation of a separate Gujarat state was now removed. Later, when Indulal was called on to defend this giveaway, he replied that only the wealthy Gujarati businessmen were concerned with holding onto Bombay City. The majority of the people of the city itself did not share this concern. Furthermore, he argued, Gujaratis in Bombay would be safer once Gujarat state came into existence and could monitor their safety and welfare.

The next question to be settled was the political placement of the Dangs, the largely tribal area on the border between Gujarat and Maharashtra. Anthropologists and survey researchers saw its people related linguistically to Gujarati. Historians saw ancient historical links. In 1958 elections for local board representatives in the Dangs, hotly contested between the MGJP and the SMS, the MGJP carried twenty-six of thirty seats, further suggesting that the Dangs should be assigned to Gujarat. Agreements also began to be reached on payments by Maharashtra to Gujarat for its loss of Bombay and its need to create a new state capital. In anticipation of an acceptable resolution of the linguistic state issue, political tempers began to cool. Membership in the MGJP declined from 182,000 in December 1956 to 37,000 in June 1958.[16]

As political pressure slackened, however, it appeared that the bilingual state might continue despite the efforts of the MGJP and the SMS. In an exchange of letters in July 1958, Nehru told Indulal that the decision on dividing the bilingual Bombay state rested with the national parliament, not with the Bombay assembly, and he seemed to suggest that parliament was not prepared to take that action. Indulal wrote, "It was now the Prime Minister of India himself who razed to the ground the towers of our hopes. Since no middle path of compromise remained, we got ready to dismember the bilingual state" (6:297).

The issue of a memorial to those slain at Congress House in 1956, Indulal wrote, "turned out to be the central point of the struggle for Maha Gujarat" (6:301). The Congress did not want a perpetual memory of the atrocity to be installed directly across the street from its headquarters, as the MGJP proposed. The government of Bombay refused permission in 1957, and Mayor Chinubhai refused permission in 1958.

The MGJP nevertheless prepared two memorial statues, each depicting a young man with his arm raised up holding a torch, and carried them in a great parade through Ahmedabad on August 8, 1958, the second martyrs' memorial anniversary. The police gave permission for the parade, but only up to Victoria Garden. Government and police had opposed the installation of the memorial statues; they wished to keep city life normal that day. The MGJP, however, depicted this as a struggle between "the power of the people and the power of authority"[17] and vowed to go ahead, creating a public confrontation before an audience of hundreds of thousands of people.

When the procession attempted to continue on to Congress House and to install the two memorials adjacent to it, to the astonishment of the marchers who had expected violent confrontation, the police gave way, allowing the marchers to proceed and to install both the memorials. Similar installations took place in the nearby towns of Kalol on August 10 and Nadiad on August 11 at locations where students had also been shot by the police. The MGJP was ecstatic.

Then, in the hours just after midnight on August 12, police removed all the memorials. This act "proved to be the signal for an unparalleled outbreak of rioting accompanied by arson, looting, and mischief on an extensive scale."[18] At dawn, when MGJP members discovered that the memorials had been removed, rioting broke out and continued for three days. Protesters burned police *chowkis* and the shops of pro-Congress businessmen. Three people were killed and forty-five injured. Indulal declared a seven-day fast against the government's actions and against the violence and destruction caused by his own colleagues in the MGJP. He walked the streets calling for peace, but to no avail. Brahmakumar Bhatt notes that antisocial elements and hooligans took advantage of the political disruption to loot property. Furious protest meetings were followed by 226 days of daily satyagraha processions in support of reconstructing the martyrs' memorials. Each day, a group of satyagraha volunteers would walk peacefully in procession westward along the main route from Manek Chowk through Three Gates toward Congress House, and would be arrested. In the course of riots and satyagraha, thousands were arrested; most were detained for a month to six weeks. Ahmedabad had become the stage for months of continuous street theater.

Chinubhai and the Nagrik Paksh continued to block the construction of a permanent memorial to the martyrs adjacent to the Congress House, despite the daily satyagraha processions. In protest, thirteen corporators quit the Nagrik Paksh and resigned their positions in the corporation.[19] In by-elections, held in December 1958, twelve of them were reelected on an MGJP-backed ticket, provisionally named the Janata Samiti.[20]

In the face of such widespread popular and political opposition, the bilingual state could not endure. In 1959, responding to a report submitted by a committee of nine appointed to inquire into the issue, the Congress high command agreed to reconsider the possibility of creating two separate states. Yashvantrao Chavan, chief minister of Bombay state, submitted a case for dividing bilingual Bombay state into the two unilingual states of Gujarat and Maharashtra. He argued that emotional integration had not taken place in the bilingual state.[21] The Congress leadership finally agreed to create Gujarat and Maharashtra, with Bombay to remain a part of Maharashtra, and with Gujarat to receive compensation toward building a new capital at Gandhinagar. On May 1, 1960, the two new states were born.

With its goal achieved, the MGJP agreed to dissolve. The mixed composition of the MGJP membership became clear as eleven of its members in the old Bombay assembly joined the Congress and five joined the new right-wing Swatantra Party in the newly created Gujarat assembly. In the Ahmedabad Municipal Corporation, forty-one members of the Nagrik Paksh rejoined the Congress; a few rejoined the PSP.

Indulal had been of two minds about disbanding the MGJP. The PSP members of the MGJP had warned him that all the members except the communists would return to their own parties; the communists would want to keep the MGJP alive as a cover for their programs. Indulal, however, was not prepared to give up public political struggles. When the left-wing and communist members of the MGJP urged him to recreate the party under a new name, he agreed. In July 1960, in Nadiad, the Nutan (New) Janata Parishad, later renamed the Nutan Mahagujarat Janata Parishad, was created with Indulal as president. Its agenda was to push for more left-wing political and economic policies and for the establishment of a martyrs' memorial.

The new MGJP did not inherit the élan of the old. With the creation of the Gujarat state, the voters seemed to forgive the Congress. In the 1961 elections to the Ahmedabad Municipal Corporation, Congress won fifty seats out of seventy; the PSP won eight; the Janata Samiti, the name under which the new

MGJP contested, won nine, none of them in the TLA-stronghold mill areas. In the 1962 elections to the legislative assembly of the new Gujarat state, Congress won 113 of 154 seats; Swatantra, which flourished primarily in rural Gujarat, 26; the PSP, 7; the Nutan MGJP, 1. In the 1962 elections to the Lok Sabha, Indulal alone was victorious on the MGJP ticket, defeating S. R. Vasavada, the candidate of the TLA and the Congress. It appeared that the new MGJP had little further reason to exist.

Critics, especially in the Congress, saw the new MGJP primarily as a front for communists, who indeed played a large part in its creation and existence. The anti-MGJP publicity of the Congress and others was strident, persistent, and shrill in its opposition to communists. In other parts of India, in West Bengal and Kerala, communist parties had begun to work within the nonviolent democratic electoral system—and to win. But the anticommunist, anti-MGJP publicity of the Congress in Gujarat painted a much harsher, more demonic picture of the threat of communism.

The MGJP during 1956–60 had been mostly a middle-class movement. It had not been able to crack the hold of the TLA in working-class industrial areas. Indeed, Indulal had not been much acquainted with these areas and had not campaigned there extensively. Now he began to see more clearly the power of the organized laboring classes. A new union of the doffers in the spinning department illustrated both the potentials and the difficulties.

The doffers' union was founded by Karsandas Parmar, a member of the scheduled castes and a local leader of Dr. Ambedkar's Republican Party. In 1957, Parmar had been elected to Parliament from Ahmedabad to a seat reserved for members of scheduled castes. Parmar could see the benefits won by the TLA for the formerly untouchable doffers, but he resented the patronizing attitudes of its leadership and the continuing discrimination that restricted scheduled caste workers to only certain jobs and certain units within the mills. Eating areas within the mill compounds continued to segregate scheduled caste workers from members of the upper castes. Pay scales for spinners and doffers were considerably lower than for weavers and others of higher castes.[22]

Parmar understood that he would nevertheless have a difficult task in competing with Congress and the TLA. Under the Bombay Industrial Relations Act of 1948, only the TLA was certified as the representative union for Ahmedabad textile workers. Only the TLA could collect its dues from the workers by a direct checkoff from their paychecks within the mills. Only the TLA was authorized to participate in collective bargaining. The TLA seemed to have more contact with the owners than with the workers, Parmar thought, but it was also much better organized than any of the new unions. The TLA stressed organization. It attended to workers' day-to-day problems and complaints and followed up systematically. By comparison, the Kamdar Sangram Samiti, an alliance of anti-TLA unions, was not organized for efficiency. The doffers' union itself lasted for only three years before its members were reabsorbed into the TLA. It demonstrated both the desire for more union alternatives and the difficulty of creating them.

The communist Mill Kamdar Union (MKU), led by Dinkar Mehta, was succeeding in some of its organizational work in Ahmedabad, and Indulal reluctantly joined in. Mehta tells of his own attempts to unionize Ambalal Sarabhai's Calico Mill in the early 1950s. Ambalal was bitterly opposed. Workers started strikes in response. They were joined in demonstrations by fellow workers from other mills. As many as 20,000 workers came each day to protest. Mehta called for a citywide strike, and fears spread of Hindu–Muslim riots in the communally mixed areas around the Calico Mill. Armed soldiers were called in. At this juncture, Indulal went to talk to Ambalal. Their conversation went on for hours and resulted in an agreement that aborted the proposed strike. Indulal wanted peace and feared rioting. Mehta, on the other hand, cited the event as an example of an early sellout by Indulal. The workers, Mehta relates, were deflated and angry when Indulal addressed a meeting at Premabhai Hall to explain the negotiations and their results. Indulal, according to Mehta, had betrayed them.[23]

The MGJP that had fought for Gujarat state had mostly addressed the middle classes. Its strongholds had been in the Khadia and Kalupur wards of the walled city, in Maninagar, and across the river in Ellisbridge. Economically, they believed that the loss of Bombay City might be more than compensated by Gujarati investors redirecting their finances to the new state. Their hopes proved at least somewhat correct, especially after the Bombay-based Shiv Sena political movement harassed Gujaratis in Bombay in the 1960s and as labor militancy under the leadership of Datta Samant alienated Bombay capitalists in the 1970s. Bombay Gujaratis redirected some of their investments toward Gujarat. Most came to the southern parts of the state, nearer Bombay,[24] but some reached Ahmedabad as well. In addition, as labor militancy in Calcutta increased in the late 1960s, Gujaratis and others in Bengal also saw the new Gujarat state as a more stable place for their investments.

Ahmedabad's mill workers did not see themselves sharing in these economic benefits, and after 1960, Indulal set out to mobilize them in earnest. He organized gate meetings, up to twenty a day during heavy campaigning. He spoke to the workers directly and used the language of the street, cursing not only the mill owners but also the TLA officials. Unlike the Gandhians of the TLA, he chain smoked, allowing the workers to feel that he was with them instead of above them. The workers loved him for his simplicity, his obvious sympathy with the poor, his idiosyncrasies, his color, and his fire.[25] On July 17,

1962, Indulal led a procession of 100,000 people to the state legislative assembly, then meeting temporarily in the new Ahmedabad civil hospital. Indulal, incidentally, opposed the construction of a new state capital at Gandhinagar; he wanted to keep the legislators in Ahmedabad, accessible to demonstrations, and he wanted to save construction costs. The Congress wanted Gandhinagar for the opposite reasons.

In the same year on December 4, during the annual celebration of Labour Day by the TLA, Indulal addressed a parallel meeting at the Kankaria football grounds, which he claimed drew 200,000 participants, ten times the attendance of the TLA celebration:

> Until now the worker of Ahmedabad was not on the map of India—he was in the pocket of the Majoor Mahajan (TLA). Today he has come out. Today is not only the day of the founding of the Majoor Mahajan, it is the day of the liberation, of the revolution, of the worker. Now a united front of free workers of Ahmedabad and Bombay will be formed. For all of India a strategy will be formed, and from it a brilliant future for the workers. (6:405, in Gujarati)[26]

The meeting set out demands for a higher cost of living allowance, an annual bonus equivalent to one month's wages, and the appointment of an expert committee to determine the cost-of-living allowance.

Indulal hammered away at the Majoor Mahajan and at the Congress. He contrasted the TLA that Gandhi had formed with the corrupt TLA of his own day: "What a Mahajan Gandhi created for the greatest benefit of he workers! and what a Mahajan it has become, boiling over with corruption!" (6:406, in Gujarati). The TLA was no longer a voice for the workers; it had become a broker between the workers and the owners. In addition, TLA officials were complicit in fostering a system of contract labor that displaced full-time, protected union labor with workers who were paid about one-fourth the salary, with no benefits. As many as 10 percent of the mill labor force was employed under contract labor schemes as union representatives took kickbacks to hide the illegal arrangement. Up to half the contract laborers were women.[27]

Indulal addressed the January 25–26, 1963, inaugural session of the Mahagujarat Kamdar (Workers) Association, applauding the formation of new militant unions. He also went to rural areas to organize peasants, agricultural laborers, bonded laborers, scheduled castes, and *adivasis*. On July 28, 1963, the Mill Kamdar Union and the communist parties in Ahmedabad staged a mass procession down Relief Road to the Sabarmati River. They denounced continually rising prices. At first Indulal ignored the procession, but, Mehta relates, when Indulal saw that 20,000 people were participating, he decided to come to the riverbed and speak. Indulal loved the excitement of the crowds, but he also seemed to feel, Mehta wrote, that if he did not participate along with the communists, he would lose out to them.[28] He was, of course, welcomed warmly.

On September 1, 1963, representatives of forty-six mills joined together to form the Kamdar Sangram Samiti (Workers Struggle Committee), with Indulal as president and Mehta as vice president. Later they formed the Mahagujarat Mill Workers Union, with 50,000 dues-paying members and twenty-six full-time party workers.

In the working-class areas of Ahmedabad, criticism of the TLA was rising, making its way even into popular poetry and songs. One of the poems, "The 'X' of the Mill and of the Vote," by Aalji Bhagat, collected by Rameshchandra Parmar in *Shramik Kavita* [Labor Poems],[29] indicted the TLA on many counts: hunger for the power and wealth of political office, corruption in choosing candidates, general lassitude, and selling out the workers' needs to the mill owners' money. The humor and sarcasm of this poem turns on the two very different significances of the mark of an "X." It could refer either to an electoral candidacy or to a new, more demanding configuration of machinery to be operated by the worker on the shop floor.

> A working couple sit by the window, talking of serious things.
> "Why so sad today, my man? You've brought home your lunch,
>> uneaten.
> Tell me the truth, my man,
> Have I done something wrong?"
>
> Says the husband, "In the mill today, many things went wrong.
> They are planning to give me the 'X.'
> That is why my heart is troubled
> And I had no wish to eat."
>
> "Oh, but dear, today people want to get the 'X.'
> They go on giving speeches, even at their own expense.
> YOU'VE gotten the 'X' mark for free!
> How can you refuse?"
>
> Says the husband, "Those who have gotten THAT 'X' get to enjoy life.
> But from the 'X' of politics to THIS 'X' is the distance from heaven
>> to earth.
> Haven't you understood at all?
> Now listen to my words:

Those who ran on the political 'X'—they are all rulers today.

But my 'X' is for running four lines of machines!

That is my problem,

And there is no escape."

Replies his wife, "Oh, my husband, our country is free,

And our TLA is strong, go and file a complaint!

They will fight your case!

No need to go on so sad!"

Says the husband, "You don't understand at all!

You give them all this credit!

The TLA and the millowners—they are all one and the same!

THEY have given me this assignment!

To whom can I complain?"

Says the wife, "Lakhs of workers roam without jobs.

From such rules the country will be ruined.

What kind of freedom is this?

Our lives are not worth living."

On August 5, 1964, the MGJP called for a statewide general strike, a Gujarat *bandh*. The agitation had begun as a weeklong protest against high prices on consumer goods, especially food, specifically cooking oil. It broadened into a call for a citywide Ahmedabad *bandh,* which grew into the call for statewide resistance. In Ahmedabad, a huge strike, parade, and meeting were organized. All the mills in the city were crippled, some shut down by strikers, some closed by owners who feared potential violence. For the first time, thousands of Harijan workers joined thousands of non-Harijans in a strike that shut down 60 percent to 70 percent of the total mill capacity. "This strike and meeting," Mehta wrote, "shook the foundations of the Congress and the TLA."[30]

In countering the strike and demonstrations, the government employed armed and mounted police against the marchers on Relief Road. Six people were killed and many were injured. Ahmedabadis were horrified at the sight of their own government once again using violence against its own citizens, as it had in 1956.

Discontent with the Congress and the TLA deepened into revulsion. The MGJP swept to power in the 1965 Ahmedabad Municipal Corporation elections. The MGJP carried forty-two seats, the Congress thirteen. Eight of the MGJP candidates campaigned from the jail cells in which they had been incarcerated for their role in the Gujarat *bandh*. For the first time, the TLA hold on the labor areas was broken. In addition, the other elected corporators were likely allies of the MGJP: nine from the PSP; five republicans (Dalits); and at least five of the nine independents.

The official investigation of the violence of August 5 and 6, conducted under the direction of Gujarat high court justice N. K. Vakil, interrogated Indulal closely about his alleged communist affiliations and his willingness to incite violence during the strike (6:472–92). Distinguishing his views from Mehta's, Indulal declared that he was not a communist, that he had quit the All India Kisan Sabha when it followed a communist line in 1942, and that he did not believe in the necessity of the violent overthrow of the government. He added that many communists also did not believe in that necessity.

"I give speeches that do not incite; they inspire," he said. He acknowledged that many of his statements were ambiguous. For example, he frequently quoted Gandhi as saying, "If inequality is not ended, violent revolution becomes inevitable" (6:426, 435, in Gujarati). When he said that the MGJP would destroy the TLA with the Sudarshan Chakra, the discus of the Lord Vishnu, which usually refers to a lethal weapon, he was in fact referring to the weapon of the strike. The term that he used for the mill owners, *saalaao,* usually a term of contempt, was not meant as an insult but was simply colloquial usage. And when he said that the owners would "have to pull up their dhotis in their hands and flee the mill," he only meant that the mills might someday be nationalized (6:488, in Gujarati). The commission accepted Indulal's slippery explanations.

At about the same time, Indulal gave a lengthy interview to the *Jansatta* newspaper in which he declared, "Do not paint me falsely as a Communist. I am a complete Gandhian, and I intend to remain so." He added, "I am not at all a materialist, but a complete believer in the soul. I believe in the soul and in the 'Great Soul,' God" (6:510, 508, in Gujarati). In an interview a few days later in another Ahmedabad daily, *Prabhat,* Indulal reflected on the extent of the changes in Ahmedabad social and political life: "The Shethias do not want to pay the cost of living allowance nor the bonus. They talk about taking these issues to the Supreme Court. Their good sense has been corrupted. Their prestige has come to an end. They have been put to shame" (6:513, in Gujarati). Indulal undertook a seven-day fast to call attention to the economic suffering of the common man.

The Congress accepted a great deal of the blame for its 1965 electoral disaster in Ahmedabad and discussed it in its weekly bulletin, *Congress Patrika.* The Congress was not doing well in several major cities, including Bangalore, Madras, and several large cities in the north Indian state of Uttar Pradesh (U.P.). Women and youth, both as voters and as candidates, were shifting to the opposition. "Rapid, fundamental change has been taking place in the values of life," and the Congress has not been keeping up. The *Congress Patrika* itself was consistently filled with appeals to the past, to the heritage of Gandhi and Patel. The negative vote had been not a vote *for* the opposition so much as a vote *against* the Congress. Congress would have to clean house.[31]

In the next four years of MGJP rule in Ahmedabad, 1965–69, both the party and the voters would learn that it was easier to protest against the party in power and to throw it out than it was to achieve good governance. The problems of the MGJP became evident immediately in its attempt to balance internal factions. Each wanted its own candidate to be mayor, so that position rotated each year. In the first year, Dr. Somabhai Desai was elected. In the second year, Mehta was selected by the thinnest of margins: Mehta nineteen; Dr. Somabhai Desai seventeen; Manubhai Palkhivala, who was later elected mayor and held that post from 1968 to 1969, seventeen. When the result of the vote of the party leadership was announced, Mehta reported that Indulal lay down on the dais dramatically and cried out, "I am half dead!" Yagnik and Mehta, the leader of the communist faction, had many sharp differences of opinion, and Indulal was not pleased to see Mehta as mayor. Meanwhile newspapers and the BBC spread the news around the world: "A Communist Mayor in a Capitalist City!"[32]

The populist legislation passed by the MGJP strained the city budget and administration. The Ahmedabad Municipal Corporation raised city workers' salaries to bring them on par with those of the central government, thus sharply increasing the city's expenditures. It increased octroi taxes on imports into the city and property taxes, especially on the more wealthy citizens. It terminated the use of khadi cloth for all its uniforms, a policy in place since Gandhi's time, enraging the Congress. The move was a combination effort to economize— khadi cloth is expensive relative to its quality and durability—and to make yet another political statement through fashion.

Mehta argued proudly that the new MGJP administration shifted the priorities of the city's expenditures to the impoverished industrial east side. Primary schools, water, lights, sewers, and toilets were provided more widely throughout the workers' *chawls* and slums. Even many of those who agreed with Mehta's assessment, however, argued that this shift of priorities had begun with the Congress and the TLA from the 1920s, and that it continued after the MGJP administration ended in 1969. Critics also argued that many of the programs of the MGJP, which seemed appropriate in theory, were not well implemented in practice. Day-to-day administration was less efficient than it had been under the Congress government. Meanwhile, under the leadership of Mehta and Indulal, the MGJP conducted regular picketing and demonstrations at Esso and Caltex gas stations throughout Gujarat, chanting,

> Americans! Imperialists!
> Quit India, Quit!
> Long Live the Revolution! (6:528)

The Congress government at the state level and the MGJP government at the municipal level often struggled in deadlock. One exception was the agreement finally reached in 1968 to construct a martyrs' memorial adjacent to Congress House.

By 1969, both the MGJP and the voters had had enough. The factions that had composed the MGJP—communists of the left and the right, United socialists and Praja socialists—ran together under the name Janata Morcha (People's Front). Of the 105 seats in the municipality, they carried only 4. The mayor, the deputy mayor, the chairman of the standing committee, and the chairs of many other committees were defeated. Congress swept back into power with sixty-five seats. After this, the MGJP virtually ceased to exist. It had carried only two seats in the state legislature in 1967.

For the fourth municipal election in a row, Ahmedabad voted to throw the rascals out—a message Indulal might well have endorsed. Although Ahmedabad had had elected officials since the late 1800s, it was only after independence that universal suffrage was introduced. In Ahmedabad, as elsewhere across India, the voters seemed eager to exercise their right to get rid of a government that they did not like, but they had not yet succeeded in electing a government that served them well. In every municipal election from 1957 until the 1980s, they consistently voted out the government they had chosen in the previous election.

Indulal, however, was reelected to the Lok Sabha consistently, in 1957, 1962, 1967, and 1971. In the last years, after the Congress split of 1969, Indulal supported Indira Gandhi in her successful opposition to Morarjibhai Desai, and he was adopted as an independent friend of her Congress (I) party. His parliamentary victory in 1971 over Jaykrishna Harivallabhdas, a staunch Congressite, wealthy mill owner, and former mayor of Ahmedabad, consolidated Indulal's reputation with Indira.

Indulal died in 1972 at the age of eighty. His body lay in Sardar Bagh for twenty-four hours as hundreds of thousands of citizens came to pay their respects. It was then carried to the Dudeshwar cremation ground in an open truck accompanied by additional hundreds of thousands of Ahmedabadis. In the history of Ahmedabad, Mehta writes, there had never been so large a funeral procession.[33] With Indulal's death, the MGJP too breathed its last.

Indulal's many campaigns revealed that the masses of Ahmedabadis were not necessarily made in the austere, controlled images of Gandhi, Vallabhbhai, and the *sheths*, or even in the compassionate, domestic mode of Anasuyaben Sarabhai. The middle classes of the walled city were inflammable, and the industrial workers in the *chawls* and slums had grown resentful of being patronized by the TLA, even though the association brought them considerable benefits. Laborers and middle classes alike could be moved by the issues and by political theater on the streets, and these Indulal provided through his oratory, his sets, and his dramatic confrontations with authority. Unlike Gandhi, he did not hesitate to approach the point of violence, and even to cross it.

Indulal's mix of contradictions had its own charms. A man of simple habits, including chain smoking, with few economic needs and hardly a home to call his own, Indulal conveyed to common people an immediate, endearing sense of a certain roguishness. A Nagar Brahmin of the highest intellect and education, an accomplished and prolific writer in both English and Gujarati, Indulal spoke with the masses on their own level—and below. Energetic, magnetic, even charismatic, he had a special attraction for students and for women, both personally and politically. In his Gujarati patriotism and his political populism, he mobilized mass sentiments, demonstrating that the political leadership, first of the Congress and later of Ahmedabad, had lost touch with the emotional and economic needs of the citizens. The masses loved him. Yet they could differentiate between his theater, which they applauded by continually reelecting him to parliament, and his political party, which they rejected when they perceived that it had no further goods to deliver.

Indulal succeeded in bringing out many submerged faces of Ahmedabad, and the people loved him for it. This was less true in the rest of Gujarat, where the Congress remained firmly in control and where Indulal's political battle cries went largely unheeded. In Ahmedabad, however, Indulal's successes demonstrated that three of the principal institutions that had dominated the city at least since the earliest days of Gandhi's regime—the Congress, the Ahmedabad Millowners Association, and the TLA—were now more fragile than they appeared on the surface. And the fourth institution, the Ahmedabad Municipal Corporation, could be captured by outsiders. In addition, the electoral and lobbying victories of his Mahagujarat Janata Parishad helped create the state of Gujarat and brought its capital to Gandhinagar, virtually a suburb of Ahmedabad.

Indulal was not an institution builder—quite the contrary—although he earned credit as one of the principal founders of Gujarat state. As a result, in Ahmedabad today, he is less remembered than the other veterans of the 1915–22 ruling circle. Nevertheless, his statue occupies one of the most prominent places in the city, Indulal Yagnik Park, at the eastern end of Nehru Bridge, visible to the hundreds of thousands of people who pass by every day. His tall, thin, powerful form, captured in bronze, carrying over his shoulder the bag of *chana,* chickpeas, that he always took with him, marches on. Ironically, the park itself was tended for many years by its nearby neighbor, the Holiday Inn, and later by its successor, Le Meridien.

PART 3

Creativity and Chaos, 1969–

Creativity and Chaos, 1969–

"Broken Bricks"

—SUNDARAM (1937)

"I Am Shattered"

—UMASHANKAR JOSHI (1952)

The Gandhian age had brought a sense of unity to Ahmedabad. Four principal institutions provided the formal organizational structures: the Ahmedabad Millowners Association, the Textile Labour Association, the Congress, and the municipality. Apart from their individual, separate missions, these institutions shared three common visions: ending British imperial rule, assuring a minimum level of social services to Ahmedabad's citizens, and preserving the peace, order, and favorable business climate of the city.

Despite these shared commitments of the city's most powerful institutions, civic tensions broke out in periodic violence. The riots of 1919, 1941, 1942, 1946, 1990, and 1992 showed that Ahmedabad was not isolated from the nationwide disturbances that accompanied the struggle for independence, partition, and communal confrontations. Violence in 1956, 1964, 1985, and 1986 over local and statewide issues further demonstrated that dedicated agitators, invoking inflammatory words and actions at critical moments, could whip latent political frustrations and social tensions into violence in the streets.

The poets were first to sense that more violence and turmoil was to come. They uttered dark premonitions of a turbulent future. Sundaram (1908–1991) was born as Tribhuvandas Luhar, a name indicating his blacksmith caste. He graduated from Gandhi's Vidyapith in 1929 and began to craft a new form of poetry that helped to create the Gandhian age of Gujarati literature. He was later hailed "as the New Poet in Gujarati who sang the songs of the poor and cried out against God."[1]

In 1937, Sundaram wrote "Intala" [Broken Bricks], an appreciation of the tough working people of the street. The poem addressed their diverse potentials for cooperation and for destruction. It played on the ambiguity of the word *intala,* literally "pieces of broken bricks," but also, in slang, "the rough peoples of the street"—people who themselves are broken and scattered by society, people who might pick up *intala* and hurl them in violent fury. Much depended on the leaders whom the *intala* would accept as their friends and guides. Sundaram's own spiritual and political guide was Gandhi, but he recognized that some *intala* might choose very different "friends" who might lead them in very different directions:

> The "intala" render their service in many forms;
> Thanks to many "friendships" they appear cultured;
> Serious and mature in many of their characteristics;
> They go on performing their tasks—many of them devious.

Waiting to see how the drama of industrial Ahmedabad and its working class citizens would unfold was ultimately not to Sundaram's taste, and in 1945, to the astonishment of the people of Ahmedabad, he left the city to take up permanent residence in the peaceful sanctuary of Sri Aurobindo's ashram in Pondicherry, where he lived until his death in 1991.

Umashankar Joshi (1911–1988) is a transitional figure among Gujarati poets. Considered, along with Sundaram, as the greatest of the Gujarati poets of the Gandhian era, he was also the first great Gujarati poet of the post-Gandhian era. "Chhinbhinn Chhun" [I Am Shattered], written in 1952, was one of the poems that marked the transition. Drawing on the existential literature of the time, much of it coming from the West, Umashankar saw the *trimurthi,* the three faces of God, no longer as the lords Vishnu, Shiva, and Brahma, but as Lust, Hatred, and Fear. Cut off from nature, in an urban, mechanical world, surrounded by hypocrisy and selfishness, Umashankar declared:

> Day and night, night and day, I despair.
> Struggling to become centered, I grow weary;
> Broken in pieces, with each beat of my heart, I am
>   shattered.

Unlike Sundaram, Umashankar remained at the center of the literary, cultural, and political life of Ahmedabad, even as it began to shatter and fragment, like his own psychological and spiritual life. Especially as vice chancellor, the highest executive officer of Gujarat University, 1967–73, he struggled to maintain educational standards at a time when civic and intellectual values came under attack.

Had the poets' power of prophesy been more precise, they might have predicted a series of eight events that would devastate Ahmedabad in the period 1969–2002:

1. The outbreak of communal violence in 1969, which turned into a massacre of Muslims, and repeated every few years, usually on a more limited scale, but in 2002 with comparable fury.

2. The emergence of the politics of personal patronage and corruption, which would even sanction violence for personal gain, a strategy pioneered by Gujarat state chief minister Chimanbhai Patel. Resistance against such politics, in the form of the Nav Nirman (Reconstruction) movement of 1974, ended in disillusionment.

3. The collapse of the Ahmedabad textile industry, the backbone of the city's economy for almost a century.

4. The concomitant collapse of the Textile Labour Association and all the support and services it provided for its 150,000 members.

5. The resulting impoverishment of the Ahmedabad Municipal Corporation.

6. New political strategies designed by Chief Minister Madhavsinh Solanki in the 1980s to create political coalitions of lower castes and classes, along with Muslims and Adivasi tribals.

7. Violent backlash riots that split apart the groups that Madhavsinh sought to unite and brought a "mafia don" bootlegger, Abdul Latif, to prominence as the defender of the Muslim community in the absence of police protection.

8. The communal violence between Hindus and Muslims in 1992, a local manifestation of the national unrest triggered by the campaign to destroy the Babri mosque in Ayodhya, north India, and replace it with a Hindu temple.

Perhaps the poets would even have foreseen Chief Minister Narendra Modi's advocacy of Hindutva, the merger of Hinduism and politics, which inspired the worst pogrom in Ahmedabad's history in 2002.

What the poets could not have foreseen, alongside this political violence born from the manipulation of class, caste, and religious identities, and the economic collapse of Ahmedabad's flagship industry, was the restructuring and rebirth of the Ahmedabadi economy. The political leaders most responsible for provoking violence were also most concerned with the economic development of Ahmedabad city and Gujarat state. The checkered careers of chief ministers Chimanbhai Patel, 1973–74 and 1990–94; Madhavsinh Solanki, 1976–77,

1980–85, and 1989–90; and Narendra Modi, 2001–, forced Ahmedabadis and Gujaratis to ask themselves just what values they wanted in their leaders and in themselves. What kind of economics would they endorse, and for whose benefit? Which political tactics were acceptable, and which were not? The age of Gandhi and his associates was over; what new age would Ahmedabadis construct for themselves?

CHAPTER 7

Communal Violence, 1969

People who have been brought up in defiance of law as an instrument to achieve independence may continue to entertain the same idea until it is discouraged by leaders of public opinion.

—Reddy Commission report

I found that small pockets of minority communities in areas of larger communities were wiped out or stood to be wiped out.

—BRIGADIER SUKHWANT SINGH

It is an open secret in Gujarat that police and anti-social elements have close ties.

—PROF. GHANSHYAM SHAH

The Breakdown of the Nonviolent Consensus

The Gandhian consensus preserved the peace in Ahmedabad from 1919 until the national agonies of the 1940s intruded on the local scene in the form of Hindu–Muslim riots in 1941 and 1946 preceding partition, and attacks on government property accompanying the Quit India movement of 1942. The violence of 1956–60 exploded out of the Mahagujarat movement. The police confrontation with Indulal Yagnik's 1964 populist campaign was specific to Ahmedabad and comparatively limited in intensity.

Communal Pogrom, 1969

The Hindu–Muslim communal warfare that suddenly erupted in 1969, however, raised violence to unprecedented levels. The street battles of September 1969, which turned into a massacre of Muslims, left an official death toll of 560, of whom 430 were known to be Muslims and 24 Hindus.[1] Private estimates by reliable witnesses put the total number at between 1,000 and 2,000, with the proportions of Muslims to Hindus unchanged. After 1947, these were the most destructive communal battles anywhere in India until the nationwide communal riots of 1992.[2] The murders shattered Ahmedabad's mystique as a center of Gandhian nonviolence. Ahmedabad was once again a shock city—for entirely new reasons.

The intensity was unexpected. Between 1947 and 1969 the state of Gujarat had witnessed Hindu–Muslim conflicts, but not of great severity, and not in Ahmedabad. The Indo-Pakistan war in 1965 had aggravated antagonisms between Hindus and Muslims, especially after the chief minister of Gujarat, Balvantrai Mehta, was killed when his plane was shot down during an inspection tour near the border with Pakistan. Nevertheless, even the war did not precipitate local violence in Ahmedabad.

The late 1960s saw a rise in separatist rhetoric among both Muslims and Hindus. (Perhaps the death in 1964 of prime minister Nehru, the leading apostle of a composite multicultural society, opened the floodgates.) On June 2, 1968, the Muslim cultural organization, Jamiat-ul-Ulema, organized a large meeting in Ahmedabad and drafted a list of sixteen resolutions. Some sounded separatist and communal—for example, calling for special facilities for Muslim government officers to offer prayers on Friday, and for opposing any change in the name and constitution of Aligarh Muslim University in north India.[3] Among Hindus, the militant cultural organization, the Rashtriya Swayamsevak Sangh (RSS), held a huge rally at the end of December addressed by one of its leaders, M. S. Golwalkar, calling for Hindu Rashtra, a Hindu nation. In March 1969, a copy of the Quran had fallen from a pushcart; the volume had been carelessly handled by a Hindu policeman. Muslims were enraged and attacked the local police station; Hindus, in turn, were agitated when the government ordered the policeman to apologize publicly.

Far from India, in early September 1969, an emotionally disturbed Christian from Australia detonated a small bomb that damaged a section of the Al-Aqsa mosque in Israeli-held Jerusalem. Muslims around the world protested this attack on one of their most sacred shrines. Most cities of Gujarat witnessed marches. In Ahmedabad, 50,000 people participated. Many Hindus resented this show of solidarity with the larger world community of Islam as unpatriotic. About a week later, in a series of talks throughout Gujarat, Balraj Madhok, leader of the Hindu-militant Jana Sangh Party, spread this allegation of foreign allegiances. (Umashankar Joshi presided over one of Madhok's meetings, but when he rose to disagree with the speaker, he was shouted down and was not permitted to continue.)

In the next week, a Muslim police officer closed down a performance of the Hindu Ram Lila play in the Behrampura area of Ahmedabad after midnight because it was against the law to use microphones at that late hour. In the pushing and shoving that followed, the officer apparently kicked a copy of the Hindu classical epic Ramayana. The government ordered an investigation. Hindus contrasted this kid-glove treatment with the immediate public apology demanded of the officer who had shown disrespect to the Quran. Two days later, Jana Sanghis and some religious leaders formed the Hindu Dharma Raksha Samiti (Committee for the Defense of the Hindu Religion).

In addition to these manifestly antagonistic events, sociologist Ghanshyam Shah adds two underlying sources of tension.[4] Traditional Hindu beliefs and rituals were under attack from a more modernized strata of society that held to more flexible philosophies and practices. In particular, a recent series of public lectures by Bhagwan Rajnishji had attacked traditional religious leaders. They responded to this challenge to their authority with greater militancy, expressed in part by hostility to Islam. Second, Shah noted, "There is a widespread belief in Gujarat that most of the street corner bullies and 'goondas' [hoodlums] belong to the Muslim community."[5] Some were bootleggers and gamblers who purchased protection from the police and the Congress government. "Hindu–Muslim alienation has thus many causes and a deep base in Gujarat and this had been sharpened by recent developments."[6]

On September 18, 1969, near the Jagannath Temple in the Jamalpur neighborhood of Ahmedabad, a densely mixed Hindu and Muslim residential area, about a thousand Muslims had gathered at a *dargah,* a mausoleum, to commemorate the death anniversary of a local saint. At about 3 PM, two Hindu sadhus were shepherding a herd of cows back to the temple, when one of the cows, reacting to the crowds, bolted, injuring a Muslim woman and her two children. Meanwhile, Muslim children were harassing one of the sadhus, a dwarf. As he raised his stick to hit the boys, he accidentally hit another Muslim woman. The Muslims began throwing stones at the sadhus, who fled into the safety of the temple. The crowds outside, however, were larger, and approximately thirteen sadhus were injured by stones. Glass frames around pictures of a deity inside the temple were broken. The match had been lit. Sadhus in the temple began a fast to protest the attack and to demand an inquiry and appropriate punishment of the guilty. The Hindu Dharma Raksha Samiti called for a public meeting the next evening. Three Muslim-owned shops were torched during the night. Rumors began to circulate.

Newspaper accounts the next morning implied, inaccurately, that the attack on the temple had been both serious and planned. By afternoon, hundreds of handbills giving exaggerated accounts of the attack were circulating. They gave false information: a cow had been killed; a Mahant, a leading priest, had been seriously injured, even killed; Muslims had entered the temple and damaged the image of a god.

By 2 PM, most of the markets were closed. Schools closed a little later. Evening shows of the cinema were canceled. By afternoon, a grim atmosphere of suspense had overtaken the city.[7] Leaders of all communities, including fifteen Muslim leaders, condemned the attack on the temple, called for punishment of offenders, and urged peace. But it was too late. Arson had begun. Despite government orders forbidding the assembly of large groups of people, the evening meeting of the Hindu Dharma Raksha Samiti was held as scheduled.

The wheels of government turned slowly and ineffectively. The chief minister, Hitendra Desai, declared the appointment of a committee of inquiry, as demanded by virtually everyone, but he did not publicize the decision. Government imposed a curfew on three of the most sensitive areas—Khadia, Jamalpur, and Kalupur—but "the rest of the city was left at the mercy of the rioters."[8] Some of the first attacks were on Muslim *goondas* in the Gita Mandir, Behrampura, and Shah Alam areas of the city. With prepared lists in hand, mobs began to identify, loot, and burn Muslim shops. Those in Hindu-owned buildings were only looted. Although the police commissioner denied that the attacks were planned, the governor of Gujarat state took the opposite position, arguing that organized groups had prepared the attacks, and they must be exposed and stopped. In light of the evidence of lists used by arsonists and looters to identify Muslim victims, and of truckloads of weapons being delivered to riot areas, the Reddy Commission, appointed to investigate the violence, agreed with the governor.[9]

About noon on September 20, a young Muslim, who had set out to revenge the destruction of his property, was seized and burned to death on a hastily improvised pyre. Hindu onlookers seemed not to protest; they even seemed to offer encouragement. "Up to now incidents of killing were sporadic; they now became frequent and on a large and organised scale."[10] A crowd of about fifty people headed for Gandhi's ashram, by now converted into a national shrine and museum, to attack the residence of seventy-year-old Gulam Rasool Kureshi, who had lived there since 1921. The ashramites protected him and his home, but the houses of his two sons, and copies of both the Quran and the Ramayana, were burnt by the mob.

The rioting spread eastward to the mill areas: Khokhara-Mehmadabad, Amaraivadi, Raipur, Rakhial, Bapunagar, Chamanpura, New Mental Hospital Colony. These became the main sites of the continuing violence. Attacks, less severe, occurred in Ellisbridge:

> Atrocities multiplied by the 20th evening when several poor laborers were either burnt alive or murdered. In some places they were thrown into fires. Scythes, axes, knives and spears were used for killing people. Women were raped or stripped bare and forced to walk naked on the

road. Children were beaten against stones or their legs were torn apart. Limbs were cut off dead bodies. Women's breasts were cut and sex organs were mutilated or torn apart.[11]

Several trains were attacked, Muslim passengers were pulled out, robbed, and killed—several on September 20, forty on September 23, when the government lifted the curfew for three hours, and seventeen on September 24. Rioting spread to other cities, but none experienced the savagery of Ahmedabad. Indulal, who had declared a three-day fast at the first outbreak of violence and began to tour the riot-stricken areas, now extended the fast for several additional days. Morarjibhai Desai fasted for eleven days.

Who was responsible for the immediate violence? Ghanshyam Shah found that

> By and large all sections of the Hindu community participated in the riots in one way or other. Some were actual participants, some were observers providing facilities for the rioters if needed, and some were sympathisers and morale-boosters. However one can say that businessmen, irrespective of caste, creed, or region did not take a direct part in the riots. Even Punjabi and Sindhi businessmen who had deep-rooted grievances against the Muslims [because of the violence of Partition] remained aloof from the riots.[12]

In my own discussions of the mob violence that afflicted Ahmedabad so frequently between 1969 and 1986, most Ahmedabadis I spoke with claimed that "outsiders" were responsible. Published newspaper accounts made the same claim, and Shah's detailed, scholarly account finds some limited truth in this disclaimer. Several textile mills had recently closed, and 6,000 to 7,000 workers had been laid off. Many were non-Gujaratis, with their own anti-Muslim biases:

> The most active participants came from textile workers, manual labourers and scavengers. . . . Devotion to Jagannath is marked among workers. Sevadasji, the chief priest of the temple, is held in high regard by them. When they heard of the attack on the temple and the sadhus, they were very angry. Later, when the rumor spread that the chief priest had been killed, they were ready to take revenge. . . . A sizeable number of labourers in Ahmedabad are non-Gujaratis. They are from U.P. [the state of Uttar Pradesh], Rajasthan, Maharashtra, and other parts of the country. . . . Workers from these regions are religious and have deep-rooted animosities towards the Muslims. Moreover, as they live alone, they have no roots in the cultural life of the city. . . . These immigrants were free from immediate family bonds. They were thus available for mob action. . . .

Among the Gujaratis themselves, Vagharis, Harijans, Bhois, and Kolis [lower-caste and Dalit groups] were in the forefront in looting and killing. Many of these castes belonged to criminal tribes till as recently as two decades ago. But Patidars and Rajputs also actively participated in killing Muslims. The former, in many cases, encouraged and financed people from the lower castes.[13]

Shah does not invoke Sundaram's reference, but he obviously presents many of the Gujarati workers, especially, as *intala* following the guidance of their "friends." The Reddy Commission report concurs. It indicts members of the militantly Hindu Jana Sangh political party and the RSS cultural–political organization as the organizers behind the riots. The commission cautioned, however, that it could not demonstrate that the Jana Sangh and RSS participated as organizations. Jana Sangh and RSS members were further implicated in the spread of rioting outside Ahmedabad, but their organizations were exonerated:

> There is evidence definitely that they took a leading part in the Districts of Amreli, Banaskantha, Mehsana and Baroda. In one of these instances there is evidence to show that they were inciting the crowds to riot. One of the District Magistrates, however, stated that there was no evidence that Jan Sangh and Hindu Mahasabha workers were working under the directions of their local party or organization.[14]

Many observers disputed this distinction. In parliament, Prime minister Indira Gandhi taunted Atal Bihari Vajpayee, asking whether it was "a coincidence that when people who belong to the RSS or the Jan Sangh go somewhere, soon afterwards there is a riot close to that place?"[15]

For an example of the riot organizers at work, the Reddy Commission highlighted a report by Brigadier Sukhwant Singh:

> I found that small pockets of minority communities in areas of larger communities were wiped out or stood to be wiped out. The religious places, rich properties, and thickly populated areas of one community became targets of attack by the other community. These target areas were isolated by the miscreants by putting barriers there on all approaches so as to prevent vehicles from passing and they were so placed that the targets were beyond the musket range from the barriers. The lookouts were also posted for giving warning signals of the approach of the police. Inside the barriers the houses and shops were looted, inmates killed and household goods were dragged outside the houses in the street and set ablaze throwing kerosene soaked rags therein. The next modus operandi was that the miscreants operated in large numbers. The weapons used were knives, swords, Bhalas [spears],

Dharias [scythes], steel pipes, iron rods, knives, acid filled bulbs and stones used as missiles. For destruction of buildings crow-bars and pavdas [clubs] were extensively used. Incendiary effect was achieved by gasoline soaked rags set to fire by matches. On approach by the police detachments the crowds used to melt in the city in lanes and bylanes. The onlookers out of fear always professed ignorance. The rumours and false information were freely circulated to divert police away from the areas of trouble.[16]

The riots stopped only after the army was called in on Sunday, September 21, and given orders to shoot on sight in case of curfew disturbances. Ahmedabad remained under almost complete curfew for ten days, and during these days, more than 5,000 persons were arrested for participating in riots.

The Reddy Commission heaped blame on the Congress government and the chief minister, Hitendra Desai, for their tardy, timid, half-hearted approach to riot control. The commission allowed, however, that the riots had been unexpected. In recent decades, Gujarat—and Ahmedabad—had a reputation for communal peace: "Even political workers, leaders of the different communities, did not dream or imagine that Ahmedabad will be visited by such widespread riots."[17] Nevertheless, recent tensions should have raised the apprehensions and the guard of government. The chief minister was late in responding to the outbreak of violence, late in calling up the army, and late in visiting the affected areas: "He and his Ministers moved round freely in all the areas and met people on a large scale only after the intensity of violence had subsided."[18]

Accusations of complicity in the riots were leveled against the government, but the Reddy Commission rejected these assertions:

> We cannot also countenance the suggestion that all this was permitted to be done either by the Government or by the police deliberately to enable the decimation or genocide of Muslims. There is, therefore, absolutely no evidence that such an idea ever entered the mind of the Government, nor do any of their actions justify such a conclusion.[19]

The police came in for much harsher blame. The Reddy Commission accused them indirectly, but clearly, of covering up for the Jana Sangh, the Hindu Mahasabha, and other "communal minded" persons in their riot activities:

> When Shri Indulal Yagnik made inquiries, the Commissioner of Police told him that Bharatiya Jan Sangh and other communal minded persons created communal trouble in the city. While this was the stand taken by the police initially, we find that in the evidence, the Commissioner sought to deny that the Hindu Dharma Raksha Samiti was formed with the participation of Jan Sangh, but instead

asserted as pointed out by us . . . that it was formed as an independent organization. It is apparent that the police were attempting to resile from the stand taken by them in their reports that Jan Sangh, Hindu Mahasabha and other communal minded Hindus were involved in the agitation and had contributed to communal tensions just before the Jagannath temple incident. . . . The evidence as a whole indicates that the police had reason to believe that some local Jan Sangh leaders and workers were actively participating in the riots, though these officers in their affidavits had not given any such indication and even in cross-examination attempts were made to prevaricate and plead ignorance of such participation.[20]

Shah was more blunt. The police were ineffective because they had become a corrupt force within a system of widespread corruption.

It is an open secret in Gujarat that police and anti-social elements have close ties. Oftener than not, illicit liquor, gambling, and smuggling which are rampant in the towns and villages of Gujarat run under police protection. For this policemen get a regular amount every month which is often many times their salaries. Such association between bootleggers and policemen has paralyzed the functioning of the police (prohibition's contribution to public life!). For the same reasons the police were reluctant to arrest known goondas. If a few were arrested, they were released on bail immediately. In the course of my investigations, I have come across a case in which a police officer informed a hooligan in advance that a warrant was to be issued against him.[21]

Many police officials were in the pay of bootleggers who ran a flourishing business in a state under complete prohibition. Bootlegging is an illegal, and often violently competitive, profession. The bootleggers often employed local toughs, hooligans, *goondas, intala.* These functionaries of everyday commercial illegality and violence could be inducted swiftly into creating communal disturbances. When the *intala* were pressed into such service, those police who were already on the take could not act against them. As an unintended legacy of Gandhi's principles, illegal business activities and violence had become entrenched in Ahmedabad.

The Reddy Commission alluded to the irony that some criminal violence might have been a by-product of the freedom struggle:

People who have been brought up in defiance of law as an instrument to achieve independence may continue to entertain the same idea until it is discouraged by leaders of public opinion. Whenever a group of people want to achieve what they think subserves their end they try to put it forward as a laudable object to be achieved even by violent methods.[22]

Religious belief had turned militant and violent in just this way. Within each religious community, and particularly among members of the RSS and Jana Sangh, increasingly strident voices argued that their religion was in danger and must be defended aggressively and even violently against others. Each group felt it had to "teach a lesson" to the others. Personal religious identities began to become more rigid and fixed.

Fear entered into the life of the city, especially in the industrial neighborhoods. Walls were constructed between neighborhoods. Gates to the *pols* in the old city, which had been unattended for decades, were restored to use. Some people living in pockets of minority residence—Hindus among Muslims, Muslims among Hindus—abandoned their homes and relocated. The 1969 riots initiated this process; later riots, discussed below, expanded it.

Government and the police failed to stop the rioting before it got out of hand. In a rapidly growing, heterogeneous, industrial metropolis, the potential for violence is always present. When social controls fail, government and the police are expected to step in. In Ahmedabad in 1969, they failed, undermining civic trust in government. Each further riot over the next thirty-three years further eroded that trust.

In the years just prior to the 1969 riots, the poet Farid Gulamnabi "Adil" Mansuri thought that he would have to leave Ahmedabad. (He did leave, for the United States, in 1985.) Mansuri registered his sadness in a poem in *ghazal* song form—a poem that remains famous today throughout the city. Indeed, it was included in the official government of Gujarat's *Gujarati Reader* for the tenth grade in high schools of the state.

Will I Ever See It Again?
by Adil Mansuri[23]

Will I ever see it again? This city at play in the sands of the river,
This vision on the screen of my memory, will I ever see it again?

Let me breathe deeply of the ocean of its fragrance,
The effect of its earth, moistened by fresh rains, for I may never sense
    it again.

Let me look to my heart's content on my friends,
These smiling faces, these sweet glances, for I may never see them again.

Let my eyes be filled with these streets, windows, walls,
This city, these passageways, this house, for I may never see them again.

Let us mourn the relations we embrace here today
For even the graves of one another we may never see again.

The faces of those who have come to bid me farewell will flash back in
    my eyes,
For on the journey ahead I may never have even one such companion
    again.

Let me anoint my head with the dust of my homeland, Adil,
Oh, this dust! For the rest of my life, I may never touch it again.

Not many left Ahmedabad as a result of the riots, but even for those who stayed, the city was being transformed into a different environment—more harsh, more violent, more criminal, more divided, less tolerant—than they had known before. Even those Ahmedabadis who remained in Ahmedabad would never see their city in quite the same way again. Ahmedabad had become a shock city not only to the rest of India, but also to its own citizens.

CHAPTER 8

Chimanbhai Patel Provokes the Nav Nirman Movement, 1974

O nly five years after communal warfare made Ahmedabad a shock city for all of India, the Nav Nirman (Reconstruction) movement, a middle-class protest against corruption and patronage in the state government, brought the city once more to center stage. Nav Nirman fused together three issues: middle-class opposition to patronage and corruption in politics; professional opposition to the commercialization and politicization of the expanding system of higher education; and urban opposition to high food prices, including apparent price gouging by rural agricultural producers in collusion with the state government. None of these issues was exclusive to Ahmedabad, but they came together here so dramatically that all of India paid attention. One of India's leading political–moral leaders, Jaya Prakash Narayan, came to the city to add his voice and prestige to this spontaneous mass movement to clean up politics.

Participants in the city and spectators across India hoped that Ahmedabad would provide a national model for political rebirth as earlier it had provided a model for ending British rule. The reality proved quite the reverse. Ultimately, prime minister Indira Gandhi came to believe that the Nav Nirman movement, and similar popular protests led by Jaya Prakash in other areas of India, threatened the stability of her government. She declared a national emergency and imposed dictatorial rule in 1975 in part as a direct fearful reaction against Nav Nirman's populism. Ahmedabad was a shock city once again.

The Nav Nirman movement revealed political philosophies in conflict. Chief minister Chimanbhai Patel crafted a politics of patronage in Gujarat, increasing his own power by bringing new constituencies, loyal to him, into public life. The Nav Nirman reformers wanted a cleaner, more open and responsive politics, not structured on patron–client relationships. Within a little more than a month, the riots achieved their first political objective: Chimanbhai's resignation. The second objective, less widely shared, came a month later with the dissolution of the state legislative assembly and a call for new elections.

Despite these apparent victories for reform, the antagonists had wrestled each other to exhaustion. Politics in Ahmedabad and Gujarat did not undergo fundamental change. Although disgraced for the moment, Chimanbhai would remain powerful in state politics. Sixteen years after his resignation, he returned as chief minister and continued in office until his death in 1994. Neither side had really won. Nav Nirman failed in its immediate concrete economic objective of bringing down the prices of everyday consumer commodities; in its intermediate goal of improving the quality of higher education; and in its long-term goal of cleansing the political system of corruption.[1]

The Increase in Prices

Nav Nirman represented a conjunction of several different movements that coalesced in early 1974. First, prices of essential food commodities in Gujarat were rising beyond the ability of most consumers to keep up. The consumer price index for Ahmedabad rose from 100 in 1960, to 171 in 1970, to 212 in 1973—and it was continuing to rise in early 1974.[2] The uncontrolled rise in prices increased the factionalism within the ruling Congress Party. For opposition parties, it provided a rallying cry. The Jana Sangh Party called for an anti–price rise week in Ahmedabad, and for daily public protest meetings beginning January 1, 1974. Most of the meetings assembled in middle-class areas of the old walled city, in Khadia, Dariapur, Relief Road, Gandhi Road, Delhi Chakla, and Kalupur, and in Saraspur outside the walls.[3] Each meeting provoked some stone throwing against government property. Unlike 1969, however, this unrest did not spread to the industrial mill workers' areas.

The general opposition to the price rise crystallized in a student revolt that gave Nav Nirman its leadership and its name. The cost of food in the college cafeterias went up even more rapidly than in the open markets, rising almost 50 percent in the month of December 1973 alone. In protest, on December 20, students at the L. D. Engineering College in Ahmedabad burned furniture and other possessions of the college rector. He resigned. Eight days later, students at the engineering college at Morbi, about a hundred miles away, destroyed furniture of that college and its cafeteria. On January 3, the L.D. students destroyed more furniture in their college and dormitory and declared a strike. Police entered the campus on January 3 and 4, beating several students and arresting approximately 300.

On January 5, 1,000 students marched to the nearby Navrangpura police station to demand the release of these students. The police constable insisted that he had no power to act, so they proceeded across the river to Congress House to address the chief minister, Chimanbhai Patel. He evaded them. The students later found out that he had gone to the opening of a new film. For the first time, student anger focused specifically on Chimanbhai. Because students and their professors played such a major part in Nav Nirman, and because Chimanbhai's early power base was in education, we examine Chimanbhai's career in Gujarat University and the significance of the entire higher educational establishment in the life of Ahmedabad, and of Gujarat at this time.

The Expansion and Politicization of Gujarat University

Chimanbhai Patel had built his first base of political power within the university. Born into a farming family in Sankheda Taluka, Vadodara district, about fifty miles south of Ahmedabad, Chimanbhai took his B.A. and M.A. degrees in economics from the Maharaja Sayajirao (M.S.) University of Baroda. He began his political activities in student politics as secretary of the Gujarat Students Congress in 1949 and as founding president of the M. S. University Student Union in 1950. He entered Congress Party politics as secretary of the Gujarat Youth Congress in 1954 and became secretary of the entire Gujarat Pradesh Congress Committee in 1962.

Chimanbhai began his teaching career, also in 1954, at the Gandhian Gujarat Vidyapith in Ahmedabad. The next year he moved to L. D. Arts College, Ahmedabad, and was elected to the university senate from the professors' constituency. In 1956 he moved to St. Xavier's College, Ahmedabad, where he served as professor of economics and dean of the faculty, and was reelected to the university senate. In 1957–58, he was elected to the university's executive council.[4]

In 1959, Chimanbhai left St. Xavier's College to explore the new financial opportunities that were beginning to open in higher education. He established a publishing house, Bharat Prakashan, for producing textbooks in a wide variety of academic subjects. Textbook publication became especially lucrative when Gujarat University, after fierce debate, voted to adopt Gujarati, rather than English, as the language of instruction. A whole new library of books and textbooks in Gujarati, either as their original language or in translation, was required.

Linking the publishing of textbooks to the management of colleges promised still greater financial rewards. In 1960, Chimanbhai founded the Gujarat Kelavani (Education) Trust, which later became the Sardar Vallabhbhai Trust. Through the trust, he began to establish colleges. The first was Sardar Vallabhbhai Arts and Commerce College in Ahmedabad (1960), of which he was the principal, the chief administrative officer. The trust founded five more colleges, four of them in Ahmedabad. Soon other educational entrepreneurs followed suit. In 1965, Chimanbhai was reelected to the university's executive council, this time from the principal's constituency.

Chimanbhai helped others to found about forty-five new colleges in rural areas of Gujarat. He assisted local people in meeting the requirements for opening a new college: gaining authorization and grant assistance from the government; procuring loans; securing affiliation to Gujarat University, the central institution that sets standards, curriculum, and examinations for all undergraduate teaching in its affiliated colleges; and appointing principals and faculty.

Education was becoming a huge growth industry in Gujarat, especially after the creation of the new state. The number of students in Gujarat multiplied nearly ten times over, from 16,800 in 1950 to more than 162,000 in 1971–72. The number of colleges affiliating to Gujarat University increased from 31 to 235. The location, standards, and styles of the colleges were changing. In 1950, the overwhelming majority of Gujarat University's affiliating colleges were urban; by 1971–72, two-thirds were rural. Accessibility was increasing not only geographically, but also linguistically. The university switched from English to Gujarati as the principal language of instruction, and the introduction of English as a subject in the high schools was postponed from the fifth to the eighth grade. Previously, admission to colleges—such as those established by the Ahmedabad Education Society and the Gujarat Law Society—had been rigorously competitive. Chimanbhai, and others, opened the doors to anyone who passed the matriculation examination.

Chimanbhai's supporters lauded him for recognizing the need of rural Gujarat for access to the new world that higher education seemed to provide. They especially noted the accessibility for women, who might not have received family permission to attend a college in the city, but who could enroll comfortably in a local rural college. They also noted that students of various castes, high and low, and of different religions would mix together in these colleges, in experiences otherwise unknown in rural areas.

Critics, however, stressed the raw commercialism of the colleges and the power that they brought to their founders and administrators. The older institutions for spreading higher education, such as the Ahmedabad Education Society and the Gujarat Law Society, had not been run as businesses. They did not, for example, interweave college administration with the publication and sale of textbooks. The new colleges were heavily weighted toward arts and commerce, the least expensive curricula to establish and administer, rather than toward the sciences, engineering, and medicine, where the demand for graduates was proportionately higher. The 136 colleges affiliated with Gujarat University in 1971 included about 35 combined arts and commerce colleges, 20 commerce colleges, 18 education colleges, 17 arts colleges, 15 arts and sciences, and 10 law; there were only 15 science colleges, 5 medical colleges, 2 engineering colleges, and 1 college of pharmacy. For students, and for society at large, this distribution created problems of educated unemployment typical of India and other developing nations, while not providing the society with adequate trained manpower in scientific and technical areas.

The new colleges cut corners for profit. Often two colleges would utilize the same building, one meeting in the morning, another in the afternoon or evening, but each college would collect a full government grant for the building premises. University rules were modified to allow part-time, rather than full-time, faculty in some positions, compromising instructional quality to save on faculty salaries. In addition, control of a college brought enormous powers of patronage: appointing the principal, faculty, and staff; setting admissions policy; establishing relationships with local political leaders, bankers, builders, and businessmen. The *sheths* who had previously funded the establishment of colleges had surely gained prestige, but the basis of their power rested in their commercial businesses. They had not usually demanded patronage and power over the administration of the colleges they supported. With controlling powers over at least fifty, and perhaps as many as seventy, colleges, Chimanbhai was in a position to dominate Gujarat University by packing its senate, the legislative center of the university, where each principal had a vote.[5] The growth in Chimanbhai's power was already evident in the 1961 election of the university vice chancellor, its chief executive officer. Chimanbhai's candidate, L. R. Desai, principal of A. G. Teachers College, defeated Vikram Sarabhai, whom we have already encountered as one of India's most distinguished scientists, the son of one of Ahmedabad's most outstanding mill owners, and the favored client of another. Most observers saw this election as a triumph for academic mediocrity. The way had been cleared for university expansion with lowered standards. Advocates described the process as providing accessibility; detractors called it a watering down of the curriculum and a politicization of the university.

Having alienated Ahmedabad's educational elites while creating a large patronage network of his own clients, Chimanbhai entered into politics full time. In 1961, he became secretary of the Gujarat State Congress Committee. In 1967, he was elected to the state legislative assembly from his home area of Sankheda in Kheda district, and was appointed minister of sports, transportation, and culture. He had attracted powerful friends and dedicated opponents.

Among the opponents were the older intelligentsia of Ahmedabad and the faculty of the university-related colleges. A union of college faculty, the Gujarat University Area Teachers' Assocation (GUATA) (named more simply in Gujarati the Adyapak Mandal, "Professors' Association"), was formed in 1962 and became active in 1965. By the early 1970s, it had about 3,000 members. Its two main grievances were conventional union issues: unsatisfactory pay and benefits, and unstable tenure and service conditions. These problems were especially severe in the commercialized urban colleges and the newly founded rural colleges—the kinds of colleges with which Chimanbhai was associated. Management in such colleges allegedly exploited teachers in a variety of ways: forcing some to sign receipts for their official wages but actually paying them less; renewing contracts on an annual basis to avoid payment of salary increments and conferral of tenure; denying the institution of pensions; sometimes defaulting on salaries or cost-of-living allowances altogether; and threatening dismissal at the slightest show of resistance.[6] Battles over salary intensified after the central government recommended higher pay scales in 1966. College administrations passively dragged their feet and actively resisted. Battles over tenure were even more hotly contested. At the end of each academic year, the contracts of hundreds of professors were terminated to ensure that they would not achieve tenured status. One of those sacked in 1972, Mahendra Purohit, a part-time teacher of statistics at one of Chimanbhai's colleges in Ahmedabad, committed suicide. Enraged at the treatment Purohit had received, faculty held an outdoor meeting at Chimanbhai's Sardar Vallabhbhai College, in the heart of Ahmedabad, and vowed to fight Chimanbhai in all spheres of the political and educational system.[7]

Gujarat University, from its headquarters in Ahmedabad, had become a major new arena of conflict in education, business, and politics. In all three spheres, Chimanbhai Patel had effectively turned the university to his own purposes. His actions had helped expand—and alienate—two academic constituencies in Ahmedabad: the students and the faculty in higher education. When the students spontaneously began their protest against high prices in the school cafeteria, hundreds of faculty were eager to encourage and support them, and to turn their anger against Chimanbhai.

Collusion with Farmers

Nav Nirman began as a protest waged by students and professors. They harbored many resentments against Chimanbhai's educational contrivances, but the immediate precipitating issue was high prices in college cafeterias. It grew into a widespread protest movement against rising food prices. Protesters complained that farmers were getting more profits than they should and that the state was not taking action.

Critics charged that higher prices were a result of Chimanbhai's political deals and corruption. In the month of December, peanut oil, the principal cooking oil in Gujarat, usually came into the market in large quantities, bringing down the price. In December 1973, however, despite bumper crops, the supply was short and the price was high. The chief minister threatened to take over the trade if the price did not come down to Rs. 4 per kilogram, but even when the price rose to Rs. 8, the government took no action. The market in food grains followed the same contrary pattern in the winter of 1973–74. In December, in an effort to limit the price increase, the export of food grains from the state was officially banned, but again, no action was taken against those who flouted the ban.

Chimanbhai's roots were in agricultural Gujarat. He was a Patel, a member of one of the cluster of castes known for their hard and successful work as farmers and village administrators. By midcentury, they were beginning to move into the cities of central Gujarat and to prosper in new business and professional careers. For many of them, Sardar Patel was a role model. Wealthier farmers—especially the Patels of Chimanbhai's native Charotar region and the cooking-oil barons of Saurashtra—were among Chimanbhai's most ardent supporters. Critics accused him of collusion with these farmers and food suppliers: Political scientist Pravin Sheth explained:

> The widely-spread report that the new government [of Chimanbhai Patel] had collected a huge sum of about Rs. 31 lakhs from oil-millers and owners of solvent plants in Saurashtra "giving them in return a free hand to exploit consumers in Gujarat" was believed to be correct by the general public. The price of edible oil, therefore, scaled new peaks and became almost oppressive.[8]

And sociologist Ghanshyam Shah added:

> The moral authority of the government had by now been seriously eroded. . . . For the first time, corruption charges had been levelled against the Chief Minister in public. And Chiman Patel lost credibility in the public eye rather quickly.[9]

National Politics Permeates Gujarat and Ahmedabad

National political leaders exploited these local grievances. In 1969, the Congress Party had split in two, with prime minister Indira Gandhi as leader of the wing that ultimately won out and Morarjibhai Desai as one of the leaders of the opposing wing. The split had profound consequences for Ahmedabad. From this time onward, factional struggles at the national level drove their tentacles into state and local politics.

Political mobilization throughout India took two turns—in opposite directions. On the one hand, public participation in politics increased, the masses became more outspoken, and democratization took root in the relatively newly independent nation. Nav Nirman was a part of this trend. On the other hand, many political leaders established their power not only by appealing directly to the masses, but also by garnering the support of local political organizers and financial contributors. Political analysts began to speak of "vote banks"—groups of voters mobilized by local leaders to deliver their votes to the politician who promised the most rewards to the mobilizer as well as to the voters. Politicians at upper levels cynically manipulated those at the middle levels, and vice versa. Both attempted to manipulate the voters. The restraint and moral discipline that Gandhi had demanded when he rallied the masses was gone. Also, the freedom struggle had a single principal goal, ending British rule, and it had been achieved. Politics in the new independent democracy was far more complex.

The world of upper-level politicians became disconnected from the world of the masses. Middle-level politicians claimed to represent the people, but they derived much of their power from the patronage of the party bosses, bribes from people seeking government favors, and *intala* employed to intimidate opponents. Their ability to deliver votes was one source of their power, but not the only source, and they found many means to procure those votes. The public became increasingly frustrated. The new system of factional politics called for their votes, but gave little in return.

Under Mrs. Gandhi as prime minister, the Congress (R) party dispensed with primary elections, in which members of the party voted to select the party candidates. Now party bosses, above all Mrs. Gandhi, selected the candidates. General elections did provide an opportunity for the voters to take revenge, to throw the rascals out, but voters were not successful in establishing stable governments over long periods of time. We have seen above that each municipal election in Ahmedabad from 1950 until 1990 produced a new government, different from the one before. Elections at the local level, as at the national level, often produced waves of massive majorities for one party in one election, followed by massive waves against them in the next. In Gujarat state politics, from 1960 to 2006, only one chief minister was able to fulfill his full five-year term, and as we shall see below, he was forced from office within a matter of months of beginning his second term.

The new style of opportunistic politics was expanding out of control. Chimanbhai Patel's rise to his position as chief minister of Gujarat was a part of that nationwide process. A prodigy and political ally of Morarjibhai Desai for many years, in 1971 Chimanbhai joined with other ministers in deserting Morarjibhai's Congress (Organizational), thus bringing down the government of Gujarat's chief minister, Hitendra Desai. Chimanbhai became the leader of the Congress (R) party in the legislature. The Congress (R) then won a massive wave victory, carrying 140 of the 168 seats in the state legislature.

In the new state assembly, Chimanbhai was one of the contestants for chief minister, but the Congress leadership in Delhi chose Ghanshyam Oza. Because the Gujarat Congress Party was split into three factions, Chimanbhai argued that the head of the state government should be chosen by the assembly itself in Gandhinagar, and not by the prime minister in New Delhi. He maneuvered Oza out of office and got himself voted in. The methods were problematic. In the first week of July 1973, Chimanbhai gathered seventy elected members of the legislative assembly (MLAs) at the Panchwati farm, about sixteen kilometers (ten miles) from Ahmedabad, and kept them there as he negotiated with them for their support. When they emerged five days later, they were prepared to vote for Chimanbhai as the new party leader and chief minister of the state.

Chimanbhai's critics charged that the legislators had been bought; Chimanbhai replied that they had been persuaded. Against her wishes, Mrs. Gandhi accepted the vote. Chimanbhai was the new chief minister.

By the time the Nav Nirman rioting broke out in January 1974, Chimanbhai certainly had his enemies: college faculty organized through their union; middle-class urbanites struggling with the increasing prices of food; citizens appalled by Chimanbhai's manipulation of politicians and the political system; and Mrs. Gandhi, who bitterly resented his successful challenge to her control of Gujarat politics. He also had his allies, especially in the rural areas, where many middle- and upper-level farmers, many of them Patels like himself, appreciated the higher prices they were getting for their products and the new colleges that their children were attending. This was the background. At first, however, Nav Nirman did not focus on Chimanbhai.

Nav Nirman—The Movement Gathers Strength

On January 5, 1974, even though Chimanbhai did not agree to meet the protesting students at the L. D. Engineering College, the police commissioner did release about 300 students who had been arrested. Some students decided to form a committee called the Yuvak Lagni Samiti (Committee on Youth Sentiment), which protested the closing of the L. D. Engineering College and the continuing increase in prices. On January 7, more than 100 student representatives from different colleges met at Sardarbagh Park, in central Ahmedabad, calling for a strike until food bills in the college cafeterias would be reduced, police atrocities would end, fees would be reduced, hoarders and profiteers would be arrested, and good-quality food grains would be distributed in public distribution shops. The Akhil Bharatiya Vidyarthi Parishad, the youth wing of the Jana Sangh political party, joined the protest, explicitly linking partisan protest with the student movement.

That night, a number of food grain shops in the city were looted. Six policemen and several students were injured in clashes. A total of 188 people were arrested. Protests continued over the next few days in Ahmedabad and other cities of Gujarat, especially in the Saurashtra region. On January 9, students held a protest meeting in the university senate hall. A few hours later, at a separate meeting in the same venue, GUATA decided to launch its own faculty protest against the vice chancellor for his policies in favor of management. Also on January 9, students blocked traffic on roads in Ahmedabad for three hours. Some looting continued. The police responded with tear gas shells, *lathi* charges, and local curfews.

The 14th August Workers Committee—mostly trade unions of white-collar employees, including GUATA, joined by the Yuvak Lagni Samiti and the Jana Sangh—called for a *bandh,* a general strike, on January 10. The Textile Labour Association did not back the move. It perceived the agitation as a dispute within the middle classes, and it saw behind the protest the hand of Mrs. Gandhi, whom they opposed. The textile mills continued to run. In the old city, however, the *bandh* was almost total. Looting, tear gas, *lathi* charges, and curfews all continued. The state reserve police were called in. So far, the protest had not turned against Chimanbhai. Indeed, three of Chimanbhai's cabinet ministers supported the student struggle against the price rise, blaming Mrs. Gandhi for the problem. Rioting spread to other cities of the state. Rural areas were immune. Farmers profited from the high prices of food.

Purshottam Mavalankar, an independent member of parliament from Ahmedabad and son of Ganesh Vasudev Mavalankar, supported the *bandh* call. In July 1973, Mavalankar had already called for the imposition of president's rule in Gujarat, charging that the political parties were interested only in their own welfare, not in their constituents.' Now he repeated that call. He specifically accused Chimanbhai's government of corruption, and he asserted that it had lost the confidence of the people.

At Mavalankar's suggestion, the students disbanded the Yuvak Lagni Samiti and reconstituted themselves as the Nav Nirman Yuvak Samiti (Youth Reconstruction Committee), including student representation from all colleges, and some more senior advisors as well. For a few days, Mavalankar served as president of the advisory committee. Then, complaining that the students did not consult him, he resigned. The Jana Sangh protested against the price increase but did not ask for Chimanbhai's resignation. A farmers' organization, the Khedut Samaj, saw the anger of the people as a danger to themselves, and they began to submit to a levy on paddy, which the government had imposed; they offered to contribute even more than asked.

Encouraged by the GUATA, the students *gheraoed* (surrounded and obstructed) the university vice chancellor, Ishwarbhai Patel, and burned furniture and records of the university. The president and secretary of the Navnirman Yuvak Samiti (Youth Reconstruction Committee), Manishi Jani and Umakant Mankad, respectively, were arrested. Protests continued and spread. GUATA, with branches around the state, fed the fire. They ensured that some agitation, somewhere in the state, was always simmering, with Ahmedabad at the epicenter of the flames.

When the chief minister agreed to negotiate the students' demands for changes on the campus, the students rejected his offer, saying that they wanted change throughout society. On January 22, female students of the H. K. Arts College, demonstrating on behalf of the agitation, were beaten by the police, further inflaming public opinion against the administration. The GUATA called for a Gujarat *bandh* on January 25. The business community opposed it;

the Textile Labour Association opposed it; the government imposed curfews in forty-four towns in Gujarat; and still the agitation grew. The army was called into Ahmedabad on January 28. Ghanshyam Shah wrote, "Hatred for Chiman Patel, who had become the symbol of an anti-people government and of corruption, was widely shared."[10] In the first week of February, a few ministers resigned, and the president of the Gujarat Congress as well as dissident leaders came out against the chief minister. On February 9, Chimanbhai Patel resigned as chief minister, the governor suspended the elected state assembly, and president's rule was imposed on Gujarat.

Nav Nirman—Phase 2

The second phase of Nav Nirman now began with the call for dissolution of the state assembly and new elections. Protesting his innocence, and wishing to spite Mrs. Gandhi and the Delhi high command, Chimanbhai Patel, too, called for dissolution. Riots continued across the state, demanding dissolution and lower prices. In a striking demonstration, repeated each evening, women in the historic central city of Ahmedabad went to the roofs of their houses and symbolically tolled the death knell of the state government by banging their wooden *lathas* (rolling pins) on their metal *thalis* (dining plates). Attempts to block the export of foodstuffs outside the state continued, along with attacks on public and private property.

The Congress was a special target, Shah reported:

> Vehicles of Congressmen were damaged or burnt. Their houses were set on fire. Water, electricity and telephone connections were cut. Some Congress leaders were beaten up and insulted by the mobs. One Congress leader was not only stripped naked, but was forced to walk several miles from village to village. Student mobs painted the face of an MLA black and forced him to ride a donkey. The Speaker of the State Assembly was beaten up in a hospital.[11]

On March 11, the state government dismissed the municipal government of Ahmedabad, placing the city under its direct administrative control. Administrator's rule continued for almost two years, until municipal elections were held once again in January 1976.

On March 12, Morarjibhai Desai began an indefinite fast in favor of new state-level elections, effectively evoking a morality and a strategy from the past. On March 16, the state assembly was dissolved and elections were called for June. The Nav Nirman movement had achieved its second goal. [12]

Once Chimanbhai resigned, however, the Nav Nirman movement lost most of its steam, and once the assembly was dismissed, it shut down almost entirely. Faculty returned to their teaching, students to their exams, and journalists to their writing; most others outside the urban middle classes had never been involved. In terms of the most basic demands, prices did not come down. The economic problems were not relieved. In the rural areas, the farmers had remained aloof from the concerns of the movement. They welcomed high prices for agricultural commodities. Many supported Chimanbhai, who presented himself as a *khedut putra,* a farmer's son. Even in the cities, the working classes did not join the movement. The university faculty union did not reach out to others, and by the end of the movement, GUATA was perceived as a trade union working for its own professional and economic interests rather than as a broad-based movement for society-wide transformation. The class divisions of Ahmedabad remained firmly in place. The movement left in its wake 104 dead (unofficially about 120), of whom 88 had been killed in police firings, 310 seriously injured, and 8,053 arrested at one time or another.[13]

Before the June election, Chimanbhai tried to vindicate his position. His lengthy statement, *Gujaratno Ghatnaono Ghatsphot,* proclaimed his innocence in each of the charges against him. He defended his record, including the following arguments: the meeting at the Panchwati farm had been an open meeting with the press present. It was not an occasion for buying off the MLAs who attended. The shortage of agricultural supplies was the work of the central government out to defeat him by cutting Gujarat's grain allocation, while demanding that the state export cooking oil to others. The student riots had been incited by politicians with their own agendas, mostly to remove him from power. Nor did the faculty participants have serious long-term goals. They abandoned the movement as soon as he had resigned. Finally, the governor of Gujarat had conducted an investigation into the charges against Chimanbhai and had announced in June 1974 that there was no substance to the allegations.

Chimanbhai pointed out in his defense that he had pressed aggressively for the economic development of his state. He emphasized his assertiveness in New Delhi on behalf of Gujarat. He took credit for initiating the huge hydroelectric project of the Narmada Dam, which would later become the pride of Gujarat and the scorn of ecologists and human rights activists throughout India and the world (see chapter 12). Chimanbhai was introducing a pattern that later chief ministers would also follow: claiming that economic progress for the city and state outweighed any criticism that might be brought against his social or political record.

Chimanbhai closed his statement with a call for a formal investigation of the charges of corruption that had been leveled against him: "I know that I am not a criminal. Those who float charges against me without giving me a chance to prove my innocence are intentionally defaming me. . . . I leave it to the people of Gujarat to render their verdict. . . . If I am a criminal, then hang me."[14] The public was not persuaded by this defense. Chimanbhai formed a new party of his own, the Kisan Majdoor Lok Paksh (Peasant, Worker, People's Party). The new party contested 128 seats, winning 12. Seventy-nine of its candidates earned less than 16 percent of the vote and forfeited their deposits. Chimanbhai himself was badly defeated in his own constituency by a relatively unknown young tribal *adivasi*. His constituents were not ready to hang him, but neither were they ready to reelect him.

Mrs. Gandhi also suffered a severe loss in this election. Her party, which had won an overwhelming majority of 140 of 168 seats in the 1972 state election, carried only 75 of 182 in 1975. This loss almost certainly reduced her confidence in her control of India's politics, and served as a background for her declaration of emergency powers later in the month.[15]

Nav Nirman had toppled the chief minister, brought down the state legislature, and precipitated new elections. It brought hope to India that political life could be cleansed of corruption through the organized protest of vigilant, active citizens. Then it stopped. Jaya Prakash Narayan, who had hailed the movement for its early potential, expressed the general disillusionment:

> The Gujarat movement was a path-finder in India's march towards democracy, with all parliamentary democracy, in which the demos, the people, are not mere passive agents but are active, demanding and in the end commanding. . . .
>
> Having said all this, I must again repeat that it was a pity (a) the Gujarat movement ended with the dissolution of the assembly, and (b) no one is trying to utilise a friendly and responsive government to re-start a revolutionary movement.[16]

Nav Nirman had a substantial boomerang impact on national politics. Mrs. Gandhi's critics, like Jaya Prakash Narayan, whom she jailed, cited Nav Nirman favorably because of its original call for radical democracy, and for its demonstration that Mrs. Gandhi's popularity had faded. They sought to reproduce that commitment at the national level and to bring down her government.[17] Mrs. Gandhi, on the other hand, cited Nav Nirman as an example of an undisciplined uprising, and she identified it as one of the reasons for declaring a national emergency and assuming dictatorial powers from June 1975 to March 1977.[18] She steamrollered and jailed her opposition, including Jaya Prakash. Despite Nav Nirman, the politics of personal patronage continued in the ascendant.

As J. P. and the movement that took his name transferred their attention from Nav Nirman in Gujarat to a larger struggle in Bihar state, the right-wing Hindu militant Jana Sangh Party and its cultural ally, the Rashtriya Swayamsevak

Sangh (RSS) came increasingly to dominate it. In April 1974, the RSS and the Jana Sangh accepted J.P.'s language of total revolution and increased their own prestige through association with him. In Gujarat, in the state elections in June, the Jana Sangh candidates within the Janata Front coalition won eighteen seats, up from three in the previous election.[19]

From the beginning of Nav Nirman in Gujarat, the main Jana Sangh connection with the movement had been through its allied youth group, the Akhil Bharatiya Vidyarthi Parishad. Three decades later, one of leaders of that group, Narendra Modi, would become the chief minister of Gujarat and a leading national spokesperson for militant Hindu nationalism (see chapter 12). Nav Nirman made Ahmedabad once again a shock city. Its consequences, intended and unintended, would continue to resonate locally, at the state level, and nationally for decades to come.

CHAPTER 9

The Mills Close, the TLA Falters, and the Municipal Corporation Goes Broke

Ahmedabad's Mills Shut Down

In the 1980s, Ahmedabad's mill industry began to shut down. The effects devastated the owners, the workers, and the city. Once again, Ahmedabad was a shock city, bearing the brunt of what became a national, and global, trend in the collapse of large-scale older industries. The closure of Ahmedabad's mills was, however, surprisingly different from the collapse taking place in wealthier, more industrialized countries. The more industrialized countries lost out to regions with lower wage rates and sometimes with newer machinery, especially to China. But Ahmedabad lost its industries not to more competitive overseas plants, but rather to indigenous Indian small-scale power loom production. Ironically, Gandhian Ahmedabad lost its mills as a result of government policies favoring small-scale industry, a legacy of Gandhian economics.

The figures tell the story: 1981 was the year of maximum employment in Ahmedabad's composite textile mills. Sixty-three mills employed an average of 155,244 workers each day. Of these, 131,560 were members of the Textile Labour Association (TLA). By 1989, the thirty-three mills that were still in business employed 62,126 workers. The union actually had more members—71,438—than there were workers in the mills because it represented them in claiming unemployment and severance benefits from the mills and the government. By 1997, only nineteen mills remained, employing 35,494 workers. Only about half, 18,172, were still in the TLA.[1]

Across India, the production of cotton cloth shifted from mill manufacture to decentralized production on power looms and hand looms. In the decade 1955–65, large-scale mills manufactured two-thirds of India's total cloth production; power looms and hand looms, about one-third. By 1990, the mills manufactured only one-sixth of the nation's cloth; power looms and hand looms, five-sixths, or 83.3 percent. Total production in the mills was cut by about 60 percent, while it rose almost five times in the power loom and hand loom sector.[2] If the mills were a catastrophe, the power looms and hand looms were a great success. Despite the decline of the composite mills, total production of cloth in India rose by two-thirds, from 6,900 million square meters annually in 1955 to 11,760 million in 1990.

This transformation was largely a result of conscious policies of the government of India to restrict the size of the mills to favor hand looms and thus put Gandhian philosophy into practice. In effect, however, power looms were usually classified with hand looms and shared in the benefits of the legislation. *Power looms* usually refers to workshops or small factories ranging from "units with 6–8 second-hand looms operated mainly with hired labor but not covered by the Factory Act, to units with 40 or more high-speed, partly or fully automatic, even shuttleless looms and many technical and organisational features of a modern textile factory."[3]

Legislation favoring these relatively small units included: severe limits on any expansion of weaving capacity in composite mills between 1956 and 1985; higher tax levies on composite mills than on hand loom and power loom production; and controls on the variety of goods that composite mills were permitted to produce. By the 1970s, Indian consumers began to buy synthetic man-made fabrics, such as terylene and rayon, rather than pure cotton. The man-made fabrics lasted at least twice as long, and this durability had the effect of reducing cloth consumption per capita. Further, until 1985, national policy forbade the composite mills from producing 100 percent synthetics. Thus the new area of greatest growth was reserved for the decentralized sector. In addition, small, decentralized power looms could frequently evade taxes that organized units could not. They were not unionized and did not have to pay the higher pay scales and provide the benefits of the organized sector.

Power looms also had many technological advantages over composite mills.[4] Perhaps the most important technological change was the availability of electricity on a commercial basis in smaller cities and towns of India after about 1940. This new supply of power enabled many footloose small-scale industries, including power looms, to locate in smaller centers where they had easier and cheaper access to labor, raw materials, processing units, and markets. In the 1950s, the power looms developed the interfirm coordination required to integrate these resources.[5] The small power looms also attracted the capital of small-scale local owners and investors.[6]

Ahmedabad mill owners not only failed to respond to the new challenges, they also mismanaged their enterprises, as some of them admitted. The owners became complacent in a sellers' market, especially during World War II, but also for many years after, as government policy sheltered the domestic market from external competition. But they were not sheltered from domestic competition, and they failed to meet it. They did not replace obsolescent and worn-out machinery; they did not increase productivity; they did not professionalize management; they did not rationalize their labor force; they did not plow profits back into reinvestments but rather paid them out in high dividends, dissipating the resources of the industry.[7]

Some of these high dividends paid out by the faltering mills were wise entrepreneurial moves to shift investment out of textiles into new, more profitable enterprises, such as chemicals. Some of the dividends went into the flourishing real estate market, in housing construction and land speculation.[8] Often the disinvestment from textiles represented sheer profit taking for personal gain rather than for commercial goals. Some of the owners of composite mills were dismantling their own mills and reestablishing them in multiple power loom workshops to save on salaries and taxes and to escape regulation.

The workers understood, but they were powerless. They watched the process of disinvestment: no new machines were introduced to upgrade the mills' productivity; current machines were removed from the premises and reinstalled in smaller work sheds. Manishi Jani, a student leader in the Nav Nirman (Reconstruction) movement a decade before, conducted interviews in 1984 among workers in mills that were about to shut down. He reported the workers' perspectives:

> "The owner of Bagicha Mill and Raipur Mill wants to sell the mills and raise Commercial Centres instead."
>
> "Our Sheth has shown a loss of Rs. 8 lakhs in accounts. He has given a reason that he is unable to pay electric bill of Rs. 4 lakhs. However, our Sheth had overnight built Motera [sports] Stadium at the cost of lakhs of rupees."
>
> "Our owners have no interest in this business. They have now other factories. Previously those factories were here in the mill premises only. Now they are shifted outside elsewhere at the cost of Rs. 1.5 crores!"[9]

Jani added critical observations of his own:

> On 6th April 1984, at 5:00 PM, the Gujarat Spinning Mill was closed down. At 5:15, I saw worried, frustrated, and excited workers visiting this closed mill. Talks with them revealed that yesterday was a day off. At night, mill people were trying to take out truck loads of machines, two trucks full of iron sheets, Dublin machines, etc., out of the mill premises. They could take out some goods but remaining goods were stopped by the workers and today in the morning they obtained a stay order from the court.

Among the veteran Ahmedabad businessmen, the ethics of mill closure also drew sharp criticism and engendered profound feelings of betrayal. Personal interviews with businessmen who supplied mill stores, with bankers who provided loans, and with academics who observed these processes revealed patterns of mill owners buying mill stores or taking out loans just days before they declared bankruptcy and closed their mills. The sellers and the lenders—along with investors—never recovered their losses. Among these businessmen, feelings of betrayal against the mill owners, people within their own community, were as powerful as the feelings of the workers who lost their jobs. The coherence of the Ahmedabad business community was shattered.

In 1983–84, an eighteen-month strike that shut down the Bombay textile industry gave Ahmedabad a short respite in the general downtrend of its mills, but the process of decline proved irreversible. The years 1984–86 were especially severe. Three successive years of drought forced up the price of cotton, the industry's basic raw material, while lowering the purchasing power of consumers.[10] In addition, in 1985, composite mills were given permission to shut down legally: "Where a unit has no expectation of becoming viable in a reasonable period of time, there may be no alternative but to allow the unit to close provided the interests of the workers are protected."[11] Until 1985, owners wishing to close their factories had found other ways to do it. Some, for example, declined to pay their utility bills, then shut down the mills when the electrical connections were cut off.[12] Between 1983 and 1987, half the mill workers of Ahmedabad lost their jobs.

Not everything was lost. Some other jobs had developed that helped to pick up the slack. Ahmedabad was not one of India's major centers of power looms; nevertheless, the number of jobs in small-scale textile factories rose from 7,790 in 1977 to 22,625 in 1986. Employment opportunities were also shifting from inside the city boundaries to more distant, peripheral areas. Although total employment in all types and sizes of textile factories decreased sharply within the legal borders of Ahmedabad City, 1977 to 1986, in the periphery—that is, the area outside the city limits but still inside Ahmedabad district—it increased.

Total factory employment of all types and sizes actually increased in Ahmedabad district from 1979 to 1987 from 635,684 to 729,696. Of this increase, 57,000 workers found their jobs in the three industrial estates established by the Gujarat Industrial Development Corporation to encourage new industries—Naroda (1963), Vatva (1964), and Odhav (1965)—that were growing on the eastern periphery of the city. The new jobs, however, usually paid less than half the wages and none of the benefits of the unionized jobs in the organized sector factories.

The Naroda industrial estate included one striking success in textile manufacture itself. In 1966, Dhirubhai Ambani founded Reliance Textile Industries with a paid up capital of Rs. 150,000, not as a composite mill but as a power loom unit. Ambani explained, "We got the license for powerlooms because the regulation was that you could not make 100 per cent filament synthetics except on licensed powerlooms."[13] Fixed assets increased from Rs. 280,000 in 1966 to Rs. 145,000,000 in 1977, when Reliance Textile Industries became a public limited company. That year, the mill earned a profit of Rs. 43.3 million on revenues of Rs. 700 million. By 1983, Reliance Textile Industries had "become India's largest composite textile mill, sprawling over 280,000 square meters, producing three million square meter of fabric per month, and employing 10,000 workers."[14] Ahmedabad did have its areas of growth, even in textiles, but they were produced by new entrepreneurs employing new business techniques and new technologies. Some of the innovations proved attractive to Ahmedabad businessmen and they followed suit, but only after several years had passed.

For owners doing less well, in 1967, the central government created the National Textile Corporation (NTC) to take over the management of "sick" mills that were operating at a loss. In 1974, the Corporation took over the actual ownership of 103 ailing mills nationally. Only in 1985 did it switch its policy to take over only mills that might be brought back to profitability. In 1986, Gujarat state founded its own Gujarat State Textile Corporation to supplement the national programs. By keeping the mills running, the NTC and GSTC functioned as job preservation programs for the workers. But, as careful economic analysis pointed out,

> the real purpose of nationalisation was different from the official argument. It was a measure to help the owners of sick mills. This is clear from the fact that a large amount of compensation was paid to millowners who were responsible for losses. . . . the payments of high compensation for the closed mills, in effect permitted the millowners to pay off the debts they had accumulated in their search for new avenues of investment.[15]

The Collapse of the TLA

Historically, the TLA had drawn strength from its alliance with the Indian National Congress during the freedom struggle and the Congress Party after independence. The split in the Congress in 1969, both nationally and locally, confronted the TLA with a dilemma; it chose to remain nonaligned. Hoping to remain powerful by bargaining with both parties, instead it was marginalized. When the layoffs came, the TLA had little leverage with government.

It did push vigorously for the workers to receive all severance pay due to them, and for government funds for retraining. Many of the retraining programs, however, were underfunded and ineffective in delivering useful vocational education and in locating new jobs. The TLA did not attempt to use government power and the courts to stop those mill owners who illegally dismantled and closed their mills.[16] The TLA lacked the creativity of its early years, and it no longer listened carefully to its members. One disillusioned TLA official later summarized the decline:

> The TLA had very little room for new ideas and a dwindling ability to face new challenges. It had become a top-down organization where the leaders had stopped listening to each other and, more important, to the members. Despite the looming changes in the textile industry, there was no real attempt to equip the workers to adapt to changing economic conditions. It was sad to watch the growing rift between the laid-off workers and the shrinking union.[17]

The Congress Party, too, even when reunified in the 1980s, lost power and credibility as workers saw that it did not help them any longer.[18] The owners got safety nets; the workers did not. They might find jobs outside the mills, but the pay was less than half. A study by the Ahmedabad Textile Industry Research Association in 1985 showed that a worker in the weaving section of the mills was earning Rs. 50 per day, while those in the power loom section were earning from Rs. 10 for workers in the preparatory processes to Rs. 25 for weavers.[19]

Further study, by Professor B. B. Patel of the Gandhi Labour Institute, Ahmedabad, looked farther afield, investigating the entire range of jobs that workers found in the years immediately following the mill closures. Only about one in five of the laid-off workers had found wage-paid employment, and many of these jobs were as casual laborers, without any benefits for sickness, leaves, insurance, or provident fund. For the most part, they also worked in the lowest-paid unskilled jobs. Many worked as contract laborers under conditions of low pay, no protection, and no benefits, but with obligations to the labor contractor.[20]

More than half were self-employed, meaning they had no regular, salaried job—a sharp contrast to their days in the mills. Many crowded into street hawking and vending, a sector already overcrowded. Patel noted "enhanced competition with and obstructions to established shops and competition even within the informal sector" and feared "the subsequent impact on the viability of such activities." Reports from the Self-Employed Women's Association affirmed that some of the laid-off workers began to prepare *agarbatti* (incense sticks) and to roll bidis (tiny cigars)—very low-paying work usually performed by women.[21]

The interviews conducted by Manishi Jani captured the despair of the struggling laid-off workers, as well as their anger and frustration, which was directed against the mill owners, the TLA, and society in general:

> Due to the closure of one mill after another, our 35–36 workers from Ahmedabad only have met with death. Some of them committed sui-

cide. Many others died of worries that led to brain hemorrhage or heart failure.

Sajju of our Marsden Mill jumped into the tank of the mill. A boy of the Bhalakia mill jumped into Kankaria lake. Dungarbhai Mahubhai of the spinning department of Marsden mill and Lalabhai Ganeshbhai of Mongoram mill died of excessive worries. . . . And we have also heard that due to the closure of he Tarun Commercial Mill one Bhikabhai, a mechanic and Chandrakant Mehta, a clerk, also died of excessive worries.

This is all politics! Neither Government, nor the owners or Union . . . nobody bothers about the workers. . . . One by one the mills are facing closure. TLA is dumb and deaf, is not raising its voice. It goes on saying that the proceedings are on . . . The workers of Gujarat are mild-natured, peace-loving! Are not struggle-minded! Something can happen only if all the workers unitedly revolt!

TLA people knew everything. Our representatives were not loyal to us. Three crores of rupees of the workers [benefit monies] were to be collected. Goods worth Rs. 3 crores were in the mill. It was decided that the mills will continue to work. . . . the workers will get weekly salary. Cost of the produced goods will be deposited in the banks. But our representatives did not pay careful attention. Our mill was not depositing money with the bank. We were kept in the dark and goods worth Rs. 1.5 crores were taken out. The representatives were also with them. They went out of station. On our inquiry, they say, "He has gone out because his uncle is sick . . ." then auntie will be ill . . . These representatives might have got money. So they kept silence and went away.[22]

Jan Breman noted that the head of the TLA told him that by the end of 1999, workers had received only about one fifth of the separation payments due to them according to their contracts. Breman saw this as a result both of welching on the part of the owners and lack of assertiveness on the part of the union.[23] In addition, a national renewal fund that the government of India set up to provide support to unemployed workers the 1990s was flawed in conception and implementation. It failed to provide significant relief to workers of closed textile mills.[24]

There are no clear figures on the number of mill workers who left Ahmedabad. Estimates ran from "a small number"[25] to about 20 percent.[26] Breman and Patel, who resurveyed 600 former mill workers in Ahmedabad in 1998, found about one-fourth of them in irregular employment where they competed with Muslims,

Dalits, other low-caste and impoverished workers, and women, heightening tensions among all these groups. Sometimes employers rejected them, fearing that their union backgrounds would leave them disgruntled and ripe for agitation. The lack of suitable employment and the lack of an organization that could fight effectively for their rights left the workers dispirited, powerless, and lacking in self-respect. The dignity of labor, a long-established tradition in industrial Ahmedabad, was undermined.[27]

The once-powerful TLA was a spent force. The unraveling of their economic and social reality left large segments of the laid-off work force as *intala,* broken bricks, a lumpen proletariat, tensely competing with other groups for inferior jobs, adrift politically from the Congress Party that had previously claimed their loyalty, intensely aware of what they had lost, and with little sense of a better future. When caste and communal riots broke out in the mill areas in 1985 and 1986, the laid-off workers felt themselves footloose, with no further ties to the mills. Where they were in the communal minority, they left. Neighborhoods that had once been integrated by community and caste, because of shared work in the mills, now disintegrated, with consequences that are discussed more fully later.

The Changing Ethos of the Business Class

The decline of the mill industry also marked a turning point in the role of Ahmedabad's business elite. Its central industry was no longer so significant in the city; the owner-managerial institution, the Ahmedabad Millowners Association (later the Ahmedabad Textile Mills Association) no longer played a critical role in the city. The ruthless and self-serving methods of many of the mill owners in disinvesting from their mills—looting their mills by paying out large dividends even while the mills were failing, with little regard for their creditors, investors, or workers—tarnished many reputations.

The textile magnates no longer controlled the city's finances. Often they competed among themselves for access to new resources controlled by the state. Ahmedabad's industry had prided itself historically on its ability to raise funds through a deposit system in which personal reputation was the principal collateral. The leading businessmen helped assess those reputations. But by 1985, new government institutions, created since statehood in 1960 and acting more or less impersonally, had become principal sources of new investment funds. In 1983–84, the Gujarat State Financial Corporation provided Rs. 38.32 crores (US$31 million) in loans; the Gujarat Industrial Investment Corporation, Rs. 122.05 crores (US$100 million). Over the twenty-year period 1964–83, the Industrial Development Bank of India had disbursed Rs. 1,476 crores in Gujarat. By 1985, Ahmedabad's business leaders had become enmeshd in political struggles for access to state funds.

The contest for control of the state's new wealth and power precipitated further changes in the ethos of the business community. In a break with Jain and Vaishnava traditions of nonviolence, their call for a five-day *bandh* (general strike) against government policy failures in June 1985, during which 33 people were killed and 150 were injured, showed that the business community was willing to risk violence in order to assert its power.

Ahmedabad's business community was no longer purely local. New, nonlocal businessmen were rising to power without integrating into the social structure of the city and its *mahajan* (guild) traditions.[28] The rise of the Ambani family of Reliance Mills was the foremost example. Although Ramniklal Ambani stayed in Ahmedabad to provide day-to-day supervision of the mill, he was a newcomer to the city and had not become active in the charitable and civic causes that united the city's Vania (merchant caste) elite. Moreover, principal control of the enterprise vested with his brother, Dhirubhai, at the family's headquarters in Bombay. For the first time in the city's history, Ahmedabad's largest, fastest-growing, and most sophisticated textile mill was controlled by an outsider.

Aging and "sick" mills were also being sold to outsiders, notably the Marwari Kanoria families who controlled the Asarwa Mills, Anil Synthetics, Omex, and New Gujarat Synthetics.[29] As in political life, power in Ahmedabad's industrial and financial life, heretofore earned by the careful tending of local contacts and concerns, could now be achieved through external connections. Ahmedabad's indigenous Vania elite no longer controlled the economy, and with it the social and political fate of the city. Nor had the newcomers been socialized to the older value system of moderation in politics.[30]

Two of the major institutional pillars of the city—the TLA and the Ahmedabad Millowners Association—were thus thoroughly undermined. Huge tracts of mill properties in the east side of the city were deserted and left unused; legal considerations and court cases blocked their sale, and economic considerations blocked their efficient utilization. Masses of workers, as well as many owners, were left frustrated and dispirited. The trust that once marked this sphere of the institutional life of the city was replaced by bitterness and frustration. Ahmedabad's rate of population growth, 39 percent from 1961 to 1971, and 28 percent from 1971–1981, dropped to 19 percent from 1981 to 1991. This 19 percent would actually have been only 6 percent but for the annexation of the lands of East Ahmedabad.

Decay in the Municipal Corporation

By the mid-1980s, many charges of incompetence were leveled against the Ahmedabad Municipal Corporation (AMC), including its failures to keep the city clean, the roads repaired, the transportation system running smoothly, the water and sewage systems expanding to meet the needs of a growing population,

the schools functioning properly, and the legal codes enforced. Critics univer-
sally noted that the city had functioned more efficiently and more honestly in
the 1950s and 1960s than it did in the 1970s and 1980s.[31] (The corporation was
not officially blamed for the failure to cope with the riots of 1981, 1985, and 1986,
discussed in the next chapter, because law and order is a state, not a municipal,
function.)

The fundamental problem was financial. In the decade 1980–81 to 1989–90,
the corporation balanced its budget only twice. In 1980–81, the mills were still
working full force and the city's economy was still strong. The success in 1986–
87 owed to the one-time jump in octroi revenues that came with the annexation
of eastern Ahmedabad. In all other years, the corporation ran a substantial deficit. In 1989–90, this deficit was Rs. 660 lakhs, the difference between revenue
of Rs. 13,545 lakhs and expenditure of Rs. 14,205 lakhs. To make up the deficits,
money was drained from the capital budget, and in the years 1989–91, the AMC
spent only about a third of its capital budget allocation. The percentage plum-
meted from 51 percent in 1988–89, to 36 percent in 1989–90, to 27 percent in
1990–91.[32]

In 1985 the AMC entered into an agreement with the World Bank for programs in solid waste management, sewerage, water supply, slum upgradation,
and institutional strengthening. The agreement was especially welcome because
in 1986, Ahmedabad annexed a vast territory to the east, equal in geographical size to the entire existing corporation. This area was largely without water,
sewerage, solid waste disposal, lighting facilities, and adequate roads. A large
part of the loan was dedicated to helping to provide these services. The project
ran for ten years and was to cost a total of Rs. 630 million rupees. By the end
of ten years, when the project was wound up, only Rs. 466 million had been
spent.[33] The municipal corporation had failed to meet its share of the project
budget, forcing the bank to limit its contribution proportionately. Much of the
infrastructure construction was canceled.

Birmingham University researcher Richard Batley described Ahmedabad
in 1991 as a municipal corporation slipping backward:

> Earlier success in the extension of conventional housing seems to have
> been followed in the 1980s with deterioration of already installed infra-
> structure and declining construction of water pipe lines, roads and
> houses. Furthermore, in 1986, with the latest in its series of doublings
> in size every quarter century, the AMC acquired new under-serviced
> areas, including large industrial estates generating serious problems of
> contamination.[34]

In the same year, the municipal commissioner also reported a deteriorating
situation. A total of 65 percent of the domestic water connections were cor-

roded. Slum and *chawl* dwellers had, at best, access to collective toilets, and an estimated 500,000 people had to resort to defecation in the open. The city suffered annual epidemics of gastroenteritis, infectious hepatitis, cholera, typhoid, and other waterborne diseases.[35]

A balanced budget is not the only indication of municipal success or failure, but persistent deficits, coupled with warfare in the streets and a plethora of complaints against the municipal administration, indicated a corporation in serious trouble, without the resources to meet its obligations:[36]

> The millowners pulled out of direct involvement in local politics and the Congress Party reoriented itself to appeal particularly to the working class and backward castes. This divorce of the business elite from municipal government was sometimes said (in interviews) to have led to a declining concern with strategic direction and financial rectitude in favour of a more populist and reactive style of political management.[37]

The days of mill owner mayors, such as Chinubhai Chimanbhai (1950–56, 1957–58, 1959–61) and Jaykrishna Harivallabhdas (1961–65)—and of a Congress Party lock on the municipal government—were over. Without a powerful, engaged civic elite, and lacking a powerful, disciplined party leadership to provide vision and drive, bureaucratic inertia further crippled the Ahmedabad Corporation.

Municipal administration in India continues to bear the legacy of colonial administration. Even when allowing limited elections, the British had kept ultimate power in their own hands. After independence, the new government retained much of the old system. The civil service administrators of the municipality were chosen not by the municipal electorate, but by higher-ranking civil servants and by state-level officials. Elected officials and appointed bureaucrats confronted each other, with different constituencies to please and often with different agendas. There was "no single line of accountability and no ultimate authority."[38] Batley pointed out at length the shortcomings of this system: "At its best, this is a system which gives due respect to professional standards and which maintains continuity through routines. At its worst, it is not a system which can be easily mobilized to achieve institutional objectives," and "there is a premium put on risk avoidance."[39] The system invites abuse. The elected leadership did not allow the administrators to carry on their jobs without interference; the administrators took advantage of the powers of their office. The processes of hiring and promotion were politicized and corrupted: "It would be only in rare circumstances that a clear political leadership combines with a clear administrative leadership in a common purpose."[40] Throughout the two decades 1969–1990, such leadership was absent:

At all levels, but particularly now in the zonal and ward offices, official procedures and programmes are vulnerable to disruption from the free access which corporators (councillors) have to any office at an time and their expectation of the satisfaction of particular complaints. . . .

The AMC has no way of ensuring output from its staff. Neither incentives nor penalties for performance are structured into the system.[41]

In 1987, Ahmedabad voters threw out the Congress and elected the Bharatiya Janata Party to power in the corporation, hoping that this political party would bring greater honesty, order, and efficiency to municipal governance. Even then, Batley saw the corporation as only "weakly disciplined."[42]

Despite all these problems with lack of finance and an unresponsive bureaucracy, as well as a slippage from earlier, higher standards, Ahmedabad was doing well compared to other municipal corporations in India—indeed, its administration was rated one of the best.[43] Ahmedabad may have compared well to other cities in India, but in comparison to its own recent history, the city seemed to be in sharp decline. Its mills were mostly closed, its mill workers out of work and demoralized, its principal union impotent, its municipal corporation financially overstretched, its business leaders discredited, and its communal fabric was rent with violence.

CHAPTER 10

Madhavsinh Solanki Invokes
the Politics of Caste and Class

The 1980s brought Ahmedabad's Gandhian era to an end. The mills collapsed, crippling the Ahmedabad Millowners Association and the Textile Labour Association (TLA), and leaving the Ahmedabad Municipal Corporation (AMC) impoverished. The leaders who had grown to maturity under Gandhian influence and had guided the city's affairs for a half century passed from the stage. Seeking to make the best of this trying situation, and to fill the leadership vacuum, the new head of the Congress Party in Gujarat, Madhavsinh Solanki, sought to create a new ruling coalition by increased recruiting of the lower castes and classes. India's prime minister, Indira Gandhi, with whom Solanki was closely allied, was attempting to implement a similar strategy at the national level, so Ahmedabad once again commanded center stage as a microcosm of Indian politics. When Solanki's strategy went down in flames in six months of urban chaos and rioting in 1985, Ahmedabad was once more a shock city for the nation.

The populist politics of the Gujarat chief minister, Madhavsinh Solanki, ignited the flames. The transfer of power from upper castes to lower that he effected in state government, and the reservations—affirmative action benefits —that he expanded on behalf of the same lower castes, provoked a violent backlash. Subsequently, and unexpectedly, the caste conflict morphed into warfare in the streets between Hindus and Muslims. Ahmedabad convulsed in violent turmoil for six months in 1985. Order returned only after Mrs. Gandhi sent in a team of high-level government and party officials to take over the task of restoring law and order and forced Solanki to resign. Solanki's Ahmedabad had come to symbolize a failed policy of lower-class mobilization.

The issue of reservations for so-called backward groups, affirmative action programs on their behalf, had been a prominent and continuing subject of national political debate and mobilization throughout India since even before independence. Ahmedabad's experience illuminates the forces supporting and opposing reservations and the rationales that they proclaim. It spotlights some of the urban groups that have advocated reservation politics as legitimate tools for increasing the status of disadvantaged groups—and as strategies for personal gain.

Article 16(4) of the constitution of India establishes reservations, or special set-aside positions within government services, electoral politics, and educational institutions for groups that are considered to be backward: members of scheduled castes (former untouchables) and scheduled tribes in proportion to their numbers within the general population, approximately 14 percent for scheduled castes and approximately 7 percent for scheduled tribes nationwide. Each state could modify reservation policies internally, although they were urged to subscribe to the common national policy.[1] In Gujarat, reservations were established at approximately 14 percent for tribals and 7 percent for scheduled castes, which was approximately their proportion within the state population.

The center also pledged to follow up at a later time with further reservations for other disadvantaged lower castes and classes, constituting about 25 percent of India's population, with considerable variation by region. These groups, usually referred to as other backward classes (OBCs), generally ranked above the scheduled castes and scheduled tribes in status, but below the higher castes and classes. However, the OBCs were difficult to identify. To some degree, economic and social backwardness correlated to caste position, but not fully. Despite older, popular views of caste as being rigidly fixed, in practice, mobility does exist in the status of castes and in the status of individuals within castes. Many advocates of reservations have therefore opposed the use of caste categories alone to identify OBCs without reference to social and economic conditions. In the face of the intellectual complexities and political minefields of extending reservations to OBCs, nothing was done at either the national level or in Gujarat. In some states, however, notably Tamil Nadu in the south—where lower castes were proportionately more numerous, and their resentment had festered and boiled over into political action decades earlier—substantial reservations for OBCs had been in effect from as early as the 1920s.[2]

In Gujarat, a new chief minister, Madhavsinh Solanki, himself a member of an OBC, built his electoral majority on a coalition of four disadvantaged groups known by the acronym KHAM: Kshatriyas (lower peasant castes, generally considered OBCs), Harijans (ex-untouchables), Adivasis (tribals, literally, original inhabitants), and Muslims. In 1980, his party, the Congress (I), won a clear majority of 51 percent of the vote for the Gujarat legislative assembly and an overwhelming 140 seats in an assembly of 182. In 1985, it repeated this victory with even greater success, winning 56 percent of the vote and 149 seats. The remarkable electoral success of the KHAM strategy attracted nationwide attention. Its fragility surfaced in Ahmedabad when Solanki began actually to implement expanded reservations for OBCs.

Madhavsinh Solanki was born in 1927, a lower-caste Kshatriya, son of a primary-school teacher. During his student days at Bombay University (B.A.,

1949), he worked under Indulal Yagnik as a subeditor for his publications, and he developed a deeper appreciation of the lives of poor people, especially the rural poor. His professional interests took him into journalism and communication —and the city of Ahmedabad. He worked for five years as subeditor of the *Gujarat Samachar,* Gujarat's largest-circulation daily newspaper, joined the AMC as publicity officer, and went on to study law and become an advocate.[3]

Solanki was elected to the legislative assembly from the Borsad constituency of Kheda district eight times in succession, beginning in Bombay state in 1957 and continuing in Gujarat state after 1960. During his legislative career, he also became an advocate in the high court. During part of this time, his law partner was a Muslim, Hamid Kureishi, son of Gulam Rasool Kureishi, whose home in Gandhi's ashram had been attacked by mobs in 1969, and grandson of Imam Sahib, who had accompanied Gandhi on his return from South Africa. Solanki often argued cases on behalf of tenant farmers and as deputy minister of land reforms, 1962–67, and cabinet minister for land reforms, 1973–74, he helped draft and legislate land reforms for tenant protection. For a short time, 1976–77, during the emergency, he served as chief minister of Gujarat.

A man of considerable charm, educational sophistication, and political dexterity, Solanki was selected by Mrs. Gandhi to head the Gujarat Congress. His alliances with the lower and backward groups paralleled her call for *garibi hatao,* "eliminate poverty." His electoral victory at the state level in 1980 paralleled hers at the national level. It brought into the legislative assembly ninety-six members of KHAM background, 69 percent of the Congress (I) total. Of the twenty-two members of Solanki's new cabinet, fifteen were of KHAM backgrounds. "For the first time in the history of the state there was not a single Patidar minister of cabinet rank."[4] Amarsinh Chaudhary became the first tribal in the state to hold cabinet rank. As minister in charge of irrigation, Chaudhary posed a potential threat to the Patidar cash-cropping farmers of Gujarat.

High and middle-peasant castes saw themselves excluded from political power. Tensions rose between Kshatriyas and Patidars; tribals and nontribals; and low caste and high caste. The frustration and anger of those who saw their power being undermined mounted: "No longer able to control their social subordinates through political or social institutions, the high and middle-peasant castes increasingly took matters into their own hands."[5] Their violent backlash was soon felt in Ahmedabad.[6]

1981

At the B. J. Medical College in Ahmedabad, a high-caste student was first in his class in pathology, but he was refused admission to further specialized study. Only one seat was available, and it was reserved for a scheduled caste student under the roster system. This roster system not only reserved a specific number of seats within specific advanced fields for Adivasis (tribals) and Dalits (ex-untouchables), but if such candidates were not available in any given year, it kept the seats temporarily empty and carried the reservation over to the next year. On December 31, 1980, infuriated by this reverse discrimination, a delegation of students from the medical college called for the immediate abolition of the roster system, a reduction in reserved seats, and an increase in unreserved seats at the postgraduate level, as well as some additional minor changes in the reservation system. The government granted some of the minor demands and agreed to increase the number of unreserved seats by exactly the number of seats that were reserved.

Once the issue of reservations had been opened, however, the students went on to demand an end to all reservations in the medical college. On January 20, they went on an indefinite strike. Students in the engineering colleges joined in. Soon students in other colleges added their support. The government closed all schools and colleges in Ahmedabad indefinitely, and all medical colleges in the state for six months, beginning January 28. The next day, leading professionals and businesspeople in the city met the chief minister to argue the students' case. Most of the Gujarati press supported the upper castes. The lines of battle were being drawn.

The social geography of the neighborhood surrounding the medical school heightened the tension.[7] The medical school was located inside Ahmedabad's sprawling new civil hospital complex, one of the largest public hospitals in Asia. This complex was situated adjacent to industrial areas of textile mills and their Dalit workers' *chawls*. This was one of the few areas of the city where Dalits and upper-caste Hindus actually came into physical proximity to one another. In addition, the core of the neighboring old Asarwa Village was home to a substantial number of Karva Patidars, whose relationships with Dalits were also quite strained.

On January 23, 1981, a minor clash between antireservation, higher-caste students and proreservation Dalit students in the medical school touched off a month of riots, first within Ahmedabad but then soon spreading to the villages of central and north Gujarat. The forces on the two sides were unequal, and for the most part, despite the existence of a Dalit Panther defense organization,[8] the Dalits suffered most. They were terrorized by higher castes living in multistory residences above who hurled rocks, flaming rags, and acid bombs down onto their shacks below, and by attacks on the roads as the Dalits returned from work. Throughout February and much of March, the police placed various neighborhoods in Ahmedabad under curfew. In total, about forty people were killed in the city, and scores were injured.[9] The army was called in to establish order, and in various parts of the city curfews continued for almost three months. In at least nineteen villages in the Ahmedabad, Kheda, and Mehsana districts, Dalit houses were burned and property looted.

Powerful interest groups arrayed themselves against the Dalits. The police often did not defend them against the attacks by the upper castes, and sometimes they joined in. In November 1980, some Dalit policemen filed a case in the Gujarat high court alleging discrimination in promotions. They noted that of 517 police subinspectors in the state, only four were of scheduled castes and two of scheduled tribes. In February 1981, the home of the Dalit subinspector who had filed the case was burned down. In the same month, the unions of police inspectors, subinspectors, and constables passed a resolution calling for the abolition of reservations, the roster system, and other programs of positive discrimination. The government banned *Aakrosh* [Rage], a magazine established in 1978 by the Dalit Panthers for publishing Dalit poetry.[10]

Further Cracks in the TLA

The rioting split the TLA. On February 21 and 22, approximately 40,000 Dalits walked out of the textile mills of Ahmedabad in a wildcat strike. Next, upper-caste workers struck for two days. Then the mill owners closed the mills for two days to allow passions to cool. The TLA made no public expression of support for the Dalits or for reservations. The leader of one wing of the organization, however, Elaben Bhatt of the Self-Employed Women's Association, spoke out in favor of peace. Her apparently neutral statement was interpreted as supportive of the Dalits and of reservations. This act of "indiscipline" was one of the grounds for the TLA leadership to expel Bhatt and the women's association, setting them on their own independent course of action. In addition, that night, a group of rioters stoned Bhatt's home and threatened to set it on fire,[11] forcing her and her husband to seek refuge in the home of a relative.

By now, political leaders had had enough of violence, curfews, strikes, and *bandhs*. The government of Madhavsinh Solanki offered to end the roster system that had been the immediate issue of contention and to add to the medical college a number of unreserved seats equal to the reserved seats. The Gujarat Chamber of Commerce and Industry and the Ahmedabad Textile Mills Association (formerly the Ahmedabad Millowners Association) advised the students to accept these terms while negotiating others, and they advised the government to reopen the medical school. By the end of March, the city was returning to normal.

The 1981 riots had many implications for Ahmedabad. Caste competition had become a public, highly politicized, and much-disputed issue that constantly threatened to explode in violence. The actual lines of alliance and conflict, however, were not yet clear. For example, the most frequently and brutally attacked Dalits, and also the most militant, were not the lowest of the low; the Bhangis, sweepers, remained outside the conflict. The Dalits most involved in the battles were the most upwardly mobile of the scheduled castes—the Vankars (traditionally weavers who make up half of the Dalit population of Gujarat)[12] and the Chamars (traditionally leather workers). Inspired by the conflict, Vankars and Garodas (the priests among the Dalits) began to evolve "a dalit literary movement, which was up to then scattered and disorganised."[13] The lower castes among the Dalits did not yet participate.

Muslims had not been much involved in the 1981 conflict, and tribals almost not at all. Even the Kshatriyas were a divided community, with some of those at the bottom providing protection and even support to the Dalits. Institutions like the TLA, which had formerly helped to contain violence in Ahmedabad, were now paralyzed by internal divisions.

Madhavsinh Solanki not only survived these riots, but he also became the only chief minister in the history of Gujarat state until that time to serve his entire five-year term (1980–85). Political scientist John Wood attributes Solanki's success to his emphasis on the economic growth—a must for Gujaratis—which he coupled with his concern for welfare measures for the disadvantaged. He launched projects to increase power generation and fertilizer production, and he sought to develop an electronics industry. During his tenure, Gujarat rose to the second position in industrial development among India's states. At the same time, in programs for the poorer sections, he introduced free midday meals for primary school students, free education for girls and women from primary school through university completion, and the distribution of free food grains to families with annual incomes below Rs. 5,000. Despite the 1981 reservation issue, Solanki launched no attacks on Gujarati capitalists or large cash-cropping farmers. His majority was large enough to withstand defections, and he could count on the support of Mrs. Gandhi in Delhi. In 1985, Congress won the Gujarat legislative assembly with an even larger majority than in 1980. The turmoil of 1981 seemed forgotten. Then the larger troubles exploded. Once again the issue was caste, the epicenter was Ahmedabad, the shocks were national, and the news coverage international.[14]

1985

Although it took no concrete action, the Gujarat Congress had actually begun to consider extending reservations to OBCs in the 1970s. To identify the OBCs, the state Congress government appointed the Socially and Educationally Backward Class Commission, headed by a retired judge, A. R. Bakshi. For three years, the Bakshi Commission sifted through information and categories of classification by caste, poverty, illiteracy, and social habits. In a much-praised final report, the Bakshi Commission identified eighty-two groups deserving of assistance: sixty-one lower-caste Hindu groups, twenty Muslim groups, and one Christian community. By the time the report was ready, however, a new state government had been voted into power, and the document was shelved. National politics, however, returned to this unresolved issue of reservations for OBCs as a Janata Party government came to power from 1977 to 1979.

In 1983, Chief Minister Solanki appointed a new committee under another retired judge of the Gujarat high court, C. V. Rane. By this time, Gujarat had reserved 14 percent of most of its government positions for scheduled tribes, 7 percent for scheduled castes, and, for a trial period of ten years, 10 percent for OBCs. The Rane Commission recommended expanding the OBC reservation by an additional 18 percent so that the total of all reservations would become 49 percent. On January 10, 1985, two months before elections, the Solanki government announced that it would implement this new schedule.

For a few weeks, the upper castes and classes did not react publicly, but by early February, the backlash had begun. Government property was attacked, buses burned, and buildings stoned. Although some violence occurred elsewhere, the main focus was Ahmedabad. Here opposition continued to build. Upper-caste and upper-class college students, supported by their parents and guardians, protested by boycotting examinations and forcing their postponement in approximately thirty institutions. All primary, secondary, and higher secondary schools in the city closed until after the election.

Meanwhile, critics examined the Rane Commission report more carefully. They found that the commission had recommended increased reservations on the basis of social, economic, educational, and occupational standards, not caste. Solanki had ignored this fundamental part of the recommendation, raising serious doubts about his transparency and honesty.

In the countdown to the election, the political opposition parties entered the fray. Student groups associated with the Bharatiya Janata Party (BJP)—a predominantly middle- and upper-caste, staunchly Hindu, urban party that had arisen out of the Jana Sangh—supported a *bandh* called by the all-Gujarat education reform committee for February 25. (BJP leaders claimed that many Congressites privately supported the *bandh*.)

In the elections, as noted, the Congress (I) Party won an overwhelming victory in an apparent triumph of the KHAM strategy. Ninety percent of the winners were new to the state assembly—and beholden to Solanki for choosing them as candidates. Many of them had no grassroots support. On March 11, the new cabinet was sworn in. Fourteen of the twenty seats and all of the major portfolios went to members of the KHAM constituencies.[15]

Schools in Ahmedabad reopened officially on March 11, but tensions ran high, and few students attended. College examinations were further postponed.

Seeking to end this impasse that had arisen among the middle and upper castes, the government declared that it would not implement the increase in reservation quotas for at least a year. Nevertheless, on March 17, students called for a *bandh* as leaders of the 1981 antireservation agitation began to reemerge. Also, as in 1981, professional organizations—primarily upper caste and upper class in composition, including the Ahmedabad Bar Association and the Ahmedabad Medical Association—voted to support the *bandh*.

Unexpectedly, on March 19, during a period of general calm in communal relations, Hindus attacked Muslims in the Dariapur area of Ahmedabad's historically walled city, killing three people and injuring eight. Violence quickly spread across the Sabarmati River to the western suburbs. Forty-five people were injured, and fires were set in many localities. Property worth Rs. 3 crores (US$2.5 million) was destroyed.[16]

Who, if anyone, had planned these communal riots? What was their relationship to the violence that had begun to break out among Hindu caste groups? Wildly differing answers were proposed. Some charged that Congress (I) politicians had encouraged communal rioting in order to divert attention from the caste riots and to unite the Hindu population.[17] Others saw the BJP as fostering communalism as a strategy for removing Solanki from power.[18] Still another explanation saw Hindu–Muslim violence as a plan by land speculators and developers to take advantage of this time of public turmoil to push people out of their homes, which could then be seized for use by the locally dominant group or for commercial sale.[19] A fourth view saw bootleggers as encouraging the riots. A few days earlier, on March 12, approximately twenty-eight people had died from drinking illicit liquor, and demands for crackdowns on bootleggers followed. The riots sidetracked this attention.[20] In addition, because the financiers of liquor sales were usually upper-caste Hindu Vanias and Patels, while the direct purveyors were Muslims and Dalits, rioting between these groups conflated the conflicts of caste and class.[21]

From this period onward, the role of bootleggers, smugglers, drug dealers, and local strong-arm *dadas*—criminal bosses—figured prominently. Gujarat's total prohibition of liquor gave them huge scope for profit. Because their work was illegal, bootleggers formed alliances for protection with both police and politicians. In return, the politicians found these illegal operators useful as sources of funds and of strong-armed thug supporters.[22]

Anthony Spaeth, writing in the *Wall Street Journal* on September 16, 1987, vividly described the role of bootleggers in the creation of riots:

> Politicians and businessmen in Gujarat say the illegal liquor business
> is fiercely competitive and frequently a Hindu bootlegger's rival is a
> Moslem in one of Gujarat's ghettos. This is where a communal riot

can come in handy. When one bootlegger wants to harm another, he creates a riot in his rival's turf, which brings about an unwanted police reshuffle in the district. It is the task of the paid-off politicians to help arrange the riot.

There are variations, according to local politicians: When the police are asking too much protection money, a bootlegger holds a riot in his own district. When a politician isn't cooperating, his district gets a riot, financed by the bootlegger and arranged by a rival politician.

In Ahmedabad, the politicians were now using their relationships with bootlegger gangs in reverse fashion. They were asking the gangs to create riots as political disturbances. The *intala* and their friends—the subjects of Sundaram's prescient poetry—had forged their alliances.

Ahmedabad's riots appeared to be an array of planned, orchestrated, professional campaigns. In the hospitals, doctors describing stab wounds noted that the attackers were striking the liver and other vital organs with an accuracy suggesting hired professional assassins, rather than simple angry retaliation among local communities.

Whatever the motives underlying the initiation of communal violence, all commentators agreed "the anti-reservation stir, launched by the students a month ago, has been pushed into the background with anti-social elements taking control and giving the agitation a communal turn."[23] The army was called in to help subdue the city.

On March 23, prime minister Rajiv Gandhi paid a brief visit to Ahmedabad to demonstrate his confidence in Solanki, but on April 1, Gujarat University postponed examinations indefinitely and declared an early start of summer vacation.

Now the police entered as combatants. From early April, they were accused of attacking innocent civilians and condemned in the press for personal indiscipline, ties with politicians and the underworld, and communal biases (on both sides). Skirmishes broke out among the police and between the police and the citizenry.

In the Asarwa industrial area, the police assaulted four students, and when one mother registered a complaint, the police beat her too. They made people open their houses, then beat up everyone in sight. It was also alleged that a notorious bootlegger was let loose in the area, threatening people with dire consequences if they reported against the police. On April 9, police atrocities shifted to Khadia in a bloody variation on those in Asarwa.[24] So many protests ensued that the metropolitan court barred the commandant of the state reserve police and the local superintendent of police from entering certain sensitive neighborhoods. Instead, the army was sent in to patrol.

On April 22, police head constable Laxman Desai was murdered while accompanying a committee of inquiry in the Khadia–Astodia neighborhood. Outraged, the police went on a rampage. They beat people in the compound of the V. S. Hospital, attacked women who were fasting for peace at the nearby town hall, and then withdrew to police headquarters for Desai's funeral.

Although the police were no longer manning their posts, the army was not given full authority to replace them. The city was exposed to an orgy of violence, which now spread beyond the walled city to the industrial Dalit areas of Ambedkar Nagar, Bapunagar, and Naroda Road in one direction, and to Ashram Road and the elite western suburbs in the other. On April 21, an anti-reservation rally of 10,000 people was held. On April 23, between seventeen people (officially) and fifty (unofficially) were killed, eighty-five injured, and hundreds of houses and huts burned down, leaving 5,000 people homeless. Most textile mills were closed. The entire walled city was under curfew. No buses moved. Police were nowhere in sight in the affected neighborhoods.

Worse, the police were in the vanguard of people who attacked, burned, and destroyed the printing presses of the largest daily newspaper in the city, the *Gujarat Samachar,* which had criticized them sensationally. The presses of the *Western Times,* a small English-language newspaper housed in the same building, were also burned down. Army guards protected two other major newspapers nearby, the *Indian Express* and *Jansatta.* Solanki seemed to condone the violence, "attributing the police behavior to 'resentment spreading through the ranks,' which was aggravated due to the anti-police stand of the press."[25]

The reservation issues surfacing in Ahmedabad had national implications. Between April 17 and 19, leaders from all over India who were opposed to reservations met in Bombay and began to plan an agitation in Maharashtra similar to that in Gujarat. From New Delhi, prime minister Rajiv Gandhi announced his continuing support for Solanki, but the continuing violent agitation endangered the political stability of the state. Calls for an end to the Solanki ministry increased.

On the night of May 8, in the Kalupur neighborhood, in the most volatile area of the walled city, police subinspector Mahendrasingh Rana was shot dead. Rana had a reputation for harsh treatment of Muslims, so Muslims were immediately blamed for the shooting, with most attention fastening on an enterprising, aggressive bootlegger and gang leader, Abdul Latif. Communal clashes resumed. Antireservation activity also continued to simmer. Because the state government had long ago withdrawn its proposal for an increase in caste reservations, it appeared that the remaining goal of the agitation was to bring down the government. Leaders of three parties—the BJP, the Janata Party, and the Lok Dal—began a hunger strike, demanding the dismissal of the Solanki ministry.

Although several Dalit meetings were held, some with the support of Muslims, Solanki did not actively mobilize his KHAM supporters. Sporadic violence sparked between rural Kshatriyas and Patidars, but the countryside, the main source of Kshatriya power, did not ignite.[26] Solanki's opponents took this as proof of his demagoguery: he had bid for KHAM voters without attending to the work of organizing them to defend their interests politically or physically.

In Ahmedabad, the Gujarat Chamber of Commerce, supported by thousands of shopkeepers, officially entered the lists on June 5. Protesting the breakdown of law and order, it announced a five-day *bandh* to close down all commerce in the state. Because every previous *bandh* had been accompanied by further outbreaks of violence, this call suggested the willingness of the business community to risk violence in exchange for Solanki's dismissal, notwithstanding its high proportion of Jains and Vaishnavas, groups normally religiously committed to nonviolence. During the period of the commercial *bandh,* other antireservationists called for an additional, parallel *bandh.* In two days, 33 people were killed and more than 150 injured. A Hindu family of eight was locked in its home and burned to death in a communal attack in Dabgarwad. Strikes spread as 65 percent of state government employees (350,000 people) left work, demanding the end of the roster system. On June 18, employees of the AMC joined the strike.

Two days later, despite intense police and government pressures to cancel or at least limit the procession, the annual Hindu Rath Yatra emerged from the Jagannath Temple and thrust its way through the neighborhoods of the old city, with its parade of elephants clearing the path for temple carts carrying images of gods followed by tens of thousands of devotees. As the Hindu procession entered Muslim neighborhoods, communal violence broke out again and continued at high levels for several days.

At last the central government began to intervene. A team of government and Congress party officials arrived from New Delhi to investigate. High-level officials of the ruling party were arrested. Former allies of Solanki—Jinabhai Darji and Sanat Mehta—publicly called for his removal. Darji had been one of the originators of the KHAM strategy in 1977 and continued to organize among Dalits and tribals. In 1985, he had been forced from power by Solanki and had come to believe that Solanki was an opportunist, lacking true commitment to the oppressed. The Congress thus divided both along caste lines and between dissident and ministerial members.

On the evening of July 6, at the directive of the prime minister, Solanki and his government resigned. (At the time, I was a resident in Ahmedabad, near the university, and was awakened from an early sleep by the firecrackers and celebrations of my upper-caste, well-to-do neighbors.) Solanki's handpicked successor, Amarsinh Chaudhary, took office as Gujarat's first chief minister of tribal origin. Chaudhary's new cabinet, apparently dictated from Delhi, broadened to include Patels and Vanias while dropping five Kshatriya members.

Julio Ribeiro, former director-general of the central reserve police and highly praised for his role in taming the Bombay underworld, arrived on July 9 as the new director-general of police. Immediately he began touring the city, emphasizing the gathering of intelligence, and bringing the police under his own control—not subject to local politicians. Ribeiro identified bootleggers as "the main trouble-makers"[27] and began to crack down on them. He located weapons manufacturers who had eluded his predecessors.

The 2,500 army troops who had been in the city since March 19 were withdrawn, but in a week of transition, as police began to reassert full control over the city, 60 people were reported killed and more than 138 injured in police and private shootings. Most confrontations were communal—not caste—based. On July 26, the new chief minister announced that police officers in whose jurisdictions bootleggers were operating would be held responsible and punished. The link between police, politicians, and illegal business activity was snapped, at least temporarily. The police now arrested several gang leaders and captured caches of arms and ammunition.

Various strikes by government workers moved toward resolution. On August 2, AMC employees ended a forty-seven-day strike. On August 17, approximately 350,000 state government and *panchayat* (local government) employees withdrew their seventy-three-day strike over a caste-based roster system. Schools reopened. Teachers and students returned to their classrooms.

Accords were achieved between the Amarsinh ministry and the two major student, parent, and guardian groups that had spearheaded the antireservation agitation: the 18 percent increase in reservations for socially and economically backward classes was scrapped until a national consensus could be achieved—which, for practical purposes, meant indefinitely. Responsibility effectively shifted from Ahmedabad to Delhi. A committee to review the 1978 reservation of 10 percent for OBCs was established and charged to report before 1988, when the ten-year provision would expire. A judicial inquiry into the violence was promised. In return, the agitation was withdrawn. After a half year of upheaval, in which 275 people had died, thousands had been injured, tens of thousands had been left homeless, and property and trade had suffered losses estimated at Rs. 2,200 crores (US$1.75 billion),[28] Ahmedabad finally returned to some sense of normality.

The Congress' Broken Chain of Command

How had Solanki, after two successive electoral triumphs, so badly lost touch with his constituents, so badly misjudged the political forces of his state and its capital city? He had not nurtured the kind of chain of command and communication that had characterized Ahmedabad and Gujarat in the days of Mahatma Gandhi and Sardar Patel. The Congress Party experienced "a spectacular dissociation between the party and its leadership."[29] This failure mirrored the decay of the Congress organization nationally under Mrs. Gandhi. Gujarat politics, like national politics, experienced waves of voter enthusiasm, often followed by disillusionment and the complete collapse of popular support.

In the course of his first ministry, Solanki forced from office many of the people who had brought him to power, including the inventors of the KHAM strategy, Jinabhai Darji, Harihar Khambholja, and Sanat Mehta. In the elections of 1985, he did not allow tickets to eleven members of his first ministry, including Mehta and Khambholja. Solanki tightened his links with the Congress high command in Delhi, but cut them with the representatives of localities and interest groups below him.

When riots broke out, the political chain of command disintegrated. Despite the continuing violence in Gujarat, the center hesitated to dispose of Solanki because of his recent second electoral triumph. They feared a backlash from his KHAM constituents, especially Kshatriyas. For four months, the center allowed chaos to prevail rather than risking action that might threaten delicate and unpredictable political balances between the center and the state, between the state government and its chief supporters, and between the caste groups within Gujarat. Under these circumstances, violence was politically effective. In the words of Upendra Baxi, professor of law and vice chancellor of the University of Delhi, "This constituted a serious crisis of legitimacy not only for the majority party but even for bourgeois liberal democracy."[30] Only after local forces had thoroughly battered Solanki, exposing the fragility of his support, did the center finally dismiss him. A struggle of such continuing violence and chaos in Gujarat would have been unthinkable from 1920 to 1969.

1986, a Contrast in Political Response

The effectiveness of a clear political chain of command in halting violence became dramatically clear in 1986, when riots once again broke out in Ahmedabad but were suppressed by the swift action of the central government. The contrast with 1985 is instructive.

In 1986, riots again broke out in Ahmedabad, killing some eighty persons, wounding hundreds, rendering thousands homeless, and registering losses to business of approximately Rs. 150 crores (US$125 million)[31] in one week of violence. The trigger was, once again, the annual Jagannath Rath Yatra, proceeding boisterously and provocatively through the heart of a city still wounded and raw. By the time the procession had completed its route on the night of July 9, eleven people were reported dead and many more were wounded, some of whom would die in the next few days. Communal riots had begun. This time, they had been expected; the quest for revenge was strong in the city in both major communities. As in 1985, complicity was charged between police and politicians in allowing, if not abetting, the attacks.

In reply to alleged Muslim attacks during the Rath Yatra—although clear responsibility was never fixed—the Hindu Raksha Samiti (Defense Committee) called for a statewide *bandh* on July 12. The *bandh* was totally effective in north Gujarat, including Ahmedabad, where observers called it the most thorough shutdown they had ever seen, with all the textile mills in the city closed for the first time in decades. It had more limited effects in other parts of the state. Nevertheless, on the day of the Gujarat *bandh,* twenty-four people were killed thoughout the state.

Now, however, the scenario diverged from 1985. P. Chidambaram, union minister of state in charge of internal security, flew to Ahmedabad. (Simultaneously, a three-man All India Congress Committee team flew in to make its own review.) After consultation with Chaudhary, and all the while affirming the chief minister's authority, Chidambaram announced that the situation would be under control within twenty-four hours. Fifty-four companies of state reserve police, central reserve police, border security forces, and other security personnel were brought in to patrol the city.

With astonishment, the *Times of India* reported on July 16, "Surprisingly the claim of the Union Minister . . . that the situation would be brought under control within 24 hours proved correct." Although sporadic violence continued, the various security forces, a rigidly enforced curfew, and the arrests of key people—for example, the secretary and the other leaders of the state branch of the militant Hindu Mahasabha—proved effective. The total arrests for the month were 3,401, of whom 61 were arrested under the National Security Act. Further, on Janmashtami Day, the birthday of Lord Krishna, August 27, the police, fearing renewed violence, successfully prevented a proposed Shobhayatra religious procession that had been called by the Hindu Suraksha Samiti (Protection Committee). Blocking three separate attempts to start the procession, they detained 1,100 people.

Meanwhile, Chidambaram, in his capacity "as cadre-controlling authority for the IAS [Indian Administrative Service] in the department of personnel, and for the IPS [Indian Police Service] in the Home Ministry,"[32] announced that the central government would hold district collectors and police superintendents directly and principally responsible for any communal violence. In accord with the Indian administrative structure in which the civil service administration is separated from the politically elected structure, the police and administrators were to report to their own service chain of command, not to local politicians. Thus, from the very beginning of the outbreak of riots in 1986, Chidambaram implemented immediately the successful policy that Julio Ribeiro had devised the year before in bringing an end to the 1985 riots. In 1986, a determined administration, freed from political considerations, halted communal confrontation and shut down violence quickly. At least temporarily, a political chain of command was in place. Gujarat was subservient to Delhi. Riot control, however, was based on suppression imposed from above rather than on any long-term construction of grassroots organization from below. This chain of command could hold so long as central, state, and city governments belonged to the same party. As we shall see, when the various levels of government were held by different parties, governance became more difficult. The cohesion that had often been provided by the Congress of Gandhi and Patel was a thing of the past.

Within the AMC, despite setbacks, the Congress held on until the mid-1980s; then it too was shattered. From 1975 to 1977, the years of the national emergency, the elected city government had been superseded and Ahmedabad had been placed under an administrator dispatched from Gandhinagar. Municipal elections in 1977 brought the Janata Morcha, a coalition government, to power for three years. The Congress was returned to power, 1980–85, and its term of office extended by order of the state government to 1987, so that municipal elections were not held during the years of rioting.

The 1987 election produced two striking, and contrary, victories. Together, they suggested the depth of the rift between Hindus and Muslims in Ahmedabad. The first was the victory of the BJP as the ruling power within the Ahmedabad Corporation. Its victory was in part a protest vote against the Congress, but the BJP was clearly identified as a militantly Hindu party that expressed substantial animosity toward the Muslims of India. Anti-Muslim bias informed at least a part of its electoral success. Second were the victories of Abdul Latif as an independent candidate in each of five different Muslim-majority electoral wards of Ahmedabad in campaigns waged from his jail cell. While the Hindus of Ahmedabad were returning a majority for the BJP, the Muslims were voting for their own representative.

Hindu Militants in the Riots of 1985

The BJP was the political-party wing of a cluster of Hindu militant organizations, which originated with the Rashtriya Swayamsevak Sangh (Association of the National Volunteers). Founded in 1925, the RSS promoted pride in Hinduism and aimed to make India a Hindu nation, not only demographically but also in official policy. It wanted all other religions to accept the supremacy of Hinduism in India, and it often represented itself as protecting Hindus and Hinduism from the aggression of other religions, especially Islam, but also Christianity. Among the other large and prominent groups in this Sangh Parivar, or ideological/cultural family of organizations, were the Vishwa

Hindu Parishad (World Hindu Assembly), established in 1964 to attempt to provide an overarching centralized structure to Hinduism, which historically flourished as a highly decentralized array of religious traditions; and the Akhil Bharatiya Vidyarthi Parishad (All India Student Assembly), established in 1948 to bring together all those involved in university education—both faculty and students—to promote Hindu ideology in higher education.[33] All these groups involved themselves in Ahmedabad's riots in 1985—more broadly to create a more Hindu public universe, and more narrowly to overthrow Solanki's government and bring the BJP to power.

Sociologist Ornit Shani has detailed the participation of the Sangh Parivar in Ahmedabad in 1985.[34] Shani's study focuses on the Dariapur ward of the old walled city, an area where caste Hindus, Dalits, and Muslims lived in close proximity to one another. Here antireservation riots among castes were transformed into communal riots of Hindu versus Muslim. By recruiting Muslims to fight against Dalits, the upper castes splintered Solanki's KHAM coalition. Shani cites the official government of Gujarat commission of inquiry, led by Judge V. S. Dave: "Communalism is not caused by religious difference [but] religion became a means to have the power."[35]

The BJP/Rashtriya Swayamsevak Sangh/Vishwa Hindu Parishad Sangh addressed each group according to its needs. For middle-caste groups experiencing downward mobility because of the closing of the textile mills, the Sangh provided jobs, job retraining, and protection from the police.[36] Dalits in the mill areas of Bapunagar reported that BJP politicians gave them money and food, indoctrinated them against Muslims, warned them of imminent attack, and provided them with clubs. In June, Dalits were invited to participate in the Rath Yatra. They began to feel accepted into the Hindu community. They turned against their Muslim neighbors. Muslims reported that during the 1985 riots, Hindus shouted, "Muslims should go" and "This is a Hindu raj, come out and bow down."[37]

Shani stresses religious ideology as the basis of organization on both sides. Congress sought to bring both Dalits and Muslims into its coalition. The BJP sought to splinter that coalition by turning Dalits against Muslims. Congress supported Muslims, so the BJP supported Dalits. The BJP acceptance of Dalits marked a change in policy. During the 1981 riots, the Dalits and Muslims had stood as one, and the BJP was seen as a party based among upper-caste Hindus, opposed to both. By 1985, the BJP was recruiting Dalits and turning them against Muslims.

Latif: The Criminal–Political–Police Connection

Under attack from the surging Sangh Parivar, the Muslim minority took some refuge in the defense provided by Abdul Latif, a bootlegger who had risen from a simple job as a young delivery boy to become the principal "don" of the "mafia" bootlegging business in Ahmedabad. His career throws light on the significance of bootlegging and organized crime in Ahmedabad's politics and economy, and in the life of many of its economically depressed neighborhoods.

Abdul Latif Abdul Wahab Sheikh was born in 1952 into a family of six brothers and two sisters in Popatiawada *pol* in the Dariapur neighborhood of the old walled city.[38] His father earned his living from a tobacco shop. Latif studied at the Khanpur Kalyani Republic high school, but he failed the secondary school certificate examination at the end of high school and left his studies. By this time, his father had died, and he had no means of earning a living.

In 1974, the bootlegger Manjur Ali, in the Saraspur neighborhood, hired Latif to deliver liquor to people's homes. When he was first charged and arrested under the Prohibition Act, Manjur Ali paid his bail, and soon Latif also became known in the gambling dens as Manjur Ali's delivery person. When the manager of an illegal gambling club in the Saraspur area offered Latif slightly more pay, he left Manjur Ali. Soon he started his own small-scale liquor den. In 1980, Latif began a small-scale business in selling foreign liquor at a stand in the Dariapur Popatiawada area. As an independent bootlegger, he paid weekly *hapta* (payoffs) to police officers and constables. He began to open new dens and stands, and he prospered as his business spread. In just five years, he became the liquor king of Ahmedabad and mixed freely in Ahmedabad's criminal world.

To improve his source of supply, Latif opened direct business relationships with Kailash Jain, of Udaipur, Rajasthan, a manufacturer and wholesaler. His monthly income from the liquor dens increased by about 50 percent. As his income increased, Latif found himself in sharper competition with other bootleggers in Ahmedabad, and the sums he paid to the police increased. Latif began to hire hoodlums armed with knives and other weapons. To equip his gangsters, Latif began to buy weapons in India and abroad. In a quarrel over payments to Kailash Jain, Latif dispatched his gang to Udaipur and had him killed. Because the murder took place in Rajasthan, Latif did not fear the local police in Ahmedabad, and it was said that he secretly sent huge bribes to the police investigators in the case.

Latif's gang began to extort protection money from other bootleggers and from the managers of liquor and gambling dens. It was rumored that some police encouraged these activities—in exchange for a share of the take. Between 1982 and 1984, the size of his gang tripled.

In Bombay, Latif met the underworld boss Alamzeb Rangrej Khan. In 1984–85, during a bloody gang war in Mumbai against the infamous gang of Dawood Ibrahim, Alamzeb fled for his life to Ahmedabad, where Latif gave him shelter. In exchange, Alamzeb equipped Latif's gang with the most up-to-date weapons and instructions on using them. Gang warfare continued. In 1984,

Dawood dispatched an assassin to kill Alamzeb. Near Jamalpur Gate, the hired man shot, but missed. Then Dawood entered into an alliance with another gang in Ahmedabad, that of Pappukhan of the Shah Alam area. In a bloody turf war, Latif's gang smashed Pappukhan and his accomplices.

Later that year, the police killed Pappukhan, and Latif and Dawood reached a compromise. Latif had warm relations with some members of the Gujarat police administration, and Dawood could now benefit from this connection. Gujarat state opened as a market for heroin and other illegal drugs, and it became a transit point for smuggling these substances into Rajasthan, Madhya Pradesh, and Maharashtra. Latif, too, entered into these new businesses and also into smuggling gold. He became a don in the underworld.

The riots of 1985, it was rumored, were kept at the boiling point by Latif's gang "in the service of a politician out of power [Chimanbhai Patel?] who wanted to disturb the existing government."[39] On the night of May 9, 1985, when Latif's gang shot up the Bhanderipol neighborhood and subinspector Mahendrasingh Rana was killed, people alleged that Latif was transported to safety in a government van, out of the neighborhood to the Sarkhej area. In the criminal proceedings, the court completely acquitted and released the members of Latif's gang. On November 12, 1985, however, the criminal investigation branch of the Ahmedabad city police administration captured Latif and remanded him to police custody.

Latif became a popular hero in Ahmedabad's Muslim neighborhoods during the 1985 riots when his gang distributed grain, milk, and vegetables in the Muslim areas that were under seemingly endless curfew. In 1987, while he was sitting in jail, Latif entered into the AMC elections as a candidate from each of five different Muslim-majority wards and won a large majority in each one. His majorities in the five wards collectively totaled more than 50,000 votes. Citywide, the BJP, a Hindu militant party, won a convincing victory to control the AMC for the first time. The two diametrically opposite victories revealed the depth of communal divisions and fears within the city.

After Latif's victories, the BJP proclaimed that criminals dominated the Muslim neighborhoods. The BJP had demonized both the man and his community by campaigning on a platform contrasting "Rama Raj"—government of the Lord Rama—against "Latif Raj." Latif's victories came in wards usually carried by the Congress. They revealed widespread displeasure with the Congress for its inability to contain the communal riots and protect the Muslim minority. Latif's popularity among the Muslim masses was undeniable—reaffirmed again by the 40,000 people who joined in the procession at his mother's funeral in 1987—and widely resented.

Under electoral law, Latif had to resign four of his wards, and he attended meetings of the corporation only twice on behalf of the fifth. He took little interest in electoral politics, although some political leaders sought to encourage him. He escaped police custody in 1987 and continued to control his gang from across the Arabian Sea, in Dubai, where he fled. He continued to strike deals with Ahmedabad and Gujarat politicians who used him as he used them. Latif was recaptured by the police—some say he surrendered willingly—in New Delhi in 1995, imprisoned in Ahmedabad, and murdered by the police in 1997 in what is usually referred to as a staged police encounter. By the time of his death, however, Latif had lost his reputation as defender of his community, a kind of Robin Hood, and was more widely viewed, even among those who had once voted for him, as an extortionist and a criminal. The newspaper accounts of his assassination noted this decline in Latif's popularity—the result of his gang's racketeering in the construction industry, even against fellow Muslims.[40]

Transformations in Ahmedabad's Social Geography

By the late 1980s, Ahmedabad's social geography had been transformed. First, the former local leaders in the neighborhoods of the old walled city, where much of the violence occurred, had departed for the new, wealthier suburbs west of the Sabarmati River. Although they maintained ties with family, friends, and former neighbors in the old city, the links had attenuated over time. (During the 1985 riots, I was visiting in the western suburbs with a longtime friend. He told me that he must return to the city to organize for peace. Twenty years previously, he had been living in the old city and would not have had to undertake such a mission as a special task. It would have come naturally to his geographical as well as his social position in the city.)

The vacancies created as residents left the walled city had been filled by heterogeneous groups of immigrants, breaking the tight social control of the compact *pol* neighborhoods.[41] Ahmedabad's outbreaks of civic violence, 1969–86, indicated not only an inability of older elites and institutions to function effectively, but also the change in the social geography of the city.

The new suburbs housed many of Ahmedabad's academic and intellectual institutions and elites. In their suburban seclusion, many of them seemed only loosely tied to the life of the rest of the city. The new research and teaching institutes that dominated the western suburbs—the cosmopolitan institutions such as the Indian Institute of Management, the National Institute of Design, the Physical Research Laboratory, and the Schools of Architecture and Planning (now the Center for Environmental Planning and Technology)—were national in their patterns of recruitment and curricula of study. To what extent were their faculty, students, and research concerned with the problems of Ahmedabad itself? To what extent should they be? These questions were widely debated, but in general, these institutions appeared to be in the city more than of the city. For example, Ashoke Chatterji, director of the National Institute of Design, wrote in the midst of the 1986 riots, "The institutions which Ahmedabad has nurtured seem curiously irrelevant to its present agony; islands in a rising tide of alienation."[42]

The departure of powerful local leaders and the arrival of heterogeneous newcomers without local ties facilitated the increase in liquor and gambling dens in the old walled city. The old neighborhoods could not defend themselves physically or politically against the new illegal encroachments. Criminal activity flourished as civic order declined. As Sundaram had feared, the *intala* had fallen into the hands of questionable friends.

Most of all, the intense rioting in the city convinced many Ahmedabadis to shift their residences. People who found themselves as minorities in communal-majority areas often shifted to areas where they would be in the majority. Hindus in Muslim-majority areas fled; Muslims within Hindu majority areas also fled—by far the more common situation. Neighborhoods became increasingly polarized. In the growing semisuburban western area of the city, the road separating Muslim Juhapura from neighboring Hindu Guptanagar was commonly referred to as the border between India and Pakistan, and it was an armed border.

In his comparative study of communal violence in various cities of India, Ashutosh Varshney chose Ahmedabad as one of his six case studies—a case in which violence was severe.[43] Varshney argues that cities in which diverse groups live in close residential proximity to one another and interact in social and economic life, promote peace and discourage violence. He cites Ahmedabad as a city with contrary relationships, where diverse groups live segregated from one another and have little social and economic interaction. By 1985 that description had become valid. The segregation, however, was new to Ahmedabad. Until 1969, and to some degree even until 1985, Hindus and Muslims lived much closer together, socialized together, and worked together. The sheer growth of the city and its suburbanization accounted for some of the change. The closing of most of Ahmedabad's textile mills also played a major role. Then each wave of violence—and more were to come—fed a vicious circle driving the communities ever farther apart. The social geography of 1985 and later was no longer that of 1965.

The increasingly segregated social fabric of the city, the violence, the collapse of the historic economic base, and the erosion of the unique institutions that had characterized Ahmedabad for more than fifty years brought an end to the Gandhian era in Ahmedabad's life. In December 1987, two of Ahmedabad's prominent institutions for urban planning, the Center for Environmental Planning and Technology and the Gujarat Institute of Civil Engineers and Architects, assembled an array of some of Ahmedabad's most distinguished citizens to discuss the current status and fate of the city. They entitled their program "Is Ahmedabad Dying?"

CHAPTER 11

Ahmedabad 2000:
The Capitalist City Out of Control

*A capitalist city is bound to have some cha-
otic development. After all, there is not one
individual or institution taking decisions.
Thousands of people are involved in the
process.*

—BIMAL PATEL

Ahmedabad rebounded from the loss of its textile industry. In the 1990s, it rebuilt its industrial economy with new initiatives in chemicals, pharmaceuticals, soaps, denim, and diamond polishing. In addition, Ahmedabad's financial sector grew to service the rapid expansion of the economy of Gujarat state. The city did not attract the international back-office call center operations that captured wide attention for Bangalore, for example, but its manufacturing enterprises supported India's large-scale entrance into the global economy. As India's economy emerged more global and more powerful, Ahmedabad was one of the shock cities that provided the thrust.

As India's economy liberalized, and government shrank, nongovernmental organizations (NGOs) also flourished. Ahmedabad's largest NGO, the Self-Employed Women's Association (SEWA), drew worldwide attention for its work with poor working women, and development experts from around the world came to observe its methods. Born as a wing of the Textile Labour Association, the union that Gandhi had helped to create, SEWA, almost alone in Ahmedabad, perpetuated the legacy of the Gandhian era.[1] Unfortunately, high levels of corruption and illegal economic activity also flourished in Ahmedabad, giving testimony to the city's more general departure from the ideals of the Mahatma.

Rajiv Gandhi, in his tenure as prime minister in the mid-1980s, began gently moving India away from the more regulated economic policies of the generation of his grandfather, Jawaharlal Nehru. Then, in 1991, came the jolt that pushed the country far more directly into the global economy. India desperately needed a loan to pay off international obligations. In granting the loan, the International Monetary Fund imposed its usual set of free-market conditions. India was required to open its markets to imports and foreign investment; to reduce sharply government employment, subsidies to the poor, and regulations on business; and to devalue the rupee and make it convertible with international currencies. The reduction in controls and regulation opened new opportunities for new entrepreneurs from outside and inside India. India's economy responded positively to this new economic regime. The gap between rich and poor increased, but in absolute terms, even the poor benefited. Ahmedabad, historically one of India's most business-oriented cities, became a shock city of the new economy, with a growth rate far higher than the national average—and with problems of growth also more severe than the national norm.

As the commercial hub of Gujarat state, Ahmedabad prospered as the state took advantage of new opportunities in industrial growth and built a highly diversified economy. With only 5 percent of India's population, Gujarat produced 11.5 percent of its industrial output.[2] The growth came in the urban sector, in industry and services. Gujarat accounted for a significant share of the national production of salt, caustic soda, fertilizers, sulfuric acid, and petrochemicals.[3] It accounted for about 20 percent of the national production of crude oil and 14 percent of the production of natural gas (1994–95). Agriculture, on the other hand, lagged badly, with a low or even negative growth rate throughout the 1980s and 1990s.[4]

Ahmedabad served as the financial and commercial hub of this flourishing economy of Gujarat—and beyond. Ahmedabad was "the only metro-centre serving Gujarat, Rajasthan and Madhya Pradesh."[5] In 1996, the Ahmedabad stock exchange, the second oldest in India, moved from its historic headquarters in an ornate building in the heart of the old city in Manek Chowk to a new, simple, and undistinguished building in western Ahmedabad. It replaced face-to-face on-the-floor transactions with online trading. The shouting and yelling (which could be heard a block away) from the buyers in the upper tiers of the old stock exchange building, receiving their orders by phone from brokers across the street, and calling them out to the sellers on the ground floor, were replaced by traders sitting quietly and staring intently at banks of glowing LED computer screens in simple, unadorned offices.

Employment

In an even newer development, during the 1990s, Ahmedabad saw the spectacular growth of a diamond-polishing industry. Bapunagar–Amraiwadi, previously a mill workers area, began to thrive with this diamond industry.

Estimates of employment in the industry were between 100,000 and 150,000.[6] The industry grew, almost overnight, as a spin-off of the much larger diamond-polishing industry in Surat, 150 miles to the south. Tens of thousands of workers were seated at their polishing tables before government statistics even took note of them.[7] The workers were all recent arrivals. The majority of the entrepreneurs and the workers were men of the Patidar castes who had immigrated from Saurashtra, western Gujarat.

Small-scale industry generally flourished in Ahmedabad district as well, with 58,332 total units registered in 2000, up from 29,661 in 1990 and 10,919 in 1980.[8] The overall figures concealed the ups and downs of the period. Liberalization brought euphoria, followed by anxiety, to the business community. First-generation entrepreneurs eagerly began to open small-scale industries, and government policies favored them. After 1991, most new product lines were automatically approved. Market information became easily accessible, bank loans easily available. Ahmedabadi entrepreneurs followed a herd mentality[9]; whatever seemed to bring profit to one soon attracted many imitators. New fields quickly became saturated. By the early 2000s, however, the weeding-out process had rid the market of many of those who were unable to compete legally and successfully.

The large-scale composite mills had closed, but textile manufacture, now mostly produced on power looms, employed 78,450 workers in Ahmedabad district in 1996, with 69,210 of them in the city.[10] The industrial estates at Naroda, Odhav, and Vatva, established in the 1960s in Ahmedabad's eastern suburbs by the Gujarat Industrial Development Corporation as incubators of new industries, provided space and infrastructure for hundreds of new ventures. New state financial agencies such as the Gujarat State Finance Corporation helped provide the necessary financing. Of the eight largest cities in India, Ahmedabad continued to have the highest percentage of workers employed in industry, at 33 percent in 1999–2000, down sharply from 44 percent in 1987–88, but still 6 percentage points above the average for metropolitan cities in India.[11]

The quality of the new jobs was problematic. More people were working, but they were earning less. Work participation rates by men increased from 49 percent in 1987–88 to 54 percent in 1999–2000, but the percentage in "regular employment" dropped sharply from 45 percent to 33 percent, exactly paralleling the drop in industrial employment. Over the same time period, work participation rates for women increased from 7 percent to 13 percent, while the percentages of women in regular employment also went down sharply. Apparently more women were pressed into the workforce to make up for the decline in work and pay available to the men in their families. This is not certain, but it is consistent with anecdotal interview evidence.[12]

The chemical industry, the largest new growth sector of both Ahmedabad and Gujarat, created serious pollution problems. Gujarat produced forty-six chemicals that were considered extremely toxic and hazardous; Ahmedabad had sixty factories that produced one or more of them.[13] The Gujarat high court closed approximately 700 small-scale chemical units in the eastern periphery of the city until a common effluent treatment plant to service the industrial estates came online in 1999. Even with the new treatment plants, biological pollution of the Sabarmati River and its watershed presented serious health hazards.[14]

The number of motor vehicles registered in Ahmedabad multiplied dramatically, from 166,000 in 1981 to 538,000 in 1991 to 1,210,000 in 2001. About three-fourths of these were two-wheel scooters and motorcycles; about one in eight was a car; about 5 percent were autorickshaws. (In 1961, there had been only 43,000 vehicles registered in the entire state.[15]) The vehicle exhausts, added to the industrial emissions, produced intense air pollution. Ahmedabad had "the highest level of SPM [suspended particulate matter] in the country."[16] Noise pollution, although not measured officially, was omnipresent. The one indispensable part of every motor vehicle in Ahmedabad was a horn, always kept in good working order.

The city and state lagged in the clean knowledge-based industries associated with cities like Bangalore. The most common explanation given for this lag was Gujarat's lack of emphasis on education in general, and English-language education in particular.[17]

Entrepreneurship

Industrial diversification fragmented Ahmedabad's business community. When Ahmedabad had been a single-industry town, most people shared the same fate: when textiles prospered, most people prospered; when textiles slumped, most people suffered. By 2000, diverse sectors had diverse fates. Pharmaceuticals might do well while construction lagged; diamonds might be in a slump while financial services boomed. Common policies did not emerge. The city had no common program for economic development.

Many new entrepreneurs stepped forward, while some established business families stumbled. For example, although the Lalbhai family's Arvind Mill was struggling following its aggressive entry into the international market in the production of denim, a new Ahmedabad company, which also went into denim production, proved successful. Ashima, founded in 1982 by Chintan Parikh with capital of US$20,000, had a net worth of about US$90 million by the end of the century.

Another newcomer to industrial entrepreneurship, Karsanbhai Patel, founded Nirma as a soap manufacturer and distributor, successfully challenging the giant multinationals, Hindustan Lever and Proctor and Gamble, for national leadership. Born in 1946, Karsanbhai came from a farming family in Mehsana district in north Gujarat to St. Xavier's College, Ahmedabad, to study chemistry. For a few years, he was employed by the state of Gujarat as a chemist in geology and mining. At night, he manufactured detergents in his backyard and sold them to neighbors and friends, going from house to house by bicycle. The technology and the chemistry of soap manufacture are not sophisticated, and Karsanbhai could sell basic soap products at one-third the price of the multinationals. In 1969, he established a small-scale factory in the Vatva industrial estate. By the 1980s, Nirma had become a major soap and detergent manufacturer, with five factories in Gujarat, each managed by a family member. By 2000, with sales of Rs. 1,718 crores, Nirma held 16 percent of India's market share in branded detergents.

Karsanbhai used some of Nirma's profits to found three new educational and research institutions along the Ahmedabad–Gandhinagar highway: the Nirma Institute of Management; the Nirma Institute of Technology; and the Nirma Institute of Diploma Studies. The goal of these institutions was not only to educate their students effectively, but also to raise the general standards of management and technical education locally and even nationally. He also contributed generously to Vaishnava religious institutions in Ahmedabad and Gujarat, notably to the construction and maintenance of Ahmedabad's ISKCON temple. But Karsanbhai did not assume a public position of leadership in the civic life of Ahmedabad.

Ahmedabad's, and Gujarat's, most significant area of growth in the last two decades of the twentieth century was in chemicals and pharmaceuticals. U. N. Mehta, founder of the Torrent Group, had created a business empire worth Rs. 2,100 crores (about US$500 million) by the end of the century. Born in a village in Palanpur district to the north, Mehta took a degree in chemistry from Wilson College, Bombay, and worked for several years as a medical representative for the multinational Sandoz company. Later, on his own, he commissioned the manufacture of antirheumatic drugs, which he then sold, shifting to Ahmedabad in 1968. In the 1970s, he began producing the tranquilizer Trinicalm Plus and followed it with cardiovascular medicines and anti-infectants. In 1991–92, when Torrent exported Rs. 157 crores in pharmaceuticals, Mehta received the President's Award from the government of India. He added a wide array of other companies, related and unrelated: in pharmaceutical production, Torrent Gujarat Biotech; in energy, the Gujarat Torrent Energy Corporation, Torrent Cables, the Surat Electricity Company, and the Ahmedabad Electricity Company; and in finance, the Gujarat Lease Financing Ltd. (with an asset base of Rs. 1,100 crores, about US$ 250 million).[18] After Mehta's death in 1999, his sons assumed principal charge of running the businesses.

I. A. Modi and Ramanbhai B. Patel founded Cadila in 1951 with an initial investment of Rs. 25,000 each, producing pharmaceuticals. The company split in two in 1995. At that time, Cadila Pharmaceuticals and Cadila Healthcare (later Zydus-Cadila) each had an annual turnover of approximately Rs. 200 crore (about US$50 million). By 2000, they had each more than doubled in size and were growing rapidly, expanding especially into export markets.

The new areas of business were welcoming to newcomers from outside the state as well. The brothers Sushil and Sunil Handa, Punjabis whose father moved to Ahmedabad to work as manager of a textile mill, also entered the production of pharmaceuticals, founding Core Healthcare in 1992. The brothers split their holdings in 1996. Sushil continued with the health care segment. Sunil opened a new company, Core Emballage, which produced various types of cardboard packaging. Sunil believed that India's future lay in education, and he pioneered a new experimental school, Eklavya, in the suburbs of Ahmedabad. He also pioneered a course in entrepreneurship at IIM, his alma mater.

Entrepreneurial curricula flourished not only at the IIM, but also in the Entrepreneurial Development Institute, also an all-India institution, for preparing new entrepreneurial talent; in the Nirma Institute of Management, a postgraduate institution; and several more locally oriented institutions. The Ahmedabad Management Association, founded originally by Vikram Sarabhai in 1957, offered midcareer education for local executives and provided a venue for public lectures and discussions of pertinent issues of management and of civic life.

Some of the new enterprises stretched and bent the rules. Although Dhirubhai Ambani, one of India's most successful "business maharajas," was not an Ahmedabadi, his Reliance plant, founded in the Naroda industrial estate in 1966 for manufacturing synthetic cloth, established new models of entrepreneurship. Ambani recognized that "the most important external environment is the government of India"[19] and of the states. The Gujarat government, like the central government, was kind to the Ambanis. Reliance repeatedly received licenses for investment, development, and importing that led others to question the propriety of its relationships. For example, he successfully registered his huge Reliance textile mill in Naroda not as a composite mill but as a power loom unit because the government allowed the production of 100 percent filament synthetics only on licensed power looms.[20]

In 1978, Ambani launched a nationwide advertising campaign that made Vimal, the brand name of Reliance's synthetic fabric, a household word. He built an India-wide distribution network to match, and "by 1983, on the eve of its entry into petrochemicals, Reliance had become India's largest composite textile mill, sprawling over 280,000 sq. meters, producing three million square meters of fabric per month, and employing 10,000 workers."[21] From this base,

Ambani proceeded to build the largest industrial empire in India. In his other industries—his polyester yarn plant at Patalganga, near Mumbai, and petrochemicals near Jamnagar and at Hazira, near Surat—Ambani demonstrated his belief that Indian manufacturing could and should be world class: Business historian Gita Piramal writes that Ambani "was the first industrialist in India to build facilities which could be compared to the best internationally, both in terms of volume of production and quality of output."[22] By 2000, the Reliance textile factory in Ahmedabad was only a tiny piece of Ambani's empire. Ambani did not otherwise play a significant, direct role in Ahmedabad, but his company did return to the area, opening the Dhirubhai Ambani Institute of Information and Communication Technology in Gandhinagar in 2001.

Ahmedabad business had always demonstrated an independent streak. The textile industry, the major example, had developed through indigenous entrepreneurship. Unlike Calcutta and Bombay, Ahmedabad industry had almost no British investment or control. Throughout its modern history, Ahmedabad had not developed its economy in response to orders from above nor as the locus of colonial enterprises nor as a branch office of multinational corporations located in metropolitan centers outside India. Now, although the large, mostly locally owned textile mills closed, Ahmedabad continued its independent fashion. Its entrepreneurship, sometimes faltering and even devious, sometimes surefooted and bold, continued to originate from within.[23] Even Ambani, although not an Ahmedabadi by birth or residence, initiated his industrial empire from Ahmedabad.

Consumerism and Culture—New and Old

Increasing wealth supported levels of conspicuous consumption that would have scandalized earlier *mahajans*. A flourishing new restaurant and club scene, as well as new shopping centers, allowed for the display of new wealth. West of the Sabarmati River, an array of international shops sprang up along C. G. Road and the Satellite sector. New malls opened along the Sarkhej–Gandhinagar highway. Even the old walled city experienced a restructuring of shopping malls on Relief Road. Two new supermarkets opened in the working-class industrial Bapunagar area of east Ahmedabad. Similarly, new restaurants opened throughout the city, and local newspapers were filled with columns on (relatively) exotic restaurants and ads for the latest, trendiest boutiques.

New private clubs—like the Rajpath Club and the Karnavati Club, both located along the Sarkhej–Gandhinagar road on the western fringe of Ahmedabad—hosted a new culture of pop music, fashion shows, and, some said, concealed gambling. Many of the old-fashioned Gandhians and the more austere traditional businessmen scorned this new culture as shallow and escapist conspicuous consumption that deracinated its participants from their traditions and insulated them from the majority of their poorer fellow citizens. These critiques did not slow the growth of the new culture. To the extent that the production of solid waste is a by-product and index of consumer culture, Ahmedabad had its proof: The quantity of solid waste per capita increased from 133 kilograms in 1980–81 to 203 kilograms in 1998–99.[24]

At the same time, Ahmedabad also housed such gems of high culture as the Darpana dance academy, founded by Mrinalini Sarabhai and kept vibrant and creative in dance, theater, and puppetry by her daughter, Mallika Sarabhai. Kumudini Lakhia's Kadamb dance academy was home to a world-famous *kathak* dance troop, producing both traditional and innovative creations. The Saptak music school trained future performers and, beginning in 1983, hosted an annual ten-day festival of classical music with the most outstanding artists from throughout India performing, along with the best of the school's own students. The city renovated the town hall, built in 1936, and the Tagore Memorial Theater, built in the 1960s, and created a new city museum in the neighboring Sanskar Kendra (Culture Center), built by Le Corbusier. Several new bookstores opened, and one of them, Crossword, part of a national chain, became a center for periodic book readings and discussions. Adjacent to Crossword, the Bandhej boutique earned an all-India reputation for elegant fashion, and newer boutiques opened regularly. Multiplex theaters replaced older, single-screen cinemas and added minimalls and play areas for children to their offerings.

Poverty Alleviation

The growth in the economy seemed to have benefited the poor as well as the rich, but less. In the lowest income category, households with incomes below Rs. 25,000 per year (at 1995–96 prices), poverty in Ahmedabad declined from 35 percent in 1985–86 to 11 percent in 1995–96.[25] Toward the end of the decade, researchers reported some increases in poverty, but the official data lagged behind the rapid pace of economic change, exact trends were unclear, and interpretations of the data differed.[26]

Economic and Political Corruption and Crime— *Maaray Shun?*

The economy and the politics that it supported were not all aboveboard. Illegalities abounded in every phase of public life: political corruption, bootlegging, tax evasion, malfeasance in business transactions, criminally shoddy building construction. Most of these activities were accepted as part of the everyday local public culture. Ahmedabadis spoke somewhat cynically of a pervasive attitude of *maaray shun:* "Why should I care? What difference does it make to me?"

Bootlegging and Smuggling

Bootlegging, which accompanied Gujarat's policy of total prohibition, corrupted the police and politicians who allowed it to flourish and encouraged the growth of criminal gangs that controlled it. By the 1990s, additional, more lucrative contraband was added. Narcotics and weapons, entering from the seacoast of Gujarat and Pakistan, traveled through Ahmedabad via overland routes to Mumbai and points south. The investigative committee appointed by the government of India "to take stock of all available information about the activities of crime Syndicates/Mafia organizations" announced what everyone knew—politicians were complicit, and not only in Ahmedabad and Gujarat: "The cost of contesting elections has thrown the politician into the lap of these elements and led to a grave compromise by officials of the preventive/detective systems. The virus has spread to almost all the centers in the country; the coastal and border states have been particularly affected."[27] The local press reported regularly on this illegal drug and weapons traffic, and on the occasional apprehension of criminals connected with it.[28]

Illegal Practices in Real Estate and Construction

The construction industry, including property development and land transfers, was riddled with illegal activity. A combination of legal restrictions on the use of urban land, especially those in the Urban Land Ceiling Act of 1976, coupled with the failure of local and regional government to provide infrastructure and building permits in timely and orderly fashion, led to unauthorized and unregulated construction throughout the urban area. These included low-end and high-end construction.

In the 1970s, much of the illegal and unauthorized construction was in slum dwellings and squatter settlements. It multiplied through the 1980s and 1990s. A census of slums undertaken by the Ahmedabad Municipal Corporation (AMC) in 1976 showed 415,103 slum dwellers in some 81,255 homes in 1,250 slum colonies. Later estimates were less systematic, but they showed about double that number of slum residents in double that number of colonies by the end of the century. The newer slum colonies sprouted in the newly developing industrial areas of the city in the east, where the new jobs were.[29]

The courts often issued injunctions halting legal evictions on humanitarian grounds.[30] About 80 percent of the slum housing was, however, quasi legal, situated on plots owned by private landlords, "a growing petty-capitalist class which has strong links to the local polity." In their study of the Ahmedabad housing market, Meera Mehta and Dinesh Mehta found that these landlords took profits "even higher than in the formal sector."[31]

Unauthorized and unregulated construction also became the norm in newer middle- and upper-middle-class areas of Ahmedabad. Achyut Yagnik, NGO leader and social critic, reported that restrictions on the use of land "encouraged the growth of a new class of quasi-criminal entrepreneurs capable of illegally occupying open land through their powerful political connections. Today [1983] it is not unusual to meet at Ahmedabad a slumlord-turned-builder who at the same time is a municipal councilor or office bearer of a national political party."[32]

Ahmedabad was so rife with bootlegging, smuggling, and illegal land dealings that many responsible observers believed that, at the highest levels, Chimanbhai Patel, chief minister of Gujarat state, 1973–74 and 1990–94, was involved. We have seen that Chimanbhai was forced out of office in 1974 on charges of corruption and spent the next sixteen years in the opposition.[33]

In 1990, he was reelected. During this term, Chimanbhai won respect for his advocacy of the state's economic development and for bringing Gujarat state to the top ranks in India in industrial development. He was held in some awe for his ability to hold together diverse and alternating coalitions of fractious politicians of different parties. He was credited with temporarily ending the appeals to communalism that had characterized both the Bharatiya Janata Party and the Congress. Many communities of rural Patels, especially in his home region of Charotar, lionized him as one of their own who had worked assiduously on their behalf.

At the same time, Chimanbhai was feared and even despised for his alleged corruption and ruthlessness. His ability to keep himself in power and to advance his programs despite shifts in national political alignments was attributed to payoffs as well as diplomacy, and his name was frequently linked with that of Abdul Latif, Ahmedabad's most notorious bootlegger and criminal gang leader. On October 9, 1992, Chimabhail's most vocal critic, the general secretary of his own Congress Party in Gujarat, Raoof Valiullah, was assassinated in broad daylight on a busy street in Madalpur, a central area of Ahmedabad. India's central bureau of investigation determined that Latif's gang was responsible for carrying out the assassination. The bureau could trace the murder no further, but many sober observers believed that the chief minister had encouraged the murder.[34]

Chimanbhai corrupted and criminalized politics, but his political skills seemed indispensable. He had found a way of negotiating the reins of power. His heart attack and death in 1994 left the city and state suddenly without clear leadership. His epitaph in the *Times of India,* published on February 18, 1994, underscored his mixed contribution:

> For all his skills as a political manager, his lack of scruples sent the
> wrong signals to the state machinery. The protection given to several

notorious underworld elements has only resulted in the widespread prevalence of corruption. In the land of *ahimsa,* the increasing lawlessness, as reflected in the communal riots and murder of political figures, will remain associated with the Chimanbhai regime.

Irregularities and illegalities did not stop with Chimanbhai's death. The floods in Ahmedabad in 2000 revealed the destructive potential of unplanned, unregulated construction. New buildings cut across and blocked the natural underground drainage canal system of the city, especially in the western areas. Businessmen built shops illegally in ground-level locations known for potential flooding and officially designated for parking spaces, and then complained about their losses.

Ahmedabad newspapers began a series of articles exposing the general illegality of much of the new construction: "At least 75 per cent of buildings in the Ahmedabad Urban Development Authority areas were found to be violating the Gujarat Town Planning Act. Most of the violations were in the non-provision of parking space and encroachment of the margin area."[35] The papers also revealed widespread noncompliance with fire codes: "An affidavit submitted to the High Court [in 1998] by the Ahmedabad Municipal Corporation states that only 9 of 268 high-rise buildings are fire safe."[36] On the other hand, many of these violations were minor. Builders argued also that many regulations—fire codes in particular—were unrealistic in light of local realities. Inappropriate regulations evoked illegal violations, a political system that encouraged graft, and an unprofessional building industry.

Builders bent the zoning rules to construct commercial offices in areas zoned for residences. The most conspicuous example was C. G. Road. On this street, running through the center of the rapidly expanding western region of the city and zoned mostly for residences and for nursing homes, builders illegally constructed shops and offices, paying bribes and fines as necessary. By 1993, they had completed 1.8 million square feet of office and retail space in fifty-four separate projects. Finally, the AMC, embarrassed by the public revelations, levied additional fines, which it called "impact fees." But it also rezoned C. G. Road, allowing it to become Ahmedabad's showcase commercial shopping street.[37]

After the damaging floods of 2000, the Gujarat high court ordered the destruction of illegal structures in some of the most exclusive areas of town. Judge B. C. Patel, who took a leading role in this campaign, observed, "It is difficult to believe that any unauthorised construction would go unnoticed by officials. It can only be due to negligence or connivance of officials with builders."[38]

The construction industry also absorbed and laundered large quantities of "black" money—illegal and untaxed profits from other business activities. In case of default in such black market transactions, the courts cannot be called on to collect debts, so builders often turned to coercion and extortion. Similarly, builders acquiring land, especially from farmers on the fringes of the city, often resorted to force and extortion. Bootlegging gangs could provide the muscle, expanding their activities into the building industry. The newsweekly *India Today* added that they could also help in engineering "communal and political riots to get rid of troublesome tenants or squatters."[39] Knowledgeable observers agreed that communal riots usually included at least some attempt to force people to leave their land and property so that others could seize it.

Cutting Corners: Criminality in Small-Scale Business

The opening of India's economy to the world, especially after 1991, led to major increases in small-scale industry. Ahmedabad shared in this growth. The original euphoria, however, led to market saturation. In order to survive, many of the new entrepreneurs cut corners, sometimes in criminal fashion. Harald Bekkers, a student of this process, wrote, "References to 'cutthroat competition' and 'fly-by-night operators' pervaded the discussions I had with entrepreneurs, government officials and providers of business services. . . . Cutthroat competition becomes economic criminality when 'corners need to be cut,' for instance by illegally tapping into electricity or by secretly dumping chemical effluents at night to save on production cost, or by bribing an officer in a bank to open his files and provide confidential information on a competitor's projects and customers."[40] By 1996–97, however, conditions were improving. The new businesses were undergoing a period of weeding out, which tended to favor entrepreneurs with vision and efficient work plans over those who cut corners and broke the law.

Tax Evasion and Municipal Impoverishment

Crime, particularly economic crime, had become a way of life in Ahmedabad. Competitive business pressures made honest compliance with the law difficult. The consequences for the city, both in lack of funds and in extraordinary cynicism, were devastating. So great was the shortfall in tax collection that before 1994, Ahmedabad was almost insolvent. Social capital, the trust that people had in government and civic institutions, was also in short supply.

Pervasive tax evasion undercut the capacity of city government to carry out its job. Evasion of property tax, for example, was widespread. Rent control legislation covering the older areas of the city limited not only the landlord's capacity to raise rent, but also the capacity of the AMC to raise taxes on its older properties. To compensate, taxes on new construction were fixed at confiscatory levels—and were generally evaded.

Octroi taxes were also evaded with impunity. Octroi is a common tax in Indian cities, levied on imports into the city. It is collected at checkpoints in railway stations, airports, and, most of all, on the highways entering the city. In Ahmedabad in most years the octroi tax yielded more than half of the city's revenue. (The tax was finally abolished in Ahmedabad in 2007. Revenues provided by the state were to take its place, although this gave the state government even more control over the city than it already had.) Octroi was evaded in several ways: officials took payments for not collecting the tax and also pocketed parts of the tax that they did collect; businessmen prepared false accounts; truckers avoided the octroi toll stations, paid off the clerks, or prepared false documentation; *goondas,* hoodlums, threatened the clerks or colluded with them.

The degree of evasion became clear in 1994 when a newly appointed municipal commissioner, Keshav Verma, cracked down. To collect property taxes efficienty and accurately, Verma created a computer database to identify defaulters. He issued notices and warrants to collect back taxes. He disconnected water supply and sewage lines on defaulting properties, published defaulters' names, attached property, and restructured and strengthened the property tax department. Property tax collection rose from Rs. 44 crores in 1993–94 to Rs. 119 crores in 1998–99.[41]

He was similarly aggressive in collecting octroi. Verma monitored all octroi collection points with round-the-clock police and video surveillance, including his own unscheduled, much-publicized spot-check investigations. He inspected warehouses, demanding to see the octroi clearance papers for the goods in storage. In five years, from fiscal 1993–94 to 1998–99, octroi collection doubled from Rs. 130 crores to Rs. 264 crores, and increased again to Rs. 309 crores in 1999–2000.[42] Verma gained the support of the business community for his diligence. In principle, the Ahmedabad business community was opposed to the octroi tax, but so long as the tax was in place, they wanted it administered fairly. All should pay equally; none should gain business advantage through tax evasion.[43]

Struggles for Improvement
Action from within the Bureaucracy

Legal provisions dating back to the era of British colonial rule allow the state government of Gujarat to supersede municipal governments on grounds of incompetence and to assume direct administration of the city. Even in normal times, the state government appoints a municipal commissioner, who wields principal executive power. Under normal circumstances, the commissioner must negotiate with the elected government of the municipality, but when the corporation is suspended, he has virtually a free hand.[44] Keshav Verma became municipal commissioner of Ahmedabad in September 1994 while the corporation was suspended (1993–95). Declaring "We mean business," he set about tackling several critical problems, boldly and dramatically, with extensive publicity, making sure that the people of Ahmedabad knew of his work. Improving tax collection was only part of his mission.

Verma arrived at a time of considerable despair about the condition of the city. The roads were in such bad condition that the Gujarat high court had ordered their repair and held the corporation in contempt for its lack of responsiveness. Verma went beyond repair to actually paving and upgrading roads throughout the city, in the working-class east as well as the upper-middle-class west. He had crews at work day and night. He ordered an immediate cleanup of the area around the high court, C. G. Road, and Ashram Road, the city's premier residential and commercial areas. He had some illegal constructions near C. G. Road ripped down. A total of 15,000 to 20,000 people came out to watch the work. On the night of December 1, 1994, he dispatched 200 trucks and bulldozers to clear encroachments from Sardar Bagh, a public park at the old city end of the Nehru Bridge. While the work was going on, merchants in the nearby heavily Muslim Three Gates area began clearing out their encroachments as well. Sensing the new opportunity, Verma dispatched some of his vehicles to push them along. He reported the operation a "blitzkrieg," with all of the Three Gates area cleared by 5 A.M. When protesters came to his home and threatened "to burn down the town," Verma met them with a counterthreat: "We will bulldoze you!"[45]

Verma's flamboyant style attracted some, repelled others, and amused and bemused still others.[46] During his three-year tenure, Ahmedabad's octroi and property tax collections more than doubled, transforming the AMC from an impoverished institution unable to meet its obligations into a proud and solvent corporation with surplus funds. To add to the funds available, Verma's administration floated a Rs. 100 crore bond issue in 1997—the first municipal bond issue in Asia.[47]

Verma's administration claimed many additional achievements: professionalization of Ahmedabad's cadre of municipal administrators; beautification of C. G. Road; renewed and expanded parks and green areas in Ahmedabad; a program to improve conditions in selected slums, with the full participation of the slum dwellers themselves; and partnership agreements between the AMC and local business houses and NGOs to achieve many of these results.[48] These projects drew mixed reviews from participants and from evaluators, and they were subject to some decay without strong, continuing support after Verma's departure.[49] The turnaround in the economic fortunes of the city, however, remained a clear and lasting contribution of his term in office.

Verma himself, a professional administrator of the Indian Administrative Service cadre, remained in office only three years and then moved on, in accord with the rules and regulations governing the office of municipal commissioner. Regardless of successes or failures, a commissioner's term is restricted to a three-year maximum. Citizens cannot count on continuity. Also, Verma could more easily achieve his contributions because during the first half of his term, the corporation had been suspended. Paradoxically, Verma's successes in introducing accountable, professional standards owed in many ways to the lack of democratic, transparent, accountable, professional standards during his own tenure.

Nongovernmental Organizations

Even before Gandhi came to Ahmedabad, the city was renowned for its voluntary nongovernmental agencies working for improvement in the lives of poor and oppressed people.[50] By the 1990s, the many important NGOs based in Ahmedabad included CHETNA, working in health care and training; SAATH, in community development; AWAG, in women's welfare; Vikas, in community empowerment and poverty alleviation; Sanchetna, in health and communal harmony; and St. Xavier's Social Service Society, in empowerment of poor people in slum neighborhoods.

Among these organizations, SEWA held a special place by reason of its size, with approximately 79,000 members in Ahmedabad, out of a total membership of 206,000 in Gujarat and 319,000 throughout India (1,100,000 by 2010); its range of programs, including union organizing, banking, microcredit, housing assistance, health care delivery, child care, health and life insurance, and legal services; and its ability to affect public policy at local, state, national, and international levels. SEWA negotiated on behalf of its members for space in the marketplace, higher wages from employers, jobs with the AMC, relief payments from state and local governments, and a range of government programs helpful to poor working women and their families. A total of 93,000 women had savings accounts with the bank, and 33,778 women took out loans in 1999. When the AMC wanted to develop programs for poor people, both men and women, it frequently turned to SEWA for cooperation and assistance.

In 1995, for example, the AMC decided to join with industrialists in a slum networking pilot project to mobilize slum dwellers to improve the physical infrastructure, social organization, and community services in a few slum neighborhoods. In each of these projects, an NGO was invited to help establish the social frameworks. Frequently SEWA served this function. In all cases, SEWA's housing trust provided motivational and financial services for the residents in paying their share of the project costs, about 30 percent of the total. In another public–private cooperative venture, SEWA participated in the city's Green Ahmedabad campaign, planting saplings in small open spaces designated by the city.

Because SEWA's membership was approximately one-third Dalit, one third Muslim, and one third higher-caste Hindu, it became a beacon for caste and communal harmony. In a city frequently beset with communal riots, harmony was critical to the livelihoods, and sometimes to the lives, of SEWA's members.

SEWA was not a conventional NGO, but an MBO, a membership-based organization, a union, responsible to its members. It had been born within the Textile Labour Association in 1972, a kind of granddaughter organization of the Mahatma. It separated from the Textile Labour Association in a rancorous dispute over its outspokenness on behalf of Dalits in Ahmedabad's caste rioting of 1981. The extraordinary vision and organizational capacity of SEWA's cofounder[51] and first general secretary, Elaben Bhatt, attracted to SEWA an illustrious group of organizers and earned for SEWA worldwide influence. Bhatt served as a member of the upper house of India's parliament and later as member of India's planning commission. She helped to found and served as chair of Women's World Banking, a worldwide association of microlenders. She served two terms as a trustee of the Rockefeller Foundation. SEWA's advocacy in the International Labor Organization, Geneva, was critical in formulating legislation on behalf of self-employed informal-sector workers around the world. Sister SEWAs formed in South Africa, Turkey, and Yemen. When visitors came to India, they put visits to SEWA on their itinerary. These visitors included Hillary Clinton of the United States; Mary Robinson, past president of Ireland; James Wolfensohn, president of the World Bank; and a host of development experts and officials from around the world.

Evaluating the impact of SEWA on Ahmedabad requires diverse criteria. SEWA inspired, mobilized, and empowered thousands of working-class women. It enabled them to hold their ground, stand up for their rights, and look policemen in the eye. It led them in a struggle for financial independence, their "second freedom." After political independence, it established a model of caste and communal harmony in this city of caste and communal rioting.

On the other hand, SEWA hardly figured in the overall economic life of the business community. In 1999 the SEWA Bank, SEWA's flagship institution, had a share capital of only Rs. 107 lakhs with a total in savings accounts of Rs 1,187 lakhs.[52] When I asked major business leaders about SEWA's role in the commercial life of the city, they seemed puzzled by the question.

SEWA's work with poor Muslim and Dalit women aroused the displeasure of some powerful vested interests. In 1997, SEWA prepared to celebrate its twenty-fifth birthday with a gala fair in Victoria Garden, opposite its headquarters, adjacent to the Sabarmati River. At the last moment, the evening before the five-day celebration was to begin, after all the elaborate preparations were in place for hosting 5,000 visitors per day, the city government, with a Bharatiya Janata Party majority, ruled that SEWA could not use the park. Negotiations continued late into the night between SEWA leaders, municipal officials, and judges. Finally permission was granted for the celebration to begin on time, in the park, with full festivities. But the last-minute confrontation demonstrated that despite—and perhaps because of—SEWA's prominence and effectiveness, certain civic leaders opposed its activities.

Varied Voices in the Search for Accountability and Professionalization

By the end of the century, Ahmedabad's business class expanded and diversified. Its businessmen were enjoying the new climate of entrepreneurial opportunity. The city was no longer controlled by a small, loosely organized regime. But the legal and civic cultures that were emerging in this new, more open environment encouraged extortion on the part of officials and lawbreaking on the part of citizens. Tax evasion, breaches of prohibition, and flaunting of the laws governing land use were commonplace. The resulting cynicism spilled over into public life in general and into politics in particular. At each election, citizens consistently voted out of office the party they had voted in just a few years earlier.

A single event in mid-2000, not particularly significant in itself, nevertheless gave me a glimpse into the array of public cultures manifest in the city. On Sunday morning, August 6, 2000, leaders of three of the city's prominent NGOs convened a public meeting in Bhaikaka Hall to gain support for a public interest litigation (PIL) suit in the Gujarat high court against local government authorities for failing to adequately prepare for the monsoon rains that had flooded the city on July 13. Ten people in the city had died; property damage was publicly estimated at upward of Rs. 1,000 crores (US$250 million).[53] The goals of the PIL were to establish accountability on the part of government and to recover damages. I attended the public meeting, seeing it as an opportunity to witness one of the most important trends of the most recent decade: the widely shared desire for accountability, transparency, and professionalism in public and private institutions.

In their own defense, the AMC and the regional Ahmedabad Urban Development Authority (AUDA) both asserted that the monsoon rains had been the most severe since 1927 and that no reasonable, cost-effective plan could have been devised to cope with such an unusual, sudden natural disaster. The AMC estimated that the cost of providing a system to defend against such a severe flood would be Rs. 300 crores (US$65 million).[54] In the previous year, the corporation's entire budget for all capital expenses had been only Rs. 81 crores.

The aspiring litigants acknowledged the unusual severity of the rains, but they rejected the official attempts to evade responsibility. They charged that municipal and AUDA authorities had continued for many years to sanction, inappropriately and even illegally, new construction that had destroyed the natural drainage channels and ponds that would have alleviated the flooding.[55] In the oldest areas of the city, by contrast, the drainage was far more effective and the property damage minimal.[56]

Local newspapers in both Gujarati and English supported this accusation. For example, on July 15, the *Times of India,* Ahmedabad edition, ran a front-page article by reporter Robin David under the headline, "Whatever You Do, Don't Blame It on the Rain." Gujarat's largest daily newspaper, the *Gujarat Samachar,* blamed official inaction. An op-ed column of July 17 signed by Devendra Patel and titled "Which Officer or Leader Is Responsible for Crores of Damage?" closed by lamenting the passing of an earlier generation of civic leaders who were widely believed to have been more responsible: "But today we have neither the Sardar [Vallabhbhai Patel] nor the people of his time."

The builders, who had built the new high-rise buildings without concern for the potential ecological consequences, now joined in the criticism of AUDA for having allowed them to get away with it. Meanwhile AUDA, which over the years had sanctioned the builders' requests or had acquiesced in them even when they were illegal, now condemned the builders' practices. More than two decades of hand-in-glove collusion between builders and AUDA seemed to be unraveling in continuing front-page squabbles.

Public and private responses to the proposed PIL suit revealed the difficulty of achieving cooperation in Ahmedabad's civic life. First, people feared retaliation from the government if they joined in the suit. For example, at the outset of the meeting, the president of the Gujarat Chamber of Commerce and Industry, Ratan Prakash Gupta, affirmed his moral and personal support for the PIL, but then he apparently surprised his hosts when he abruptly changed course: "The Chamber of Commerce being a trade body neither has the time nor can it afford to become party to any litigation against government agencies."[57]

A second rationale for not joining in the PIL became clear as another NGO leader exclaimed to me privately, "What cheek! We were invited to participate in the PIL. When our members' slum houses are flooded every year, do *they* care? But now, when they are hit, they want us to join in their litigation! Nothing doing!" Festering class resentment made cooperation impossible.

A third negative response, also expressed privately, suggested that this PIL had less to do with bringing accountability into public affairs than with bringing aggrandizement to its organizers and to their organizations. Again, a lack of trust, a lack of social capital, prompted another potential participant to remain outside the prospective coalition.

A fourth reason for not joining in the PIL: a substantial proportion of the property losses had occurred in illegal, unauthorized constructions. The owners of these properties saw no purpose in claiming damages, nor in joining the PIL.

A fifth reason for not joining the PIL was the understanding that litigation normally drags on for years—and, of course, it might fail. Suing the government is difficult, and proving negligence in the face of natural disaster would be especially difficult.

A sixth reason for not joining the PIL came in the form of a suggestion of an ad hoc alternative strategy. After his earlier declaration that the Chamber of Commerce and Industry would not join in the PIL, Mr. Gupta proposed an immediate ad hoc alternative: low-interest, long-term, soft loans from the government that would allow businessmen and householders to begin rebuilding as quickly as possible. To paraphrase a similar situation reported from Boston, Massachusetts, a century earlier, the businessmen were seeking "help, you understand; none of your law and justice, but help."[58]

The diverse cultures of public life in Ahmedabad confronted one another in the auditorium of Bhaikaka Hall: the desire for accountability, transparency, and professionalism; recognition that this call carried risks of political and economic retaliation from powerful government officials; a lack of trust in cooperation, perhaps mixed with some envy of the organizers; an unwillingness to forge alliances across class lines; an admission that many losses were the result of illegal business practices and therefore not recoverable through legal process; recognition that the inefficiencies of the legal system made appeal through the courts impractical. All of the apprehensions concerning legal action combined to give greater force to an alternative perspective: the request for immediate ad hoc financial relief in the form of soft loans. This ad hoc solution would not lead toward greater accountability or transparency in government operations, but it would yield immediate relief and let people get on with their lives and their businesses. Each of these seven perspectives on public culture intersected one another constantly in Ahmedabad, and each was important in the life of the city. The call to prepare a PIL was just one occasion that allowed them to surface.

A generation ago, social scientists, fixated on the supposed conflict between tradition and modernity, might have speculated on the eventual victory of one or another of these public cultures. They might have predicted the victory of efficiency, transparency, and professionalism.[59] Today, most political scientists seem far more skeptical. They write of the difficulty of building up social capital, mutual trust, and a sense of common obligations. Scholars like Douglass North,[60] James Coleman,[61] and Robert Putnam[62] regard this process as a long historical struggle, with no predetermined, inevitable outcome.

Everyday Ahmedabadis, even without specialized training in the social sciences, would have agreed. They commonly described the widespread cynicism and lack of participation in public affairs with the simple and ubiquitous *maaray shun*. Personal experience taught them the practical obstacles to creating an accepted system of legal, formal, public accountability. Many were skeptical about even trying.

Nevertheless, important sectors of the urban community dedicated themselves to building up social capital, despite the difficulties of the process. They felt the need to rebuild a sense of community in the public life of their city after several decades of urban upheavals had undermined an earlier regime of urban cohesion. They nostalgically recalled that earlier in the century, Ahmedabad had enjoyed a period of social, political, and economic cohesion. No one wished to go back to that control. The pattern was too restrictive for current sensibilities, and in any case, it was no longer a viable alternative. But many of Ahmedabad's citizens did seek some new forms of civic cohesion to meet the challenges of a new era.

No wonder Ahmedabad spoke with so many different voices when it addressed issues of urban governance, economic development, and public culture at the end of the twentieth century. A half century earlier, it had been a city of less than one million people under the control of an economic and political elite still inspired by the ideals of the freedom struggle and the Gandhian ethic. Then for forty years it had been out of control as it multiplied in population and area four times over. New voices on the left encouraged the working classes to assert their rights and take up battle stations against vested interests and institutions. Politicians reconfigured this 1960s call for working-class mobilization into the institutionalized caste and class struggles of the 1980s. Communal violence from 1969 to the end of the century indicated both the fragility of the social contract and the unscrupulousness of politicians in exploiting social cleavages. Culture wars that attempted to validate some voices and silence others, frequently through violence, further inflamed the city's many divisions: ideological, social, caste, communal, and religious. Widespread criminal activity undermined the integrity of elected officials, politicians, police, and businessmen—the entire public order from top to bottom. Public positions that had previously carried respect and prestige now did not. Private citizens, apparently law abiding, as well as organized gangs of criminals evaded taxes and used their influence, and strong-arm tactics, to bend or break the law. An industry that had been the mainstay of the city for almost a century collapsed. Premier families in the city fell on difficult times.

Meanwhile, government programs and finances facilitated new economic opportunity, often for new people. New entrepreneurs opened new enterprises. New opportunities seemed available for the right person at the right time, for the entrepreneur who could seize new opportunities, although many also failed. More entrepreneurial models also appeared in government, as Keshav Verma demonstrated during his term as municipal commissioner. NGOs, too, offered a role for entrepreneurial talent as they nurtured new constituencies and partnered with government at all levels, sharing in new opportunities for funding and program development.

With recent experiences like these, no wonder Ahmedabad at the end of the century pulled in many different directions. Unmoored from its Gandhian heritage, Ahmedabad was now on the front lines, facing the new world of liberalization at home and globalization abroad. As Bimal Patel, one of Ahmedabad's outstanding young architect planners, remarked, "A capitalist city is bound to have some chaotic development. After all there is not one individual or institution taking decisions. Thousands of people are involved in the process: the builders, the businessmen, the architects, the authorities, the common man, a host of others."[63] That diverse, chaotic development was Ahmedabad in 2000.

CHAPTER 12

Godhra, the Gujarat Pogrom, and the Consequences

The real task of tomorrow is the rehabilitation of "hearts and minds," of getting people to live and work together in the same occupations, and to study together in the same schools. We have to organise and join hands in the same organization. That is the India to which we belong. That is our tomorrow.

—Self-Employed Women's Association, Shantipath (2002)

A book on the twentieth century would normally end with the year 2000. But the pogrom of 2002, which left almost 1,000 people dead in Ahmedabad, another 1,000 dead in the rest of Gujarat, and rendered about 140,000 people temporarily homeless, makes that impossible in this case. This pogrom, one of the worst in India since independence, made Ahmedabad once again a shock city for India, in both senses of the word.[1] The events were shocking in themselves, and they vividly represented the communal conflicts that afflicted many parts of India, as well as the degraded social and economic situation of most Muslims in India generally. The pogrom also brought Ahmedabad to world attention. The city's mixed record of rapid physical and economic growth on the one hand, and profound failure to achieve social equity among its diverse inhabitants on the other must have seemed familiar to residents of New York, Paris, Berlin, and numerous other metropolises around the globe, although the complete failure of government to keep the peace among them in 2002 put Ahmedabad in a special category. In many ways, Ahmedabad had become a shock city to the world.

Kulturkampf: Culture Wars and Communal Violence

Communal violence returned to Ahmedabad in the 1990s, although not so severely as in the 1980s or as in other parts of India. The trigger was a 1990 religious procession that traversed large swaths of north India, aiming ultimately to reach and destroy the Babri Masjid, a Muslim mosque in the city of

Ayodhya, and replace it with a Hindu temple. The organizers of the procession, the Sangh Parivar, argued that nearly 500 years earlier, the builders of the mosque had destroyed a temple that marked the birthplace of the Lord Rama. They now intended to restore what they claimed was the original order. They called their movement Rama Janmabhoomi, the campaign for the birthplace of Lord Rama.

The Sangh Parivar, the family association of militant Hindu organizations, succeeded in raising the Rama Janmabhoomi issue to national consciousness. The Sangh included its parent organization, the RSS (Rashtriya Swayamsevak Sangh, National Volunteers Organization), a cultural organization, and its offspring: the Vishwa Hindu Parishad (VHP, World Hindu Assembly), a religious organization; the Bharatiya Janata Party (BJP, Indian People's Party), a political party; the Bajrang Dal, a youth organization; the Akhil Bharatiya Vidyarthi Parishad (ABVP, All India Student Assembly), a university-based student-faculty organization; and a wide variety of others. Through a series of Rath Yatras, religious chariot processions that traveled thousands of miles across north India, the Sangh succeeded in politicizing and inflaming the issue. The largest of the Rath Yatras, launched on September 25, 1990, by L. K. Advani, president of the BJP, was credited with increasing the votes for his party, especially in Gujarat. It also precipitated communal riots that killed 116 people across India, 26 of them in Gujarat. In subsequent violence related to the temple movement, 1,342 people died, 258 in Gujarat.[2]

In Ahmedabad, in support of the 1990 procession, BJP and VHP leaders called for a *bandh,* a general strike, and forcibly shut down Muslim shops that did not acquiesce, leading to violence in the industrial areas of the city. The wealthier residential areas, the home of the city's new cultural and educational institutions, had relatively few Muslim residents; some of them were now attacked. Muslim-owned shops in exclusive shopping areas were burned down. Goods were burned or stolen. A young Muslim pharmacist was killed. Telephone cables worth Rs. 30 million were destroyed, and some railway tracks were damaged. Random stabbings occurred in the city. A second general strike called for October 30 brought violence against property so severe that the army was called in. In the suburban outskirts, upper-caste Hindus and Muslims attacked each other and torched each others' homes. In the industrial areas, Dalits and Muslims shot at each other with handmade guns and hurled homemade acid and petrol bombs. The divisions hardened: "By the end of 1990, residents of most Dalit *chawls* in the industrial areas had erected high walls around them. At places where Muslims lived side by side with Dalits, the dominant sentiment was one of fear and mistrust."[3] The Rath Yatra had begun on September 25; the riots continued until November 6, 1990.

The year 1992 began violently in Ahmedabad. During the annual kite-flying festival of Makar Sankranti, January 14, when hundreds of thousands of Ahmedabadis take to their roofs to fly kites in celebration of the end of winter and the coming of spring, communal riots in the walled city and Bapunagar claimed twelve lives. On July 2, the 115th annual Rath Yatra chariot procession through the walled city, originally meant to signify the unity of the city, saw forty-five dead by nightfall.

The destruction of the mosque in Ayodhya, on December 6, 1992, brought enormous violence across India. The *Times of India* reported on December 8 that twenty-six had already been killed in Ahmedabad. Seven people had been locked in their home in Shahpur and roasted alive, charred beyond recognition. Most of the walled city and the communally mixed working-class areas outside the walls were placed under round-the-clock curfew. On December 9, the BJP called for, and enforced, a statewide *bandh*. By the end of the day, five more were dead in Ahmedabad, forty-six across the state. Even a part of Ellisbridge, on the west side of the river and usually peaceful, was put under curfew. By December 12, the city death toll had reached fifty-six, including a sixty-year-old man and his wife, burned to death in the industrial area of Vatva. Nevertheless, violence was beginning to abate, and the *Times of India* reported "Ahmedabad Peaceful." Curfew relaxation began on December 15, and was lifted entirely in some areas, reduced to nighttime hours in others. Violence continued sporadically through the rest of December and January.

Ahmedabad reinforced its reputation for political violence. Political scientist Ashutosh Varshney reports that for the period 1950 to 1995, "The West Indian state of Gujarat . . . has the highest per capita rate of deaths in communal indicents, at around 117 per million of urban population."[4] The next highest was Bihar, far behind at eighty, with Maharashtra third at forty-five. Within Gujarat, the cities of Ahmedabad and Vadodara accounted for 75 percent of the deaths.[5]

Kulturkampf: Culture Wars for Political Gains

Hindu militancy proved politically rewarding. The BJP's electoral vote for state assembly seats in Gujarat rose steadily, from 15 percent in 1985 to 27 percent in 1990, 43 percent in 1995, and 45 percent in 1998; the number of seats multiplied from 11 in 1985 to 67 in 1990 to 121 in 1995, with a slight falloff to 117 in 1998.[6] The 1995 election gave the BJP sole control of the state government, without the need for alliances with any other parties, which it has continued to hold continuously until today (2010). The BJP and the Sangh Parivar therefore often referred to Gujarat as a laboratory for Hindutva, a state in which they could implement their cultural, religious, and political agendas with the fewest obstacles.

In 1995, the additional director general of police (prisons), V. Kannu Pillai, was awarded a Ph.D. in sociology from Gujarat University. His dissertation, *A Social Study of the Communal Violence in Gujarat,* analyzed police data on the causes of 106 major communal riots in Gujarat state between 1987 and 1991 and concluded "that political rivalry [22.6%] and conflicts during elections [17.9%] account for 40.5% of communal riots in Gujarat. Politics is interwoven with religion in Gujarat as elsewhere. The BJP is a dominant political party with its appeal to Hindus and hatred against Muslims."[7] Pillai also gave a number of public speeches similarly critical of the BJP. His dissertation was withdrawn from the university library when the chief minister, Keshubhai Patel, and the jail minister, Ashok Bhatt, accused Pillai of conspiring with the Pakistan Inter-Services Intelligence to blow up a part of the high-security Sabarmati central jail to facilitate the escape of hard-core terrorists. The charges were fantastical, and in 1998, the central bureau of intelligence completely exonerated Pillai. But freedom of speech and academic expression had been violated. The warning to potential critics was clear.

In 1997, arsonists invaded the Husain-Doshi Gufa (since renamed the Ahmedabad Gufa), an art museum at the campus of the Center for Environmental Planning and Technology, and burned canvases of M. F. Husain, one of India's most senior, respected, and famous painters, and a Muslim. The paintings, representing the goddess Saraswati as bare breasted, had attracted no special criticism at the time they had been first created in 1976. But now, two decades later, they were attacked as disrespectful to the Hindu goddess and to Hindus. The paintings had not changed, but the cultural climate had.[8]

On July 20, 1998, in a separate incident, the Center for Environmental Planning and Technology campus was invaded by about a hundred thugs claiming to be taking revenge for "ragging," or hazing, on campus. The attack was widely attributed to the Bajrang Dal, the youth organization of the Sangh, attempting to stifle the freedom of expression for which the campus was known.[9] Later in the year, fashion parades and beauty contests were forcibly interrupted. In early December, Hindu militants forced the Rupam cinema in central Ahmedabad to stop its screening of the film *Fire,* by Shabana Azmi, one of India's most celebrated and controversial filmmakers and actresses. *Fire* was forced from the screen for its depiction of lesbianism and wife burning, although, as critics of the suppression pointed out, elsewhere in Ahmedabad, "at least eight to ten cinema halls are running pornographic movies violating different provisions of the Indian Cinematographic Act, 1952, with the authorities turning a blind eye towards the violation."[10]

Hired Santa Clauses, displayed as advertising during the Christmas season by owners of some of Ahmedabad's most exclusive shops, were frightened off by Bajrang Dal youth activists. In other parts of Gujarat state, although not in

Ahmedabad, attacks were made on Christian churches. In a review of the year's events, Bharat Desai wrote in the *Times of India,*

> In no other state, with the exception of perhaps Maharashtra, has the "moral police" been so active as in Gujarat. Be it fashion shows, beauty pageants or "disco dandiyas," "Big Brother" is always frowning. The state government and the police seem to be quite helpless in dealing with situations which involve the Vishwa Hindu Parishad–Bajrang Dal combine. . . . The police would like to handle these cases with kid gloves because both the "culture cops" and the "swadeshi brigade" are seen as part of the present [BJP] regime.[11]

The symbolism inherent in names was also contested. In the 1990s, when the BJP held power simultaneously in the Ahmedabad Municipal Corporation and in the state government, it proposed changing the name of the city itself. Ahmedabad was named for the Muslim sultan who had founded the city in 1411. The BJP city and state governments proposed Karnavati instead—the name of a Hindu town that had flourished in the vicinity in the 1200s. The issue mirrored the nationwide militant Rama Janmabhoomi struggle at Ayodhya: both were attempts to characterize the Muslims as invaders who had captured and destroyed an earlier Hindu civilization, and to depict the Sangh Parivar as the restorers of that earlier, pristine, proper culture. Opponents of the change argued that Karnavati had never been a major city, as Ahmedabad had become. The capital of Gujarat before Ahmedabad had been some fifty miles north, at Patan. The central government, under Congress control, rejected the proposed name change. The BJP municipal government, however, continued to print "Karnavati" on its official stationery.

Meanwhile, the local neighborhood *shakhas* (branches) of the RSS continued to multiply. By 1998, the RSS itself had established its presence in about one-fourth of the villages of the state.[12] Its *shakhas* in Ahmedabad increased from 150 in 1998 to 305 in 1999.[13] In July 1999, another Hindu–Muslim riot took place in Ahmedabad; eight persons were killed, mainly Muslims, in twelve days of communal rioting.[14] In January 2000, the RSS organized a *sankalp shibir* (training camp) in Ahmedabad attended by about 26,000 *swayamsevaks.*[15] By August–September 2001, many of the younger leaders had attended weekly camps organized by the Bajrang Dal. There, the main targets of hatred were Muslims, and participants were assured of protection from the police in the coming "war."[16]

The Sangh Parivar was strengthened by support from overseas Indians. Many nonresident Indians (NRIs) made their homes overseas but stayed actively in touch with India and supported Indian institutions. They often sent remittances back to their families in India. Their foreign residence, professional success, and Westernized manners suggested that they preferred overseas opportunities and ways of life, but their persistent visits and contacts suggested the strength of Indian culture in their lives and reinforced the sense of vitality in India's religious traditions.[17]

The Muslim Community and Its Image

The Sangh Parivar sought to mobilize Hindus in part by demonizing Muslims. The soil had been well prepared. Over the years Ahmedabad's religious communities had learned to fear, even hate, one another. Julio Ribeiro, head of the police force that had suppressed the riots and brought peace to Ahmedabad in 1985 and in charge of an investigating committee in 2002, cited this hatred as the most significant obstacle to bringing peace to Ahmedabad:

> There was a widely prevalent perception in the minds of the Hindu upper and middle classes that the revenge that was taken in Ahmedabad was for the good of the city, the state and the country as it would serve as a good lesson to recalcitrant Muslims. They harboured deep misgivings about the Muslim minority, its absolutist religious dogma, its perceived penchant for violence and its belief in a brotherhood that extended beyond the borders of the country and was possibly loyal more to this brotherhood than to the land of their birth. They had succumbed to the propaganda that Muslims were a pampered lot and that it was the Congress which had pampered them because of votebank politics. . . .
>
> What I worry about most is that the communal poison has spread so deep in the hearts and minds of the Hindu middle class that it will have to be extracted by super-human efforts before we can hope to re-establish any semblance of communal unity.[18]

Statements by local and national political leaders testify to the accuracy of Ribeiro's lament. India's prime minister, Atal Bihari Vajpayee, in justifying the pogrom of 2002, charged the Muslim community with spreading terror, threats, and calls for jihad, holy war:

> But these days, militancy in the name of Islam leaves no room for tolerance. It has raised the slogan of Jehad. It is dreaming of recasting the entire world in its mould. . . . Wherever Muslims live, they tend not to live in co-existence with others, not to mingle with others; and instead of propagating their ideas in a peaceful manner, they want to spread their faith by resorting to terror and threats.[19]

The fact that Gujarat shares a border with Pakistan increased the fear that local Muslims were potential allies of India's most feared and hated enemy.

Reports of smuggling of contraband into the state, especially guns and drugs, has become a staple of police and news reports. Whenever an assault takes place by Muslims in Gujarat, the hand of Pakistan is seen either directly or indirectly—and correctly or incorrectly—as further inflaming the climate for violence.

Muslims were seen as transgressing the bounds of both civil and political behavior. The bootlegging, violence, and municipal electoral victories of Abdul Latif in the 1980s further nurtured this image.[20] Continuing illegal activities of some Muslim thugs reinforced it. Consider the following article in the *Times of India,* August 8, 2006:

Gangster Fazlu Lands in Police Net

Several influential businessmen in Gujarat are likely to heave a sigh of relief after hearing [of] the gangster's arrest. Fazlu's name first cropped up in December 1997 when his gang kidnapped an Ahmedabad-based businessman, Gautam Adani, for a huge ransom. . . . In 2000, Fazlu became active in Gujarat after a shootout at C Somabhai tea manufacturers' office at Ellisbridge in September to target Jayant Somabhai reportedly for a ransom of Rs. 50 lakhs. . . . During this time, Nirma chief Karsan Patel [one of Ahmedabad's most prominent businessmen] also figured in the Dubai-based Fazlu's hit list. . . . Fazlu . . . has at least 30 cases of extortion and murder registered at police stations across the country.

Repeatedly, in formal interviews and in general conversations, I heard the remark that until 2002, "we Hindus lived in fear of the Muslims; now they will live in fear of us. We have taught them a lesson." In an interview cited in the *Telegraph,* Hareshbhai Bhatt, vice president of the Bajrang Dal, put it most bluntly:

The Hindu community today is not what it was in 1984. In the years since then, the VHP has given it a spine and the courage to react. There are a whole range of feelings that have come into play, chiefly the perception that we are meek—we send our army to the border but dare not wage war; our people get driven out of the inner-city, but dare not return. After 28 February 2002, those perceptions stand corrected.[21]

As a result of the continuing communal warfare, especially after 1985, Hindus and Muslims no longer lived in the same neighborhoods. Each had withdrawn into its own community ghettos. In many neighborhoods, they referred to the streets that divided the area of one community from the other as borders, and the communities themselves as India and Pakistan. This became standard terminology even in casual conversation, and a walk down one of these streets, immediately confirmed the reality of the border and the terminology.[22] Walls were constructed along many of these border streets, reinforcing the separation.

The Muslim ghetto in the vicinity of the Shah Alam Mosque and Lake Chandola at the southern limit of the city grew into a large Muslim slum ghetto, while the Juhapura area at the western side of the city mushroomed, from the mid-1980s until today, into a Muslim ghetto of some 250,000 people. Ashutosh Varshney has made the point that communities that live and interact together on a day-to-day basis are far less likely to experience violence than those that are separated.[23] Ahmedabad, which in the heyday of its mill industry did have such interactions in residential and work patterns, saw those relationships ripped apart over a generation of rioting, demagoguery, and violence.

My own first visit to Ahmedabad in 1964–66 was to a very different city socially than existed by 2002. In those days, people from various communities had friendships and apparently easy relationships with one another. By 2002, this was not the case. I have discussed this social separation with many friends and colleagues in informal conversations, and with officials in more formal settings. All—from the most devoted advocate of a composite society to the general secretary of the Vishwa Hindu Parishad—have agreed that this perception of the decline in personal relationships across religious lines is accurate.

Even advocates of a multicultural society, however, have suggested that Muslims have contributed to their own isolation by accepting a religious leadership that has rejected social and economic integration into mainstream India.[24] These accusations often seemed to blame the victim, but some voices even within the liberal Muslim community in Ahmedabad agreed with them.[25]

The 2002 Violence: Description and Significance

The assaults began on February 27, 2002, after an attack by Muslims in the town of Godhra, approximately 100 miles to the east, on a train carrying hundreds of *kar sevaks,* Hindu pilgrims, returning from Ayodhya. The pilgrims harassed Muslim kiosk owners on the Godhra station platform, and the Muslims, perhaps believing that one or two Muslim girls had been abducted, responded with their own attack on the train. During the melee, a fire broke out in a train carriage. Fifty-nine passengers were burned to death.[26] First reports blamed it on the Muslim attackers; later investigations suggest it may have been a train-related coincidental accident. The issue is so politicized that probably no interpretation of the evidence will ever be fully accepted.[27]

The Hindu Response

Within about twenty-four hours of the attack in Godhra, Hindus throughout the state, but mostly in its north and central areas, began retaliatory raids on Muslims. The raids appeared to be preplanned: "That it was well planned was obvious from how well-equipped the rioters were with gas cylinders, swords, petrol-bombs, and mobile phones besides voters' lists and sales tax details for identifying the Muslim shops. . . . Obviously the homework for all this had been done much earlier and very systematically."[28]

For the first three days, the bloodiest period, the police, apparently under orders from the state's chief minister, did little to intervene. Sometimes they joined in the attacks. The attacks thus became a pogrom—an assault by one community on another in which the government turns a blind eye or actually supports the attackers.[29] After about eight weeks of violence, the official estimate of the dead throughout the state of Gujarat was announced at 822, but most unofficial estimates placed it closer to 2,000. About half of these casualties occurred in Ahmedabad. Up to 114,000 people, overwhelmingly Muslims, were forced to take shelter in relief camps in Ahmedabad, with tens of thousands more in other parts of the state.

Many different class groups participated in organizing and carrying out the violence,[30] and for the first time, Dalits, ex-untouchables, goaded on by Hindutva partisans, participated in substantial numbers in violence against Muslims. In previous communal riots, the Dalits had usually remained aloof or had defended Muslims in an alliance of the downtrodden.[31]

The Confederation of Indian Industries estimated the economic losses incurred in the first five days of violence at Rs. 2,000 crores, about US$500 million.[32] The homes of 100,000 families and 15,000 business establishments (including 1,100 Muslim-owned restaurants and eating establishments), 3,000 handcarts, and over 5,000 cars, trucks, taxis, and autorickshaws were badly damaged or completely destroyed in an attempt to cripple the Muslim community economically.[33] The *Statesman* newspaper reported on April 4, 2002, that Hindu militants were "circulating leaflets urging Hindus to boycott Muslims economically."[34]

Communal violence brought destruction to some but economic rewards to others. The gangs of arsonists and looters who targeted Muslim-owned shops, restaurants, and businesses, especially in the first days of the violence, took their spoils. The "land-grabbing and blatant looting of whatever little assets people had"[35] could be considered an habitual characteristic of communal rioting in Ahmedabad. This time, however, a new element also appeared: middle-class people drove their cars up to stores and looted them, sometimes even when captured in the act and widely broadcast by television[36]: "A section of Ahmedabad's elite excitedly rushed to the stores, grabbed whatever they could and filled their cars with such goods. They even sent messages on mobile phones informing their friends of the booty."[37]

Gangs of young thugs roamed the streets and issued threats during the violence and for weeks afterward. Their activities reached the international news services when thugs broke up a peace meeting in Ahmedabad's historic Gandhi ashram, on April 7, forcing some of Gujarat's best-known figures, including dancer, actress, and activist Mallika Sarabhai—daughter of Vikram, granddaughter of Ambalal—to flee. Sarabhai, an outspoken critic of Gujarat chief minister Narendra Modi at a time when few dared be so public or so critical, subsequently was confronted by menacing groups threatening her home and her Darpana dance academy. The ashram itself closed its doors to further peacekeeping efforts.

To stifle the press, Hindu militants attacked a car carrying one team of reporters and beat up a reporter from another, also burning his camera; "in some areas of Ahmedabad cable operators were even warned to black out news telecasts."[38] Nevertheless, "the Indian networks covering the violence provided saturation coverage, with gruesome images of the violence beamed round-the-clock."[39]

Militants targeted Muslim students in the schools as well, threatening them physically and attempting to have them expelled. "Headmasters of English medium schools in Ahmedabad are being terrorized so that they throw Muslim pupils out of their institutions. Worried headmasters have called Muslim parents and quietly urged them to remove their wards as they can no longer guarantee their safety. As if to drive the point home, gangs of VHP hoodlums ominously hang around school gates hoping to identify Muslims."[40]

Even the dead were not immune from attack. In efforts to blot out glories of the Muslim legacy in Ahmedabad, tombs of revered saints and scholars were vandalized, destroyed, and paved over, sometimes with state resources. The tomb of the famous seventeenth-century Urdu poet, Shah Wali Gujarati,[41] located just outside the city's main police headquarters, was destroyed on March 2, and a makeshift Hindu temple with a saffron flag was briefly put in its place. On March 3, that temporary shrine was leveled, and by March 5, 2002, the site was paved over, removing it from view and from memory.[42]

Sadism amplified the horror. Kapilaben, a Self-Employed Women's Association (SEWA) organizer from working-class Gomtipur, an area of mixed Hindu and Muslim population, reported,

> What can I tell you? I have seen terrible scenes—everything happened in front of my eyes. I have seen mobs of 4000 to 5000 men stalking the city with guns and swords, burning and looting. I have seen one man's hands cut off, another's stomach ripped open and intestines hanging out. I have also seen the police actively participating in all of this. I have seen the dead and injured lying on the road with no first aid. I have seen death, blood, suffering, fear—I have seen things like never before. I can never forget what I witnessed.[43]

Some reporters and analysts discreetly held back details of the brutality of the attacks on women especially:

> One of the worst-hit areas is Naroda where the entire colony of more than 5,000 inhabitants was repeatedly attacked, subjecting women to unprintable atrocities. Ram Sanjeevan Saroj who was a witness to the attack said about 15,000 people roamed the area from 9 AM till late in the night. The police were conspicuously absent, leaving the locality completely under the control of the armed mob.[44]

A pamphlet issued by the VHP and signed by the general secretary of the state branch of the organization circulated in Gujarat during the riots included the following poem:

> The volcano which was inactive has erupted
> It has burned the arse of the miyas [Muslim men] and made them
> dance nude
> We have untied the penises that were tied till now
> We have widened the tight vaginas of the bibis [Muslim women].[45]

Mobs destroyed the Gulbarg Society neighborhood and thirty-nine persons were burned alive, including the former Congress Party member of parliament, Ehsan Jafri: "Mr Jafri, a prominent personality of the city, kept phoning various authorities, including the Police Commissioner, various politicians he knew, and others, but no police help came. . . . Ehsan Jafri ultimately met with a violent death along with 19 members of his family and 20 others in the Chamanpura colony."[46] Eyewitnesses further reported the gang rapes of many young girls in the neighborhood before their subsequent burning to death.

The violence went on for months, although in less intense and more scattered form. In early May, when incidents of violence spiked, the central government dispatched the former director general of the Punjab police, K. P. S. Gill, to serve as advisor to Chief Minister Modi on bringing the city and state back to normal. Gill encouraged dialogue between Hindus and Muslims. He had many police officers who had been allied with the Hindu mobs transferred out of their positions and replaced by others. Three months later, Gill reported that his work was done: "There is no question of Gujarat plunging into chaos again. I think the job has been done. The new set of police officers who took over their postings in Ahmedabad and elsewhere know how to deal with the situation. They are now a confident lot."[47] Gill also noted that Ahmedabad was the key: "I must tell you that officers in Ahmedabad were transferred because we realised Ahmedabad was the key and if things came under control in this city, the rest of the state would follow. That is why it was necessary to induct new officers in the city police."[48]

The Press, Television, and Civil Society

Investigations into the causes of the violence cited the Gujarati language press as a force instigating and perpetuating the violence. Both *Gujarat Samachar* and *Sandesh,* the most widely circulated Gujarati newspapers, each of which sells nearly a million copies each day across the state, ran false stories of the murder and sexual mutilation of Hindu women by Muslims in Godhra. *Sandesh* later published a retraction, buried in a corner of an inside page, but it was too late. The claims spread of violation of Hindu honor further exaggerated by extreme sexual violence and bestiality.[49] The English-language press was generally more cautious and more restrained.

Most of the leading literary and cultural figures kept silent. Some publicly condoned the violence. K. K. Shastri, a past president of the Gujarat Literary Society and chairman of the VHP, spoke out in appreciation of the violence against Muslims: "It had to be done, it had to be done. We don't like it but we were terribly angry. Lust and anger are blind . . . the rioters were well bred Hindu boys . . . charged because in Godhra women and children were burnt alive. The crowd was spontaneous. All of them were not VHP people . . . They are angry because Hindutva was attacked."[50]

Fear of violent retaliation muted the voices for peace. A few did speak out. Esther David, an Ahmedabad writer and artist, published "The Night is Long, the Swords Unsheathed," a poem that captured some of the shock and horror as mobs of thousands raged through the city and around her own home situated in Guptanagar, one of the borders between Hindu- and Muslim-majority areas:

> Blood flows in our city of sorrow.
> Clogging our lives with shrouds without forms.[51]

Some, but not many, old-line Gandhians spoke out. SEWA, representing approximately 200,000 working women in Ahmedabad and another 300,000 across the state, about a fourth of whom were Muslims, was criticized for its silence. SEWA leaders called it caution: "We thought it wise to keep away from the mass media in such a turbulent, vitiated, and complex atmosphere. . . . In an environment where peace making was impossible—especially in the initial weeks, could we have done more? We chose to work quietly among all affected communities. We saw that our first priority was to heal wounds and keep people together."[52] SEWA also revealed that two pipe bombs had been uncovered on the front doorstep of its headquarters office.

One feminist poet, Saroop Dhruv, did speak out against the violence, writing passionately in defense of Muslim victims, and especially Muslim women. In her book of poems, *Hastakshepa* [Interference], Dhruv, a Hindu, identified with Muslim women who were attacked and violated: "I am not separate or distant from Suraiya, Salma, Fatima, Shahnaz or Amina [specifically Muslim names]. Whenever evil hands strip them of their clothes, I feel someone undressing me. When violent animals touch, open, smell, press, suck, penetrate their body making it bleed, I also feel violated by a thousand communal penises."[53]

The business community was generally silent—not wanting to be on the wrong side of the government[54]—and perhaps tacitly approving of the violence. Despite the large proportion of Jains, for whom *ahimsa* is a fundamental principle, and of Hindu Vaishnavas, for whom it is also an important value, business organizations did not speak out against the violence. In my own unsystematic interviews with business leaders, I repeatedly heard that "it was time to stop living in fear of Muslims," time "to teach Muslims a lesson," although most who spoke with me did not approve of the level of violence that occurred.

Failure of Government: From Riot to Pogrom

The greatest shock of the 2002 violence, however, was the failure of government to quash the violence quickly and firmly. At the highest levels, the government chose not to intervene but rather to inflame the situation. Almost immediately on receiving the news of Godhra, the Gujarat government announced that the Pakistan government had planned the attack as a terrorist operation, but then quickly withdrew that explanation. When the VHP insisted on bringing the bodies of all fifty-nine victims of the Godhra carnage to the Sola civil hospital in Ahmedabad, Chief Minister Modi agreed to their demand even though only twenty-six of the victims were from Ahmedabad—the rest were from Mehsana, Sabarkantha and Anand—and despite fears that this public demonstration would provoke further communal violence.[55]

By the evening of February 27, the VHP called for a statewide *bandh,* for the next day. Historically, at times of such acute tensions, such *bandhs* served as only vaguely disguised calls for rioting and violence. Gordhan Zadaphia, a senior VHP activist and minister of state for home, said, "We will teach a lesson to those who have done this (burning of the bogie) [railway car]. No one will be spared and we will make sure that the forces behind this act will never dare to repeat it."[56] At 8 PM, the BJP released a press note announcing its support of the *bandh.*[57] The chief minister convened the police officials to prepare them for the *bandh. Outlook* newsmagazine described the meeting on the basis of participants' accounts: "By the end of it, the CM ensured that his top officials— especially the police—would stay out of the way of Sangh parivar men. The word was passed on to the mobs."[58]

The BJP government allowed the violence to explode, and in many cases further encouraged it. *The Concerned Citizens Tribunal Report, People's Union for Civil Liberties,* for example, called Godhra the pretext, rather than the cause, of the massacres; the perpetrators had already been mobilized.[59] Rahul Sharma, an officer in the police intelligence bureau, cited "records of mobile phone conversations between top politicians and police officers in the first three days of the violence, which reveal that key riot-accused were in regular touch with the police, politicians and VHP leaders during the time of the massacres."[60] First information reports, the necessary first step in establishing a criminal case, were not filed, were changed, or were lost. High-ranking officers who protested were transferred.[61] Conscientious non-Muslim police officers who actively intervened in the situation and did not allow violence to spread were also transferred from field duties to office work.[62] Reliable official and semiofficial analysts—the National Human Rights Commission, the National Commission on Minorities, Human Rights Watch, and citizen groups' independent inquiries—severely criticized Chief Minister Modi for his actions and inactions. The National Human Rights Commission concluded that there was a "comprehensive failure of the State to protect the Constitutional Rights of the people of Gujarat."[63] The president of India himself, R. K. Narayanan, charged that the violence in Gujarat was a "conspiracy" between the national and state governments. Narayanan further asserted that India's prime minister, Atal Bihari Vajpayee, had ignored his letters pressing for deploying the army in Gujarat with shoot-at-sight orders to control the riots.[64]

Experience in Ahmedabad and Gujarat demonstrated that when the government used its powers forcefully, violence could be contained and sometimes even prevented entirely. Police responded when higher authorities made it clear that they were expected to, and they failed when they did not.[65] Recognizing the role of government in controlling or allowing violence, the people of Ahmedabad regularly speak of violence being "engineered," usually for political purposes.[66]

Elections—The Real Trigger

Why had the violence been so brutal, and why had the government not acted forcefully to stop it? Politics was the key. The 2002 pogrom was not just a reaction to Godhra. It became part of the electoral campaign of the BJP and of its institutional allies, the RSS and the VHP. Despite their overwhelming majority in the Gujarat legislature, the BJP found governing more difficult than getting elected. The voters had brought the BJP back to power with 117 seats of 182 in the state legislature in 1998. By late 2001, however, the BJP was in disarray in Gujarat because of internal factionalism among its leaders and scandals concerning BJP ties to builders whose buildings collapsed during an earthquake in 2001 as a result of shoddy construction. It appeared they would lose their large majority in the next elections, which were to be held no later than March 2003. The party was not doing well nationally, having lost state assembly elections in three northern states. It was also doing poorly within Gujarat.[67] Seeking to recapture its earlier electoral successes, the RSS national leadership chose Narendra Modi to replace Keshubhai Patel as chief minister in August 2001.[68]

Narendra Modi's adult lifetime had been spent primarily as a *pracharak*, an organizational worker, of the RSS. Born in 1950, Modi was running a canteen on contract in the Gujarat Road transport office in Ahmedabad in 1968 when he was recruited to the RSS. He earned an M.A. in political science from Gujarat University. As a leader in the Akhil Bharatiya Vidyarthi Parishad, the RSS student organization, he participated in the Nav Nirman (Reconstruction) political agitation that overthrew the state's government, 1974–75. In 1986, he was drafted into the Gujarat BJP as organization secretary and became general secretary beginning 1988–89. Modi effectively piloted the BJP's electoral campaigns in Gujarat between 1986 and 1995, the period in which the BJP first won control of the state government. L. K. Advani recruited Modi as an organizer of his 1990 Rath Yatra. In a Hindu militant party dominated by upper castes, Modi was a member of a "backward" caste.

Modi was sent to Delhi in 1995 to serve as general secretary of the BJP for three northern states. In 1998, he became national general secretary of the party. On October 3, 2001, Modi was appointed chief minister of Gujarat state. Up to this point, he had no experience in governance, but party leaders believed that the current chief minister, Keshubhai Patel, would not be able to win the next election, and the RSS and Advani believed that Modi could.[69]

Four pieces of evidence suggest that Modi, as chief minister, accepted the concept of pogroms for their electoral value. First was his very appointment as chief minister. Modi's background was not in running a government but in running election campaigns, including the use of incitement to violence as a means of attracting votes. Second, almost immediately after the worst of the pogrom, and while violence continued, the BJP began to call for early elections in the belief that the violence would increase their electability. The election commission of India dispatched an investigative team, however, and concluded that Gujarat was not yet ready for fair and free elections.[70] The commission finally set the election for December 12.[71]

The tenor of the election campaign itself gave a third indication that the post-Godhra violence was orchestrated to win the coming election. Modi was already giving speeches throughout the state in mid-July. In September, he began a Gaurav Yatra, a procession of pride, crisscrossing the state, reasserting the good name of Gujarat and Gujaratis who, he claimed, had been wrongfully vilified in the international press.[72] Sometimes he spoke of economic and social development—for example, bringing Narmada River water to Gujarat, and getting girls from the most backward villages into schools. Mostly, however, he represented himself as Gujarat's bulwark against Muslim violence and terror, both from within India and from across the Pakistan border. That message stirred the crowds to adulation. As the state election campaign moved into its final stage, *India Today International,* India's most popular overseas weekly, featured Modi on its cover, with the caption, "Riding the Hate Wave."

On election day, December 12, 2002, the BJP scored a smashing victory, taking 126 seats in the state legislature, with 51 percent of the vote, to 51 seats for the Congress, with 38 percent. The party's most lopsided victories were in the regions where the assaults had been most severe: the central and northern parts of the state, and its eastern regions with substantial proportions of Adivasis. As *India Today International* reported, "The BJP bagged 79 of the 102 seats in the 13 riot affected districts in central, north, and south Gujarat."[73] Maya Kodnani, accused (and later found guilty) of inciting riots in labor neighborhoods of Ahmedabad in March, won her seat in just those areas with 75 percent of the vote.[74] In areas where violence had been less, the BJP did less well. In Saurashtra, the deposed Keshubhai Patel's base, the Congress gained fourteen seats over 1998, the BJP lost thirteen; in South Gujarat, the Congress gained four, the BJP lost four; in the north, the Congress gained three, the BJP lost two. The BJP's triumph came in the central region, where it gained thirty-eight seats while the Congress lost twenty-three. Communal violence proved to be the ticket to political victory. On January 6, 2003, *India Today* designated Modi newsmaker of the year for 2002. Once again, they put his picture on their cover, with a caption reading, "Narendra Modi: MASTER DIVIDER."

The fourth and most striking evidence that the violence early in 2002 was a government-sanctioned pogrom rather than a simple, spontaneous outbreak of violence came in late 2002, when the government of Gujarat demonstrated that when it chose, it could exercise restraint in the face of communal provocation. On September 24, 2002, just seven months after the Godhra incident, two masked murderers leapt over the wall into the precincts of the Akshardham temple in Gandhinagar, "spraying bullets indiscriminately"[75] and tossing grenades. They murdered one swami and four volunteers of the temple, two state policemen, one member of India's elite national security guard, and twenty-three visitors to the site before they themselves were killed.

The Akshardham attack could be considered even more heinous and provocative than Godhra: dozens of innocent people were killed in a premeditated attack on one of Gujarat's most prominent and elegant Hindu temples in the heart of the state capital, adjacent to some of its most important offices and residences, by two Muslims, later identified as Pakistanis. The government's response, however, was entirely different from Godhra, and as a result, there was no public reaction in reply to the action. Deputy prime minister L. K. Advani, whose constituency was Gandhinagar, arrived on the scene on the evening of the attack. Prime minister Vajpayee arrived the next day. *India Today* reported that they warned Modi "that a repeat of the post-Godhra violence would be disastrous. Aside from being a severe embarrassment, it would have had an impact on the Supreme Court case on the Election Commission's decision to delay the Gujarat assembly elections. [Also] the chief minister [himself] did not want an interruption in his perceived smooth ride to the elections."[76] Further, "district police chiefs were activated within an hour. As soon as the VHP announced its *bandh,* the army was alerted. The corpses of the victims were not assembled together in procession, as they had been after Godhra."[77]

Even before the Akshardham attack, several Hindu and Jain priests had already called on the BJP government to exercise greater restraint.[78] Now, the leadership of the Akshardham temple itself called for peace. Modi was not asked to speak at the memorial ceremony for the dead, attended by about 15,000 mourners.[79] At that service, Pramukh Swami, the head of the temple and its Swaminarayan sect, declared, "All religions are good. Everyone must have a sphere to observe his religion."[80] (Vajpayee, on the contrary, issued a vengeful message: "This is a question related to the unity and security of the country. This attack will never be forgotten. The blood may dry, but the impressions will remain forever."[81])

The BJP, in anticipation of reelection, wished to demonstrate that it could properly maintain law and order, and it succeeded. No wonder most Ahmedabadis believe that communal violence is engineered. It could be provoked, and it could be suppressed. Government policy was the key.

Paying the Price for Violent Hindutva
A Fractured Social Geography

For at least two decades, from the Hindu–Muslim violence of 1985 until 2002, Ahmedabad's social geography had continued to fracture. Hindus perceived danger in living in Muslim-majority areas, and, far more typically, Muslims felt even more endangered in Hindu-majority neighborhoods. Waves of migration followed each outbreak of violence as Hindus and Muslims sought the safety of their own homogeneous ghettos. Some constructed walls around these ghettos. Inside the old city, residents of many *pols* repaired old gates, which could close off each *pol* from the rest of the city, to ensure that they were functioning properly, and in some cases, they replaced older wooden gates with new iron ones.[82] As the Sangh Parivar became increasingly effective at winning over Dalit support in attacking Muslims, barriers were often erected separating contiguous Dalit and Muslim neighborhoods. In more extreme cases, Muslims and Dalits migrated to segregate themselves from one another.[83]

The year 2002 intensified the segregation. Even the administration of relief camps, which housed more than 100,000 people in Ahmedabad alone during the 2002 pogrom, reflected and magnified the intense social divisions. In the immediate aftermath of violence, Muslims from the affected areas were shifted straight to relief camps:

> These camps came up overnight. Durgahs [shrines], school compounds, large open grounds in larger Muslims areas and burial grounds became camp sites within the city of Ahmedabad. They were constructed, and largely administered, without support from the government. They were set up mostly by men, who had prior experience with running camps in the past and also individuals who had some sort of an informal control or standing within the area. In most cases, the local Goondas [strongmen, criminals; cf. Latif in the 1980s] of the area set up these relief camps. Two of the biggest camps in the city were run by the Goondas of that area. I was told "decent people don't come out to help. . . . . . they are busy in building more gates for their houses. . . . we need these Dadas [bosses]. Even if they are not very nice people, they stand by us."[84]

The government closure of relief camps as the violence died down left the displaced Muslims with very few options. They would either have to go back to their original place of residence—where they were often not welcome—or relocate into the larger Muslim ghettos within the city. Pravin Togadia, the general secretary of the VHP, rejoiced in this uprooting of Muslims from their homes: "In Gujarat, for the first time there has been a Hindu awakening and Muslims have been turned into refugees. This is a welcome sign and Gujarat has shown the way to the country."[85]

Kulturkampf: The Battle for the Culture of Gujarat Continued

The violence and the cultural struggles in Ahmedabad claimed the attention of the nation and were reported and discussed widely in the media. Bollywood also paid attention. The film *Dev* (2004), directed by Govid Nihalani, based on a screenplay by Meenakshi Sharma and starring Amitabh Bachchan and Om Puri, was based on many riots, but the allusion to Ahmedabad 2002 resonated clearly. In the film, a state chief minister orders his police force to allow attacks against the Muslim population under his jurisdiction. Om Puri plays the police official who acquiesces in the wishes of the chief minister and carries out his demands. Bachchan, India's most honored film idol, plays his antagonist, a police official who rebels against the illegal orders, at the price not only of his office but also of his life.

In Ahmedabad itself, the violence of the pogrom silenced much opposition, but not all. Especially after the worst was over, more voices spoke out. Prashant (a center for human rights, justice, and peace) and the Indian Social Action Forum organized a poetry recital in Ahmedabad in June 2002. Poets from different communities from Gujarat and other parts of the country recited poems of anger and pain over the violence and opposition to communal propaganda.[86] We have noted above the even earlier contributions of Saroop Dhruv and Esther David.

In 2003, a new Gujarati play by Saumya Joshi, *Dost! Chokkas Ahi Nagar Vastun Hatun* [My Friend, Surely There Was a City Here][87] opened and played about fifty-six times across India, including major performances in Mumbai and Delhi. Forty-three of the performances were in Gujarat, about thirty-five in Ahmedabad. The play imagined two anthropologists in 4003 uncovering the remains of a destroyed city on the site of Ahmedabad. As they excavate, the ruins tell them of the communalism and class warfare in the dead city: The destroyed Nehru Bridge, for example, answered the archaeologists' queries: "Were there two kinds of human beings in those days?" one of the archaeologists asks. The response: "There weren't two kinds of people. There just were two communities. And this abstract, invisible, meaningless difference triumphed over all the similarities. This difference was the main cause of the city's burial." They envision a politician who instigated the killings between communities distributing daggers among his followers: "People will suddenly swell with the pride of belonging to a community. They will have a new adversary now, not hunger, not thirst, not illness. The new enemy will be every person of the other community."

International Repercussions

In March 2005, the United States government refused to issue a visa to Gujarat chief minister Narendra Modi in light of his failure to protect the minority citizens of his state. Modi was scheduled to come to the United States to address the Asian American Hotel Owners Association on March 24–26, 2005, in Florida. In addition, Sangh members in the United States formed the Association of Indian Americans of North America and invited Modi to speak in New York City on March 20. He was to come on a diplomatic visa. In opposition to this visit, a coalition against genocide formed in the United States, with thirty-eight organizations and ten supporting groups and individuals, to "demand accountability and justice in response to the Gujarat genocide":

On March 18, Modi was denied a diplomatic visa . . . by the U.S. Embassy in New Delhi, as this was not a diplomatic visit, and his tourist and business visa was revoked . . ."as an official responsible for carrying out severe violations of religious freedom," under Section 3 of the IRF [International Religious Freedom] Act of 1998."[88]

Modi then canceled a three-day trip to England from March 25 to 27. He was advised by the home ministry that there were concerns about his security. Civil rights campaigners were preparing to picket him, and there was a movement to serve him with an arrest warrant. The British foreign office made it clear that it would have no contact with Modi; nor would it provide official security. Three British citizens had been killed in the violence of 2002.[89]

Quests for Revenge and for Justice: Terrorism and the Courts

As a few years passed quietly after Godhra and the pogrom, many in Ahmedabad hoped, and even assumed, that the passage of time would bring forgetting and forgiving. But there was no closure. On July 11, 2006, bombs were detonated almost simultaneously in the first-class train compartments of seven different commuter trains in Mumbai; "a large number of people killed and injured were Gujaratis. At least seven people, mostly diamond traders, were killed in the explosions, while another eight diamond traders were reported missing." The *Times of India* seemed to have little doubt that these explosions— and some other smaller ones previously—were revenge for 2002.[90] The *Times* added a headline story a few weeks later, adding to the siege mentality: "Saudi NRIs [nonresident Indians] funded 7/11 to Avenge Gujarat Riots."[91]

In Ahmedabad itself, on July 26, 2008, nineteen bombs exploded within an hour and ten minutes of each other, killing 55 and injuring about 150.[92] The most deadly, and most repulsive, of the explosions occurred inside the civil hospital. Set to go off last, at about the time the injured from earlier bombs arrived at the hospital, it killed at least thirty-one. In Surat, 150 miles to the south, about twenty-seven bombs were also found, beginning the next day. As a result of faulty triggering mechanisms and the work of police in defusing the bombs, none exploded.[93] Clearly, however, the second largest city in the state was also vulnerable.

A few minutes before the first of the explosions, a group calling itself the Indian Mujahideen sent an e-mail to Ahmedabad media claiming responsibility. It opened with the words, "The Rise of Jehad—Revenge of Gujarat."[94] For six years, since 2002, the chief minister, Narendra Modi, had repeatedly declared that Gujarat remained free of terrorist attacks because of his protection. His words now came back to haunt him.[95] Modi himself was generally cautious in his responses to the bombs: granting payments to the families of the dead, offering rewards for information on the murderers, and dispatching army flag marches into communally sensitive areas of Ahmedabad to keep the peace. In the face of these new terrorist attacks, Ahmedabad and Gujarat would need time to formulate their responses.

While some sought revenge in the streets, Zakia Jafri sought justice through the courts. From the time her husband was murdered in the communal attack on the Gulbarg Society, along with sixty-seven others, she sought to show that the government had been complicit in allowing the attack to occur. Finally, in 2009, the supreme court of India appointed a Special Investigation Team (SIT) to look into accusations that Chief Minister Modi had instructed his police force not to assist Jafri and the others, despite numerous phone calls to him as the mobs gathered outside his home and even as they began their attack. In the course of their investigation, the SIT called Modi to an interrogation, on March 27, 2010, that went on in two shifts for nine hours. At this writing, in mid-2010, the results are not in, but however the investigation turns out, *Frontline Magazine* reported, Modi was "the first Chief Minister in the country to have been questioned on a criminal complaint."[96]

It seemed unlikely, however, that the turmoil continuing to spill over from the violence of 2002 would derail Ahmedabad from its growth, geographically and economically: A 146-kilometer ring road, named for Sardar Patel, was built in just a year and a half, connecting 300 villages to each other and to Ahmedabad. Shepherded along by the chairman of the Ahmedabad Urban Development Authority (AUDA), Surendra Patel, it proceeded with the cooperation of all groups affected by it and without legal dispute. Simultaneously, the state government expanded the political boundaries of the city to the new outer ring road, increasing the geographical area of the city by more than 100 percent, raising the population of the Ahmedabad Municipal Corporation from about 3.5 million to about 4.4 million, and establishing a framework for systematic city planning for the future.[97]

Some waters of the Narmada River, channeled for irrigation projects in Gujarat, were diverted to the Sabarmati River bed in 2004, turning what had been a monsoon-driven river into a year-round body of water. Then the Sabarmati Riverfront Development Corporation began the restructuring of an eleven-kilometer stretch along both sides of the river from the Narmada canal in the north to the Vasna barrage in the south. The project would provide a public walkway, amenities for recreation, and private land development that would pay for the project and enhance Ahmedabad's commercial life. The project, formulated by local architect and urban planner Bimal Patel, attracted national attention.[98]

National programs helped the city to expand. Ahmedabad was declared a megacity in the Indian national budget of 2005–6, making it eligible for increased financial support from the central government. Even more funds became available the next year through the national government's Jawaharlal Nehru National Urban Renewal Mission of the Ministries of Urban Development and Housing and Urban Poverty Alleviation.[99]

City business leaders also looked forward to the benefits of new special economic zones (SEZs), parcels of land cleared and set aside for industrial development and offering a ten-year income-tax holiday. The SEZ concept, introduced throughout India by the central government, was highly controversial. The terms were so friendly to industrialists that many critics called it an only lightly disguised land grab. In one year, 2005–2006, the state of Gujarat sanctioned 150 SEZ projects, six of them in and around Ahmedabad, with two more awaiting clearance and three more applications expected. These included SEZs dedicated to the production of pharmaceuticals, engineering industries, ready-made clothing, and electronics.[100]

Gujarat chief minister Narendra Modi was promoting "Brand Ahmedabad," a marketing program to encourage investment from within India and abroad "in an attempt to reinvent, rediscover and repackage the 600-year-old city."[101] Modi enlisted some of the city's most prominent business leaders to carry the banner of the city and state as international ambassadors. On the fifth anniversary of Godhra, in 2007, Pankaj Patel, head of Zydus-Cadila and president of the Gujarat Chamber of Commerce and Industry, asserted that "Gujarat today is about good governance, pro-active bureaucracy, solid infrastructure."[102] Businesspeople from across India increased their investments. In 2009, Tata Motors moved the production of its new small Nano automobile to Sanand, virtually an industrial suburb of Ahmedabad. Azim Premji, head of Wipro, one of India's leading information technology companies, and a Muslim, who had hesitated to deal with Gujarat in the wake of the 2002 pogrom, returned to the state in 2009 to talk business in a well-publicized session with chief minister Modi.[103]

So by mid-2010, at the time of this writing, Ahmedabad continues as a shock city for India in two quite different dimensions. Its economic and physical development is among the most impressive in India, but its levels of communal violence and segregation are among the most extreme. Two of the most fundamental transformations of turn-of-the-twenty-first-century India— economic liberalization and political Hindutva—manifested themselves here most clearly and dramatically.

Historically, in less democratic and populist times, Ahmedabad had produced important leaders—Mahatma Gandhi, Sardar Vallabhbhai Patel, Anasuyaben Sarabhai, Ambalal Sarabhai, Kasturbhai Lalbhai, and Indulal Yagnik—who had grappled as best they could with the challenges of their day. In an era of intense politicization, it remained to be seen whether any leader or group of leaders could at once promote growth, heal social and economic divisions, and win the votes necessary to govern.

Ahmedabad's experience of rapid economic growth, in a sprawling city, with many centers and subcenters, with great wealth concentrated in the hands of a few, moderate growth spread more widely, and only minimal economic progress at the bottom, accompanied by the suppression and exclusion of important minorities, resonated with that of many cities in an age of globalization. For example, American central cities had their festering minority slums and growing gaps between rich and poor; European cities, notably Paris and Berlin, had their immigrant neighborhoods with their youth in revolt against government policies of exclusion; Xianjiang and Tibet in China had their cities, such as Kashgar and Lhasa, where indigenous peoples, Uighurs and Tibetans, were suppressed, while newly immigrant ethnic Chinese were imported by the national government in order to alter the demography and power structure of the city.

Each of these cities was unique, and yet together they shared important similarities: high rates of economic growth that benefited the elites, minimal trickle-down effects reaching the working classes and the poor, urban sprawl that challenged the concept of urban centralization, and political policies that excluded minorities.[104] Indeed, the Los Angeles school of urbanists, studying new patterns of emerging urbanization, cited this array of characteristics as the defining pattern of the contemporary city.[105] Ahmedabad's experiences around the turn of the twenty-first century fit this pattern. Despite its four and a half million people and its prominence in India, Ahmedabad's name was not immediately recognized around the world. But for those who observed it carefully, Ahmedabad had become a shock city not only for India but for the world.

GLOSSARY

Adivasi: Literally, aboriginal peoples. People usually living in remote areas, usually not part of mainstream Hinduism, widely believed to have inhabited India before the arrival of Aryan/Hindu settlers. Often referred to as tribals.

Ahimsa: Nonviolence.

Akhada: Gymnasium, usually where traditional Indian sports and exercises are practiced.

Backward: So-called backward groups, frequently referred to as other backward castes or other backward classes (OBC). People historically low in the Hindu hierarchy, and now often eligible for government assistance.

Bandh: A shutdown of public life and business as a sign of protest against some offense, often against the government. A general strike.

Bhangi: The caste of sweepers, or a member of that caste. The lowest of the untouchable castes.

Brown sugar: Heroin.

Chawl or *chalis:* neighborhoods of single-story, one- or two-room walk-through row homes, usually built of brick, usually without running water or toilet facilities, usually for working-class people.

Charkha: Spinning wheel. Gandhi made it a symbol of the nationalist movement. Gandhians were expected to spin and weave their own cloth.

Crore: 10,000,000. Often used as shorthand for a crore of rupees.

Dalit: Literally, oppressed. Currently the most commonly used term to denote the group that were formerly called untouchables. A term indicating protest against existing oppressive conditions.

Dargah or durgah: A Muslim mausoleum, burial place of a person considered holy.

Gaddi: A padded mat or cushion serving as a seat, sometimes symbolizing a position of power.

Garba: Traditional folk dances of Gujarat, usually including the folk songs to which they are performed.

Gherao: To surround and detain someone, often in his office. A method of coercing a political official.

Goonda: Hoodlum, ruffian,

Harijan: Literally, person or people of God. Gandhi's preferred term for people who had been called untouchable. Ultimately the term was viewed as patronizing, and *Dalit* came to be used instead.

Hartal: A shutdown of business, usually in opposition to a government program. A general strike in which businesses close down.

Hindutva: A political/religious philosophy and action program calling for politics to be strongly influenced by Hinduism and for Indian public life to be increasingly Hindu, and often exhibiting antipathy toward other religions, especially Islam and Christianity.

Holi: A Hindu holiday commemorating the burning of a demon in a bonfire, from which a hero emerged untouched; by extension, any bonfire.

Jallianwala Bagh: Literally, the public garden in Amritsar, Punjab, where British troops massacred hundreds of unarmed Indians protesting against harsh colonial laws in 1919. Figuratively, any example of violent colonial oppression.

Kar Sevak: Hindu pilgrim, especially a pilgrim to Ayodhaya.

Khadi: Hand-spun, hand-woven cloth. Popularized by Gandhi as a sign of nationalism and identification with the poor.

KHAM strategy: An organizational and electoral strategy advanced by Madhavsinh Solanki to bring together lower-caste, lower-class, and minority citizens into political power: Kshatriyas (warriors), Harijans (ex-untouchables), Adivasis (tribals), and Muslims.

Khilafat: A movement in the Islamic world protesting the British dismissal of the Khalif, or titular spiritual leader of the Islamic world, after World War I. Gandhi convinced the Indian National Congress to join in support of this protest movement.

Kulturkampf: From the German, struggle over cultural policies; culture wars.

Kshatriya: The group of castes associated with rule, with military fighting, and with control of land; and members of those castes. In recent times, mostly considered middle to low castes.

Kuchha: Literally, built of impermanent materials, like a house built of mud. Figuratively, anything of inferior, impermanent quality.

Lakh: 100,000. Often used as shorthand for a lakh of rupees.

Lal Vavta: Literally, Red Flag. The symbol of a left-wing or communist labor union.

Lathi: Police club, nightstick.

Leadership Regime: A term used by some political scientists to indicate the small group of people who actually run the politics of a region or institution.

Mahant: Temple supervisor.

Majoor: A worker; a laborer.

Maaray shun?: What is it to me? What do I care? A slang phrase in Gujarati expressing indifference.

Mohalla: The basic neighborhood unit in central cities in northern India. Compares with the *pol* in Ahmedabad.

Mukkadam: A mill employee with supervisory responsibilities, sometimes for hiring and firing personnel.

Nagarsheth: Combination of *nagar,* "city," and *sheth,* "businessman," to indicate the leading businessman of a city—the one who publicly represents the business interests of the city and who sometimes represents the collective interests of the entire city.

Nav Nirman: New Construction, New Creation, Reconstruction—a movement in 1974–75 to cleanse Gujarati politics of corruption and excessive self-interest on the part of politicians.

Other Backward Classes/Castes (OBC): A designation covering people of lower castes or classes but above the ex-untouchables, usually classified in order to qualify for government assistance.

Octroi: Term from the French indicating an import tax, or tariff, levied on goods coming into a city. Until very recently, a major source of revenue, especially in Ahmedabad.

Parivartan: Transformation; radical, fundamental change.

Patidar: Another term for Patel, a person who owns village land, who has a *patta,* or deed, showing ownership. Sometimes a village headman with legal responsibilities for representing the village.

Pol: A narrow, twisty residential street, in the central area of a city, historically occupied by a single caste or religious group, giving it a strong degree of solidarity. Usually gated. The basic residential form in the historic walled city of Ahmedabad.

Pracharak: Political organizer, especially for the Bharatiya Janata political party.

Rakhi: A decorative bracelet made of thread that a sister ties around her brother's wrist on the holiday of *raksha bandhan,* invoking his duty to protect her.

Rath yatra: A religious chariot procession.

Reservations: Set-asides for former-untouchables, Adivasis (tribals), or other low-caste or low-class groups, reserving for them a percentage of places in elected government, in government offices, and in educational institutions.

Sadhu: A Hindu holy man or saint.

Satyagraha: Literally, firmness in the truth. Gandhi's term for his form of nonviolent civil resistance.

Savkar, Saukar, Sahukar: A moneylender.

Scheduled caste/tribe: An administrative, neutral term to designate the people who had been called untouchables (and Harijans and Dalits) and tribals (and Adivasis). Refers to the schedule, or list, drawn up by the government to designate groups which receive affirmative action treatment.

Shakha: Branch of an organization (or of a tree).

Sheth, shethia: A businessman. Sometimes used for a prosperous businessman as a kind of title, like "doctor," "esquire," or "professor."

Slum networking: A twofold strategy for improving the lives of people living in slums: first, to bring together a wide variety of social and technical services to assist them; and second, to link many slums together to work for their mutual benefit.

Swadeshi: Literally, of one's own country. A commitment or movement to use only goods produced within one's own country.

Vaishnava: A sect within Hinduism, devoted more to Lord Vishnu than to other gods, with a disproportionate number of businesspeople among its followers.

Vania: In Gujarati, a businessperson by caste, or those castes composed of businesspeople. In Hindi, Bania.

Vote bank: A block of votes that a subordinate politician claims to be able to deliver to his patron in exchange for some favor, either personal or for the voters.

NOTES

Introduction

1. Asa Briggs, *Victorian Cities* (London: Odhams Press, 1963; reprint, Berkeley: University of California Press, 1993), 56.

2. Cited in Stephen Hay, ed., *Sources of Indian Tradition*, 2nd ed. (New York: Columbia University Press, 1988), 351.

3. Richard Sennett, ed., *Classic Essays on the Culture of Cities* (New York: Appleton-Century-Crofts, 1969), presents a selection.

4. Robert E. Park, Ernest W. Burgess, and Morris Janowitz, *The City: Suggestions for Investigation of Human Behavior in the Urban Environment* (Chicago: University of Chicago Press, 1984).

5. Edward Soja and Allen J. Scott, eds., *The City: Los Angeles and Urban Theory at the End of the Twentieth Century* (Berkeley: University of California Press, 1996).

6. Sam Bass Warner, *The Private City: Philadelphia in Three Periods of Its Growth* (Philadelphia: University of Pennsylvania Press, 1968).

7. Floyd Hunter, *Community Power Structure: A Study of Decision Makers* (Chapel Hill: University of North Carolina Press, 1953).

8. United Nations Habitat Report, *The Challenge of Slums: Global Report on Human Settlements, 2003* (Sterling, Va.: Earthscan Publications, 2003).

9. Clarence Stone, *Regime Politics: Governing Atlanta, 1946–1988* (Lawrence: University Press of Kansas, 1989).

10. K. Mossberger and G. Stoker, "The Evolution of Urban Regime Theory: The Challenge of Conceptualization," *Urban Affairs Review* 36 (2001): 810–35.

PART I. The Gandhian Era, 1915–1950

1. For Gandhi's institution building, see especially Judith M. Brown, *Gandhi's Rise to Power: Indian Politics, 1915–1922* (Cambridge: Cambridge University Press, 1972), and Judith M. Brown, *Gandhi and Civil Disobedience: The Mahatma in Indian Politics, 1928–34* (Cambridge: Cambridge University Press, 1977).

CHAPTER 1. Gandhi Chooses Ahmedabad

1. Mohandas Karamchand Gandhi, *An Autobiography, or The Story of My Experiments with Truth,* trans. Mahadev Desai (Ahmedabad: Navajivan Publishing House, 1927), 5.

2. Mohandas Karamchand Gandhi, *Collected Works of Mahatma Gandhi* (New Delhi: Government of India. Publications Division. Ministry of Education and Broadcasting, 1969), 23:117

3. Gandhi, *Autobiography,* 363.

4. Ibid., 364.

5. Ibid., 450.

6. Ibid., 452.

7. Ibid., 93.

8. Ibid., 87–95.

9. Ibid., 343–44.

10. Fortunately, in addition to official, formal governmental documentation, several studies of Ahmedabad in this period provide summary pictures of the growing city. These include Kenneth Gillion's *Ahmedabad* (Berkeley: University of California Press, 1968), Ratnamanirao Bhimrao Jhote's *Gujaratnun Patnagar Ahmedabad* [Gujarat's Capital City, Ahmedabad] (Ahmedabad: Gujarat Sahitya Sabha, 1929), several biographies of major figures in the city, journalistic writings on the contemporary mill industry, and a number of analytic articles, including those by Makrand Mehta, "Gandhi and Ahmedabad, 1915–20," *Economic and Political Weekly,* January 22, 2005, 291–99, and by Howard Spodek, "The 'Manchesterization' of Ahmedabad," *Economic Weekly,* March 13, 1965, 483–90. Dwijendra Tripathi's *Dynamics of a Tradition: Kasturbhai Lalbhai and His Entrepreneurship* (Delhi: Manohar, 1981), illuminates the city's business history through the work of a single entrepreneur. Devavrat Nanubhai Pathak and Pravin Natvarlal Sheth's *Sardar Vallabhbhai Patel: From Civic to National Leadership* (Ahmedabad: Navajivan Press, 1980) similarly examines politics through a single political professional. Makrand J. Mehta, *The Ahmedabad Cotton Textile Industry: Genesis and Growth* (Ahmedabad: New Order Book Co., 1982), gives an overview of the city's early textile industry. A 1990 dissertation by Kunjalata Shah at SNDT University in Bombay, "Ahmedabad: Pre-Industrial to Industrial Urban Centre (1859–1930)," and another by Siddharth Raychaudhuri at Cambridge University in England, in 1997, "Indian Elites, Urban Space, and the Restructuring of Ahmedabad City, 1890–1947," provide academic analyses, while Indulal Yagnik's *Autobiography,* trans. Devavrat Pathak, Howard Spodek, and John Wood (New Delhi: Manohar Books, forthcoming), especially volumes 1 and 2, give an insider's personal, thoughtful, engaged perspective.

11. Indulal, *Autobiography,* vol. 2, chap. 3.

12. Shah, "Ahmedabad," 491.

13. Ibid., 500.

14. India, Tariff Board, *Report of the Indian Tariff Board (Cotton Textile Industry Enquiry), 1927* (Bombay, 1927), 1:86–87.

15. Jains are not usually considered as Hindus by religion, but within the social structure, they are thought of as Vanias, and intermarriage between Jains and Vaishnavite Vanias is sanctioned and frequent.

16. E. W. Hopkins, "Ancient and Modern Hindu Guilds," in *India: Old and New* (New York: Scribners, 1901), 176.

17. After 1892, the Indian Councils Act provided one representative in the Bombay legislative assembly for the Ahmedabad Millowners Association, and later the AMA was allocated one representative in the central legislative assembly.

18. Gillion, *Ahmedabad,* 21.

19. Spodek, "Manchesterization," 485.

20. Spodek, "Manchesterization," 487. Bengal was also the center of bomb attacks on British officials in the early years of the century. In Ahmedabad, this was uncommon, but on November 13, 1909, two bombs were thrown at the carriage of Lord Minto, the viceroy of India, and his wife. Neither bomb exploded. A third bomb also exploded a little distance away, as the viceroy's carriage moved through the streets. It blew off the hand of an innocent bystander. *New York Times,* November 15, 1909.

21. Mohandas Karamchand Gandhi, *Hind Swaraj, or Indian Home Rule* (1909; Ahmedabad: Navajivan Publishing, 1938), 94.

22. Gandhi, *Collected Works,* 13:510.

23. For deeper discussions of Gujarati cultural identity at this time, see Riho Isaka, "Gujarati Intellectuals and History Writing in the Colonial Period," *Economic and Political Weekly* 37, no. 48 (November 30–December 6, 2002): 4867–72.

24. Gillion, *Ahmedabad*, 63.

25. See Yagnik, *Autobiography*, vol. 1, esp. chap. 8.

26. Gandhi, *Collected Works*, 13:16.

27. Gillion, *Ahmedabad*, 140.

28. Ibid., 142.

29. Mehta, "Gandhi and Ahmedabad."

30. Shah, "Ahmedabad," 484.

31. Shankarlal Banker, *Gandhiji ane Majooropravrutiyo* [Gandhi and Labor Activities] (Ahmedabad: Navajivan Press, 1965), 79.

32. Ganesh Vasuder Mavalankar, "Introduction," in Bansidhar Govardhandas Parekh, *Sheth Mangaldas Girdhardas: Jivan ane Karya* [Life and Works] (Ahmedabad: Sheth Mathuradas Mangaldas, 1955), 12.

33. Banker, 104, 188–89.

34. Gandhi, *Autobiography*, 294.

35. Erik Erikson, *Gandhi's Truth: On the Origins of Militant Non-Violence* (New York: Norton, 1969).

CHAPTER 2. **Gandhi Assembles New Leadership**

1. Judith M. Brown, Gandhi's foremost political biographer, discusses his skills in assembling an array of leaders from across India to support his work at the national level in *Gandhi: Prisoner of Hope* (New Haven, Conn.: Yale University Press, 1989), 309.

2. Maganbhai was Ambalal's biological great-grandfather, but his grandfather by adoption. Maganbhai had no children of his own, so he adopted Ambalal's father, the son of his daughter, as his own.

3. Indulal Yagnik, *Atmakatha* [Autobiography], 6 vols. (Ahmedabad: Various publishers, 1955–72), 1:119–20. Citations to this text are presented parenthetically in text.

4. Ambalal, letter dated June 27, 1926, from the archives of the Gandhi Ashram Museum. I am grateful to Ami Bhatt Potter for calling this document to my attention.

5. For information on Ambalal's industrial policies, and on entrepreneurship in the industry in general, see Howard Spodek, "The 'Manchesterization' of Ahmedabad," *Economic Weekly*, March 13, 1965, 483–90.

6. The principal source of information on Indulal Yagnik is his own six-volume autobiography. A translation by Devavrat Pathak, Howard Spodek, and John Wood is forthcoming (New Delhi: Manohar Books, forthcoming). Digant Oza, ed., *Indulal Yagnik: Gujaratni Asmitana Swapnadrashtra* [Life and Times of Indulal Yagnik] (Ahmedabad: R. R. Sheth, 2007), provides a collection of recent assessments.

7. For Sharadaben's sympathetic views of Indulal and his later struggles against the leadership of the Gujarat Congress, see Sharadabeh Mehta, *Reminiscences: The Memoirs of Sharadaben Mehta,* compiled and translated by Purnima Mehta Bhatt (New Delhi: Zubaan Publications, 2008).

8. The first, and most useful, full-length biography of Vallabhbhai Patel, especially on his early years in Gujarat, is Narhari D. Parikh, *Sardar Vallabhbhai Patel*, 2 vols. (Ahmedabad: Navajivan Press, 1953, 1978).

9. For Vallabhbhai's career in the Ahmedabad Municipality from an admiring point of view, see Devavrat Nanubhai Pathak and Pravin Natvarlal Sheth, *Sardar Vallabhbhai Patel: From Civic to National Leadership* (Ahmedabad: Navajivan Press, 1980).

10. Rizvan Kadri, *Sardar Patel: Ek Sinhpurush* [Sardar Patel: A Lion of a Man] (Ahmedabad: Rizvan Kadri, 2003), 14–18.

11. Ganesh Vsudev Mavalankar and Chandulal Bhagubhai Dalal, *Rashtriya Chalvalmaan Amdavad Municipalitino Falo* [The Contribution of the Ahmedabad Municipality in the National Movement] (Ahmedabad: Navajivan Press, 1962), 52.

12. Howard Spodek, "Sardar Vallabhbhai Patel at 100," *Economic and Political Weekly* 10, no. 50 (December 13, 1975): 1925–36.

13. Cited in Pathak and Sheth, *Sardar Vallabhbhai Patel,* 50–51.

14. Information on Anasuyaben comes primarily from M. V. Kamath and V. B. Kher, *The Story of Militant but Non-Violent Trade Unionism* (Ahmedabad: Navajivan Press, 1993).

15. Ibid., 60.

16. Information on the workers individually is not available, but collective information appears in the *Bombay Gazetteer* (1879), the *Report of the Indian Factory Commission of 1890,* the 1892 *Bombay Provincial Report on the Working of the Indian Factories Act,* and the Bombay Government's *Royal Commission on Indian Labour: Memorandum from the Government of Bombay* (Bombay: Government of Bombay, 1929), as well as the periodic reports and publications of the Ahmedabad Millowners Association and the Textile Labour Association. The decennial censuses of India also include information on occupation. In Shankarlal Banker's *Gandhiji ane Majooropravrutiyo* [Gandhi and Labor Activities] (Ahmedabad: Navajivan Press, 1965), Banker, one of the earliest and most active supporters of the Textile Labour Association, gives a firsthand account of the conditions of workers' lives and recounts Gandhi's activities in helping establish the TLA through the period 1916 to 1940. See Salim Lakha's *Capitalism and Class in Colonial India: The Case of Ahmedabad* (New Delhi: Sterling Publishers, 1988), Sujata Patel's *The Making of Industrial Relations: The Ahmedabad Textile Industry, 1918–1939* (New York: Oxford University Press, 1987), important chapters in Rajnarayan Chandavarkar's *Imperial Power and Popular Politics: Class, Resistance and the State in India, 1850–1950* (Cambridge: Cambridge University Press, 1998), and Kamath and Kher's 1993 *The Story of Militant but Non-Violent Trade Unionism.* Jan Breman, *The Making and Unmaking of an Industrial Working Class: Sliding Down the Labour Hierarchy in Ahmedabad, India* (New Delhi: Oxford University Press, 2004), is mostly concerned with the demise of the mills, the union, and the organized workforce in the late twentieth century, but it begins with a general historical survey.

17. Breman, *Making and Unmaking,* 38; Bombay Government, *Royal Commission on Indian Labor.*

18. Cited in Kenneth L. Gillion, *Ahmedabad: A Study in Indian Urban History* (Berkeley: University of California Press, 1968), 100.

19. Bombay Government, *Royal Commission on Indian Labor.*

20. Banker, *Gandhiji ane Majooropravrutiyo,* 99.

21. Ibid., 98. See also Arup Kumar Sen, "Mode of Labour Control in Colonial India," *Economic and Political Weekly* 37 no. 38 (Sept. 21–27, 2002), 3956–66.

22. Kacharabhai Bhagat et al., *Mahajan Nahote Tyaru* [Before the Mahajan] (Ahmedabad: Jammadas Bhagvandas Trust, 1970), 5.

23. Kunjalata Shah, "Ahmedabad: Pre-Industrial to Industrial Urban Centre (1859–1930)" (Ph.D. diss., SNDT University, Bombay), 436–37.

24. Kacharabhai Bhagat, *Mahajan Nahote Tyaru,* 9; cf. Sundaram's short story, "Maja Velanun Mruthyu."

25. Shah, "Ahmedabad," 441.

26. Kamath and Kher, *Story of Militant but Non-Violent Trade Unionism,* 64.

27. Ibid., 66.

28. Bimal Hasmukh Patel, "The Space of Property Capital: Property Development and Architecture in Ahmedabad" (Ph.D. diss., University of California, Berkeley, 1995), 55–57, based on 1986 data from Ahmedabad Study Action Group (ASAG).

29. Mavalankar and Dalal, *Rashtriya Chalvalmaan,* 454–55.

30. Banker, *Gandhiji ane Majooropravrutiyo,* 180–81.

31. Bhagat, *Mahajan Nahote Tyaru,* 9.

32. Cited in Lakha, *Capitalism and Class,* 99–100.

33. Cited in Makrand Mehta, *Hindu Varnavyavastha, Samaj Parivartan, ane Gujaratna Dalito* [The Hindu Caste System, Social Restructuring, and the Dalits of Gujarat] (Ahmedabad: Ami Publications, 1995), 96–97.

34. Mahadev Desai. A Righteous Struggle (Ahmedabad: Navajivan Publishing, House, 1951).

35. Erik Erikson, *Gandhi's Truth: On the Origins of Militant Non-Violence* (New York: Norton, 1969).

36. Kamath and Kher, *Story of Militant but Non-Violent Trade Unionism,* 95.

37. Ibid., 121.

38. Ibid., 130.

39. Ibid., 132.

40. Ibid.

41. Ibid., 198.

42. Kenneth Gillion provides a summary of the events in his book, *Ahmedabad* (Berkeley: University of California Press, 1968), and in more detail in his article, "Gujarat in 1919," in *Essays on Gandhian Politics: The Rowlatt Satyagraha of 1919,* ed. Ravinder Kumar (Oxford: Clarendon Press, 1971), 126–44.

43. Kamath and Kher, *Story of Militant but Non-Violent Trade Unionism,* 214.

44. Tripathi, *Dynamics of a Tradition,* 172.

45. Gita Piramal, *Business Maharajas* (New Delhi: Penguin Books, 1996), 333.

46. Dinkar Mehta, *Parivartan: Atmakatha* [Transformation: An Autobiography] (Ahmedabad: Lokaayat Gnaankendra Trust, 1968), 294–95.

47. Mohandas Karamchand Gandhi, *Hind Swaraj, or Indian Home Rule* (1909; Ahmedabad: Navajivan Publishing, 1938), 95.

48. Mohandas Karamchand Gandhi, *Collected Works of Mahatma Gandhi* (New Delhi: Government of India, Publications Division, Ministry of Education and Broadcasting, 1969), 13:510.

49. Mavalankar and Dalal, *Rashtriya Chalvalmaan,* 483.

50. Siddharth Raychaudhuri, "Indian Elites, Urban Space, and the restructuring of Ahmedabad City, 1890–1947" (Ph.D. diss., St. Catharine's College, Cambridge University, 1997).

51. Rizvan Kadri's account of the early years of the Congress in Gujarat, as well as his study of Sardar Patel's early years in the Ahmedabad municipality, appear in *Sardar Patel.* Frequent reference is made to Muslims in city government, but their roles do not transcend local, relatively routine issues, as do those of the leaders cited here.

CHAPTER 3. Vallabhbhai Patel Builds the Congress Political Machine

1. In the mid-1930s, even after he had shifted his principal residence to Bombay City, Vallabhbhai affirmed his rural roots in choosing his telex address: POWERFARM.

2. Narhari D. Parikh, *Sardar Vallabhbhai Patel,* 2 vols. (Ahmedabad: Navajivan Press, 1953, 1956), 1:281.

3. October 4, 1925, cited in Devavrat Nanubhai Pathak and Pravin Natvarlal Sheth, *Sardar Vallabhbhai Patel: From Civic to National Leadership* (Ahmedabad: Navajivan Press, 1980), 271.

4. Parikh, *Sardar Vallabhbhai Patel,* 1:270.

5. Ratnamanirao Bhimrao Jhote, *Gujaratnun Patnagar Ahmedabad* [Gujarat's Capital City, Ahmedabad] (Ahmedabad: Gujarat Sahitya Sabha, 1929), 388.

6. Parikh, *Sardar Vallabhbhai Patel,* 1:278.

7. Ganesh Vsudev Mavalankar and Chandulal Bhagubhai Dalal, *Rashtriya Chalvalmaan Amdavad Municipalitino Falo* [The Contribution of the Ahmedabad Municipality in the National Movement] (Ahmedabad: Navajivan Press, 1962), 74.

8. Ibid., 78.

9. Ibid., 311.

10. Ibid., 313–15.

11. *Ahmedabad District Gazetteer.* Gujarat State Gazetteers (Ahmedabad: Government of Gujarat, 1984), 163.

12. India, Census Commissioner, *Census of India, 1931, Bombay Presidency* (Delhi: Manager of Publications, 1932), part 1, 5.

13. Parikh, *Sardar Vallabhbhai Patel,* 1:152.

14. *Ahmedabad District Gazetteer,* 1984, 160.

15. Indulal Yagnik, *Atmakatha* [Autobiography], 6 vols. (Ahmedabad: Various publishers, 1955–72), 11: 297.

16. Cited in Rizvan Kadri, *Sardar Patel: Ek Sinhpurush* [Sardar Patel: A Lion of a Man] (Ahmedabad: Rizvan Kadri, 2003), 108.

17. Cited in Pathak and Sheth, *Sardar Vallabhbhai Patel,* 212–13.

18. From *Praja Bandhu,* November 18, 1923, cited in ibid., 242.

19. Siddharth Raychaudhuri, "Indian Elites, Urban Space, and the Restructuring of Ahmedabad City, 1890–1947" (Ph.D. diss., St. Catharine's College, Cambridge University, 1997), stresses this point.

20. Pathak and Sheth, *Sardar Vallabhbhai Patel,* 242.

21. Ibid., 240.

22. Parikh, *Sardar Vallabhbhai Patel,* 1:301.

23. Similarly, in about 1929, reviewing Patel's role in keeping the peace during various nationalist political agitations, the police superintendent of Ahmedabad, Mr. Heeley, wrote to the government that "without Vallabhbhai it will be impossible for you to maintain law and order." Parikh, *Sardar Vallabhbhai Patel,* 1:104.

24. Parikh, *Sardar Vallabhbhai Patel,* 2:287.

25. Mavalankar and Dalal, *Rashtriya Chalvalmaan,* 230.

26. Indulal, *Atmakatha,* chap. 6, 2:154.

27. Ibid., chap. 6, 2:158.

28. Ibid., chap. 6, 2:159.

29. Ibid., chap. 1, 3:161.

30. Ibid., chap. 1, 3:17.

31. Ibid., chap. 1, 3:30–31.

32. Indulal Yagnik, *Gandhi as I Know Him* (Delhi: Danish Mahal, 1943), 209–11.

33. Ibid., chap. 13, 3:269. Indulal reports that spinning was first introduced at the Vidyapith on January 13, 1921 (2:299).

34. Ibid., chap. 13, 3:252–53. These discussions of Indulal's political and cultural clashes with Patel are drawn from the third volume of his autobiography, published in 1956, and from primary materials from 1921 that he cites. In between, he published a remarkable anti-Gandhian attack entitled *Gandhi as I Know Him* (Delhi: Danish Mahal, 1943).

35. Parikh, *Sardar Vallabhbhai Patel*, 2:193.

36. Dinkar Mehta, *Parivartan: Atmakatha* [Fundamental Change: An Autobiography] (Ahmedabad: Lokaayat Gnaankendra Trust, 1968), 144.

37. Aparna Basu, *Mridula Sarabhai: Rebel with a Cause* (Delhi: Oxford University Press, 1996), 58, citing a letter (mis)dated 16 April 1992—more likely 1932.

38. Pathak and Sheth, *Sardar Vallabhbhai Patel*, 321, citing the *Bombay Chronicle*.

39. Rajmohan Gandhi, *Patel: A Life* (Ahmedabad: Navajivan Press, 1990), 189–90.

40. Bombay CID 2/INC/36(8), in Howard Spodek, "Sardar Vallabhbhai Patel at 100," *Economic and Political Weekly* 10, no. 50 (December 13, 1975), 1929.

41. On the importance of these electoral experiences in Ahmedabad to Patel's national leadership, see Spodek, "Sardar Patel at 100," and the Rajendra Prasad Papers in the National Archives of India.

42. Manekbhai Patel, *Amdavad Kathaa* [Ahmedabad Stories] (Ahmedabad: Gurjar Granthratna Karyalaya, 1996), 111–25.

43. Pathak and Sheth, *Sardar Vallabhbhai Patel*, 354.

44. Ibid., 353.

45. Raychaudhuri, "Indian Elites."

46. Mavalankar and Dalal, 519.

47. Basu, *Mridula Sarabhai*, based on Mridula Sarabhai report, 89.

48. Raychaudhuri, "Indian Elites," 218.

49. Ibid.

50. Basu, *Mridula Sarabhai*, 88–91.

51. From *Collected Works of Mahatma Gandhi* (New Delhi: Publications Division, Government of India, 1958–94), 74:26, cited in Achyut Yagnik and Suchitra Sheth, *The Shaping of Modern Gujarat: Plurality, Hindutva and Beyond* (New Delhi: Penguin Books, 2005), 220.

52. V. S. Dave, *Report of the Commission of Inquiry into the Incidents of Violence and Disturbances which Took Place at Various Places in the State of Gujarat since February, 1985 to 18th July, 1985*, 2 vols. (Gandhinagar: Government Central Press, 1990), 1:69.

CHAPTER 4. Anasuyaben Sarabhai Engages Ahmedabad's Working Classes

1. The continuing role of Anasuyaben and her family in funding early union activity is not clear. Ambalal supported her early work in the Amarpura slums with land and money. Shankarlal Banker reports receiving an additional pledge from him, about 1920, of Rs. 500 per month for a period of three years for workers' education in Ahmedabad. Approximately Rs. 13,500 were available from private funds to support strike activities and for worker relief in the strike of 1918. In 1926, the union hospital and two dispensaries cost Rs. 11,928. The fifteen night schools, eleven day schools, kindergarten, and reading room, as well as the publication of the union's weekly, *Majoor Sandesh*, cost Rs. 34,322. Were these funds built up from workers' contributions? From Anasuyaben's purse? From a combination of these resources and others?

2. Shankarlal Banker, *Gandhiji ane Majooropravrutiyo* [Gandhi and Labor Activities] (Ahmedabad: Navajivan Press, 1965), 128.

3. Salim Lakha, *Capitalism and Class in Colonial India: The Case of Ahmedabad* (New Delhi: Sterling Publishers, 1988), 104.

4. Rajnarayan Chandavarkar, *Imperial Power and Popular Politics: Class, Resistance and the State in India, 1850–1950* (Cambridge: Cambridge University Press, 1998), 286, cited from *Young India,* May 10, 1928.

5. Royal Commission on Labour in India, *Report,* 1931, 337, cited in Lakha, *Capitalism and Class,* 126.

6. Dinkar Mehta, *Parivartan: Atmakatha* [Fundamental Change: An Autobiography] (Ahmedabad: Lokaayat Gnaankendra Trust, 1968), 150–51.

7. M. V. Kamath and V. B. Kher, *The Story of Militant but Non-Violent Trade Unionism* (Ahmedabad: Navajivan Press, 1993), 206.

8. Lakha, *Capitalism and Class,* 109, based on Royal Commission on Labour in India, *Report,* 1929, 188.

9. Ibid., 111.

10. In her helpful book, *The Making of Industrial Relations: The Ahmedabad Textile Industry, 1918–1939* (New York: Oxford University Press, 1987), Sujata Patel analyzes the clash.

11. Banker, *Gandhiji ane Majooropravrutiyo,* 113–16, and Patel, *Making of Industrial Relations,* 150.

12. Patel, *Making of Industrial Relations,* 58–63.

13. Royal Commission on Labour in India, *Report,* 1929, 201, cited in Lakha, *Capitalism and Class,* 109.

14. Patel, *Making of Industrial Relations,* 62.

15. Ratnamanirao Bhimrao Jhote, *Gujaratnun Patnagar Ahmedabad* [Gujarat's Capital City, Ahmedabad] (Ahmedabad: Gujarat Sahitya Sabha, 1929), 556. Many of the complaints concerned *mukkadams. Mukkadams* frequently alleged arbitrary treatment against them by management, and each year, they waged a few unauthorized, localized strikes against management in individual mills. From the other direction, shop laborers had many complaints against the *mukkadams,* alleging unjust fines for poor-quality production, the extortion of bribes, and sexual harrassment. In an attempt to monitor and regulate these relationships, the TLA formed a union of jobbers and *mukkadams* in 1926.

16. *Praja Bandhu,* August 31, 1924, cited by Patel, *Making of Industrial Relations,* 81n.

17. Banker, *Gandhiji ane Majooropravrutiyo,* 144–50.

18. Ibid., 144.

19. Ibid., 218.

20. Khandubhai Desai, *Textile Labour Association Ahmedabad: An Indigenous Experiment in Trade Union Movement* (Ahmedabad: Textile Labour Association, 1948), 13, cited in Lakha, *Capitalism and Class,* 116.

21. Anasuyaben did, however, ask Vallabhbhai to press for bathing facilities for women in the industrial area, and he secured a sum of Rs. 12,000 for that purpose in the 1929 municipal budget.

22. Cited in Kamath and Kher, *Story of Militant but Non-Violent Trade Unionism,* 147–48.

23. Banker, *Gandhiji ane Majooropravrutiyo,* 153.

24. Ibid., 160.

25. Patel, *Making of Industrial Relations, 104–10.*

26. Banker, *Gandhiji ane Majooropravrutiyo,* 166.

27. Mehta, *Parivartan,* 141.

28. From annual reports of the AMA collected by Patel, *Making of Industrial Relations,* 98, 113.

29. TLA papers, cited in Patel, *Making of Industrial Relations,* 121.

30. R. J. Soman, *Peaceful Industrial Relations: Their Science and Technique* (Ahmedabad: Navajivan Press, 1957), 285.

31. Ibid., 279.

32. Ibid., 277, cf. 287.

33. Historian Makrand Mehta reconstructs the 1931 visit, using as his sources Ahmedabad's pro-Gandhian *Praja Bandhu* newspaper and *Harijan Bandhu,* the newsletter of the Gandhian Mahagujarat Harijan Samaj. Makrand Mehta, *Hindu Varnvyavastha, Samaj Parivartan, ane Gujaratna Dalito* [The Hindu Caste System, Social Restructuring, and the Dalits of Gujarat] (Ahmedabad: Ami Publications, 1995), 136.

34. Ibid., 137.

35. Rameshchandra Parmar and Ashok Chaudhuri, "At the Turn of the Century: A Dialogue," *Seminar* 470 (October 1998): 66.

36. Banker, *Gandhiji ane Majooropravrutiyo,* 185.

37. Mehta, *Hindu Varnvyavastha,* 141.

38. Patel, *Making of Industrial Relations,* 120.

39. Ibid., 127.

40. Banker, *Gandhiji ane Majooropravrutiyo,* 217.

41. Lakha, *Capitalism and Class,* 115.

42. Patel, *Making of Industrial Relations,* 131.

43. Mehta, *Parivartan,* 192.

44. Kamath and Kher, *Story of Militant but Non-Violent Trade Unionism,* 327.

45. Ibid., 334.

46. Ibid.

47. Mehta, *Parivartan,* 282. Communists opposed the Quit Indian movement.

48. Manekbhai Patel, *Amdavad Kathaa* [Ahmedabad Stories] (Ahmedabad: Gurjar Granthratna Karyalaya, 1996), 111–25.

49. Lakha, *Capitalism and Class,* 115, from Desai, *Textile Labour Association Ahmedabad,* 8, 10.

CHAPTER 5. Ambalal Sarabhai and Kasturbhai Lalbhai Build an Industrialized, Westernized, Prosperous, Cultured, World-Class, Company Town

1. *Shethia,* or *sheth,* is Gujarati for businessman, or wealthy man, usually a member of a caste associated with business. The term is used informally as something of a title, like "doctor," "professor," or "esquire."

2. In 1964–66, when I was carrying out research on the Ahmedabad textile industry, I often visited the office of the president of the Ahmedabad Textile Millowners Association. I was surprised to see a large oil painting of Gandhi, dressed in his khadi dhoti, sitting at a spinning wheel, on the wall behind the desk of the president. Gandhi's khadi and the textile millowners' offices seemed an incongruous match. But of course, in addition to being the father of his country, Gandhi had also brought labor peace to

Ahmedabad through the unique labor union that he helped to found, and the *swadeshi* movement he led served as a kind of people's tariff in limiting imports to India. Gandhi's contribution to the welfare and profitability of the industry was immense. His picture was well placed.

3. "The average dividend on paid-up capital, reserves, and depreciation funds together in these years of what the Bombay mill industry regards as the worst depression the mill industry in this country has experienced have worked out at 3³⁄₂₅% [1923], 3³⁄₁₀% [1924], and 4⁴⁄₅% [1925]." India, Tariff Board, *Report of the Indian Tariff Board (Cotton Textile Industry Enquiry), 1927* (Bombay, 1927), 1:25. See also a Bombay government report of 1933, cited in Gita Piramal, *Business Maharajas* (New Delhi: Penguin Books, 1996): "In the last four years, when the whole world was suffering from widespread depression, the Ahmedabad textile industry had developed, earned profits and distributed good dividends" (347).

4. Ratnamanirao Bhimrao Jhote, *Gujaratnun Patnagar Ahmedabad* [Gujarat's Capital City, Ahmedabad] (Ahmedabad: Gujarat Sahitya Sabha, 1929). 500–501.

5. Ibid., 503.

6. Personal interview with S. A. Kher, 1965.

7. Two biographies of Kasturbhai, Dwijendra Tripathi's *Dynamics of a Tradition: Kasturbhai Lalbhai and His Entrepreneurship* (Delhi: Manohar, 1981), in English, and Dhirubhai P. Thakar's *Parampara ane Pragathi. Sva. Sri Kasturbhai Lalbhainun Jivancaritra* [Tradition and Progress: The Biography of the Late Sri Kasturbhai Lalbhai] (Mumbai: Vakilsa, Phephara, Enda Sayamansa, 1984), in Gujarati, give good accounts. I also interviewed Kasturbhai extensively in 1974–75.

8. Chinubhai memorial volume, published for private circulation, cited in Howard Spodek, "Sardar Vallabhbhai Patel at 100," *Economic and Political Weekly* 10, no. 50 (December 13, 1975): 1925–36.

9. Here and throughout the discussion of the 1941 riot, I follow the account presented by Siddharth Raychaudhuri, "Indian Elites, Urban Space, and the Restructuring of Ahmedabad City, 1890–1947" (Ph.D. diss., St. Catharine's College, Cambridge University, 1997), chap. 6.

10. From India, Supreme Court, *Report of Proceedings in the Appeal from Award of the Industrial Court Gujarat. The Ahmedabad Millowners Association Ahmedabad & Ors. versus The Textile Labour Association, Ahmedabad* (New Delhi, 1965), annexure 5, p. 400, and annexure 8, p. 403, in Textile Labour Association argument. Gross managing profits include managing agency commission and depreciation.

11. Tripathi, *Dynamics of a Tradition,* 98.

12. Ibid., 93.

13. Ibid., 119.

14. Ibid., 93.

15. Aparna Basu, *Mridula Sarabhai: Rebel with a Cause* (Delhi: Oxford University Press, 1996), 21.

16. Kamla Chowdhry, "Institution Builder," in *Vikram Sarabhai: The Man and the Vision,* ed. Padmanabh Joshi (Ahmedabad: Mapin Publishing, 1992), 79–80.

17. Kasturbhai Lalbhai, "A Great Visionary," in Joshi, *Vikram Sarabhai,* 87–88.

18. Government of India, Monopolies Inquiry Committee, New Delhi, 1965, 119.

19. Jon Lang, Madhavi Desai, and Miki Desai, *Architecture and Independence: The Search for Identity—India, 1880 to 1980* (New York: Oxford University Press, 1997).

20. Ahmedabad Municipal Corporation (Town Development Department), draft revised development plan, 1975–85; P. R. Shah, "Background Papers," Ahmedabad Municipal Corporation (Town Development Department), 142.

21. Draft revised development plan, 1975, 1:178.

22. Ibid., 1:177.

23. Shah, "Background Papers," 143.

24. Ibid.

25. Bimal Hasmukh Patel, "The Space of Property Capital: Property Development and Architecture in Ahmedabad" (Ph.D. diss., University of California, Berkeley, 1995).

26. Draft revised development plan, 1975, 1:83.

27. Ibid., 1:84.

28. Shah, "Background Papers," 151.

29. Draft revised development plan, 1975, 3.

30. Devavrat N. Pathak's monograph, *Municipal Corporationni Chuntani, 1961* [Municipal Corporation Election, 1961] (Ahmedabad: Gujarat University Press, 1961), presents the details.

31. Ibid., appendices, 45–46.

32. Ibid., 23–32.

chapter 6. Indulal Yagnik Challenges the Gandhian Consensus

1. Indulal Yagnik, *Atmakatha* [Autobiography], 6 vols. (Ahmedabad: Various publishers, 1955–72), vol. 2, *Gujaratman Navajivan* [New Life in Gujarat] (Ahmedabad: Gurjar Granthratna Karyalaya, 1955). Subsequent citations to Indulal's autobiography refer to these publications and are cited parenthetically.

2. Indulal tells of a last-ditch effort by Anasuyaben to keep him in Ahmedabad. Indulal told her that he would stay if he could carry on the work of translating books of international significance into Gujarati and publishing them. Anasuyaben took the suggestion to her brother, Ambalal, who seemed favorably disposed to funding it. Then, Indulal reports, Ambalal put down a condition:

> "Everything else is all right. Only you shall have to show me the books before they are published."
> . . . . I failed to understand his objective. Just as he was running his profession, why should I not independently carry on my work according to my abilities? . . .
> "But if you print some book about Lenin?"
> . . . . I had absolutely never thought of bringing out a book or biography on Lenin. . . . It appeared as a challenge to my self-respect and I flared up. "I shall definitely print a book on Lenin. Our people must know something about him also." . . .
> "Then we cannot carry on." Ambalal summed up the discussions with a decisive voice.
> Within a few days I took the decision to go to Bombay. (chap. 13, 3:266)

3. Indulal Yagnik, *Shyamaji Krishnavarma: Life and Times of an Indian Revolutionary* (Bombay: Lakshmi Publications, 1950).

4. Brahmakumar Bhatt, *Le Ke Rahenge Mahagujarat* [We Will Not Rest until We Have Mahagujarat] (Ahmedabad, 1994), 133–34.

5. Dinkar Mehta, *Krantini Khojmaan* [In Quest of Revolution] (Ahmedabad: Lokayat Gnaankendra Trust, 1984?), 60.

6. Commission of inquiry investigating the movement under Justice S. P. Kotval, cited in Devavrat N. Pathak, M. G. Parekh, and Kirtidev D. Desai, *Three General Elections in Gujarat* (Ahmedabad: Gujarat University, 1966), 58.

7. Bhatt, *Le Ke Rahenge Mahagujarat,* 62.

8. Dinkar Mehta, *Krantini Khojmaan,* 107.

9. Bhatt, *Le Ke Rahenge Mahagujarat,* 98–99.

10. Cf. John R. Wood, "The Political Integration of British and Princely Gujarat: The Historical–Political Dimension of Indian State Politics" (Ph.D. diss., Columbia University, New York, 1972).

11. Information on the municipal elections of 1957 and 1961 is from Devavrat N. Pathak, *Municipal Corporationni Chuntani, 1961* [Election, 1961] (Ahmedabad: Gujarat University Press, 1961).

12. Ibid. Pathak does not indicate why he does not consider the election for reserved seats as part of the partisan contests, although they appear to be. His charts and figures, which are otherwise extremely useful, do not indicate the party of the candidates for reserved seats.

13. Bhatt, *Le Ke Rahenge Mahagujarat,* 126.

14. Dinkar Mehta, *Krantini Khojmaan,* 124.

15. So did Bhaikaka Patel. Patel, one of the founders of the new Vallabh Vidyanagar University at Anand and leader of the emerging Swatantra, the rightist party based in central Gujarat, became Indulal's most important mentor in these years, especially on issues of Mahagujarat. Indulal acknowledges Patel's role as a key intermediary between the MGJP and the Samyukta Maharashtra Samiti.

16. Sohrab Peshotan Kotval, *Report of the Commission of Inquiry on the Cases of Police Firing at Ahedabad on the 12th, 13th and 14th August 1958* (Bombay: Director, Government Printing, Publications and Stationery, 1959), 21. The Kotval Commission looked into the violence surrounding the Mahagujarat movement.

17. Bhatt, *Le Ke Rahenge Mahagujarat,* 144.

18. Statement by district magistrate in Kotval Commission judicial inquiry report, 44.

19. Bhatt, *Le Ke Rahenge Mahagujarat,* 167.

20. Pathak, *Municipal Corporationni Chuntani, 1961,* 6.

21. Pathak, Parekh, and Desai, *Three General Elections,* 87.

22. Personal interview with Rameshchandra Parmar, February 23, 1999.

23. Dinkar Mehta, *Krantini Khojmaan,* 62.

24. Aseema Sinha, *The Regional Roots of Developmental Politics in India: A Divided Leviathan* (Bloomington: Indiana University Press, 2005), 183.

25. Interview with Rameshchandra Parmar.

26. Indulal Yagnik, *Atmakatha* [Autobiography] vol. 6 (Ahmedabad: Mahagujarat Seva Trust, 1973), 405. The last section of this volume, 324–729, is a collection of Indulal's later speeches and writings, edited by Dhanvant Oza. They have not been published in English translation.

27. Renana Jhabvala, *Closing Doors* (Ahmedabad: SETU, 1985), 21–25, and interviews with Elaben Bhatt.

28. Mehta, *Krantini Khojmaan*, 200.
29. Rameshchandra Parmar, ed., *Shramik Kavita* [Labor Poems] (Ahmedabad, n.d.), 17–18.
30. Dinkar Mehta, *Krantini Khojmaan*, 199.
31. *Congress Patrika*, May 22, 1965.
32. Dinkar Mehta, *Krantini Khojmaan*, 213, 216.
33. Dinkar Mehta, *Krantini Khojmaan*, 241.

PART 3. Creativity and Chaos

1. Tushar Bhatt, *Sketches in the Sand* (Ahmedabad: Image Publications, 1994), 50.

CHAPTER 7. Communal Violence, 1969

1. The P. Jaganmohan Reddy Commission of Inquiry, Ahmedabad, September 1969, 179–81, cited in A. R. Desai and Wilfred D'Costa, *State and Repressive Culture: A Case Study of Gujarat* (Bombay: Popular Prakashan, 1994), 102.
2. The official judicial inquiry under the direction of Justice P. Jaganmohan Reddy reported, "The riots in Ahmedabad were unprecedented and the city was affected as no other city had ever been affected." P. Jaganmohan Reddy, *Commission of Inquiry on Communal Disturbance at Various Places in the State of Gujarat on and after 18th September 1969* (Gandhingar: Government Central Press, 1970), 222.
3. Ghanshyam Shah, "Communal Riots in Gujarat: Report of a Preliminary Investigation," *Economic and Political Weekly,* January 1970, 5.
4. Ibid.
5. Ibid., 7.
6. Ibid.
7. Ibid., 9.
8. Ibid., 10.
9. Reddy, *Commission*, 216–18.
10. Shah, "Communal Riots," 11.
11. Ibid., 11–12.
12. Ibid., 13.
13. Ibid., 13–14.
14. Reddy, *Commission*, 306.
15. Lok Sabha Debates, 10th sess., 4th ser., vol. 41, no. 58, May 14, 1979 (New Delhi: Lok Sabha Secretariat), 323, cited in Steven Wilkinson, *Votes and Violence: Electoral Competition and Ethnic Riots in India* (Cambridge: Cambridge University Press, 2004), 21.
16. Reddy, *Commission*, 217.
17. Ibid., 213.
18. Ibid., 222.
19. Ibid., 214.
20. Ibid., 218.
21. Ibid., 16.
22. Ibid., 228.
23. Mohammed Farid Gulamnabi Mansuri, "Malay na Malay," in *Satat,* (Ahmedabad: Vora, 1970). Translation here by Raymond Parmar and Howard Spodek.

CHAPTER 8. Chimanbhai Patel Provokes the Nav Nirman Movement, 1974

1. Information on Nav Nirman is drawn here primarily from Gujarat University political scientist Pravin Sheth's *Nav Nirman and Political Change in India: From Gujarat 1974 to New Delhi 1977* (Bombay: Vora, 1977); a lengthy report and analysis by Ghanshyam Shah, "Communal Riots in Gujarat: Report of a Preliminary Investigation," *Economic and Political Weekly* 5, no. 3–5 (January 1970): 187–200, and later reprinted in *Protest Movements in Two Indian States: A Study of the Gujarat and Bihar Movements* (Delhi: Ajanta Publications, 1977); a study of "The Scholars' Rebellion: Educational Interests and Agitational Politics in Gujarat," by American scholars Dawn Jones and Rodney Jones, which appeared in *Journal of Asian Studies* 36, no. 3 (May 1977): 457–76, emphasizing the role of university professors and politics in the movement; Chimanbhai Patel's own account and self-defense, *Gujaratni Ghatnaono Ghatsphot* [The Events in Gujarat Revealed] (published privately as a manifesto, 1995); contemporary newspaper accounts; and interviews with several of the participants.

2. Sheth, *Nav Nirman and Political Change*, 8, from the quarterly bulletin of the Bureau of Economics and Statistics, Gujarat State, 1974.

3. Shah, *Protest Movements*, 34.

4. Biographical data from *Hum Hindustani* (March, April, May 1994), edited by Chimanbhai's widow, Urmilaben Patel; interview with Urmilaben Patel, April 11, 1999; and Jones and Jones, "Scholars' Rebellion." In cases of minor discrepancies in dates, I have followed the chronology presented in *Hum Hindustani*.

5. Jones and Jones, "Scholars' Rebellion."

6. Ibid., 15.

7. Interviews in 1999 with union leaders Kanubhai Shah, M. R. Patel, and Ujamshi Kapadia. Jones and Jones, "Scholars' Rebellion," provides further detail on the continuing bitter confrontation between Chimanbhai and the faculty union.

8. Sheth, *Nav Nirman and Political Change*, 10.

9. Shah, *Protest Movements*, 28.

10. Ibid., 46.

11. Ibid., 57.

12. Manekbhai Patel, *Ahmedabad Kathaa* [Ahmedabad Stories] (Ahmedabad: Gurjar Granthratna Karyalaya, 1996), 247, 175–79.

13. Sheth, *Nav Nirman and Political Change*, 191.

14. Patel, *Gujaratni Ghatnaono Ghatsphot*, 22.

15. Bipan Chandra, Mridula Mukherjee, and Aditya Mukherjee, *India after Independence, 1947–2000* (New Delhi: Viking, 1999), 249.

16. Jayaprakash, *Prison Diary*, cited in Sheth, *Nav Nirman and Political Change*, preface.

17. Ibid., 180–81.

18. Ibid., 178–79.

19. Christophe Jaffrelot, *The Hindu Nationalist Movement and Indian Politics, 1925 to the 1990s* (New Delhi: Penguin Books, 1996), 271.

CHAPTER 9. The Mills Close, the TLA Falters, and the Municipal Corporation Goes Broke

1. From 1975–97, figures supplied by the Ahmedabad Textile Mills Association. Data on TLA membership supplied by the TLA (personal communication).

2. Shuji Uchikawa, *Indian Textile Industry: State Policy, Liberalization, and Growth* (New Delhi: Manohar, 1998), 96–97; Government of India, *Indian Textile Bulletin, Annual Report,* cited in Uchikawa, *Indian Textile Industry.* Some of the statistical data given for the years 1966 to 1975 do not add to the exact totals given.

3. Tirthankar Roy, "Development or Distortion? 'Powerlooms' in India, 1950–1997," *Economic and Political Weekly,* April 18, 1998, 897.

4. Roy has argued this point in a series of articles, especially ibid.

5. Cf. Douglas Haynes on Surat: *Rhetoric and Ritual in Colonial India: The Shaping of a Public Culture in Surat City, 1852–1928* (Berkeley: University of California Press, 1991).

6. Roy, "Development or Distortion?," 907.

7. Praful Anubhai, chairman of the Ahmedabad Textile Mills Association from 1979 to 1981, laid out the dimensions of the problem in "The Textile Industry in Ahmedabad: The 2001 Scenario," *Times Research Foundation Seminar,* vol. 3 (Ahmedabad: Times of India, 1988).

8. Dinesh Mehta and Meera Mehta, *Metropolitan Housing Market: A Study of Ahmedabad* (New Delhi: Sage, 1989), 56.

9. Manishi Jani, *Textile Workers: Jobless and Miserable* (Ahmedabad: SETU, 1984), 14, 21, 19.

10. L. V. Saptarshi, "Ahmedabad Textile Industry in the National Context," in *Seminar on Ahmedabad, 2001,* vol. 3 (Calcutta: Times [of India] Research Foundation Urban Studies Center Seminar, 1988).

11. Cited in Uchikawa, *Indian Textile Industry,* 152.

12. Jan Breman, *The Making and Unmaking of an Industrial Working Class: Sliding Down the Labor Hierarchy in Ahmedabad, India* (New Delhi: Oxford University Press, 2004), 158.

13. Gita Piramal, *Business Maharajas* (New Delhi: Penguin Books, 1996), 24.

14. Ibid., 26.

15. Uchikawa, *Indian Textile Industry,* 142–43.

16. Breman, *Making and Unmaking,* 167.

17. Ela Bhatt, *We Are Poor but So Many: The Story of Self-Employed Women in India* (New York: Oxford University Press, 2006), 14.

18. Breman, *Making and Unmaking,* 229.

19. Cited in Uchikawa, *Indian Textile Industry,* 113, from Ahmedabad Textile Industry Research Association (ATIRA), *Rehabilitation of the Textile Industry* (Ahmedabad: Ahmedabad Textile Industry Research Association, 1985), 105.

20. B. B. Patel, *Workers of Closed Textile Mills* (New Delhi: Oxford University Press and IBH Publishing, 1988). Cf. S. Roy Chowdhury, "Industrial Restructuring, Unions, and the State: Textile Mill Workers in Ahmedabad," *Economic and Political Weekly* 31, no. 8 (February 24, 1996): *Review of Labour,* L-7–L-13; and Jivan Thakore, *Hum ane Maaree Mill* [Me and My Mill], *Naya Marg* 1 and 16, September 2002.

21. Patel, *Workers of Closed Textile Mills,* 32; Renana Jhabvala, *Closing Doors* (Ahmedabad: SETU, 1985).

22. Jani, *Textile Workers,* 7, 9, 12–13.

23. Breman, *Making and Unmaking,* 157–59.

24. Patel, *Workers of Closed Textile Mills.*

25. Indira Hirway and Darshini Mahadevia, *Gujarat Human Development Report, 2004* (Ahmedabad: Mahatma Gandhi Labour Institute, n.d.), 45.

26. Patel, *Workers of Closed Textile Mills.*

27. Breman, *Making and Unmaking,* 162–69, 182–89.

28. For Ahmedabad's historic guild traditons, see E. W. Hopkins, "Ancient and Modern Hindu Guilds," in *India: Old and New* (New York: Scribners, 1901), 176–79.

29. Ahmedabad Textile Mill Association annual report, 1985.

30. *India Today,* August 15, 1986, 88–95, and August 31, 1986, 113; *Imprint,* July 1986, 16–27, and August 1986, 1–2, 54–57.

31. Seminar papers by Girish Patel, Kirit Raval, and Kirtee Shah, presented at "Is Ahmedabad Dying?," Center for Environmental Planning and Technology (CEPT) and the Gujarat Institute of Civil Engineers and Architects, Ahmedabad, 1987.

32. *Statistical Outline of Ahmedabad City* (Ahmedabad: Ahmedabad Municipal Corporation, 1994–95), 52–63.

33. Richard Batley, "Urban Management in the State of Gujarat: Ahmedabad," in *Urban Management in India* (Birmingham: University of Birmigham, 1992), 89.

34. Ibid., 78.

35. Ibid., 51.

36. The 1991 report of the Municipal Commissioner, "The Environmental Profile of the City of Ahmedabad, Gujarat State, India," cited in Batley, "Urban Management," 50.

37. Batley, "Urban Management," 40.

38. Ibid., 66.

39. Ibid., 128, 74.

40. Ibid., 80.

41. Ibid., 125, 128.

42. Ibid., 79.

43. Ibid., 95, citing an unpublished report by Dinesh Mehta.

CHAPTER 10. Madhavsinh Solanki Invokes the Politics of Caste and Class

1. Government of India, *India, 1998: A Reference Annual* (New Delhi: Government of India, Ministry of Information and Broadcasting, Publications Division, 1998), 197–98.

2. Eugene F. Irschick, *Politics and Social Conflict in South India: The Non-Brahman Movement and Tamil Separatism, 1916–1929* (Berkeley: University of California Press, 1969).

3. Personal interview with Madhavsinh Solanki, 1986.

4. Achyut Yagnik and Anil Bhatt, "The Anti-Dalit Agitation in Gujarat," *South Asia Bulletin* 4, no. 1 (Spring 1984): 49.

5. John Wood, "Reservations in Doubt: The Backlash against Affirmative Action in Gujarat, 1985" (paper presented at the International Seminar on Gujarat Society, Surat, December 1986), 10.

6. Yagnik and Bhatt, "Anti-Dalit Agitation"; Wood, "Reservations in Doubt."

7. Yagnik and Bhatt, "Anti-Dalit Agitation."

8. The name was borrowed from the Black Panther organization of alienated and militant African Americans in the United States.

9. Yagnik and Bhatt, "Anti-Dalit Agitation," give precise details on the deaths of fifteen Dalits during the course of the Ahmedabad riots.

10. Achyut Yagnik, introduction to Joseph Macwan, *The Stepchild: Angaliyat* (New Delhi: Oxford University Press, 2004), xvi.

11. Jennifer Sebstad, *Struggle and Development among Self Employed Women* (Washington, D.C.: United States Agency for International Development, 1982). See also Ela Bhatt, *We Are Poor but So Many: The Story of Self-Employed Women in India* (New York: Oxford University Press, 2006), 14–15.

12. Rita Kothari, "Short Story in Gujarati Dalit Literature," *Economic and Political Weekly* 36, no. 45 (November 10, 2001): 4311.

13. Ibid., 4308.

14. *New York Times,* April 19, May 10, June 8 and 25, July 19.

15. Pravin Sheth and Ramesh Menon, *Caste and Communal Time Bomb* (Ahmedabad: Golwala Publications, 1986); Wood, "Reservations in Doubt."

16. Asghar Ali Engineer, "Ahmedabad: From Caste to Communal Violence," *Economic and Political Weekly,* April 13, 1985, 628–30.

17. *Times of India,* Ahmedabad edition, July 30, 1985.

18. Asghar Ali Engineer, "Communal Fire Engulfs Ahmedabad Once Again," *Economic and Political Weekly,* July 6, 1985, 1116–20.

19. Ibid., and Mahesh Vijaypurkar, "Ahmedabad: Fury of Fundamentalism," *Frontline,* July 26–August 8, 1986, 13.

20. *Times of India,* March 29, 1985.

21. Engineer,"Communal Fire."

22. N. M. Miyabhoy *Prohibition Policy Inquiry Commission Report* (Ahmedabad: Government of Gujarat, 1983); Achyut Yagnik, "Paradoxes of Populism," *Economic and Political Weekly,* August 27, 1983; *Indian Express,* June 24, 1985.

23. *Times of India,* March 19, 1985.

24. Upendra Baxi, "Reflections on the Reservation Crisis in Gujarat," in *Mirrors of Violence: Communities, Riots, and Survivors in South Asia,* ed. Veena Das (Delhi: Oxford University Press, 1990), 231–32.

25. Ibid., 234.

26. *Times of India,* April 28, 1985.

27. *India Today,* August 15, 1985, 61.

28. Ibid., August 13, 1985, 60 and 119.

29. Baxi, "Reflections," 238.

30. Ibid., 230.

31. *Times of India,* July 21, 1986, editorial.

32. Ibid., July 21, 1986.

33. Christophe Jaffrelot, ed., *The Sangh Parivar: A Reader* (New Delhi: Oxford University Press, 2005), 1–22, provides an excellent introduction to the array of Sangh institutions.

34. Ornit Shani, "The Rise of Hindu Nationalism in India: The Case Study of Ahmedabad in the 1980s," *Modern Asian Studies* 39, no. 4 (2005): 861–96. See also Ornit Shani, *Communalism, Caste, and Hindu Nationalism: The Violence in Gujarat* (Cambridge: Cambridge University Press, 2007).

35. Shani, "Rise of Hindu Nationalism," 875.

36. Ibid., 876.

37. Ibid.,888.

38. The information on Latif is drawn primarily from a lengthy biographical sketch published in the *Jansatta* daily newspaper on November 30, 1997, the day after Latif was murdered by the police. See also *India Today,* February 28, 1987, 57, 59.

39. *Jansatta,* November 30, 1997.

40. My own random interviews and conversations during the days immediately after Latif's death were consistent with that viewpoint.

41. Anjana Desai, *Environmental Perception: The Human Factor in Urban Planning* (New Delhi: Ashish Publishing House, 1985); Harish Doshi, *Traditional Neighborhood in a Modern City* (New Delhi: Abhinav Publications, 1974).

42. Ashoke Chatterji, "Ahmedabad: A Culture of Confidence," *Times of India,* Ahmedabad edition, August 24, 1986.

43. Ashutosh Varshney, *Ethnic Conflict and Civic Life: Hindus and Muslims in India* (New Haven, Conn.: Yale University Press, 2002).

CHAPTER 11. **Ahmedabad 2000**

1. Because much of the organization was structured as an array of unions, SEWA preferred to call itself a membership-based organization (MBO) to distinguish itself from nongovernmental organizations (NGOs), which might or might not have large memberships.

2. Indira Hirway and Darshini Mahadevia, *Gujarat Human Development Report, 1999* (Ahmedabad: Mahatma Gandhi Labour Institute, 1999), 245.

3. *Gujarat State: Socio-Economic Review, 1999–2000* (Gandhinagar: Directorate of Economics and Statistics, 2000), xviii.

4. Indira Hirway and Darshini Mahadevia, *Gujarat Human Development Report, 2004* (Ahmedabad: Mahatma Gandhi Labour Institute, n.d.), 26.

5. Pravin Visaria and Sudarshan Iyengar, "Economic Prospects," *Seminar* 470 (October 1998): 26.

6. *Times of India,* July 26, 2000, cites Vallabh Patel, president of the Ahmedabad Diamond Association, stating that the number of workers engaged in diamond polishing in the city had gone up from 25,000 to 200,000 in the past ten years: "Most of these workers were employed with the textile industry and switched over to diamonds when the mills started closing down." Another diamond merchant cited in the July 26, 2000, *Indian Express* claimed 250,000 workers in 1,500 diamond units.

7. While exploring the Bapunagar area of the city on a visit in 2001, I came across dozens of these new diamond-polishing workshops. When I talked about them with some of my academic colleagues, they noted that the workshops had not yet been registered in government data.

8. Indira Hirway and Darshini Mahadevia, *Gujarat Human Development Report, 2004* (Ahmedabad: Mahatma Gandhi Labour Institute, n.d.), 31. Data from State Directorate of Economics and Statistics (2002).

9. Harald Bekkers, "Between Fixing and Forecasting: Provincial Ahmedabad Brokered into a Bridgehead for Globalization from Below" (Ph.D. diss., University of Amsterdam, 2005).

10. Chief inspector of factories, Ahmedabad, cited in Shyam Dutta with Richard Batley, *Urban Governance, Partnership and Poverty,* Working Paper No. 16, Ahmedabad (Birmingham: University of Birmingham, School of Public Policy, 1999), 31.

11. Data from National Sample Surveys, cited in Darshini Mahadevia, *Metropolitan Employment in India* (Ahmedabad: Centre for Development Alternatives, n.d.).

12. Ibid.

13. Hirway and Mahadevia, *Gujarat Human Development Report, 1999,* 86.

14. Apparently based on statistics from 1995. Hirway and Mahadevia, *Gujarat Human Development Report, 2004,* 95–96.

15. Ahmedabad Municipal Corporation and Ahmedabad Urban Development Authority with Technical Support from CEPT University, *City Development Plan: Ahmedabad, 2006–2012,* unpublished report for the Jawaharlal Nehru National Urban Renewal Mission.

16. Hirway and Mahadevia, *Gujarat Human Development Report, 2004,* 96.

17. Ibid., 32, 43–45.

18. "Shri U N Mehta," flyer provided by Torrent Group Public Relations office.

19. Cited in Gita Piramal, *Business Maharajas* (New Delhi: Penguin Books, 1996), 19.

20. Ibid., 24.

21. Ibid., 26.

22. Ibid., 8.

23. Bekkers, *Between Fixing and Forecasting,* develops the point more fully.

24. Hirway and Mahadevia, *Gujarat Human Development Report, 2004,* 96–97.

25. Shyam Dutta with Richard Batley. *Urban Governance: Partnership and Poverty,* Working Paper No. 16, Ahmedabad (Birmingham: University of Birmingham, International Development Department, School of Public Policy, 1999).

26. Conversations with Indira Hirway and Darshini Mahadevia, and with Elaben Bhatt of SEWA.

27. *Vohra Committee Report* (New Delhi: Lok Shakti Abhiyan, 1997).

28. For examples, see the account of the involvement of Latif's gang in narcotics smuggling in his lengthy and fascinating obituary, *Jansatta,* November 30, 1997; "Narco-Terrorism 'High' on the List," in the review of the year's events, *Times of India,* December 25, 1998; Leena Misra, "Gujarat May Be Fast Emerging as a Base for Mumbai's Underworld," *Times of India,* July 26, 2000.

29. Bimal Hasmukh Patel, "Urban Housing Policies of the State in Gujarat, India, 1954–1986: An Analysis of the State's Role in Urban Housing Production Based on a Study of Housing in Ahmedabad" (M.A. thesis, University of California, Berkeley, 1988), 56.

30. Bimal Hasmukh Patel, "The Space of Property Capital: Property Development and Architecture in Ahmedabad" (Ph.D. diss., University of California, Berkeley, 1995), 144–46.

31. Meera Mehta and Dinesh Mehta, *Metropolitan Housing Market: A Study of Ahmedabad* (New Delhi: Sage, 1989), 84.

32. Achyut Yagnik, "Paradoxes of Populism," *Economic and Political Weekly,* August 27, 1983, 112–13.

33. Ghanshyam Shah, *Protest Movements in Two Indian States: A Study of the Gujarat and Bihar Movements* (Delhi: Ajanta Publications, 1977); Dawn Jones and Rodney Jones, "Urban Upheaval in India: The 1974 Nav Nirman Riots in Gujarat," *Asian Survey* 16, no. 11 (November 1976): 1012–33; Jones and Jones, "The Scholars' Rebellion: Educational Interests and Agitational Politics in Gujarat," *Journal of Asian Studies* 36, no. 3 (1977): 457–76. Pravin N. Sheth, *Nav Nirman and Political Change in India: From Gujarat 1974 to New Delhi 1977* (Bombay: Vora, 1977). Chimanbhai Patel represented his own view of the events in *Gujaratni Ghatnaono Ghatsphot* [The Events in Gujarat Revealed] (published privately, 1995).

34. Harish Khare, "An Unending Struggle for Gujarat's Political Soul," *Seminar* 470 (October 1998): 17–23, esp. 17.

35. *Times of India,* July 17, 2000.

36. Ibid.

37. Patel, "Space of Property Capital," 144–46.

38. *India Today,* international ed., December 18, 2000, 20.

39. Ibid.

40. Bekkers, *Between Fixing and Forecasting,* 110.

41. Brad Johnson and Chetan Vaidya, "Revised Draft: Lessons Learned: Ahmedabad Municipal Bond and Water Supply and Sewerage Project" (New Delhi: United States Agency for International Development [USAID], n.d.), 12–13.

42. Ibid.; Ahmedabad Municipal Corporation, *Sonari Sapnanun Shaher* [City of Our Golden Dreams] (Ahmedabad: Ahmedabad Municipal Corporation, 2000), 56.

43. Interview with Keshav Verma, June 12, 2000, Washington, D.C., and several interviews with P. U. Asnani in Ahmedabad, 1997–99.

44. Marina R. Pinto, *Metropolitan Governance in India* (New Delhi: Sage, 2000).

45. "Forging Urban Partnerships" and other publicity materials prepared by the Ahmedabad Municipal Corporation.

46. Janelle Plummer, *Municipalities and Community Participation: A Sourcebook for Capacity Building* (London: Earthscan Publications, 1999).

47. The bond issue was shepherded along by the then–deputy municipal commissioner, P. U. Asnani, who was also working as the Urban Environment Infrastructure Representative for India with the USAID agency in New Delhi.

48. Dwijendra Tripathi, *Alliance for Change: A Slum Upgrading Experiment in Ahmedabad* (New Delhi: McGraw-Hill, 1998); Dwijendra Tripathi and Jyoti Jumani, "Change after Alliance: The Sequel to a Slum Upgrading Experiment in Ahmedbad" (unpublished manuscript, 2000).

49. Plummer, *Municipalities and Community Participation,* esp. 124.

50. Kenneth Gillion, *Ahmedabad* (Berkeley: University of California Press, 1968).

51. Cofounder with Arvind Buch of the TLA.

52. *SEWA in 1999: Annual Report* (Ahmedabad: SEWA, 1999), 63.

53. *Indian Express,* July 16, 2000, wrote of Rs. 1,000 crores of damage; *Times of India,* July 16, 2000, wrote of business losses of Rs. 500 crores; the conveners of the public meeting claimed up to Rs. 10,000 crores. The floods, the damage, and the public response were the major news stories for several successive days for these newspapers and for Ahmedabad's major Gujarati-language newspapers as well, including *Gujarat Samachar, Sandesh,* and *Jansatta.*

54. Sarita Kaushik, "The Floods in Retrospect; Lessons Not Yet Learned," *Times of India,* August 18, 2000, 2.

55. Flyer distributed at the public joint meeting.

56. *Times of India,* July 17, 2000.

57. *Indian Express,* August 7, 2000.

58. Lincoln Steffens, *The Autobiography of Lincoln Steffens* (Chautauqua, N.Y.: Chautauqua Press, 1931), 618.

59. James S. Coleman, *Foundations of Social Theory* (Cambridge, Mass.: Harvard University Press, 1990).

60. Douglass C. North, *Institutions, Institutional Change and Economic Performance* (Cambridge: Cambridge University Press, 1990).

61. Coleman, *Foundations.*

62. Robert Putnam's careful study of the contrasting political cultures of northern and southern Italy, *Making Democracy Work* (Princeton, N.J.: Princeton University Press,

1993), makes especially clear the importance of historical experience in the formation of political cultures. Putnam's more recent work, *Bowling Alone* (New York: Simon and Schuster, 2000), carries a similar analysis to contemporary America.

63. Cited in *Times of India,* July 19, 2000. This quote is entirely consistent with Patel's view expressed to me in many interviews and conversations, 1997–2010.

CHAPTER 12. Godhra, the Gujarat Pogrom, and the Consequences

1. The literature on the Ahmedabad and Gujarat pogrom of 2002 is abundant and continues to grow as new information surfaces. For a description, analysis, and summary, see Howard Spodek, "In the Hindutva Laboratory: Pogroms and Politics in Gujarat, 2002," *Modern Asian Studies* 44, no. 2 (March 2010): 349–99.

2. Ashis Nandy et al., *Creating a Nationality: The Ramjanmabhumi Movement and the Fear of Self* (New Delhi: Oxford University Press, 1997). The section discussing Gujarat (102–23) was contributed by Achyut Yagnik, a highly respected journalist and civil rights activist in Ahmedabad.

3. Achyut Yagnik and Suchitra Sheth, *The Shaping of Modern Gujarat: Plurality, Hindutva, and Beyond* (New Delhi: Penguin Books, 2005), 260.

4. Ashutosh Varshney, *Ethnic Conflict and Civic Life: Hindus and Muslims in India* (New Haven, Conn.: Yale University Press, 2002), 97.

5. Ibid., 103.

6. P. Patel, "Sectarian Mobilization, Factionalism and Voting," in *Economic and Political Weekly,* August 21, 1999, 2423–33, cited in *The Sangh Parivar: A Reader,* ed. Christophe Jaffrelot (New York: Oxford University Press, 2005), 300.

7. V. Kannu Pillai, "A Social Study of the Communal Violence in Gujarat" (Ph.D. diss., Gujarat University, Ahmedabad, 1995), 90.

8. Esther David, "The Sacred and the Profane," *Times of India,* December 28, 1997, 15.

9. *Times of India,* December 27, 1998; July 21, 1998; and continuously for several days afterward. See also year-end review of events, December 27, 1998.

10. Sanjay Pandey, "Fire Extinguished, Porn Blaze Continues," *Gujarat Age,* December 24, 1998.

11. "'Culture Cops' and Minority-Bashing Pervade the Scene," *Times of India,* December 25, 1998, 5.

12. Jaffrelot, *Sangh Parivar,* 299.

13. Christophe Jaffrelot, "The BJP at the Centre: A Central and Centrist Party?," in *The Sangh Parivar: A Reader,* ed. Christophe Jaffrelot (New York: Oxford University Press, 2005), 302.

14. Ibid., 301–2.

15. Ibid., 299. The RSS and the VHP conducted training camps for youth and for prospective leaders throughout India. Most of these camps were routine, but one, conducted on the outskirts of Ahmedabad in 1992, was quite different. It was later identified as the training grounds for the Ayodhya attack itself. *Times of India,* Ahmedabad, December 20, 1992, 1.

16. Francine Frankel, *India's Political Economy, 1947–2004,* 2nd ed. (New Delhi: Oxford University Press, 2005), 743.

17. Praveen Togadia interview, August 3, 2006.

18. Julio Ribeiro, "Lost Middle Ground: A Community Loses Hope in Gujarat," *Times of India,* April 23, 2002, reprinted in *Gujarat Carnage,* ed. Asghar Ali Engineer (Hyderabad: Orient Longman, 2003), 157–58.

19. Frankel, *India's Political Economy,* 753. The prime minister's office released a transcript that read, "Wherever such Muslims live . . ." Members of the audience reported that the word *such* did not appear in the speech. A videotape confirmed this. Later, under questioning in Parliament, the prime minister admitted this. *Hindu,* May 17, 2002, cited in Siddharth Varadarajan, ed., *Gujarat: The Making of a Tragedy* (New Delhi: Penguin Books, 2002), 26.

20. Journalist Dionne Bunsha, in "Riding the Hate Wave," *Frontline* 19, no. 26 (December 21, 2002–January 3, 2003), http://www.frontlineonnet.com/fl1926/stories/20030103007812600.htm, notes that bootlegging was also politicized. She cites a local police officer as saying: "After the BJP government came, Hindu bootleggers have become more powerful than the Muslim ones."

21. Varadarajan, *Gujarat,* 31.

22. I report this from personal experience. See also Rubina Jasani, "'Sarkar nadi ke us-par rehne wale logon ke liye hay' [The state exists for the people living on the other side of the river]—Violence and Minority Citizenship in Ahmedabad" (unpublished paper delivered at annual conference of European Association for South Asian Studies, Leiden, the Netherlands, June 27–30, 2006); and Rubina Jasani, "Violence, Re-construction and Islamic Reform: Stories from the Muslim 'Ghetto'" (paper presented at the South Asian Anthropologists' Group Meeting, Goldsmith's College, London, "The Future for South Asia: Revolution? Disaster?," July 3–4, 2006.

23. Ashutosh Varshney, *Ethnic Conflict and Civic Life: Hindus and Muslims in India* (New Haven, Conn.: Yale University Press, 2002).

24. Swami Agnivesh and Valson Thampu, eds., *Harvest of Hate: Gujarat under Siege* (New Delhi: Rupa, 2002), 38–39.

25. Hanif Lakdawala, head of Sanchetna, an NGO based in Ahmedabad, working primarily with Muslims and Dalits, interviewed by Yogi Sikand, November 15, 2005 (http://www.zmag.org/content/showarticle.cfm?ItemID=9123).

26. This number is frequently reported as fifty-eight, the number reported at the time. Another victim of the fire died a few days later, bringing the total to fifty-nine.

27. Spodek, "In the Hindutva Laboratory."

28. Engineer, *Gujarat Carnage,* 19.

29. In the heat of the debates about the violence, some referred to the attacks as genocide. This term is exaggerated, used beyond its normal definition, signifying an attempt to wipe out an entire population. The term *pogrom,* however, identifying the complicity of the state in the organized attacks, is accurate.

30. Varadarajan, *Gujarat,* 418, citing Ghanshyam Shah from EPW.

31. Valjibhai Patel, interviewed by Yogi Sikand, November 15, 2005 (http://sam-maditthi.net/dialogue/dialogue_vpatel.asp).

32. Sajeda Momin, *Statesman,* April 4, 2002, cited in Engineer, *Gujarat Carnage,* 116.

33. Frankel, *India's Political Economy,* 743.

34. Engineer, *Gujarat Carnage,* 115.

35. SEWA (Self-Employed Women's Association), *Shantipath: Our Road to Restoring Peace* (Ahmedabad: SEWA, 2002), 41.

36. Nalin Mehta, "Modi and the Camera: The Politics of Television in the 2002 Gujarat Riots," *South Asia: Journal of South Asian Studies* 29, no. 3 (December 2006): 395–414.

37. Bunsha, "Riding the Hate Wave."

38. Engineer, *Gujarat Carnage,* 27.

39. Nalin Mehta, "Modi and the Camera: The Politics of Television in the 2002 Gujarat Riots," 401.

40. Sajeda Momin, "In the Ghetto," in Engineer, *Gujarat Carnage,* 114.

41. Shah Wali Gujarat was a seventeenth-century Urdu poet who pioneered *ghazal* writing in its present form. He also was the first poet to have compiled a collection of prose, *Divan-e-Vali,* which contained hundreds of *ghazals* and other forms of poetry.

42. Rubina Jasani, *Indian Express,* March 13, 2002.

43. SEWA, *Shantipath,* 6.

44. K. N. Panikkar in Engineer, *Gujarat Carnage,* 94–95. In contrast to the previous episodes of violence between Hindus and Muslims within the city of Ahmedabad, where the violence would begin from the walled city or the old city and spread to other parts, especially to the labor areas, in 2002, the violence began in the outer suburban labor neighborhoods of Ahmedabad. The areas that saw maximum violence were Chamanpura, Naroda Patia, Saijpur Bogha, and Meghaninagar, located on the northeastern periphery of the city. These areas were located in close proximity to the old textile mill areas and comprised migrant Muslims who lived in *chawls* (one- and two-room tenements built like long walk-throughs).

45. Tanika Sarkar, "Semiotics of Terror in India: Muslim Children and Women in Hindu Rashtra," *Economic and Political Weekly* 37, no. 28 (July 13, 2002): 2874.

46. Bunsha, "Riding the Hate Wave," 39, summarizing eyewitness reports in the Human Rights Watch report, *"'We have no orders to save you': State Participation and Complicity in Communal Violence in Gujarat* (http://www.hrw.org/legacy/reports/2002/india/).

47. Interview with former director general of Punjab police Kanwar Pal Singh Gill by Onkar Singh, Rediff.com, July 30, 2002 (http://www.rediff.com/news/2002/jul/30inter1 .htm).

48. Ibid.

49. Cited in Engineer, 305, from A Women's Fact Finding Panel, which visited Gujarat and issued its report, "The Survivors Speak." Engineer, *Gujarat Carnage,* titled the reprint, "How the Gujarat Massacre Affected Minority Women."

50. Frankel, *India's Political Economy,* 750.

51. *Times of India,* national ed., March 20, 2002.

52. SEWA, *Shantipath,* 34, 33.

53. Reference and translation provided by the Gujarati poet Panna Naik in "The Outsider-Muslim in Gujarati Literature" (paper delivered at the Association of Asian Studies annual meeting, 2004, San Diego, Calif.).

54. Bunsha, "Riding the Hate Wave," on the Confederation of Indian Industry.

55. Testimony of former additional chief secretary (home) Ashok Narayan before Nanavati-Shah Commission of Inquiry, in Bunsha, "Riding the Hate Wave," 32.

56. Cited in Engineer, *Gujarat Carnage,* 8, 9, and in Frankel, *India's Political Economy,* 750.

57. Bunsha, "Riding the Hate Wave," 32.

58. *Outlook,* June 3, 2002; Engineer, *Gujarat Carnage,* 424. Five years later, just before Gujarat's 2007 election, the investigative newsmagazine *Tehelka* published the results of a sting operation it had performed, capturing on audio- and videotape statements of participants who affirmed the complicity of the state government that had been reported in 2002. "Gujarat 2002—The Truth: Full Coverage," *Tehelka* 4, no. 44

(November 17, 2007) (http://www.tehelka.com/story_main35.asp?filename=Ne031107 Conspirators.asp).

59. Human Rights Watch, *"We have no orders to save you."*

60. Bunsha, "Riding the Hate Wave," 59.

61. Ibid., 15, 57–58.

62. Engineer, *Gujarat Carnage,* 20.

63. Frankel, *India's Political Economy,* 742.

64. Bunsha, "Riding the Hate Wave," 9.

65. Cf. the report issued by Julio Ribeiro on the emasculation of the Gujarat police force by the state's political leadership; *Times of India,* April 23, 2002, reprinted in Engineer, *Gujarat Carnage,* 156–57.

66. This common understanding of the engineering of violence finds expression, more academically, in the extensive writings of political scientist Paul Brass. Brass explains further that after the violence is engineered, attempts are made by the engineers to disguise their work: "Their violent manifestations appear spontaneous, undirected, unplanned—and even the most carefully planned and well-organized assaults on the other community are *designed* to appear so. Since such riotous violence is illegitimate and the elements of preplanning in it are disguised, the struggle that takes place afterwards to explain it—that is, to control its interpretation—is crucial. The most common explanation is that the violence was in fact an unplanned, spontaneous expression of the deep feelings of an aggrieved people, but there are many others . . . Here I want to note mostly the multiple functions served by capturing the meaning of a Hindu–Muslim or any other intercommunal, interreligious, interethnic riot in a particular way. These include legitimizing illegitimate violence, concealing the extent of preplanning and organization that preceded it, and maintaining intact the persons, groups, and organizations most deeply implicated in the violence by preventing punishment of the principal perpetrators." Paul Brass, *The Production of Hindu–Muslim Violence in Contemporary India* (Seattle: University of Washington Press, 2003), 14.

67. Usha Thakkar, "The Gujarat Assembly Elections 2002—Results and Ramifications," in *Current Domestic Policy Challenges and Prospects in South Asia,* ed. Institute of Regional Studies (Islamabad: Institute of Regional Studies, 2003), 62–80.

68. Ibid.

69. Ibid.

70. *Order of the Election Commission of India,* No. 464/GJ-LA/2002, August 16, 2002, reprinted in M. L. Sondhi and Apratim Mukarji, eds., *The Black Book of Gujarat* (New Delhi: Manak Publications, 2002), 448–49; full report, 420–53.

71. Ibid., 453.

72. *India Today International,* November 25, 2002, 20, and December 30, 32.

73. Ibid., December 30, 2002, 33

74. Ibid., 38.

75. *India Today,* October 7, 2002, 13.

76. Ibid., 17.

77. Ibid., 17–18.

78. Bunsha, "Riding the Hate Wave," 129.

79. Pravin Sheth, *Global Terrorism: Melting Borders, Hardened Walls* (Jaipur: Rawat, 2005), 246.

80. Ibid.

81. Ibid.

82. "Amdavadis Turn to Walls, Iron Gates to Replace Trust," *Times of India,* May 30, 2002.

83. Jasani, "Sarkar nadi ke us-par rehne wale logon ke liye hay" and "Violence, Re-construction and Islamic Reform"; and Darshini Mahadevia, "A City with Many Borders—Beyond Ghettoization in Ahmedabad," in *Indian Cities in Transition,* ed. Annapurna Shaw (New Delhi: Orient Longman, 2006), 132–69.

84. Jasani, "Violence, Re-construction and Islamic Reform," 6. Cf. also the denunciation of the state for inaction in the statement of Harsh Mander, a high-ranking civil servant who left his position after the riots: Harsh Mander, "Cry, the Beloved Country," in Agnivesh and Thampu, *Harvest of Hate,* 138.

85. Varadarajan, *Gujarat,* 23, cited from *Asian Age,* June 7, 2002. The director of SEWA's health and insurance program remarked to me that on a site visit in Juhapura, she was warmly received and residents helped her with her work, yet as she walked through the area, a child called out, "Look, there is a Hindu woman over there," as if she were a visitor from another world—which in a way she was. Personal conversation with Mirai Chatterjee, SEWA, 2008, and in e-mail exchange, 2009.

86. "Of Dark Clouds and Silver Linings," *Hindu Online,* October 27, 2002 (http://www.hinduonnet.com/thehindu/mag/2002/10/27/stories/2002102700240400.htm).

87. The translation is by Jayant Joshi, the playwright's father. Neither the play nor the translation has yet been published.

88. A. G. Noorani, "Modi and His Visa," *Frontline* 23, no. 8 (April 9–22, 2005): 47–50 (http://www.frontlineonnet.com/fl2208/stories/20050422000704700.htm).

89. Ibid., 51.

90. *Times of India,* July 15, 2006.

91. Ibid., August 2, 2006.

92. These numbers continued to fluctuate slightly because the numbers of injured were reported differently and because some of the wounded later died of their injuries. *DNA,* July 29, 2008, 1. *DNA-City,* July 30, 2008, 2. *Times of India,* August 3, 2008, 2.

93. *Times of India,* August 1, 2008, 1.

94. Ibid.

95. *Times of India,* August 3, 2008, 1. *DNA* noted July 31, 2008, 1, that Modi had also said that any terrorist who targeted Gujarat would be arrested within twenty-four hours.

96. Anupama Katakam, "Time to Answer," *Frontline* 27, no. 8 (April 10–23, 2010), http://www.flonnet.com/fl2708/stories/20100423270803400.htm.

97. *Times of India,* July 21, 2006.

98. Ibid.; see also V. Nagarajan, "Ahmedabad Real Estate Mart: Up, Up and Away," MagicBricks.com, January 10, 2007 (http://property.magicbricks.com/news_tracker/ahmedabad.html).

99. Darshini Mahadevia and Harpreet Singh Brar, "Changes and Continuities in Development Priorities: Ahmedabad," in *Inside the Transforming Urban Asia,* ed. Darshini Mahadevia (New Delhi: Concept Publishing, 2008), 132.

100. *Times of India,* August 1 and 14, 2006.

101. "'Brand Ahmedabad' Set to Rediscover the City," *Hindu Business Line,* December 23, 2006, http://www.thehindubusinessline.com/2006/12/23/stories/2006122302891900.htm.

102. Reported by Reuters, February 27, 2007, http://in.today.reuters.com/news/ newsArticle.aspx?type=topNews&storyID=2007-02-27T105047Z_01_NOOTR_ RTRJONC_0_India-289315-1.xml.

103. *Ahmedabad Mirror,* May 5, 2010, http://www.ahmedabadmirror.com/index.asp x?page=article&sectid=59&contentid=2009122420091224030927698988c4478.

104. The plight of the poor is the subject of constant reporting. See, for example, "30,000 People Homeless after Demolition Drive," *Times of India,* Ahmedabad, November 18, 2009. For the viewpoint of a distinguished public interest lawyer, see Girish Patel, *Public Interest Litigation and the Poor in Gujarat* (Ahmedabad: Girish Patel Sanman Samiti, 2009).

105. Among the many studies of Los Angeles through the prism of a "Los Angeles School" are Edward Soja, *Postmodern Geographies: The Reassertion of Space in Critical Theory* (New York: Verso, 1989), and William Fulton, *The Reluctant Metropolis: The Politics of Urban Growth in Los Angeles* (Baltimore, Md.: Johns Hopkins University Press, 2001).

BIBLIOGRAPHY

Agnivesh, Swami, and Valson Thampu, eds. *Harvest of Hate: Gujarat under Siege*. New Delhi: Rupa, 2002.

Ahmedabad District Gazetteer. Gujarat State Gazetteers. Ahmedabad: Gujarat State, 1984.

Ahmedabad Municipal Corporation. *Sonari Sapnanun Shaher* [City of Our Golden Dreams]. Ahmedabad: Ahmedabad Municipal Corporation, 2000.

———. *Statistical Outline of Ahmedabad City*. Ahmedabad: Ahmedabad Municipal Corporation, 1994–95.

Ahmedabad Municipal Corporation and Ahmedabad Urban Development Authority with Technical Support from CEPT University. *City Development Plan: Ahmedabad, 2006–2012*. Unpublished report for the Jawaharlal Nehru National Urban Renewal Mission, 2006.

Ahmedabad Textile Industry Research Association (ATIRA). *Rehabilitation of the Textile Industry*. Ahmedabad: Ahmedabad Textile Industry Research Association, 1985.

Anubhai, Praful. "The Textile Industry in Ahmedabad: The 2001 Scenario." *Times Research Foundation Seminar*, vol. 3. Ahmedabad: Times of India, 1988.

Banker, Shankarlal. *Gandhiji ane Majooropravrutiyo* [Gandhi and Labor Activities]. Ahmedabad: Navajivan Press, 1965.

Basu, Aparna. *Mridula Sarabhai: Rebel with a Cause*. Delhi: Oxford University Press, 1996.

Batley, Richard. *Urban Management in India, Part II: Urban Management in the State of Gujarat, Ahmedabad*. Institutional Framework of Urban Government Case Study No. 8. Birmingham: University of Birmingham, International Development Department, 1992.

Baxi, Upendra. "Reflections on the Reservation Crisis in Gujarat." In *Mirrors of Violence: Communities, Riots and Survivors in South Asia*, edited by Veena Das, 215–39. Delhi: Oxford University Press, 1990.

Bekkers, Harald. "Between Fixing and Forecasting: Provincial Ahmedabad Brokered into a Bridgehead for Globalization from Below." Ph.D. diss., University of Amsterdam, 2005.

Bhagat, Aalji. "The 'X' of the Mill and of the Vote." In *Shramik Kavita* [Labour Poems], edited by Rameshchandra Parmar. Ahmedabad, n.d.

Bhagat, Kacharabhai, et al. *Mahajan Nahote Tyaru* [Before the Mahajan]. Ahmedabad: Jamnadas Bhagvandas Trust, 1970.

Bhatt, Brahmakumar. *Le Ke Rahenge Mahagujarat* [We Will Not Rest until We Have Mahagujarat]. Ahmedabad, 1994.

Bhatt, Ela. *We Are Poor but So Many: The Story of Self-Employed Women in India*. New York: Oxford University Press, 2006.

Bhatt, Tushar. *Sketches in the Sand.* Ahmedabad: Image Publications, 1994.

Bombay Government. *Gazetteer of the Bombay Presidency: Gujarat.* Vol. 4, *Ahmedabad.* Bombay: Government Central Press, 1879.

———. *Royal Commission on Indian Labour: Memorandum from the Government of Bombay.* Bombay: Government of Bombay, 1929.

Brahmabhatt, Aniruddh, ed. *Ramanbhai Nilkanth* [Ramanbhai Nilkanth: A Collection of Critical Essays]. Bombay: Ashok Prakashan, 1973.

Brass, Paul. *The Production of Hindu–Muslim Violence in Contemporary India.* Seattle: University of Washington Press, 2003.

Breman, Jan. "Ghettoization and Communal Politics: The Dynamics of Inclusion and Exclusion in the Hindutva Landscape." In *Institutions and Inequalities: Essays in Honour of André Beteille,* edited by Ramachandra Guha and Jonathan D. Parry, 259–84. New Delhi: Oxford University Press, 1999.

———. *The Making and Unmaking of an Industrial Working Class: Sliding Down the Labour Hierarchy in Ahmedabad, India.* New Delhi: Oxford University Press, 2004.

Briggs, Asa. *Victorian Cities.* London: Odhams Press, 1963. Reprint, Berkeley: University of California Press, 1993.

Brown, Judith M. *Gandhi and Civil Disobedience: The Mahatma in Indian Politics, 1928–34.* Cambridge: Cambridge University Press, 1977.

———. *Gandhi: Prisoner of Hope.* New Haven, Conn.: Yale University Press, 1989.

———. *Gandhi's Rise to Power: Indian Politics, 1915–1922.* Cambridge: Cambridge University Press, 1972.

Bunsha, Dionne. *Scarred: Experiments with Violence in Gujarat.* New Delhi: Penguin, 2007.

Chandavarkar, Rajnarayan. *Imperial Power and Popular Politics: Class, Resistance and the State in India, 1850–1950.* Cambridge: Cambridge University Press, 1998.

Chandra, Bipan, Mridula Mukherjee, and Aditya Mukherjee. *India after Independence, 1947–2000.* New Delhi: Viking, 1999.

Chowdhry, Kamla. "Institution Builder." In *Vikram Sarabhai: The Man and the Vision,* edited by Padmanabh Joshi, 79–80. Ahmedabad: Mapin Publishing, 1992.

Chowdhury, S. Roy. "Industrial Restructuring, Unions, and the State: Textile Mill Workers in Ahmedabad." *Economic and Political Weekly* 31, no. 8 (February 24, 1996), , L-7–L-13.

Coleman, James S. *Foundations of Social Theory.* Cambridge, Mass.: Harvard University Press, 1990.

Dave, V. S. *Report of the Commission of Inquiry into the Incidents of Violence and Disturbances which Took Place at Various Places in the State of Gujarat since February, 1985 to 18th July, 1985.* 2 vols. Gandhinagar: Government Central Press, 1990.

Desai, Anjana. *Environmental Perception: The Human Factor in Urban Planning.* New Delhi: Ashish Publishing House, 1985.

Desai, A. R., and Wilfred D'Costa. *State and Repressive Culture: A Case Study of Gujarat.* Bombay: Popular Prakashan, 1994.

Desai, Khandubhai. *Textile Labour Association Ahmedabad: An Indigenous Experiment in Trade Union Movement.* Ahmedabad: Textile Labour Association, 1948.

Dhruv, Saroop. *Hastkshep* [Collection of Poems]. Ahmedabad: Sanvedan Sanskrutik Manch, 2003.

Doshi, Harish. *Traditional Neighborhood in a Modern City.* New Delhi: Abhinav Publications, 1974.

Dutta, Shyam, with Richard Batley. *Urban Governance, Partnership and Poverty.* Working Paper No. 16, Ahmedabad. Birmingham: University of Birmingham, School of Public Policy, 1999.

Engineer, Asghar Ali. "Ahmedabad: From Caste to Communal Violence." *Economic and Political Weekly,* April 13, 1985, 628–30.

———. "Communal Fire Engulfs Ahmedabad Once Again." *Economic and Political Weekly,* July 6, 1985, 1116–20.

———, ed. *Communal Riots in Post Independence India.* Hyderabad: Sangam Books, 1984.

———, ed. *Gujarat Carnage.* Hyderabad: Orient Longman, 2003.

Erikson, Erik. *Gandhi's Truth: On the Origins of Militant Non-Violence.* New York: Norton, 1969.

Frankel, Francine. *India's Political Economy, 1947–2004.* 2nd ed. New Delhi: Oxford University Press, 2005.

Fulton, William. *The Reluctant Metropolis: The Politics of Urban Growth in Los Angeles.* Baltimore, Md.: Johns Hopkins University Press, 2001.

Gandhi, Mohandas Karamchand. *An Autobiography, or The Story of My Experiments with Truth.* Translated by Mahadev Desai. Ahmedabad: Navajivan Publishing House, 1927.

———. *Collected Works of Mahatma Gandhi.* Volumes 1–100. New Delhi: Publications Division, Government of India, 1958–94.

———. *Hind Swaraj, or Indian Home Rule.* 1909. Ahmedabad: Navajivan Press, 1938.

Gandhi, Rajmohan. *Patel: A Life.* Ahmedabad: Navajivan Press, 1990.

Gillion, Kenneth. *Ahmedabad.* Berkeley: University of California Press, 1968.

———. "Gujarat in 1919." In *Essays on Gandhian Politics: The Rowlatt Satyagraha of 1919,* edited by Ravinder Kumar, 126–44. Oxford: Clarendon Press, 1971.

Government of India. *India, 1998: A Reference Annual.* New Delhi: Government of India, Ministry of Information and Broadcasting, Publications Division, 1998.

Guha, Ramachandra. *India after Gandhi: The History of the World's Largest Democracy.* London: Macmillan, 2007.

Gujarat State: Socio-Economic Review, 1999–2000. Gandhinagar: Directorate of Economics and Statistics, 2000.

Hay, Stephen, ed. *Sources of Indian Tradition.* 2nd ed. New York: Columbia University Press, 1988.

Haynes, Douglas. *Rhetoric and Ritual in Colonial India: The Shaping of a Public Culture in Surat City, 1852–1928.* Berkeley: University of California Press, 1991.

Hirway, Indira, and Darshini Mahadevia. *Gujarat Human Development Report, 1999.* Ahmedabad: Mahatma Gandhi Labour Institute, 1999.

———. *Gujarat Human Development Report, 2004.* Ahmedabad: Mahatma Gandhi Labour Institute, n.d.

Hopkins, E. W. *India: Old and New.* New York: Scribners, 1901.

Hunter, Floyd. *Community Power Structure: A Study of Decision Makers.* Chapel Hill: University of North Carolina Press, 1953.

India, Census Commissioner. *Census of India, 1931, Bombay Presidency.* Delhi: Manager of Publications, 1932.

India, Supreme Court. *Report of Proceedings in the Appeal from Award of the Industrial Court Gujarat. The Ahmedabad Millowners Association Ahmedabad & Ors. versus The Textile Labour Association, Ahmedabad.* New Delhi, 1965.

India, Tariff Board. *Report of the Indian Tariff Board (Cotton Texile Industry Enquiry), 1927.* Bombay: Government Central Press, 1927, 1:25.

Irschick, Eugene F. *Politics and Social Conflict in South India: The Non-Brahman Movement and Tamil Separatism, 1916–1929.* Berkeley: University of California Press, 1969.

Isaka, Riho. "Gujarati Intellectuals and History Writing in the Colonial Period." *Economic and Political Weekly* 37, no. 48 (November 30–December 6, 2002): 4867–72.

Jaffrelot, Christophe. "The BJP at the Centre: A Central and Centrist Party?" In *The Sangh Parivar: A Reader,* edited by Christophe Jaffrelot, 268–317. New York: Oxford University Press, 2005.

———. *The Hindu Nationalist Movement and Indian Politics, 1925 to the 1990s.* New Delhi: Penguin Books, 1996.

———, ed. *The Sangh Parivar: A Reader.* New Delhi: Oxford University Press, 2005.

Jani, Manishi. *Textile Workers: Jobless and Miserable.* Ahmedabad: SETU, 1984.

Jasani, Rubina. "'Sarkar nadi ke us-par rehne wale logon ke liye hay' [The state exists for the people living on the other side of the river]—Violence and Minority Citizenship in Ahmedabad." Paper presented at the European Association for South Asian Studies, Leiden, the Netherlands, June 27–30, 2006.

———. "Violence, Re-construction and Islamic Reform: Stories from the Muslim 'Ghetto.'" Paper delivered at South Asian Anthropologists' Group Meeting, Goldsmith's College, London, "The Future for South Asia: Revolution? Disaster?" July 3–4, 2006.

Jhabvala, Renana. *Closing Doors.* Ahmedabad: SETU, 1985.

Jhabvala, Renana, and Usha Jumani. "Ahmedabad 2001—Planning for the Poor: A Focus on Self Employed Women." In *Seminar on Ahmedabad, 2001.* Vol. 6, part B. Calcutta: Times [of India] Research Foundation Urban Studies Center Seminar, 1988.

Jhaveri, Bipinchandra. *Ramanbhai Nilkanth.* Ahmedabad, 1953.

Johnson, Brad, and Chetan Vaidya. "Revised Draft: Lessons Learned: Ahmedabad Municipal Bond and Water Supply and Sewerage Project." New Delhi: United States Agency for International Development (USAID), n.d.

Jones, Dawn, and Rodney Jones. "The Scholars' Rebellion: Educational Interests and Agitational Politics in Gujarat." *Journal of Asian Studies* 36, no. 2 (May 1977): 457–76.

———. "Urban Upheaval in India: The 1974 Nav Nirman Riots in Gujarat." *Asian Survey* 16, no. 11 (November 1976): 1012–33.

Joshi, Saumya. *Dost! Chokkas Ahi Nagar Vastun Hatun* [My Friend, Surely There Was a City Here]. 2003. Unpublished play. Performed in Ahmedabad and elsewhere under the direction of Saumya Joshi.

Joshi, Umashankar. "Chhinbinn Chhun" [I am shattered]. In *Abhijna*. Ahmedabad: 1967. Translated as "Fragmented" in "An Analysis of 'Fragmented' by Umashankar Joshi in the Rasa-Dhvani Tradition," by Ramanlal Joshi, *East-West Poetics at Work,* 257–66. New Delhi: Sahitya Akademi, 1994.

Jhote, Ratnamanirao Bhimrao. *Gujaratnun Patnagar Ahmedabad* [Gujarat's Capital City, Ahmedabad]. Ahmedabad: Gujarat Sahitya Sabha, 1929.

Kadri, Rizvan. *Sardar Patel: Ek Sinhpurush* [Sardar Patel: A Lion of a Man]. Ahmedabad: Rizvan Kadri, 2003.

Kamath, M. V., and V. B. Kher. *The Story of Militant but Non-Violent Trade Unionism.* Ahmedabad: Navajivan Press, 1993.

Kashyap, S. P. "Industrial Perspective for Ahmedabad Metropolitan Region." *Seminar on Ahmedabad, 2001.* Vol. 2. Calcutta: Times [of India] Research Foundation Urban Studies Center Seminar, 1988.

Khare, Harish. "An Unending Struggle for Gujarat's Political Soul." *Seminar* 470 (October 1998): 17–23.

Kothari, Rita. "Short Story in Gujarati Dalit Literature." *Economic and Political Weekly* 36, no. 45 (November 10, 2001): 4308–11.

Kotval, Sohrab Peshotan. *Report of the Commission of Inquiry on the Cases of Police Firing at Ahedabad on the 12th, 13th and 14th August 1958.* Bombay: Director, Government Printing, Publications and Stationery, 1959.

Lakha, Salim. *Capitalism and Class in Colonial India: The Case of Ahmedabad.* New Delhi: Sterling Publishers, 1988.

Lang, Jon, Madhavi Desai, and Miki Desai. *Architecture and Independence: The Search for Identity—India, 1880 to 1980.* New York: Oxford University Press, 1997.

Macwan, Joseph, ed. *The Stepchild: Angaliyat.* Translated by Rita Kothari. New Delhi: Oxford University Press, 2004.

Mahadevia, Darshini. "A City with Many Borders—Beyond Ghettoization in Ahmedabad." In *Indian Cities in Transition,* ed. Annapurna Shaw, 132–69. New Delhi: Orient Longman, 2006.

———. *Metropolitan Employment in India.* Ahmedabad: Centre for Development Alternatives, n.d.

———, ed. *Inside the Transforming Urban Asia.* New Delhi: Concept Publishing, 2008.

Mahadevia, Darshini, and Harpreet Singh Brar. "Changes and Continuities in Development Priorities: Ahmedabad." In *Inside the Transforming Urban Asia,* ed. Darshini Mahadevia, 132–69. New Delhi: Concept Publishing, 2008.

Mansuri, Mohammed Farid Gulamnabi. "Malay na Malay." In *Satat.* Translated by Raymond Parmar and Howard Spodek. Ahmedabad: Vora, 1970.

Mavalankar, Ganesh Vsudev, and Chandulal Bhagubhai Dalal. *Rashtriya Chalvalmaan Amdavad Municipalitino Falo* [The Contribution of the Ahmedabad Municipality in the National Movement]. Ahmedabad: Navajivan Press, 1962.

Mehta, Dinesh, and Meera Mehta. *Metropolitan Housing Market: A Study of Ahmedabad.* New Delhi: Sage, 1989.

———. *Modelling Urban Housing Strategies for Ahmedabad Urban Area.* Ahmedabad: Center for Environmental Planning and Technology, 1992.

Mehta, Dinkar. *Krantini Khojmaan* [In Quest of Revolution]. Ahmedabad: Lokaayat Gnaankendra Trust, [1984?].

———. *Parivartan: Atmakatha* [Transformation: An Autobiography]. Ahmedabad: Lokaayat Gnaankendra Trust, 1968.

Mehta, Makrand. "Gandhi and Ahmedabad, 1915–20." *Economic and Political Weekly,* January 22, 2005, 291–99.

———. *Hindu Varnvyavastha, Samaj Parivartan, ane Gujaratna Dalito* [The Hindu Caste System, Social Restructuring, and the Dalits of Gujarat]. Ahmedabad: Ami Publications, 1995.

Mehta, Makrand J. *The Ahmedabad Cotton Textile Industry: Genesis and Growth.* Ahmedabad: New Order Book Co., 1982.

Mehta, Nalin. "Modi and the Camera: The Politics of Television in the 2002 Gujarat Riots." *South Asia: Journal of South Asian Studies* 29, no. 3 (December 2006): 395–414.

Mehta, Sharadaben. *Reminiscences: The Memoirs of Sharadaben Mehta.* Compiled and translated by Purnima Mehta Bhatt. New Delhi: Zubaan Publications, 2008.

Mehta, Sumant. *Atmakatha* [Autobiography]. Ahmedabad: Gurjar Granthratna Karyalaya, 1971.

Miyabhoy, N. M. *Prohibition Policy Inquiry Commission Report.* Ahmedabad: Government of Gujarat, 1983.

Mossberger, K., and G. Stoker. "The Evolution of Urban Regime Theory: The Challenge of Conceptualization." *Urban Affairs Review* 36 (2001): 810–35.

Naik, Panna. "The Outsider-Muslim in Gujarati Literature." Paper presented at the Association of Asian Studies annual meeting, 2004, San Diego, Calif.

Nandy, Ashis, et al. *Creating a Nationality: The Ramjanmabhumi Movement and the Fear of Self.* New Delhi: Oxford University Press, 1997.

North, Douglass C. *Institutions, Institutional Change, and Economic Performance.* Cambridge: Cambridge University Press, 1990.

Nussbaum, Martha. *The Clash Within: Democracy, Religious Violence, and India's Future.* Cambridge, Mass.: Harvard University Press, 2007.

Oza, Digant, ed. *Indulal Yagnik: Gujaratni Asmitana Swapnadrashtra* [A Visionary of Gujarat's Identity]. Ahmedabad: R. R. Sheth, 2007.

Parekh, Bansidhar Govardhandas. *Sheth Mangaldas Girdhardas: Jivan ane Kaarya* [Sheth Mangaldas Girdhardas: Life and Works]. Ahmedabad: Sheth Mathuradas Mangaldas, 1955.

Parikh, Narhari D. *Sardar Vallabhbhai Patel.* 2 vols. Ahmedabad: Navajivan Press, 1953, 1978.

Park, Robert E., Ernest W. Burgess, and Morris Janowitz. *The City: Suggestions for Investigation of Human Behavior in the Urban Environment.* Chicago: University of Chicago Press, 1984.

Parmar, Rameshchandra, and Ashok Chaudhuri. "At the Turn of the Century: A Dialogue." *Seminar* 470 (October 1998): 63–68.

Patel, B. B. *Workers of Closed Textile Mills.* New Delhi: Oxford University Press and IBH Publishing, 1988.

Patel, Bimal Hasmukh. "The Space of Property Capital: Property Development and Architecture in Ahmedabad." Ph.D. diss., University of California, Berkeley, 1995.

———. "Urban Housing Policies of the State in Gujarat, India, 1954–1986: An Analysis of the State's Role in Urban Housing Production Based on a Study of Housing in Ahmedabad." M.A. thesis, University of California, Berkeley, 1988.

Patel, Chimanbhai. *Gujaratni Ghatnaono Ghatsphot* [The Events in Gujarat Revealed]. Published privately, 1995.

Patel, Girish. *Public Interest Litigation and the Poor in Gujarat.* Ahmedabad: Girish Patel Sanman Samiti, 2009.

Patel, Gordhanbhai I. *Vithalbhai Patel—Life and Times.* Bombay: Shree Laxmi Narayan Press, 1951.

Patel, Manekbhai. *Ahmedabad Kathaa* [Ahmedabad Stories]. Ahmedabad: Gurjar Granthratna Karyalaya, 1996.

Patel, Sujata. *The Making of Industrial Relations: The Ahmedabad Textile Industry, 1918–1939.* New York: Oxford University Press, 1987.

Pathak, Devavrat N. *Municipal Corporationni Chuntani, 1961* [Election 1961]. Ahmedabad: Gujarat University Press, 1961.

Pathak, Devavrat N., M. G. Parekh, and Kirtidev D. Desai. *Three General Elections in Gujarat.* Ahmedabad: Gujarat University, 1966.

Pathak, Devavrat Nanubhai, and Pravin Natvarlal Sheth. *Sardar Vallabhbhai Patel: From Civic to National Leadership.* Ahmedabad: Navajivan Press, 1980.

Pillai, V. Kannu. "A Social Study of the Communal Violence in Gujarat." Ph.D. diss., Gujarat University, Ahmedabad, 1995.

Pinto, Marina R. *Metropolitan Governance in India.* New Delhi: Sage, 2000.

Piramal, Gita. *Business Maharajas.* New Delhi: Penguin Books, 1996.

Plummer, Janelle. *Municipalities and Community Participation: A Sourcebook for Capacity Building.* London: Earthscan Publications, 1999.

Putnam, Robert. *Bowling Alone.* New York: Simon and Schuster, 2000.

———. *Making Democracy Work.* Princeton, N.J.: Princeton University Press, 1993.

Raychaudhuri, Siddharth. "Indian Elites, Urban Space, and the Restructuring of Ahmedabad City, 1890–1947." Ph.D. diss., St. Catharine's College, Cambridge University, 1997.

Reddy, P. Jaganmohan. *Commission of Inquiry on Communal Disturbance at Various Places in the State of Gujarat on and after 18th September 1969.* Gandhinagar: Government Central Press, 1970.

Roy, Tirthankar. "Development or Distortion? 'Powerlooms' in India, 1950–1997." *Economic and Political Weekly,* April 18, 1998, 897–911.

Saptarshi, L. V. "Ahmedabad Textile Industry in the National Context." In *Seminar on Ahmedabad, 2001.* Vol. 3. Calcutta: Times [of India] Research Foundation Urban Studies Center Seminar, 1988.

Sarkar, Tanika. "Semiotics of Terror in India: Muslim Children and Women in Hindu Rashtra." *Economic and Political Weekly* 37, no. 28 (July 13, 2002): 2874.

Sebstad, Jennifer. *Struggle and Development among Self Employed Women.* Washington, D.C.: United States Agency for International Development, 1982.

Sen, Arup Kumar, "Mode of Labour Control in Colonial India," *Economic and Political Weekly* 37, no. 38 (Sept. 21–27, 2002), 3956–66

Sennett, Richard, ed. *Classic Essays on the Culture of Cities.* New York: Appleton-Century-Crofts, 1969.

SEWA (Self-Employed Women's Association). *Shantipath: Our Road to Restoring Peace.* Ahmedabad: SEWA, 2002.

Shah, Ghanshyam. "Communal Riots in Gujarat: Report of a Preliminary Investigation." *Economic and Political Weekly* 5, no. 3–5 (January 1970): 187–200.

———. *Protest Movements in Two Indian States: A Study of the Gujarat and Bihar Movements.* Delhi: Ajanta Publications, 1977.

Shah, Kunjalata. "Ahmedabad: Pre-Industrial to Industrial Urban Centre (1859–1930)." Ph.D. diss., SNDT University, Bombay.

Shani, Ornit. *Communalism, Caste, and Hindu Nationalism: The Violence in Gujarat.* Cambridge: Cambridge University Press, 2007.

———. "The Rise of Hindu Nationalism in India: The Case Study of Ahmedabad in the 1980s." *Modern Asian Studies* 39, no. 4 (2005): 861–96.

Shaw, Annapurna, ed. *Indian Cities in Transition.* New Delhi: Orient Longman, 2006.

Sheth, Pravin. *Images of Transformation: Gujarat and Narendra Modi.* 2nd ed. Ahmedabad: Team Spirit, 2007.

———. *Nav Nirman and Political Change in India: From Gujarat 1974 to New Delhi 1977.* Bombay: Vora, 1977.

Sheth, Pravin, and Ramesh Menon. *Caste and Communal Time Bomb.* Ahmedabad: Golwala Publications, 1986.

Sinha, Aseema. *The Regional Roots of Developmental Politics in India: A Divided Leviathan.* Bloomington: Indiana University Press, 2005.

Soja, Edward. *Postmodern Geographies: The Reassertion of Space in Critical Theory.* New York: Verso, 1989.

Soja, Edward, and Allen J. Scott, eds. *The City: Los Angeles and Urban Theory at the End of the Twentieth Century.* Berkeley: University of California Press, 1996.

Soman, R. J. *Peaceful Industrial Relations: Their Science and Technique.* Ahmedabad: Navajivan Press, 1957.

Sondhi, M. L., and Apratim Mukarji, eds. *The Black Book of Gujarat.* New Delhi: Manak Publications, 2002.

Spodek, Howard. "From Gandhi to Violence: Ahmedabad's 1985 Riots in Historical Perspective." *Modern Asian Studies* 23, no. 4 (1989): 765–95.

———. "In the Hindutva Laboratory: Pogroms and Politics in Gujarat, 2002." *Modern Asian Studies* 44, no. 2 (March 2010): 349–99.

———. "The 'Manchesterization' of Ahmedabad." *Economic Weekly,* March 13, 1965, 438–90.

———. "Sardar Vallabhbhai Patel at 100." *Economic and Political Weekly* 10, no. 50 (December 13, 1975): 1925–36.

———. "Traditional Culture and Economic Entrepreneurship: A Case Study of Ahmedabad, India." *Economic and Political Weekly,* February 22, 1969, M-27–M-31.

Steffens, Lincoln. *The Autobiography of Lincoln Steffens.* Chautauqua, N.Y.: Chautauqua Press, 1931.

Stone, Clarence. *Regime Politics: Governing Atlanta, 1946–1988.* Lawrence: University Press of Kansas, 1989.

Sundaram [Tribhuvandas Purushottamdas Luhar]. *Selected Poems of Sundaram.* Translated by Dhanavanti. Gandhinagar: Gujarat Sahitya Academy, 2001.

Thakar, Dhirubhai P. *Parampara ane Pragati. Sva. Sri Kasturbhai Lalbhainun Jivancaritra* [Tradition and Progress: The Biography of the Late Sri Kasturbhai Lalbhai]. Mumbai: Vakilsa, Phephara, Enda Sayamansa, 1984.

Thakkar, Usha. "The Gujarat Assembly Elections 2002—Results and Ramifications." In *Current Domestic Policy Challenges and Prospects in South Asia,* edited by the Institute of Regional Studies, 62–80. Islamabad: Institute of Regional Studies, 2003.

Thakore, Jivan. *Hum ane Maaree Mill* [Me and My Mill]. *Naya Marg* 1 and 16, September 2002.

Times (of India) Research Foundation. *Ahmedabad 2001—Imperatives Now: Towards a New Metropolitan Management Strategy.* 18 vols. Calcutta: Times Research Foundation, 1988.

Tripathi, Dwijendra. *Alliance for Change: A Slum Upgrading Experiment in Ahmedabad.* New Delhi: McGraw-Hill, 1998.

———. *Dynamics of a Tradition: Kasturbhai Lalbhai and His Entrepreneurship.* Delhi: Manohar, 1981.

Tripathi, Dwijendra, and Jyoti Jumani. "Change after Alliance: The Sequel to a Slum Upgrading Experiment in Ahmedabad." Unpublished manuscript, 2000.

Uchikawa, Shuji. *Indian Textile Industry: State Policy, Liberalization, and Growth.* New Delhi: Manohar, 1998.

United Nations Habitat Report. *The Challenge of Slums: Global Report on Human Settlements, 2003.* Sterling, Va.: Earthscan Publications, 2003.

Varadarajan, Siddharth, ed. *Gujarat: The Making of a Tragedy.* New Delhi, India: Penguin Books, 2002.

Varshney, Ashutosh. *Ethnic Conflict and Civic Life: Hindus and Muslims in India.* New Haven, Conn.: Yale University Press, 2002.

Visaria, Pravin, and Sudarshan Iyengar. "Economic Prospects." *Seminar* 470 (October 1998): 26.

Vohra Committee Report. New Delhi: Lok Shakti Abhiyan, 1997.

Warner, Sam Bass. *The Private City: Philadelphia in Three Periods of Its Growth.* Philadelphia: University of Pennsylvania Press, 1968.

Wilkinson, Steven. *Votes and Violence: Electoral Competition and Ethnic Riots in India.* Cambridge: Cambridge University Press, 2004.

Wood, John R. "The Political Integration of British and Princely Gujarat: The Historical-Political Dimension of Indian State Politics." Ph.D. diss., Columbia University, New York, 1972.

Wood, John. "Reservations in Doubt: The Backlash against Affirmative Action in Gujarat, 1985." Paper presented at the International Seminar on Gujarat Society, Surat, December 1986.

Yagnik, Achyut. "Introduction" to Joseph Macwan, *The Stepchild: Angaliyat,* xi–xxxi. New Delhi: Oxford University Press, 2004.

———. "Paradoxes of Populism." *Economic and Political Weekly,* August 27, 1983, 112–13.

Yagnik, Achyut, and Anil Bhatt. "The Anti-Dalit Agitation in Gujarat." *South Asia Bulletin* 4, no. 1 (Spring 1984): 49.

Yagnik, Achyut, and Suchitra Sheth. *The Shaping of Modern Gujarat: Plurality, Hindutva, and Beyond.* New Delhi: Penguin Books, 2005.

Yagnik, Indulal. *Atmakatha* [Autobiography]. 6 vols. Ahmedabad: Various publishers, 1955–72.

———. *Autobiography.* Translated by Devavrat Pathak, Howard Spodek, and John Wood. New Delhi: Manohar Books, forthcoming.

———. *Shyamaji Krishnavarma: Life and Times of an Indian Revolutionary.* Bombay: Lakshmi Publications, 1950.

Yajnik, Indulal K. *Gandhi as I Know Him.* New ed. Delhi: Danish Mahal, 1943.

INDEX

Page numbers in italics indicate maps and tables. Photo gallery appears after page 114.

HOWARD SPODEK is Professor of History at Temple University. He is author of *The World's History*, editor (with Doris Meth Srinivasan) of *Urban Form and Meaning in South Asia*, translator (with Devavrat N. Pathak and John Wood) of Indulal Yagnik's *Autobiography* (forthcoming), and producer/writer of the documentary film *Ahmedabad: The Life of a City in India*.